The McGraw-Hill Guide to

ENGLISH
LITERATURE

The McGraw-Hill Guide to

ENGLISH
LITERATURE

Volume Two
William Blake to
D. H. Lawrence

KAREN LAWRENCE
BETSY SEIFTER
LOIS RATNER

McGraw-Hill Publishing Company

New York   St. Louis   San Francisco   Auckland   Bogotá
Caracas   Hamburg   Lisbon   London   Madrid   Mexico   Milan
Montreal   New Delhi   Oklahoma City   Paris   San Juan
São Paulo   Singapore   Sydney   Tokyo   Toronto

THE MCGRAW-HILL GUIDE TO ENGLISH LITERATURE

3 4 5 6 7 DOC/DOC 9 9 8 7 6 5 4 3 2 1 0

ISBN 0-07-036705-1

LIBRARY OF CONGRESS CATALOGING IN PUBLICATION DATA
(Revised for volume 2)

Lawrence, Karen
 The McGraw-Hill guide to English literature.

 Bibliography: p.
 Includes indexes.
 Contents: v. 1. Beowulf to Jane Austen—v. 2. William
 Blake to D. H. Lawrence.
 1. English literature—History and criticism.
I. Seifter, Betsy. II. Ratner, Lois. III. Title.
PR85.L4 1985   820.9   84-12626
 ISBN 0-07-036704-3 (v. 1)
 ISBN 0-07-036705-1 (v. 2)

The editor for this book was Karl Weber; the editing supervisor was Marthe Grice.

BOOK DESIGN BY PATRICE FODERO

This book is dedicated to our three supportive husbands, Peter Lawrence, Julian Seifter, and Stephen Ratner, and to the children who came into being during the seven years of its composition: Andrew and Jeffrey, Andrew and Charles, and Philip and Peter.

PREFACE

Like guides who lead their companions through unfamiliar terrain, making sense of the territory, this book attempts to illuminate some of the vast expanse of English literature. The uniqueness of *The McGraw-Hill Guide to English Literature* lies in its format and completeness. It provides questions and answers on works by almost all the major authors of English literature from medieval to modern times. By example rather than prescription, the guide attempts to teach students fruitful ways to think and write about different kinds of literature, including fiction, poetry, drama, and the essay. The dual purpose of the guide is to demonstrate general approaches to literature and to give useful analyses of specific texts that college students are likely to encounter in their classes. This book certainly is not meant to replace the study of the texts themselves but is intended to serve as a useful supplement to them. Without sacrificing the richness, complexity, or variety of English literature, we attempt to cover the most significant aspects of these texts.

The guide appears in two volumes, corresponding to the division in most year-long survey courses and anthologies. Volume 1 includes Old English through eighteenth-century literature and is divided into seven parts: Old English literature, Middle English literature, the Renaissance, the seventeenth century, the Restoration, the neoclassical age, and the emergence of the novel. Volume 2 includes nineteenth- and twentieth-century literature and has five parts: the romantic age, Victorian poetry and prose, the Victorian novel, modern poetry, and the modern novel and drama. To provide a context for the discussions of individual texts, each part is introduced with a timeline which charts important political and literary events of the period. Chapters are divided according to individual authors (except, of course, in the case of anonymous texts), and a short chronology is provided for each author, listing the important dates and events in his or her life. In addition, each chapter includes a list of suggested readings for further study. The initials at the end of each chapter indicate the writer responsible for the material in that chapter.

This book has been written primarily for the college student who desires help in the study of English literature. Although some students may want to read through the guide, most will dip into it for help on particular writers being studied. It may prove especially useful in preparing students for the type of essay exams one is likely to encounter in literature courses. The guide should also be a valuable resource for the teacher of literature, who will find it a repository of significant questions on, as well as helpful analyses of, individual texts. As teachers of literature, we have tried to provide material that is beneficial to class preparation.

No other guide of this kind and comprehensiveness exists today. We hope that students and teachers will find *The McGraw-Hill Guide to English Literature* a helpful and stimulating companion in their study of literature.

K.L.
B.S.
L.R.

ACKNOWLEDGMENTS

In the seven years from the conception of this project to its fruition, a few people have been indispensable to our efforts. Chief among them is Barry Weller at the University of Utah, who read the manuscript in draft form and offered us the benefit of his considerable critical intelligence. He made insightful changes, both editorial and substantive, throughout the work.

Karl Weber has been the other significant participant in this enterprise, and for Karl's editorial expertise we are extremely grateful. We would also like to thank Karl and Teresa Carriero for their joint efforts in producing the timelines.

Finally, we would like to thank Dr. John V. Antush of Fordham University, who contributed the chronologies in Volume 2.

K.L.
B.S.
L.R.

CONTENTS

Part One

THE ROMANTIC AGE

T I M E L I N E

The Age

1750: Founding of Methodism by John Wesley

1755: Publication of Johnson's *Dictionary*

1756: Outbreak of Seven Years' War

1757: Victory by Clive at Plassey secures English control of India

1760: Death of George II; accession of George III

1763: Treaty of Paris

1765: Publication of Percy's *Reliques of Ancient Poetry*

1775: Outbreak of American War of Independence

1783: American independence won

1789: French Revolution

1799: Napoleon takes control of French government

1801: Preface to *Lyrical Ballads*

1804: Napoleon named emperor of France; war throughout Europe

1810: George III insane; the Regency

1815: Napoleon's final defeat at Waterloo

1820: Accession of George IV

1825: First English railway opened

1830: Death of George IV; accession of William IV

1832: Passage of Reform Bill

1837: Death of William IV; accession of Queen Victoria

1845: Great Famine in Ireland

1848: Revolutions in France, Italy, Austria; publication of *Communist Manifesto*

The Authors

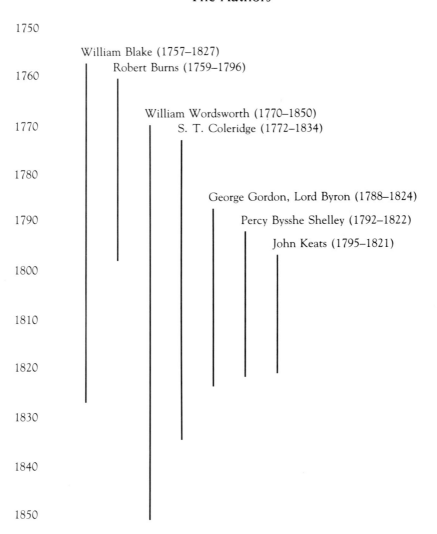

1750

1760

William Blake (1757–1827)
Robert Burns (1759–1796)

1770

William Wordsworth (1770–1850)
S. T. Coleridge (1772–1834)

1780

George Gordon, Lord Byron (1788–1824)

1790

Percy Bysshe Shelley (1792–1822)

John Keats (1795–1821)

1800

1810

1820

1830

1840

1850

WILLIAM BLAKE

C H R O N O L O G Y

1757	Born in London. Son of James Blake, a shopkeeper, and Catherine Harmitage Blake, both probably religious dissenters.
1761	Sees God "put his head against the window"; first of many religious visions he will experience.
1767	Is sent to a drawing school conducted by Henry Pars; will receive no regular schooling, though he educates himself through reading and study.
1772	Is apprenticed to engraver James Basire, engraving being a practical means of earning a living through artistic talent. Around this time begins writing plays and poems and composes music for his own lyrics.
1774	Basire assigns Blake the task of sketching the memorials in Westminster Abbey, a job commissioned by the Society of Antiquaries; it provides valuable artistic experience.
1779	Enters the Royal Academy of Arts, where he meets some of the leading artists of the day, including Sir Joshua Reynolds, who advises him to improve his drawing (a "slight" resented by the proud Blake).
1780	Meets the Swiss artist Henry Fuseli and the sculptor John Flaxman, who become his longtime friends. Exhibits a watercolor at the Royal Academy.
1782	Marries Catherine Boucher. Although she was uneducated—it is not certain whether she was literate—their marriage was by all accounts an unusually happy one and highly supportive for Blake as artist and poet. Mrs. Blake

shared her husband's religious beliefs and helped him in the production of his books.

1783   Printing of *Poetical Sketches,* a collection of early poems, arranged by several friends. The book apparently is not publicly sold.

1784   Death of Blake's father. With his small inheritance, Blake opens a printshop in partnership with James Parker; it soon fails. Blake exhibits more drawings at the Royal Academy and writes the prose satire *An Island in the Moon.*

1787   Blake's brother Robert, age 19, dies; Blake sees Robert's spirit ascend to heaven, "clapping its hands for joy." Blake later has a dream in which Robert teaches him the method of printing, called illuminated printing, that Blake will use for his own works.

1788   Blake publishes two small books, *There Is No Natural Religion* and *All Religions Are One,* by illuminated printing. (Words and illustrations are engraved; the printed pages are colored by hand, with each copy slightly different from the others.)

1789   Blake and his wife take part in the founding of a new church based on the writings of Swedish mystic and theologian Emanuel Swedenborg; within a few years, however, Blake apparently breaks with this group. Publishes *Songs of Innocence* and *The Book of Thel,* one of the earliest of his so-called prophetic poems.

1790   Around this time Blake begins a long career as an engraver of illustrations to books by others. This supports him and his wife while he continues to work on poetry and illuminated editions of his own works. Writes *The Marriage of Heaven and Hell,* setting forth his heretical religious views.

1791   Blake meets advanced democratic thinkers Thomas Paine and William Godwin; writes his prophetic poem *The French Revolution,* which is typeset but never published.

1792   Laws limiting freedom of speech in Britain passed; Blake's revolutionary religious and political ideas become increasingly dangerous.

1793   Publishes *Songs of Experience.* This collection of lyrics forms a counterpoint to the earlier *Songs of Innocence,* and from this time on the two are printed together by Blake. Also publishes prophetic poem *America* and the emblem book *The Gates of Paradise.*

1794   Publishes *Europe* and *The Book of Urizen.* Begins receiving commissions from Thomas Butts, a longtime patron, for various works of art.

1796   Illustrates Edward Young's book of poems *Night Thoughts.* Exhibits a painting of *The Last Supper* at the Royal Academy.

1797   Begins work on *The Four Zoas*, a massive prophetic work which he never completes.

1800   Meets William Hayley, who helps Blake financially but does not fully understand his gifts and so is treated satirically by Blake in many epigrams. Moves to a cottage at Felpham made available by Hayley.

1803   Blake drives a soldier named Scholfield from his garden; is said to shout "Damn the King" in doing so. Charges of sedition brought against Blake; penalty of death is possible. Blake moves back to London.

1804   Defended by lawyer Samuel Rose, a friend of Hayley's, Blake is acquitted of sedition. Begins work on prophetic poems *Milton* and *Jerusalem*.

1809   Publishes *Milton*. Exhibits paintings of the *Last Judgment* and other subjects at a London gallery.

1815   Begins work as an engraver of illustrations for a Wedgwood pottery catalogue.

1821–   Illustrates an edition of *Pastorals of Virgil* with his only known woodcuts;
1826   though little liked at the time, they are powerful and expressive. Also illustrates Bunyan's *Pilgrim's Progress* and the Book of Job; the series of illustrations for Job is often considered his masterpiece.

1822   Publishes his last illuminated work, the play *The Ghost of Abel*; it is dedicated to Lord Byron.

1827   Death of Blake. He is said to have spent his final hours singing of the things he was seeing in heaven. Is buried in Bunhill Fields, the dissenters' cemetery, but with the rites of the Church of England (at his request).

ESSAY QUESTIONS WITH ANSWERS

"Introduction" to *Songs of Innocence*

1.1. Characterize Blake's vision of innocence as suggested by this poem.

Answer The *abab* rhyme scheme and the lilting tetrameter rhythm lend an air of untroubled serenity to Blake's "Introduction." The vision in the poem is a pastoral one, with the traditional features of a golden world or prelapsarian Eden. Instead of turning to the inspiration of the muse, the poet finds inspiration in the voice of a child. Indeed, throughout the *Songs of Innocence* the persona, if not in fact a child, often conveys childlike qualities of naiveté and purity.

The advice of the child to "pipe a song about a Lamb" (line 5) evokes both the pastoral environment and the Christian scheme in which the lamb is a traditional symbol for Christ as redeemer. The world is consequently a happy place, blessed with rural "chear" and with God's presence. Even the tears in the poem ("he wept to hear" [line 8]) turn out to be tears of happiness ("he wept with joy to hear" [line 12]).

The creative process, too, is seen as happy and spontaneous; the poet moves from festive piping to joyful singing to, finally, writing "that all may read" (line 14). Like a good shepherd-poet, he writes with natural implements, plucking "a hollow reed" (line 16) for a pen and staining water for ink.

By beginning the book with this simple lyric, Blake establishes a dominant tone for the *Songs of Innocence.* He invokes the ideas of unspoiled nature and spontaneous wisdom which come from the pastoral tradition, postulating an Edenic phase in the cycle of human life.

1.2 Is Blake's world of innocence perfect or imperfect? Defend your answer.

Answer The state of innocence represented in the "Introduction" is on the surface a perfect realm of unblemished beauty. The whole poem serves to establish an image of perfection, an unsullied state of pure delight held up before the reader as an ideal. This ideal is connected with childhood, or rather with the nostalgic vision of childhood which the adult, experienced self harbors. Thus there is a repeated emphasis on joy and happiness ("pleasant glee," "merry chear," "happy chear," "happy songs"), and the landscape, with its valleys and clouds, inhabited by child and lamb, is a pastoral haven. Blake uses the nursery rhyme format to portray the initial phase of human life as a state of purity and bliss and to evoke the sensations of security and pleasure associated with an innocent time. In Blake's myth of human existence, the realm of innocence is identical with "Beulah," a springtime world of unconflicted peace and love.

However, the state of innocence suggested in the poem is severely limited. By confining himself to the singsong rhythms and simple images of a nursery rhyme, Blake implies that the innocent world is a precarious one that can exist only by the exclusion of real experience. In the "Introduction," he complicates this idyllic vision by subtly suggesting in the last two lines that only a child could derive pure pleasure from the *Songs of Innocence* ("And I wrote my happy songs/Every child may joy to hear"). There is a further hint of irony in the line "And I stain'd the water clear" (line 18). Although the shepherd-poet is ostensibly describing how he made his ink, the implication is that the clarity and purity of innocent perceptions are somehow stained, unwittingly darkened or compromised, by a more knowing perspective. The line "Pipe a song about a lamb" (line 5) also hints at a darker vision; viewed from another angle, the lamb is meat and wool, a victim ripe for the slaughterhouse. The laughing child of the poem may be another such sacrificial victim, with an innocence perilously allied to vulnerability and ignorance.

Except from an entirely naive and childlike perspective, the songs are not purely joyful, for they are too simple and trite to reflect the complexities of experience. Blake suggests, by the very fact that the *Songs of Innocence* are followed by the *Songs of Experience,* that innocence is only one of the "two contrary states of the human soul." Thus, the "perfect Eden" is circumscribed by the fallen world and can be criticized as a half-truth or incomplete vision. In Blake's comprehensive philosophical system, "Beulah," the springtime realm of repose and artless innocence, is only the initial phase of a cycle that leads through the harsh world of generation or experience to the creative energy and fulfillment of the true Eden. Blake was in fact an accomplished ironist who often presented ideas in the form of oppositions and "contraries." Thus evidence from outside a given poem may be an especially useful critical tool in fully understanding the Blakean perspective.

"The Chimney Sweeper" I and II

1.3   Why is Blake's first "Chimney Sweeper" poem included in *Songs of Innocence?*

Answer   Partly, the lyric does embody the innocent perspective in that it is spoken by a child. In the first stanza, the narrator tells the gruesome history of his young life with an apparent ignorance of its pathos. When he begins the tale of "little Tom Dacre" (line 5), he displays a naive optimism in that the cruel shaving of the head becomes a means of "protecting" the boy's white hair from soot. Furthermore, the story of Tom's dream is told as a wondrous vision with a happy ending: "And the Angel told Tom, if he'd be a good boy,/He'd have God for his father & never want joy" (lines 19–20). The narrator reinforces the "cheerful" tale with his own moral: "So if all do their duty, they need not fear harm" (line 24). Thus a naive facade is preserved throughout.

However, dramatic irony is at work in the poem, undercutting every serene statement with grim evidence of the misery experienced by children in the urban slums of eighteenth-century England. The selling of the child-narrator when still a lisping infant, the soot in which he sleeps, Tom Dacre's shaved head, and the vision of the resurrection of the young chimney sweeps from black coffins all attest to the bitter, loveless, and cruelly abbreviated lives of child laborers. The Angel who promises Tom joy is in fact promising him death. Thus the sole instance of pastoral imagery in the poem ("Then down a green plain, leaping, laughing they run,/And wash in a river and shine in the Sun" [lines 15–16]) clearly alludes to life after death, when the sweeps are set free from their "coffins" (which suggests the deathlike confinement in the chimneys that the boys must undergo). There is a paradoxical reversal of terms, with life described as death (in terms of sadness, darkness, imprisonment) and death pictured as life (joy, brightness, freedom). As Blake employs the paradox, it is not only the conventional consolation of Christian elegy, "we die to live," but also a harshly critical and ironic social statement. The duty exacted by the life of the sweeps is too harsh, and the harm is all too evident.

The phrases of reassurance and comfort in the poem ("never want joy" [line 20], "need not fear harm" [line 24]) and the singsong rhythms are also part of the lyric's double technique; they contribute to the serene surface while implying the vast discrepancy between the naive narrator and his pitiful existence. In this lyric, at least, Blake's realm of "innocence" is profoundly compromised by the intrusion of bitter experience.

1.4 Compare "The Chimney Sweeper" from *Songs of Innocence* with "The Chimney Sweeper" from *Songs of Experience*.

Answer The poems are alike in subject matter, with Blake using the figure of the chimney sweep in both to underscore the miseries of urban life in the early industrial age. A white-and-black palette predominates in both poems, and there is even a repetition of the pun " 'weep, 'weep," referring both to the sweeper's street cry and to weeping. Parental figures (mother and father) and spiritual presences (Angel and God) also appear in both poems. Finally, the rhyme schemes (*aabb, abab*) and rhythms (four-beat lines) are similar in both, producing the effect of a children's song.

However, despite similarities in the cast of characters, setting, and rhythm, the two lyrics display one important difference in technique. In the "innocent" version, the persona is a naïf, a child who is unaware of the implications of the story he is telling. In the "experienced" version, the persona is that of an experienced, streetwise child of the slums. The poet establishes the scene in two swift lines of impersonal narration, with a pitiable soot-blackened creature, "a little black thing," abandoned in the snow; but it is the answer that the child gives to the narrator's question ("Where are thy mother & father? say?" [line 3]) that launches a frontal attack on the hypocrisies of parents, God, Priest, and King, "who make up a heaven of our misery" (line 12). The childlike Eden of innocence is only briefly alluded to ("Because I was happy upon the heath" [line 5] and "because I am happy, & dance & sing" [line 9]). The child has been betrayed by his parents, who put him to work as a sweep ("They clothed me in the clothes of death" [line 7]) and by church and state, institutions which sanction the inhumanity of child labor. The child is thus a knowing martyr, consciously attacking the false pieties of his age. Unlike the narrator of the earlier poem, who believes in the Angel's vision of heaven where the sweeps will "rise upon clouds, and sport in the wind" (line 18), in the later poem the child sees heaven as a pretense, something concocted by adults to justify their exploitation of innocents (" . . . God & his Priest & King,/. . . make up a heaven of our misery" [lines 11–12]).

In the realm of experience, social injustice becomes the overt target of a narrator who is an unbeliever and a skeptic. In the realm of innocence, cruelty and misery are criticized only indirectly by the discrepancy between the speaker's optimism and his terrible tale. This latter approach is perhaps more highly charged emotionally because it increases the poignancy of the child's situation; he is more completely the victim in his vulnerability and credulity.

"The Sick Rose"

1.5   Compare Blake's use of the rose as a symbol with that of Burns in "A Red, Red Rose."

Answer   Robert Burns employs traditional symbolism in his love ballad, drawing on the association of the rose with springtime vitality and beauty. He simply asserts a similarity, using the established connotations of the flower as a kind of shorthand to describe and compliment his beloved: "O My Luve's like a red, red rose/That's newly sprung in June" (lines 1–2). This simile, like the following one comparing the mistress to a melody "that's sweetly played in tune," produces an effect of graceful decoration with a reticent, allusive quality. Instead of explicit statement, Burns relies on convention, those agreed-upon meanings known to both reader and writer, to suggest the nature of the likeness between mistress and rose.

In contrast, Blake's strategy is bolder and more immediate. Instead of simile he uses metaphoric substitution, directly addressing the rose in the first line of the poem and presenting a drama in which the rose and the worm are actors. By beginning with the idea of disease ("O Rose, thou art sick"), Blake is announcing, in the tone of a prophet, the calamity that has befallen Burns's pure rose of love. In the modern world, sexual love has become pathological.

In the context of Blake's central metaphor of a rose diseased, the phrase "thy bed of crimson joy" has ambiguous and ambivalent connotations. The crimson joy is not the natural burgeoning of Burns's red, red rose but an un-healthy self-gratification; the rose's joy precedes the arrival of the worm and furthermore is concealed, for the bed must be "found out" by the worm. Both rose and worm have "secret" loves, as compared with the open, straightforward love that the persona of Burns's lyric brings to his mistress. "The Sick Rose" offers an implicit drama that exploits rather than simply presents the conven-tional symbol of the rose. Burns draws on the role of the rose in a stable iconographic scheme, while Blake shows the fate of the rose in a dynamic, unfolding sequence. The use of extended metaphor rather than condensed simile energizes the whole poem and at the same time lends it an enigmatic, riddling quality. "The Sick Rose" is a poem of and about experience, while "A Red, Red Rose" is innocent in that it confines itself to a single sweet gesture of compliment, excluding any negative or repellent features that the "rose" might possess.

1.6   Discuss the central metaphor of the poem.

Answer   The poem is saturated with sexual connotations; the rose suggests the female genitalia, and the worm the phallus. Only a specifically sexual reading accounts most fully for the physical properties of rose and worm as well as for the references to "bed," "crimson joy," and "dark secret love." Thus the burrowing of the worm into the "bed of crimson joy" is a metaphor for sexual intercourse. The hidden bed of the rose and the secret love of the worm imply the polarity between the sexes, their self-protective isolation and concealment before the act that unites them. In Blake's terms, the sexual relationship is inherently a form of conflict, with the male in pursuit and the female in hiding.

Blake ends the poem with an image of destruction: "And his dark secret love/Does thy life destroy." However, Blake's pessimistic view of sexuality applies to sex of a particular kind. In the poem the worm is an "invisible" one that "flies in the night/In the howling storm" (lines 3–4). The language implies that the worm is a kind of incubus, a demon lover called up in a nocturnal fantasy of agitated desire and longing, and that the intercourse is imaginary. Thus the eroticism of the worm is dark and secret, life-denying rather than life-enhancing. Blake hints that the sickness of the rose is repressed passion, which issues in autoerotic fantasy and delusion. It is this kind of "love," self-involved and self-defeating, that is destructive.

Blake's use of metaphor to sketch this drama of involuted desire is highly effective, since it allows him to condense a complex analysis of sexual conflict into eight short lines. The basic horticultural conceit, a rose devoured by a pest, also provides the poem with its emotional texture, conveying a sense of waste and repugnance. The poem is thus a graphic illustration of one of Blake's "Proverbs of Hell": "He who desires but acts not, breeds pestilence."

"The Tyger"

1.7   What does the tiger represent?

Answer   The tiger is not solely a symbol but a concrete, literal being heightened by the poet's perception of him. The image of the beast "burning bright/In the forests of the night" (lines 1–2) underscores his physical presence, the tawny brilliance of the animal gleaming against the dark background of the jungle. Thus the tiger has an intense "quiddity," or "whatness," an idiosyncratic and individual self. As the poem progresses, however, with the poet questioning and wondering as he ponders this being, the tiger begins to embody something other than or more than simply himself. In general, he seems to represent some morally ambiguous force or potency in the universe, an aggressive, self-assertive energy in absolute contrast to the tameness and tractability of the lamb. The lamb is humanly comprehensible as both the sign of Christ's role as the sacrifice for the sins of humanity and, like the lamb who lies down with the lion, an emblem of the human aspiration to peace and love. In contrast, the tiger is the "other," all that is nonhuman and uncivilized. He is not only in the night but a manifestation of the night, the imagery of fire and burning suggesting an intense and unconstrained vitality foreign to the daylight world of ordinary being. The tiger is alien and incomprehensible; his symmetry is "fearful" (line 4), inspiring awe, and he possesses "deadly terrors" (line 16), as though to approach him were fatal. The "dread hand," "dread feet," and "dread grasp" (lines 12, 15) suggest the awesome might of the Creator who "dare[s] seize the fire" (line 8) in the act of creation. At the same time, these references to "dread" seem to apply to the tiger himself, his own limbs constituting a source of dread and wonder.

This awesome being, so alien and so "other," symbolizes not only an essential being or an amoral vitality but the exemplary result of God's act of creation in Genesis; he is one of the strange and wonderful beings with which the Creator populated his universe. Blake's conception of God is that of the patriarchal deity who created heaven and earth, man and beast. But this patriarch is also literally father to the Lamb, Christ. Part of the mystery and force of the poem derives from the line "Did he who made the Lamb make thee?" (line 20). Paradoxically, God is the source of both good and evil, meekness and savagery, restraint and unbridled energy, of both the stars which "bristle" with spears and the heavens which weep with compassion.

On yet another level, Blake is referring to the act of artistic creation. The images in the poem allude to different kinds of "making." Thus, seizing the fire, twisting the sinews, stoking the furnace, and pounding the anvil evoke the art of the sculptor and the craft of the welder and blacksmith. Beneath Blake's allusions to these various kinds of handiwork is a latent reference to the poet's work in "hammering out" his lines. (These references may also derive from Blake's own experience of creating art out of material substance. A painter and engraver as well as a poet, he printed his books from metal plates dipped in an acid bath; the texts thus produced represent his "handiwork" in a far more literal sense than is true of most writers.)

Blake attributes to the artist not only a mysterious creativity but a daring which approaches hubris. The line "On what wings dare he aspire?" (line 7) alludes to a traditional symbol for the artist, Icarus, who attempted to overreach his human condition by fashioning wings of wax which melted when he flew too near the sun. The connection between art and rebellion is reinforced by the line "What the hand, dare seize the fire?" (line 8), referring to Prometheus, who stole fire from the gods as a gift to humanity. Thus, in his vitality and daring energy, the poet is linked to the tiger he depicts. He goes beyond moral categories in the act of imitating creation.

Part of the difficulty of the poem lies in the conflict between the two very different answers possible to the question posed by the speaker: Who created the tiger? The persona seems to lean toward the orthodox answer, God, in the line "Did he who made the Lamb make thee?" (line 20). But the references to the human daring of Icarus and Prometheus suggest that at least momentarily, he is thinking of humankind as the creator of the tiger. Although the speaker twice calls the agent "immortal," the images of making in the poem suggest that the "hand or eye" that "framed" the tiger is human, immortal only in the sense that the artist contains within himself the divine spark of creativity. The urgent accumulating questions, which receive no explicit answer, suggest a tension in the speaker, who seems poised between an attitude of reverence before the one Creator and the recognition, itself daring, that each person is a creator whose fierceness and originality equal God's.

1.8   Discuss the metrics of the poem.

Answer   Blake uses the usual short tetrameter line of his lyrics in this poem. However, the preponderance of trochees (a foot with a stressed syllable followed by an unstressed) and spondees (a foot with two stressed syllables) in the lines changes the overall rhythm from an iambic lilt (unstressed, stressed) to a pounding driving beat. Thus in the first stanza, the first three lines are trochaic and the fourth line begins with a spondee, producing a kind of incantatory urgency. A more extreme example of the driving rhythm is the line "What dread hand? & what dread feet?" (line 12), in which every syllable except "&" can be read as stressed, giving the line a thrusting quality. The "beat" of a line such as this suggests the stroke of a hammer on an anvil, a throbbing pulse, or even drums in the primeval forest. The rhythms of the poem thus convey multiple connotations, simultaneously suggesting the activity of making, an emergence into being and consciousness, and a mysterious pulsation, a life force which underlies all creation. Part of the tension of the poem derives from the discrepancy between the simple lyric format which recalls the *Songs of Innocence* (four-line stanzas, *aabb* rhyme scheme, tetrameter lines) and the intermittent intrusion of a new driving tempo which suggests the urgency and fierceness of "experience."

1.9   Compare "The Lamb" with "The Tyger."

Answer   "The Lamb" consists of two stanzas, one posing a question and the other supplying an answer. The implication is that in the realm of innocence every question has its answer, and the world is thus both comprehensible and unified. The "integrated" quality of innocence is further reinforced by the explicit equation in the second stanza between child, lamb, and the Lamb of God ("I a child & thou a lamb,/We are called by his name" [lines 17–18]). Observer (child) and observed (lamb) become inseparable as children of the Lamb, God. Blake implies that the child's feeling of belonging to and embracing nature is justified by the fact that the Creator, the common source and maker of all things, has imbued all his creations with meekness, mildness, and joy. The sense of kinship that the child expresses is not a fallacy but a true spiritual perception.

In keeping with this radically simple vision, the diction is childlike and the images accessible and familiar. The soft, woolly lamb, feeding on the bounty of nature and bleating with a "tender voice," is a picture book illustration which evokes the joys of childhood. The parablelike statements in the second stanza ("He is meek & he is mild,/He became a little child" [lines 15–16]) exploit the pastoral connotations of Christian theology to leap to a recognition of oneness in the universe. The closing of the lyric is a prayer of benediction ("Little Lamb God bless thee/Little Lamb God bless thee" [lines 19–20]), once again suggesting a simple and spontaneous comprehension of God's goodness. God's "making" and "blessing" are one, just as his "making" is, in the first stanza, equivalent to "giving" ("Little Lamb who made thee?/Gave thee life . . . /Gave thee clothing . . . /Gave thee such a tender voice"). With one gesture God creates, gives, and blesses.

In contrast, "The Tyger" suggests that God and his creation are alien and incomprehensible. Instead of question and answer, the poem consists almost entirely of questions which go unanswered. Indeed, the questions increase in tempo, breaking up the lines with staccato bursts and truncating the full syntax of statements (e.g., "What dread hand? & what dread feet?" [line 12], "What the hammer? what the chain?" [line 13]). The implication is that the universe does not readily yield answers and, further, that the energizing power of experience lies in its mystery. The insistence on the separateness of observer and observed reinforces this sense of an innate mystery in life and in creation. The tiger is seen as strangely bright and frighteningly awesome; it is thus the "other," an alien and potentially aggressive being.

Blake suggests something about the relationship between the two poems in the line from "The Tyger" "Did he who made the Lamb make thee?" (line 20). He refers the reader back to the earlier vision in the *Songs of Innocence,* where the lamb symbolizes human identification and integration with nature, as well as spontaneous sympathy and goodness. The tiger seems to violate this simple conception of God, thus suggesting the limitations of innocence. The realm of experience is wider than the closed world of childhood; it includes the terrible beauty of fierceness and unconstrained self-assertion.

"The Proverbs of Hell"

1.10 How "serious" is Blake's intention in the "Proverbs"?

Answer "The Proverbs of Hell" are full of contradictions and tonal ambiguity. Not only does the tone shift between proverbs, but a single adage can be read as parodic and serious at the same time. The title indicates a "devilish" and playful intention to parody the Book of Proverbs in the Old Testament, and indeed Blake often capriciously turns the conventional wisdom of moral maxims on its head. For example, instead of prudence and the golden mean, the poet advises a wild abandon:

The road of excess leads to the palace of wisdom.

Prudence is a rich ugly old maid courted by Incapacity.

However, the celebration of excess is not just a playful rhetorical inversion, for it has thematic significance in the "Proverbs" as a whole. According to Blake, the violation of restraints ends in an enhancement of being and a deepening of knowledge. Thus instead of the temperateness of the familiar adage "Enough is as good as a feast" (recorded in John Heywood's *Proverbs* [1546]), with its admonition to be content with a sufficiency, Blake seems to advocate intemperance: "Enough! or too much." Interested in plenitude and fullness, he urges "enough" as every person's proper portion, but if the right measure cannot be found, "too much" is better than too little. In fact, he suggests that the proper measure can never be found without going beyond it: "You never know what is enough unless you know what is more than enough." A similar belief in exceeding limits is implied in Blake's definition of "Exuberance" (literally, "to come forth abundantly") as "Beauty." Again, in his comparison between the cistern which contains and the fountain which overflows, he implicitly prefers the fountain. After all, one can only "expect poison from the standing water." Against the orthodoxies of self-restraint, self-interest, and prudence, Blake poses an ethic of self-expression and daring. Indeed, the riddling quality of many of the proverbs is Blake's way of attacking convention and asserting a personal credo.

In his thoroughgoing parody of proverbial wisdom, Blake inverts not only admonitory maxims but moral fables. Using traditional animal allegory, he reverses the usual system of values by praising the vices conventionally exemplified by various beasts:

> The pride of the peacock is the glory of God.
>
> The lust of the goat is the bounty of God.
>
> The wrath of the lion is the wisdom of God.

Beneath the ostensible rebelliousness and immorality of such assertions is the idea that being true to the passions and to the self is more valid than abiding by an externally imposed system of law.

Blake's outrageous slogans are, in fact, paradoxical truths. Implied in his inversion of proverbial wisdom is a serious system of belief which values intense feeling, individuality, and energy. His revolutionary upheaval of received wisdom constitutes a means to a serious end, an attempt to shake human beings awake so that they may fully realize their individuality and humanity.

In this system, Blake makes room for aphorisms of a more conventional sort, as one of the two poles between which humanity inevitably moves:

> The busy bee has no time for sorrow.
>
> The most sublime act is to set another before you.
>
> The thankful reciever [sic] bears a plentiful harvest.

Thus the traditional values of industry, self-sacrifice, and gratitude find a place in Blake's scheme alongside the specifically Blakean values of self-expression, sensual awareness, and experiential freedom. Still, the revolutionary statements far outnumber the orthodox dicta, for in Blake's view the thrust of growth depends on the violation of strictures. As he puts it, "Damn braces: Bless relaxes."

The belief in creative experiment as a precondition for self-realization becomes part of Blake's artistic creed. Thus our understanding of the world derives from the daring and genius of people who felt free to imagine: "What is now proved was once only imagin'd." In Blake's view, absolute freedom of thought leads not to idle fantasy but to a vision of reality ("Everything possible to be believ'd is an image of truth"), and the mind's vagaries, as opposed to reason, are the pathway to imaginative comprehension ("Improv[me]nt makes strait roads, but the crooked roads without Improvement, are roads of Genius"). Indeed, Blake was fiercely opposed to the late eighteenth-century ideal of reason as the supreme good, and for him the scientific "improvers" Locke and Newton were symbolic representations of death and tyranny.

Blake's rhetorical strategy of inversion and paradox is in itself a "crooked road" which veers and changes direction, expressing truths in a startling and original style. "The Proverbs of Hell" thus constitute a verbal enactment of those qualities of excess, exuberance, and revolutionary fervor which Blake recommends as a style of life and art.

B.S.

SUGGESTED READINGS

Adams, Hazard, *William Blake: A Reading of the Shorter Poems* (1963).
Bloom, Harold, *Blake's Apocalypse: A Study in Poetic Argument* (1963).
Frye, Northrop, *Fearful Symmetry: A Study of William Blake* (1947).
Frye, Northrop, (ed.), *Blake: A Collection of Critical Essays* (1966).

ROBERT BURNS

C H R O N O L O G Y

1759   Born at Alloway, near Ayr, Scotland. Son of William Burnes, a gardener and tenant farmer, and Agnes Broun Burnes. Burns's Scottish background and upbringing are crucial for his literary career; he is immersed from childhood in the Scottish vernacular language and in fairy tales, legends, and ballads.

1765   Burns and his brother Gilbert begin studying under schoolmaster John Murdoch; they read the Bible and "elegant extracts" from writers such as Addison and Pope.

1766   Family moves to a rented farm at Mount Oliphant; by Burns's account, life there is hard and lonely. Burns works as a plowboy (later known and romanticized as the "plowboy poet").

1773   Burns spends several weeks studying grammar and French with Murdoch in Ayr; also dabbles in Latin. Is a ready pupil and a voracious reader. Probably writing poetry by this time.

1775   Attends dancing school, where he outgrows much of his shyness and begins to display the charm for which he will be famous. Studies at Kirkoswald during the summer.

1777   Family moves to a larger farm at Lochlea; for a time, at least, their fortunes improve; they escape the near poverty in which they had been living.

1780   Burns helps form the Tarbolton Bachelors' Club, a young men's society; he gives speeches and takes part in debates there.

1781	Burns's father begins a prolonged legal dispute with his landlord. Burns probably first reads the poems of the Scottish poet Fergusson at this time; he decides to use only the Scottish vernacular language for his own writing.
1783	Burns rents Mossgiel farm in partnership with his brother Gilbert; begins a trying and ultimately unsuccessful career as a farmer. Begins to keep a commonplace book, a journal containing thoughts and maxims, and resolves to pursue a career as poet.
1784	Burns's father, his health in decline, finally wins his lawsuit against his landlord but dies soon thereafter. Robert and Gilbert Burns suffer financial problems in their operation of the Mossgiel farm. Burns enters into the most prolific period of his poetic career, writing numerous lyric and narrative poems in a Scottish dialect of English, often based on old Highland ballads. He begins a love affair with Elizabeth Paton.
1785	Elizabeth Paton bears a daughter named Elizabeth; Burns is ordered to pay a fine and do penance by the local court. He meets and falls in love with Jean Armour; they marry, but under pressure from her disapproving family, she disavows the marriage.
1786	Jean Armour bears twin children by Burns. Disheartened by his failures, Burns plans to emigrate to Jamaica. First, however, he arranges publication of a volume of his poems (the Kilmarnock edition). It achieves an unexpected success and is reprinted in Edinburgh.
1787	Having given up plans of emigrating, Burns travels around Scotland; his book has won praise from critics and made him a well-known poet, though he has earned little money from it. James Johnson, in the process of compiling a collection of old Scottish ballads, persuades Burns to contribute; between this date and 1796, Burns gathers and reworks almost 200 Scottish lyrics to be published in Johnson's *Scots Musical Museum*. This is his main literary work after this time.
1788	Jean Armour and Burns acknowledge their marriage and settle at Ellisland. She bears twins, both of whom die within a month. Burns begins seeking a post as exciseman.
1789	Son Francis born. Burns is appointed exciseman, with a stipend of £50 a year; this sum, together with the small income from his still-struggling farm, will enable him and his family to survive.
1790	Burns writes "Tam o' Shanter," his major original work of poetry dating from the years after his marriage.
1791	Birth of a son, William, to Jean and an illegitimate daughter, Elizabeth, to Anne Park.

1792   Burns is promoted to Dumfries port division. Is invited by George Thomas to help in the compiling of his *Select Collection of Original Scottish Airs*, another anthology of Scottish ballads. Jean gives birth to a daughter named Elizabeth.

1793   Second Edinburgh edition of Burns's poems is published (two volumes).

1794   Birth of son James. The final edition during his lifetime of Burns's poems is published in Edinburgh. Burns is promoted to acting supervisor.

1795   Burns is severely ill with a heart condition.

1796   Death of Burns; he is buried on the day his son Maxwell is born.

ESSAY QUESTIONS WITH ANSWERS

"A Red, Red Rose"

2.1 "This poem is boring and trite; it echoes the sentiments of hundreds of other love lyrics and has nothing special to recommend it." How accurate is this criticism of "A Red, Red Rose"?

Answer It is true that Burns draws on conventional images in his love ballad. However, the skillful use of simile, metaphor, and hyperbole, coupled with subtle rhythmic cadences, indicates that the lyric is not the product of a naive sensibility but rather an artful creation.

The opening line, "O My Luve's like a red, red rose," with its four strong stresses, constitutes a simple, bold assertion of the poet's feeling. The lover draws on the conventional association of love with nature's bounty; his mistress, like a rose, represents beauty, blossoming, awakening life, and springtime vitality. The next simile, which attributes the sweetness and harmony of music to the beloved, is equally simple and straightforward: "O My Luve is like the melodie/That's sweetly played in tune" (lines 3–4).

Having characterized his mistress, the poet attempts to quantify the depth of his feelings. First, he "measures" his own boundless love by reference to his lady's infinite beauty ("As fair art thou . . ./So deep in luve am I" [lines 5–6]). This device serves to compliment the lady while at the same time asserting the depth of the poet's devotion. The implication is that her beauty is in fact immeasurable, like the poet's love. The poet then explores another dimension of love, its length or duration, offering a series of images which convey the notion that his love will last forever. He will love her "Till a' the seas gang dry," till "the rocks melt wi' the sun," and "while the sands o' life shall run" (lines 9, 10, 12). These images suggest the poet's psychological situation. With a lover's impetuosity, he claims that he will love her until the world ends, while the hourglass reference ("the sands of life") adds a poignant admission of the transience of mortal life and the evanescence of even an "undying" love. "Luve" is not only as beautiful but as fragile as any rose "newly sprung in June." The poem ends with another hyperbole, the poet's heroic vow that he will overcome not only immeasurable time but vast distance to be by his mistress's side. The fleeting suggestion of the impending separation of the lovers gives the lyric a touch of drama and urgency.

In addition, the balladlike rhythms of the four stanzas enhance the poem's lyricism. In part, Burns achieves this songlike quality through repetition. Thus the iterated lines "And I will luve thee still, my dear,/Till a' the seas gang dry" and "And fare thee weel, my only luve,/And fare thee weel awhile!" not only provide rhetorical emphasis but constitute a musical refrain. The word "love" is itself repeated many times, as if to insist on the basic emotion expressed in the poem. The urgency and passion are contained within an unassuming format; the simple rhyme scheme (*abcb*) and the tripping rhythm (iambic tetrameter) provide a songlike "setting" for the poem's insistent repetitions and headlong hyperboles. The ballad setting connects the individual lover, caught up in the throes of a particular passion, with all lovers. Although certain rhetorical features of the poem suggest the poet's personal psychology, his impetuosity and desire, the ballad elements evoke the universal experience of love, lending the lyric the quality of a spontaneous, anonymous song which almost sings itself.

Part of the appeal of the poem lies in this evocation of folk song. In fact, "A Red, Red Rose," like many of Burns's songs, incorporates elements from several folk songs of the day. The obvious "Scottishness" of the poem is thus authentic. Here, as in other lyrics, Burns made accessible to English readers an otherwise unfamiliar dialect as well as the remnants of a folk culture which had apparently survived longer in the rural hinterlands of Scotland than it had in England. Because of its traditional ballad motifs and dialect words, the poem has the effect of putting the reader in contact with an older and simpler, although by no means naive, sensibility. Its qualities of directness and honesty are derived, at least partly, from its kinship with traditional native songs.

"To a Mouse"

2.2   Discuss the levels of diction in the poem.

Answer   "To a Mouse," which consists of a continuous direct address to the mouse, is written for the most part in colloquial Scots dialect. Features of this "low" (that is, nonliterary) style include the elision of syllables ("cow'rin', tim'rous beastie"); the use of diphthongs or elongated vowel sounds which suggest

Scottish inflections ("I would be laith [loath]" in line 5 and "art no thy lane [are not alone]" in line 37); the frequent occurrence of onomatopoeic words ("bickering brattle," "stibble . . . nibble . . . dribble"); the use of many diminutives ("beastie," "breastie," "housie," "mousie"); and the employment of dialect words, especially relating to weather—*snell* ("bitter") and *cranreuch* ("hoarfrost")—and agriculture—*pattle* ("plowstaff") and *coulter* ("cutter blade"). Taken together, these linguistic devices suggest an intimate, colloquial style and stress the connection between the poor farmer and the wee "beastie" on whom he lavishes compassion; both are of humble origin and spend their lives in obscure toil on the land.

However, at several points in the poem, Burns adopts a more elevated language, introducing a second style which suggests an educated consciousness. For example, in stanza 2, a cluster of Latinate words occurs: "dominion," "union," "opinion," "companion." These polysyllabic words contribute to a shift in tone as the poet formally elaborates on the implications of his theme. The farmer commiserates with his victim because they are alike in their earthborn mortality; both belong to an integrated and coherent natural order ("Nature's social union") which "man's dominion" callously violates. But the connection between farmer and mouse is clearly a conscious act of sympathy rather than an intuitive identification, for the formal diction illustrates the gap between the "beastie," who can only react instinctively, and the man, who can philosophically reflect on their shared plight. The shift in styles allows Burns to convey both emotional connection and explicit interpretation.

In stanza 2, Burns comes close to puncturing his dramatic fiction, speaking in what one could call the poet's own voice, as distinct from the farmer's. But he quickly returns to the homely dialect associated with the farmer in the next four stanzas, which amplify the pitiable situation of the mouse. In the last two stanzas, Burns employs a middle style as the farmer expounds on the proverbial wisdom implied by the tale and reflects on his personal fortunes. The mouse becomes an illustration of the maxims that "foresight may be vain" and that "the best-laid plans o' mice an' men/Gang aft agley" (lines 39–40). The diction here is closer to that of standard English, with only a sporadic dropping of final consonants and the single idiomatic phrase "gang aft agley"; the more formal style suggests a shift from dialogue to meditation, although ostensibly the farmer is still addressing the mouse. "But och! I backward cast my e'e/On prospects drear!" (lines 45–46) evokes the image of a person wincing in pain while naming his or her regrets and fears.

The modulations up and down the scale of diction provide a means of combining emotional pathos with philosophical reflection. The farmer seems to move close to the mouse in the dialect passages and to stand back from him when he moralizes in the middle and high styles. Burns thus creates two levels of meaning, one intimate and "homely," the other more formal and public, while retaining a consistent persona. The consistency of the persona derives in part from the pervasive dialect elements and idiomatic expressions, which occur even in the more formal passages. And in part, the consistent rhythmic texture of the verse, with its regular elongations and contractions (three tetrameter lines, a two-beat line, a tetrameter line, and a two-beat line) itself seems to characterize the speaker, giving him an idiosyncratic speech pattern. Thus the stylistic discontinuities are absorbed by the coherent rhythms of the poem.

2.3   Until the last stanza, Burns emphasizes the common lot of "mice an' men." However, at the very end of the poem, he introduces a distinction between the farmer and the field mouse. Analyze the significance of this distinction.

Answer   In a sense, the last stanza of the poem is a commonplace, expressing the familiar idea that dumb animals are fortunate compared with people. Thus Burns says to the mouse, "But thou art blessed compared wi' me!" (line 43). He implies that the gift of reason enjoyed by human beings has an ironic double edge. Though it endows people with the ability to think and plan, it also burdens them with memory and anticipation. The mouse's "foresight" is instinctive; his whole existence is involved, really, in the present moment only. For the individual, the present moment is complicated by regretful recollection of past troubles (the backward looks on "prospects drear" [line 46]) and fearful imagination of future ills (what the farmer can "guess an' fear" [line 48]). Instead of freeing the farmer from bondage to his immediate physical hardships, memory and anticipation haunt him, circumscribing his life of toil with troubled reflections.

This final observation on the unhappy fate of mortals expands and enriches the poem. By abandoning a simple parallel between the mouse and the man, Burns goes beyond anthropomorphism to provide insight into a condition specifically human. In his emphasis on the limitations of this condition, he offers an implicit critique of reason as humanity's highest good. Burns's pessimistic view of human nature and his melancholy focus on the yearnings and fears which haunt the sensitive, conscious individual are characteristically romantic.

2.4 Is "To a Mouse" sentimental? Defend your answer.

Answer "To a Mouse" has certainly struck some readers as sentimental. The tender feeling lavished on the "cow'rin, tim'rous beastie" and his "wee-bit housie" may seem excessive; a mouse, of course, could not really be as heart-broken over the devastation of his "home" as a person would be. The identi-fication of the speaker with the mouse may appear faintly ridiculous, reflecting the poet's romantic bias and an overwrought attempt to create poetry out of absurdly mundane material.

However, although rich in sentiment, the poem is not sentimental. A major means by which Burns prevents the poem from descending into bathos is the humorous tone; the farmer's pity for the mouse might seem exaggerated if it were not expressed with a chuckle. The idiomatic dialect, the endearments, and the strategy of direct address contribute to the indulgent, half-amused tone of the speaker. At the same time, these rhetorical devices create an intimate situation in which genuine emotion persists. But the mouse is not the sole object of the empathetic compassion that is expressed in the poem, for throughout there is a stress on the connection between the human and animal realms. People, too, must be pitied, for they also are subject to the whims of chance and weather. Thus, a line like "A daimen-icker [an occasional ear of corn] in a thrave/'S a sma' request" (lines 15–16) has an underlying reference to the human estate as well. The need of a poor person for food, small request though it be, may be denied by the indifference of the elements or by the callousness of fellow human beings. Indeed, the whole fable of the mouse has an allegorical quality. The house, built with hard labor and anxious care and casually destroyed by "man's dominion," is the house of poverty, and the laboring farmer is as much a victim of the caprices of nature, both physical and human, as the frightened, homeless mouse. The emotion expressed in the poem is thus ap-propriate to the basic theme, which is the fate of mice *and* men.

"Tam o' Shanter"

2.5 Analyze the mock-heroic techniques used in the poem.

Answer "Tam o' Shanter" parodies heroic narrative by presenting a bawdy, boisterous tavern tale as though it were a tragic story with moral implications.

The story of Tam's midnight encounter with the devil is ostensibly an admonitory tale warning against the sins of drunkenness and lechery, but its "tragic" consequences are comically displaced onto Maggie, Tam's trusty nag. Thus, the closing moral is bathetic rather than pathetic, comic rather than somber:

> Now, wha this tale o' truth shall read,
> Each man and mother's son, take heed;
> Whene'er to drink you are inclined
> Or cutty-sarks rin in your mind,
> Think! you may buy the joys o'er dear;
> Remember Tam o' Shanter's mare.
> (lines 219–224)

The absurd catastrophe, the ripping off of Maggie's tail by Nannie the witch, is the climax, or rather anticlimax, of an "epic" plot which includes prophecy (wife Kate's prediction "that, late or soon,/Thou would be found deep drowned in Doon" [lines 29–30]), foreshadowing ("That night, a child might understand,/ The Deil had business on his hand" [lines 77–78]), and a well-defined peripety, that moment when the hero commits the tragic error and begins the fatal descent (Tam, watching the witches dance, breaks his silent vigil and "roars out, 'Weel done, Cutty-sark!'/And in an instant all was dark!" [lines 188–189]). Through this parody of epic conventions, the anecdote of a drunken fool becomes a hero's adventure, but the hero is a mock-hero rather than a genuine one. The satire cuts two ways; not only is Tam shown up as a besotted, benighted swaggerer, a sorry excuse for an epic hero, but the epic conventions themselves seem suspect.

The language of epic is also used in a double-edged way. It simultaneously undercuts the narrative's pretensions to grandeur and subverts the claims of the high style to a privileged literary status. Burns's lavish expenditure of linguistic resources exposes the subject as comically inadequate to the style while also exposing the pretensions of the epic style itself, with its exclamatory apostrophes, extended similes, elaborate catalogues, and studied personifications.

Apostrophe occurs with great frequency in "Tam o' Shanter," producing an effect of continual emotional exaggeration. As one of the more patently artificial rhetorical devices, apostrophe invites parody as a pretentious stylistic tic. The poet addresses Tam ("O Tam!" [line 16], "Now Tam, O Tam!" [line 151], "Ah Tam! ah Tam!" [line 201]), the reader ("Ah, gentle dames!" [line 33], "Every man and mother's son" [line 220]), liquor ("inspiring bold John Barleycorn!"

[line 105]), and Meg, Tam's horse ("Now do thy speedy utmost, Meg" [line 205]). The drama of the story clearly does not justify all this exclamation and exhortation, nor is the apostrophe a mark of genuine sentiment or emotion.

Burns achieves a similar burlesque effect through accumulated similes. These clustered comparisons with their lofty rhetoric constitute an ironic comment on the lowly events of the narrative; they also possess a self-reflexive irony suggesting the inherent tendency of language to digress and "show off." Thus the line "But pleasures are like poppies spread" (line 59) leads to "Or like the snow," "Or like the borealis race," and "Or like the rainbow's lovely form" (lines 59–66), and Maggie the mare takes off at the critical moment like angry bees from a hive, or dogs after a cat, or a market crowd after a thief (lines 193–199).

Anaphora, which refers to the repetition of a word or phrase, is another technique used for purposes of amplification and accumulation. Describing the time of Tam's ride, Burns repeats "hour" three times in a comically melodramatic periphrasis:

> The hour approaches Tam maun ride;
> That hour, o' night's black arch the keystane,
> That dreary hour, he mounts his beast in;
> (lines 68–70)

The ford Tam crosses is described as a place of accumulated horrors and grisly accidents: "Where in the snaw the chapman smoored; . . ./Where drunken Charlie brak's neck bane; . . ./Where hunters fand the murdered bairn; . . ./ Where Mungo's mither hanged hersel" (lines 90–96). These accidents, murders, and suicides contribute to the mock-heroic tone by stressing the ominousness of Tam's course of action, but at the same time they display a playful rhetorical *copia*, or abundance. The reader is as aware of the linguistic surface, the energetic pileup of words, as of the substance, that is, the actual horrors cited. Part of the comedy derives from the discrepancy between the verbal exhibitionism and the melancholy topic.

Playfulness likewise informs the catalogue of "relics" on the holy table in the kirk (lines 130–142). The murderer's bones, unchristened "bairns," thief, five tomahawks ("wi' blude red rusted"), five scimitars ("wi' murder crusted"), garter, and knife, while suggesting tragic evocations of terror and pity, in fact lose their terror because of the comic emphasis on the sheer number and variety of these ghastly items.

Personifications and epithets are also subjected to satirical distortion, conveying an effect of bathos rather than epic grandeur. For example, Burns personifies "Care" as a tippler who "mad to see a man sae happy,/E'en drowned himsel amang the nappy" (lines 53–54) and prosaically describes the devil himself, "auld Nick," as "a touzie tyke" (line 121), that is, a shaggy dog.

The language of the poem, then, satirizes both Tam's boozy adventure and the epic tradition of patterned and embroidered narrative. A final function of the poem's rhetoric is to characterize the speaker or persona; the narrator sounds inebriated, as though drink had loosened his tongue so that he cannot stop his teeming brain from adding just one word more. His verbal flights and descents create both the mock-heroic tone and the general air of indecorousness, for his rhetoric is as drunken as Tam himself.

The narrator is not only a drunk but a Scot. Indeed, one of the ways in which Burns's mock-epic differs from other exemplars of the genre is its Scottishness. The poem's connection with the folk ballads and superstitious tales of a particular culture gives it an idiosyncratic quality, a tone all its own, just as Pope's *The Rape of the Lock* derives its specific tonality from the customs and values of polite eighteenth-century society. In each case, the parody is not solely a linguistic phenomenon. To satirize the model of epic narrative, the authors introduce not only an array of rhetorical devices but a setting, and a set of assumptions, at a vast remove from the culture and morality of ancient Greece and Rome. For example, in "Tam o' Shanter" the conventional voyage to the underworld takes the form of a drunken hallucination:

> And vow! Tam saw an unco sight!
> Warlocks and witches in a dance!
> Nae cotillon brent new frae France,
> But hornpipes, jigs, strathpeys, and reels,
> Put life and mettle in their heels.
>
> (lines 114–118)

These peculiarly Scottish denizens of hell, for whom auld Nick himself plays the pipes, are for the most part old hags, and the repeated emphasis on their "sarks" (the shirts which remain after they throw off their clothes) has the effect of indecorous sexual innuendo. Old witch Nannie's "cutty sark," "in longitude though sorely scanty," seems to stimulate Tam's lust so that, unable to contain himself any longer, he cries out admiringly, "Weel done, Cutty-sark!", thus provoking the "hellish legion" to pursue him.

In this poem, the vision of hell thus takes the form of a drunken party, and the hero's "sin" is a kind of bleary-eyed concupiscence. In contrast, Pope's underworld is the Cave of Spleen, where dissatisfied prudes and disappointed old maids live with their perverted fantasies and thwarted desires. Burns's folk-tale, with its bawdy, farcical quality, and Pope's fantasy, with its pointed misogynistic satire, each embroider on the epic motif of a descent into a strange and awful netherworld, but in ways that reveal specific cultural biases. The swaggering, leering masculinity of Scottish tavern life contributes to the specific tonal quality of Burns's mock-epic, just as the flirtatious, manipulative femininity of eighteenth-century drawing rooms contributes to Pope's.

B.S.

SUGGESTED READINGS

Crawford, Thomas, *Burns: A Study of the Poems and Songs* (1960).
Daiches, David, *Robert Burns* (1950).

WILLIAM WORDSWORTH

C H R O N O L O G Y

1770	Born at Cockermouth in Cumberland. Son of lawyer John Wordsworth and Anne Cookson Wordsworth.
1778	Death of Wordsworth's mother. William is sent to live with Ann Tyson in Hawkshead; he attends the grammar school there, studying for the next nine years under William Taylor.
1787	Enters St. John's College, Cambridge University.
1789	French Revolution begins. Wordsworth is an enthusiastic supporter of it at first; later, his democratic sympathies cool, and he will end his life as a staunch conservative.
1790	With Robert Jones, Wordsworth takes a walking tour through France, Italy, and Switzerland during summer holiday.
1791	Receives A.B. from Cambridge. Visits France in November.
1792	At Orléans, meets Annette Vallon, the 25-year-old daughter of a surgeon; she bears him a daughter, Caroline. Returns to England in December.
1793	Takes a walking tour through southern England and Wales, including a visit to Tintern Abbey, inspiration of one of his most famous poems. Publishes *An Evening Walk* and *Descriptive Sketches*. Secretly visits Annette Vallon and daughter Caroline in October.
1794	Visits Lake District. Spends last portion of year caring for his friend Raisley Calvert, who is dying.

1795   Upon death of Calvert, receives a legacy of £900. Uses this money to set up a home with his sister Dorothy in Dorsetshire. Meets William Godwin and Samuel Taylor Coleridge.

1796   Writes play *The Borderers*.

1797   Moves with Dorothy to Alfoxden in Somersetshire, largely to be near Coleridge, who is living nearby and with whom a close friendship has developed.

1798   Wordsworth and Coleridge conceive the idea for the *Lyrical Ballads*, a collection of poems written by the two in close collaboration and intended as an experiment in poetry written in "the natural language of men." The book is published anonymously; it will come to be regarded as the inauguration of the English romantic movement. Coleridge accompanies the Wordsworths on a trip to Germany.

1799   In Germany, Wordsworth writes the "Lucy" poems and begins work on the autobiographical poem later published as *The Prelude*. Later, Wordsworth and Dorothy settle at Dove Cottage in Grasmere.

1800   Writes "Michael" and "The Recluse," among other poems.

1801   Second edition of *Lyrical Ballads* published, containing Wordsworth's famous "Preface," a "manifesto" of romanticism and a milestone in the history of literary criticism.

1802   Visits France with Dorothy; spends several weeks with Annette Vallon and Caroline. On return to England, marries Mary Hutchinson; she comes to live with William and Dorothy at Dove Cottage. At work on many fine poems including the famous sonnets and the "Immortality" ode.

1803   Visits Scotland with Dorothy; meets novelist and poet Sir Walter Scott.

1804   At work on *The Prelude*. Coleridge leaves England for Malta.

1805   Death of Wordsworth's brother John in a shipwreck.

1806   Coleridge returns from Malta, resumes friendship with Wordsworth.

1807   Publication of *Poems, in Two Volumes*.

1808   Moves to Allan Bank, Grasmere; Coleridge resides nearby.

1809   Contributes to *The Friend*, periodical edited by Coleridge. Publishes political tract *The Convention of Cintra*.

1810   Wordsworth and Coleridge quarrel and become estranged.

1812   Death of Wordsworth's children Catherine and Thomas. Reconciliation with Coleridge.

1813   Moves to Rydal Mount; is named stamp distributor for Westmoreland, a
            government sinecure. ,

1814–   Publishes *The Excursion*, *Collected Poems*, and *The White Doe of Rylstone*.
1815

1817   Meets John Keats.

1818   Wordsworth's political liberalism all but dead by this time; publishes election
            pamphlets on behalf of the Tories.

1820   Visits Europe; publishes *The River Duddon*, an uninspired sonnet sequence.

1822   Publishes *Ecclesiastical Sketches*, setting forth conservative religious views.

1831   Last meeting with Coleridge.

1834   Death of Coleridge.

1839   Receives honorary doctorate from Oxford University. By this time, Doro-
            thy's mental health is in decline. Wordsworth is at work revising *The Prelude*.

1842   Publishes *Poems, Chiefly of Early and Late Years*. Receives a pension of £300
            per year from the government.

1843   Named poet laureate.

1849   Final edition of collected poems during his lifetime.

1850   Death of Wordsworth; buried at Rydal Mount. *The Prelude* is published
            posthumously. Wordsworth is survived by Dorothy (d. 1855) and by his
            wife, Mary (d. 1859).

ESSAY QUESTIONS WITH ANSWERS

"Preface" to the Lyrical Ballads

3.1   Compare Wordsworth's critical theory with that generally espoused by eighteenth-century critics.

Answer   Wordsworth's theory, as stated in the 1801 "Preface" to *Lyrical Ballads*, attacks the central tenet of eighteenth-century critical doctrine: the theory of decorum. That theory, which called on poets to choose corresponding subject matter and style according to a hierarchy of genres ranging from humble pastoral to lofty epic, had been a feature of poetic theory since the Greeks and Romans. As codified by eighteenth-century critics such as Pope and Johnson, the theory influenced the "neoclassical" character of that period so that much of the poetry produced conformed to definite kinds or genres in theme, structure, and style.

By insisting on a new "contract" between writer and reader, Wordsworth modified traditional notions of the proper domain of poetry. The contract Wordsworth proposes in his "Preface" involves the poet's fidelity to his own mood and feelings as he expresses "the essential passions of the heart" and "the beautiful and permanent forms of nature." Instead of applying external rules of composition according to preestablished convention (for example, fitting an elevated style to the epic themes of love and war), Wordsworth postulates an organic decorum springing from the writer's own intimate experience with nature and articulated in a "natural" idiom.

This new decorum suggests a different kind of subject matter. Because, in Wordsworth's view, the "passions" exist in their purest form in simple rural life, ordinary people and humble activities become acceptable poetic themes. This rural life can be presented realistically, rather than cloaked in the allegorical trappings of the pastoral mode, because it has value in and of itself. In addition, the poet's own passions become a proper domain of poetry. One consequence of the autobiographical themes of the romantics is a more frequent use of lyric modes, such as the ode, sonnet, or meditative poem, which provide arenas for the presentation of the poet's persona, the "I."

Wordsworth's attack on the old theory of decorum includes hostility to the rhetorical figures of speech and consciously elevated diction which many eighteenth-century critics applauded as delightfully "artificial." Against the canon of artifice, Wordsworth poses a doctrine of sincerity and authenticity. In his view, the poet is not primarily a skilled artist but rather "a man speaking to men." Poetic language, then, must be the common currency of humanity, not a specialized vocabulary addressed to an elite. Even the Wordsworthian definition of poetry reflects the newness of his aesthetic approach. According to Wordsworth, poetry is "the spontaneous overflow of powerful feelings; it takes its origin from emotion recollected in tranquillity." This definition of poetry treats it not as a product, a formal "end," but a creative process which originates in mood, feeling, and sensation.

Wordsworth's proposals were revolutionary in that they opened up the subject matter of poetry to include the realistic presentation of common experience and common life as well as broadening the linguistic resources available to the poet. At the same time, however, many of Wordsworth's ideas were linked to eighteenth-century views on poetry. Like the neoclassicists, he insists on treating nature, including human nature, as a repository of moral significance and standards. He implicitly upholds the classical and neoclassical formula that the purpose of poetry is to delight, move, and instruct the reader. Furthermore, he subscribes to the neoclassical doctrine of imitation in which the poet holds the mirror up to nature, reflecting the world in words. It is in what Wordsworth sees in the mirror that he differs from the neoclassicists: instead of types of people and ideal actions, he sees individuals and a world of psychological experience. Thus, Wordsworth's greatest poems—"Tintern Abbey," the "Immortality" ode, *The Prelude*—form a kind of spiritual autobiography. It is only by faithfully recording the intimate experience of an individual—himself—that Wordsworth arrives at a sense of the universal and the ideal.

3.2   Analyze Wordsworth's literary theory as presented in the "Preface," and relate it to his practice in the *Lyrical Ballads* themselves.

Answer   In the "Preface," Wordsworth's argument seems to have two thrusts. One part of the discussion is devoted to a redefinition of the proper domain and themes of poetry, the other to questions of style and diction. The two components are intimately related, for Wordsworth's new aesthetic appears to depend on a new concept of theme. Thus Wordsworth combines form and content in his description of his poetic purpose: "to choose incidents and situations from common life, and to relate or describe them . . . in a selection of language really used by men," with the aim of illustrating "the manner in which our feelings and ideas are associated in a state of excitement." "Low and rustic life" is suitable matter for poetry because "in that condition the essential passions of the heart find a better soil in which they can attain their maturity, are less under restraint, and speak a plainer and more emphatic language." The plainer language is necessary in order to imitate those "essential passions" which constitute the truth of human nature.

Again and again in the course of the "Preface," Wordsworth implies that the task of a true poet is to strip away the false accretions of ornament in order to reveal the beauty and wonder of nature in all its simplicity. When he describes poetry as the "spontaneous overflow of powerful feelings," identifies the poet as "a man speaking to men," and characterizes the poet's art as "an acknowledgement of the beauty of the universe," Wordsworth seems to be calling for purging art of false rhetoric and conventional gestures and reconstituting it as a genuine, sincere, impromptu communication between writer and reader.

This enterprise of getting back to nature, as it were, is somewhat naively presented by Wordsworth as fundamentally a matter of "true" imitation. The poet's fidelity to what he feels and sees, as well as to the "real" language of men, is all that is required. Wordsworth's friend, the poet and critic Samuel Taylor Coleridge, in several essays in his *Biographia Literaria*, pointed out as early as 1815 the imprecision of this formula. Although acknowledging Wordsworth's "remonstrance in behalf of truth and nature" (Chap. XVII), Coleridge resists the idea that poetry's only subject should be low and rustic life and that its only style should be a common, prosaic language. Coleridge questions the notion of a "real" or common language spoken by people, pointing out the great linguistic variety exhibited by individuals and social classes. He further suggests that only in drama "or other professed imitation" can particular class usages be precisely imitated, for a poem requires certain omissions and changes in diction in order to retain its essential identity as a unified metrical composition.

Coleridge's remarks reveal one of Wordsworth's weaknesses as a literary critic: a failure to define his ideas in a consistent and systematic way. The "Preface" is also flawed by a tendency toward self-contradiction, a consequence of Wordsworth's attempt to purge art of art. In trying to define a new poetic which is true to common experience and ordinary speech, Wordsworth is in fact substituting for the old rules of rhetoric and composition a new canon of art, although one that masquerades as artless. In his remarks about language, he is actually invoking the classical *genus humilis,* the low style, except that he severs its traditional connection with the pastoral and extends it to all poetry. In his remarks about subject matter, he is implicitly arguing against the whole idea of genre or kind in poetry, rejecting the conventional themes associated with particular genres for an all-inclusive if somewhat vague poetic subject: the excited passions of ordinary people, particularly when "incorporated with the beautiful and permanent forms of nature." In insisting on the emotional truth exhibited by rustic life, he seems to be promoting a pastoral based on realistic norms instead of allegorical convention.

This new rhetoric does not, indeed cannot, entirely jettison all the features of the old, and thus it lands Wordsworth in some apparent contradictions. For example, Wordsworth insists on the importance of "selection" "for removing what would otherwise be painful or disgusting in the passion" which the poet is so faithfully and realistically imitating. He thus retains the neoclassical concept of the idealizing, generalizing function of the poetic imagination, for the object of poetry is "truth, not individual and local, but general and operative." He emphasizes the pleasures of meter even while arguing that there is no "essential difference between the language of prose and metrical composition." This "new" poetry is, then, in many respects conservative, retaining the aesthetic properties of selection, idealization, and meter traditionally associated with the craft.

The poems in *Lyrical Ballads* show what Wordsworth meant far better than his uncertain attempt at systematic argumentation. For example, the idea of a "new" pastoral emerges more clearly in "Michael: A Pastoral Poem" than in all the earnest extolling of rustics in the "Preface." This tale of a shepherd, sustained through hardship and loss by his profound connection with nature, blends an insistence on the real rigors of rural life with eloquent pathos and sentiment. The poem is both "low" and "high," both realistic by comparison with the never-never land of conventional pastoral and idealistic in its elevated moralizing strain. Similarly, "The Old Cumberland Beggar" aggrandizes its humble subject by means of the persona's meditations on the moral regeneration of a whole community wrought by a vagrant who is almost anonymous in his decrepitude. In "Lines Composed a Few Miles above Tintern Abbey" (the title itself suggesting an improvisation rather than a formal piece produced by rule in the study), Wordsworth shows the approach of humanity to the "beautiful and permanent forms" of nature and dramatizes the act of "recollecting emotion in tranquillity."

Thus, in the longer, more complex poems of *Lyrical Ballads,* Wordsworth exhibits his characteristic themes. In these poems, he also employs the signature style that he attempts to describe with only partial success in the "Preface." This style is simple and direct, depending on repetition and the gradual accumulation of striking phrases to achieve its effect.

The shorter poems of the *Lyrical Ballads* exhibit many of the same features of theme and style in condensed form. Taken together, they constitute Wordsworth's "songs of innocence," celebrating the power of nature, the vivid sensations of childhood, and the inherent dignity of humble persons through a kind of compressed assertion. Striking phrases and epithets are frequent: "A wise passiveness" ("Expostulation and Reply"), "Love, an universal birth" ("To My Sister"), and "One impulse from a vernal wood" ("The Tables Turned") all suggest the eloquence Wordsworth brings to bear on the ordinary incidents of life.

In the "Preface," Wordsworth expresses a somewhat naive faith in a mirror relationship between humanity and nature, person and person, in which the poet participates as "an upholder and preserver, carrying everywhere with him relationship and love." With the possible exception of "Tintern Abbey," which is essentially about coping with doubt, the poems of *Lyrical Ballads* express this faith thematically and stylistically; they persuade by virtue of their music and rhetoric.

"Tintern Abbey"

3.3 Analyze the treatment of time in the poem.

Answer "Tintern Abbey" is a meditative poem in which a visit to a familiar landscape triggers remembrances of time past. Wordsworth uses verse paragraphs to signal shifts among his present experience of the scene, memories of his earlier visit to the Wye, and memories from the intervening years. This fluid movement from one moment in time to another suggests the rambling of the mind as it plays over the physical landscape.

The opening stresses the lapse of time between the present experience and the original visit five years before: "Five years have passed; five summers, with the length/Of five long winters!" (lines 1–2). The poet then goes on to paint the particulars of the present scene, representing earth, sky, hedgerows, and farms as parts of a fused, organic whole.

As the poem progresses, we learn how the poet has arrived at this unified vision of the forms of nature. In the second paragraph (lines 23–48), he begins to describe the operations of his memory on the forms of physical experience and to show how these memories have become integrated in his moral life. His mind has turned and returned to the original scene in order to gain solace in the midst of the "joyless daylight" (line 52) of worldly cares: "How oft, in spirit, have I turned to thee,/O sylvan Wye! thou wanderer through the woods,/How often has my spirit turned to thee!" (lines 55–57). Time becomes layered as the poet superimposes past sensations on present experience. The influence of the past is suggested in the condensed "autobiography" of paragraph 4 (lines 58–83), where Wordsworth remembers his adolescent self—haunted, sensual, impulsive, seeking escape in nature. That initial encounter with the landscape is recalled as fevered and passionate, with the young Wordsworth projecting his own emotional turmoil onto the natural forms around him.

The poet returns to the present in the second half of paragraph 4 (lines 83–111), elaborating on his mature philosophy of the illuminating interchange between self and scene, subject and object, which yields a recognition of a presence in nature beyond the realm of sense, animating both the beholder and the thing beheld.

The last development in the poem is the invocation in the fifth paragraph (lines 112–159) of "my dearest Friend," Wordsworth's sister, who becomes yet another means of endowing the present with the emotional riches gleaned from experiences in the past. His sister's "wild ecstasies" (line 138) recall Wordsworth's past, that is, his adolescent impulses, and suggest the future, that is, the "sober pleasure" (line 139) which is Wordsworth's current mood and which shall be his sister's in years to come as the operation of memory within her deepens the moral and emotional significance of her present experience. Using the process of free association as the mind wanders through time, Wordsworth blends past, present, and future into a fluid medium which traces the timeless values that he sees as immanent in nature. In doing so, he reveals the reassuring continuities of the individual's imaginative life.

3.4 Discuss the themes and significance of the passage (lines 88–111) which begins

> . . . For I have learned
> To look on nature, not as in the hour

Of thoughtless youth; but hearing oftentimes
The still, sad music of humanity
(lines 88–91)

Answer   The passage begins with a comparison between time past and time present. The difference between "the hour/Of thoughtless youth" (line 90) and the poet's more mature perspective is the addition of the element of thought. No longer limited to sensual appetite, the narrator now experiences in the presence of nature something beyond the reach of the senses. The emphasis on metaphysical sensations—"hearing oftentimes/The still, sad music of humanity" (lines 90–91) and "And I have felt/A presence which disturbs me with the joy/Of elevated thoughts" (lines 93–95)—suggests that the poet's interaction with the scene is not solely perceptual; rather, it has become psychological and creative, partly a projection of Wordsworth's emotions into nature and partly a transfiguration of nature by the power of imagination. Detailed visual description is replaced by generalized reference ("the light of setting suns,/And the round ocean and the living air" [lines 97–98]), implying that mere vision, the coarser appetitive response of his adolescent self who "had no need of . . . any interest/Unborrowed from the eye" (lines 81–83), has been subdued. It would seem that only this relative defeat of the "eye" allows the poet to experience "a sense sublime/Of something far more deeply interfused" (lines 95–96).

At the same time, Wordsworth does not simply turn away from physical nature in order to celebrate a quasi-divine revelation. He insists on a complex simultaneity of response that integrates the individual's mental life with the world outside. Imagination has the primary role in achieving this difficult integration. Thus the lines "the mighty world/Of eye, and ear—both what they half create,/And what perceive" (lines 105–107) refer both to the physical world apprehended by the senses and to an internal, animated version of this world created in the mind. In this crucial passage, as elsewhere in the poem, Wordsworth alludes to the difficulty of arriving at a full imaginative comprehension of nature. The "serene and blessed mood" (line 41) he invokes early in the poem is countered by "a sad perplexity" (line 60); a sense of "loss" precedes the "abundant recompense" (lines 86–87). The individual, after all, can only "half create" the world anew, and although "nature and the language of the sense" (line 108) produce a feeling of internal continuity and moral certitude in the poet, he needs the further support of his young sister, who will repeat, heighten, and clarify his own experience, lest he allow his "genial spirits to decay" (line 113). The mature perspective, transforming the "wild ecstasies" of sensual youth into a "sober pleasure" compounded of memory and imagination, is achieved only through an active effort of creative will.

"Ode: Intimations of Immortality"

3.5 In what sense does Wordsworth intend the statement "The Child is father of the Man"? How does the "Immortality" ode communicate this idea?

Answer The statement sounds like a riddle, but it offers in epigrammatic form Wordsworth's theories of psychological development and imaginative growth. Appearing as part of an epigraph to the ode, the line was originally used in Wordsworth's short lyric "My Heart Leaps Up." In that poem, Wordsworth evoked a vivid emotional state engendered by the sight of a rainbow, a state he had entered again and again from his life's beginning to the present moment. Thus the child's excited response to nature, the heart's "leaping," is the source, or "father," of the adult's sensations of pleasure in the same event. This crucial link connecting childhood with maturity and old age is a major theme in Wordsworth's psychology of natural revelation.

In the ode, the poet expands on the concept of the child's special powers of vision. From early memories of his own vivid experience of nature, Wordsworth infers a state of preexistence (existence of the soul before birth) somewhat analogous to the Christian conception of an afterlife. Both preexistence and afterlife are celestial states, where the soul abides close to God. Thus the role of the child may be seen as that of an intercessor for the original "Father" of our being, reminding adults of their former glory and future destination.

Wordsworth's method here, which is characteristic of his mature lyrics, is to move back and forth between two different states of experience, childhood and maturity. Each state is only partial. The child is incomplete because of radical innocence and ignorance of the world of suffering and knowledge; the adult is crippled by the inability to retrieve the child's sense of glory. Only when bound together through the poet's imaginative power do the two states form an organic whole. The repeated references to springtime creatures—birds and lambs— and to "Thou Child of Joy" evoke one pole of experience toward which the poet yearns. Contrasting sections describe the narrator's recurrent sense of loss, desolation, and deprivation:

> Whither is fled the visionary gleam?
> Where is it now, the glory and the dream?
> (lines 56–57)

This technique of juxtaposition allows Wordsworth to explore the relationship between "radiant" childhood and "shadowy" age, with the adult still preserving some faint recollection of the faded glory and a sense of "primal sympathy" which has been inherited from the childhood self. However, Wordsworth does not entirely reconcile the two poles. The child is "Father" in the further sense of a lost original, a distant source; the splendor and beauty of childhood haunt the adult like the memory of an irrecoverable Eden.

3.6 Where is the climax of the poem?

Answer The ode's climax begins in stanza 9. The lines "O joy! that in our embers/Is something that doth live" (lines 130–131) signal a shift from the regret expressed at the end of stanza 8, where the poet contemplates the child's future: "Full soon thy Soul shall have her earthly freight,/And custom lie upon thee with a weight,/Heavy as frost, and deep almost as life!" (lines 127–129) Wordsworth suggests that he has escaped the cold stillness of "frost" because of the fire that yet burns within him, even if only as "embers." The whole of stanza 9 is about the solace he has gained over the years from "Those shadowy recollections/Which, be what they may,/Are yet the fountain light of all our day,/Are yet a master light of all our seeing" (lines 150–153). Although somewhat diminished in fire and radiance, the past is contained in the present. No matter how far we have come "inland" on our journey through life, still "Our Souls have sight of that immortal sea/Which brought us thither" (lines 164–165). There is comfort for the poet in an ember, a shadow, a glimpse.

Although the turn from regret to consolation occurs in stanza 9, the full emotional climax of the poem is reached in stanza 10, where joy predominates and the poet expresses himself with greater confidence. In this stanza, he returns to the present scene of springtime festivity and celebrates his mature recognition of the proper relationship between humanity and nature. Wordsworth begins the stanza with an invocation of the inhabitants of the pastoral landscape (birds, lambs, pipers, shepherds), asserting his sympathetic identification with their rites of spring: "We in thought will join your throng" (line 172). Although he briefly acknowledges his sense of loss, at the same time he names his source of consolation:

> Though nothing can bring back the hour
> Of splendor in the grass, of glory in the flower;

> We will grieve not, rather find
> Strength in what remains behind;
> In the primal sympathy
> Which having been must ever be;
>   (lines 178–183)

In these lines, Wordsworth encapsulates the essential meaning of the ode: as people grow older and suffer the loss of radiant apprehension, they can still find a sense of oneness with nature through meditation, memory, and the powers of the "philosophic mind" (line 187).

Thus stanza 10 is climactic in part because it offers in a striking and condensed form the central theme of the poem. After the resounding assertions of this passage, the final stanza has the effect of a coda. Its lowering of tension enacts the process described by the poet whereby the individual approaches nature with serene comprehension. One last time Wordsworth reads the book of nature, extracting a moral lesson about human life from "the meanest flower that blows" (line 203). Nostalgia, doubt, and joy may have led the poet to this final "reading," but they have also led him beyond mere emotion or "tears" to a profound philosophic acceptance:

> Thanks to the human heart by which we live,
> Thanks to its tenderness, its joys, and fears,
> To me the meanest flower that blows can give
> Thoughts that do often lie too deep for tears.
>   (lines 201–204)

3.7   Discuss the conception of life presented in stanza 7.

Answer   Stanza 7 begins by describing a child's playing at life, pretending various adult activities, but as the passage develops, the literal context fades and the description becomes a portrait of human life as a series of roles played out upon the "humorous stage" (line 104). The implicit metaphor of the world as a stage and the individual as an actor, together with the reference to "humors," links this description to Jaques's famous speech in Act II of Shakespeare's *As You Like It* ("All the world's a stage"). Jaques's cynical caricatures of the human gallery from infancy to old age suggest a melancholic view of people as posturing fools. Though Wordsworth's catalogue is less biting, it too suggests the quality of empty gesturing: "As if his whole vocation/Were endless imitation" (lines

107–108). The whole stanza, with its allusions to stratagems and roles—"some little plan or chart" (line 91), "newly-learned art" (line 92), "dialogues of business, love, or strife" (line 99), "The little Actor cons another part" (line 103—implies a superficial showmanship and a life lived externally. Thus the stanza provides a vivid contrast to Wordsworth's ideal conception of life, in which the individual is moved from within by a "primal sympathy" (line 182) to seek a true relationship and identification with nature and with other people.

"I Wandered Lonely as a Cloud"

3.8 What are the central subject and the theme of the poem?

Answer The poem has the outlines of a narrative. The poet wanders through a landscape, is struck by the sight of a field of daffodils, and later, in moments of solitude, recalls the experience, seeing the field again in his mind. However, this sketch does not fully explain what happens in the poem, for Wordsworth develops the vision of the daffodils as the central event, emphasizing the act of seeing and exploring its philosophical significance. Thus the imagery describing the scene becomes particularly important, for it is through figurative language that Wordsworth explores the relationship between subject and object, humanity and nature.

The first image of the poem, "I wandered lonely as a cloud" (line 1), immediately establishes both the poet's solitude and his connection with the natural world. He "floats above" the scene and yet is part of it. The sense of a living nature which reaches out to the observer deepens as Wordsworth describes the field of daffodils. He compares the flowers to the "stars that shine/And twinkle on the milky way" (lines 7–8) and to the "sparkling waves" (line 14) of a nearby lake. Thus a kind of fusion occurs by which heaven, earth, and water are joined in the vision of the dancing flowers. Both images convey the qualities of radiance and movement ("twinkle," "sparkle"). Together with the repetitions of the word "dance," these images create a picture of nature as vital, animated, and glowing.

The relationship between poet and landscape is one of intimate union, suggesting an identity of mood between subject and object:

> A poet could not but be gay,
> In such a jocund company;
> (lines 15–16)

Finally, then, the experience of seeing ("I gazed—and gazed—") becomes the subject of the poem. The vision and the attendant emotion are what the poet brings away from the experience and later recreates in memory.

3.9   Discuss what the poem implies about "that inward eye/Which is the bliss of solitude."

Answer   The idea of solitude is central to the poem. The image of the poet wandering "lonely as a cloud" (line 1) opens the poem and establishes the atmosphere in which the poetic vision occurs. Solitude is once again the poet's condition at the end of the poem as he lies on his couch, apart from nature yet still somehow connected to it through the power of imagination.

The last stanza as a whole describes the operation of imagination on the fragments of past experience. A single brief event which occurred in a distant summer landscape has brought the poet permanent "wealth" (line 18) in terms of the ability both to recall the visual scene and to recapture the emotional mood. The idea of recurrence is suggested by the "flash" (line 21) of vision, which is connected with the radiance of the original flowers, and by the "danc-ing" (line 24) of the poet's heart, which recalls the animation of the scene. Thus, "that inward eye/Which is the bliss of solitude" is the creative imagination, the human capacity to remember and reproduce experience. This creative power, common to all people, is more highly developed in the poet, who composes poems out of "emotion recollected in tranquillity."

"The World Is Too Much with Us"

3.10   Discuss the structure of the poem.

Answer   The poem is a sonnet, its fourteen lines divided into octave (the first eight lines) and sestet (the last six lines). Employing only four rhymes (*abbaabba, cdcdcd*), Wordsworth creates a unified structure in which sound and sense are tightly woven together.

The major turn occurs in line 9, where a monosyllabic statement is followed by a dash and exclamation: "It moves us not—Great God! I'd rather be . . . ." The sonnet breaks in two at this point, with the former part devoted to a picture of humankind's alienation from nature and the latter devoted to a vision of the human position in a pantheistic universe. Thus, in the opening octave, Wordsworth conveys the ideas of separation from nature and existential emptiness. The first four lines describe the "world" as a place of mercantile activity which exploits people's "powers" (line 2) and "hearts" (line 4) for the futile purposes of "getting and spending" (line 2). In the next four lines, images of a living nature—the maternal sea, the sleeping winds—suggest only the human disharmony with nature: "For this, for everything, we are out of tune;/It moves us not" (lines 8–9).

By breaking the line in the middle with an exclamatory burst ("Great God!"), Wordsworth creates an emotional climax as he moves into the sestet. In the closing movement of the sonnet, he imagines a state very different from the world-weary condition described in the octave. Placing himself in a particular landscape ("this pleasant lea" [line 11]), he invokes the spirits of pagan deities as a metaphor for a nature alive with meaning. Wordsworth uses all six lines of the sestet to elaborate his imaginative "glimpse" of natural divinity, thus making it a persuasive answer to the despair expressed in the octave.

3.11   What is the point of the classical allusions at the end of the poem?

Answer   The classical allusions create an aura of magical animism which permeates the imagined universe as the poet gazes out to sea. Proteus, a sea god who can change shape at will, and Triton, another deity of the sea who served as herald for Neptune, are personifications of the great force of nature brooding in the deeps of the ocean. Ironically, the poet must turn to pagan mythology for images of nature's vital power, for though the "creed" of the ancient Greeks is "outworn" (line 10), that is, no longer a viable system of belief in the modern era, the Greek legends are nourishing, "suckling" the pagan by providing a sense of connection to nature's living force. The images of Proteus and Triton constitute a way of making nature ours again, a way of humanizing the physical universe by means of anthropomorphic transfiguration.

The Prelude

3.12   Explain what the following episodes in *The Prelude* have in common: the boat ride (I, 357–400, meaning Book I, lines 357–400), skating with friends

(I, 425–463), the rising moon (I, 567–580), the walk home after the dance at sunrise (IV, 309–338), and meeting the shepherds (VIII, 256–293).

Answer All these episodes represent what Wordsworth calls "spots of time" (XII, 1), those moments in life which charge the imagination and lend the perceiver a sense of power. They are scattered throughout *The Prelude* as a sign of the continuous influence of nature on the poet's mind. All suggest an animated universe that is rich in significance.

Some of these incidents are triggered by an optical illusion which suddenly suggests to Wordsworth the presence of a vital force permeating the scene. For example, in narrating his nighttime foray in the stolen boat, Wordsworth describes his destination, a craggy ridge, as a monster rearing up from the deep:

> . . . the grim shape
> Towered up between me and the stars, and still,
> For so it seemed, with a purpose of its own
> And measured motion like a living thing,
> Strode after me
>
>   (I, 381–385)

Similarly, when Wordsworth describes his sudden stop while skating, the landscape seems to come alive, continuing to sweep by him with a movement of its own:

> . . . yet still the solitary cliffs
> Wheeled by me—even as if the earth had rolled
> With visible motion her diurnal round!
>
>   (I, 458–460)

Both these incidents forge a link between the youthful poet's mind and the breathing world of nature which surrounds him.

A related theme is the power of the landscape to bind the poet to other people. In Book VIII, Wordsworth depicts his encounter with a solitary shepherd, who appears like a "giant" in the mist and then, stepping into the sun, like an angel transfigured by light:

> His form hath flashed upon me, glorified
> By the deep radiance of the setting sun.
>
>   (VIII, 269–270)

From this visual perception, Wordsworth moves to a recognition of the inherent dignity and worth of the individual:

> . . . Thus was man
> Ennobled outwardly before my sight,
> And thus my heart was early introduced
> To an unconscious love and reverence
> Of human nature;
>   (VIII, 275–279)

The other two episodes listed, the risings of moon and sun, suggest the poet's active role in the interchange between humanity and nature. The poet is not merely the passive recipient of visual sensations but a creator of meaning through the subjective power of his mind. Thus Wordsworth's eye moves over the waters shining in the moonlight, "gathering . . . new pleasure like a bee among the flowers" (I, 578–580). His description of the sunrise, with the sky "kindling," the sea "laughing," and the mountains "shining" (IV, 319–332), suggests that the benevolent power of the scene comes in part from the animating vision of the poet's own eye. As he says elsewhere, of a sunset:

> . . . An auxiliar light
> Came from my mind, which on the setting sun
> Bestowed new splendor;
>   (II, 368–370)

These "spots of time" knit the fabric of the poet's experience, creating a continuous thread of revelation which connect the major crises of the poem. It is through these momentary flashes of insight that Wordsworth develops the habit of meditation which prepares him for the great illuminating visions of the Simplon Pass and Mt. Snowdon.

3.13 What is the structure of The Prelude?

Answer Wordsworth designed the structure of The Prelude to mirror the subject of the poem: the "growth of a poet's mind." The major principle of organization is that of mental association, or the power of the mind to connect disparate incidents into a coherent framework. Thus one "spot of time" follows another in a continuous stream, as Wordsworth illustrates the operation of creative thought on the physical forms of experience. A strictly chronological report of events is abandoned in favor of a more faithful rendering of the poet's spiritual autobiography, which consists in fact of an accumulation of timeless visions.

Beyond this fabric of associations, the poem contains several other organizing patterns. One of these—a pattern of ascent and decline or crisis and recovery—depends on a magnified version of the spots of time motif. Thus the visions occurring at the Simplon Pass and Mt. Snowdon represent climactic moments in the poet's experience, when the simple train of associations becomes charged with religious and moral significance and the poet fully realizes and articulates his philosophy of life. As these two moments represent the zenith of the poet's inner existence, so others represent its nadir. The episodes involving an urban milieu—Wordsworth's residence in London (Book VII), the fair at Smithfield (Book VII), and his sojourn in Paris (Books IX–XI)—represent humanity alienated from nature, struggling with the "blank confusion" (VII, 722) of the city and the terrible conflict of political ideologies. These crises in Wordsworth's life illustrate "a heart that had been turned aside/From Nature's way by outward accidents" (XI, 290–291), suggesting a descent into error on the spiritual journey from which the poet can recover only by renewed contact with the natural world.

These patterns of timeless vision and of crisis and resolution are superimposed upon a rough chronology, extending from the childhood memories of Books I and II through the years at Cambridge (Books III–VI) to the short stay in London (Book VII) and the sojourn in France (Books IX–XI). But Book VIII, which reviews the first twenty-one years of Wordsworth's life, and Books XII through XIV, which amplify the theme of imagination, reflect the general tendency of the poem to wander from strict chronology in order to mirror the poet's inner thoughts and associations. It is significant that the climactic ascent of Mt. Snowdon, which occurs in the final book (Book XIV), is an event drawn from the poet's early twenties but reserved for the end of the work because of its spiritual meaning.

A final organizing pattern consists of the passages of direct address to the "Friend," identified with the poet Samuel Taylor Coleridge. These passages create a kind of critical apparatus in which Wordsworth directly comments on his methods of turning raw experience into poetry, the very poetry, in fact, which we are reading.

Thus the design of the poem reflects Wordsworth's highly developed self-consciousness as a poet. The small associations and large climaxes represent his fidelity to the raw material of his perceptions, while the continuing appeals to Coleridge as fellow poet, critic, and even mentor show his attention to the poetic craft of translating feelings into words.

3.14 Compare the passage describing the Simplon Pass (VI, 562–640) with that describing the vision on Mt. Snowdon (XIV, 1–129).

Answer Both passages figure as climactic "spots of time" in the poem, representing two ascents, both literal and figurative, which culminate in visionary insight. On both occasions, Wordsworth experiences the natural scene as an invitation to reflect on and celebrate the power of imagination to transfigure and illuminate the visible world. Although the two incidents differ in some respects, their similarity is striking, with the second passage largely echoing the first. This reiterative quality is characteristic of *The Prelude* as a whole and is a significant feature of Wordsworth's portrayal of the "growth of a poet's mind."

In the first incident, the narrative suggests an initial disappointment with the merely visible, for the poet discovers not from any divinely illuminated landscape but rather from a humble passerby that he has "*crossed the Alps*" (VI, 591). Out of his disappointment Wordsworth fashions his encomium of the imagination, which is indebted not to external nature but rather to a feeling of expectation and "something evermore about to be" (VI, 608). Humanity's glory and greatness, Wordsworth feels, lie in the striving for "infinitude" (VI, 605), that moment "when the light of sense/Goes out, but with a flash that has revealed/The invisible world" (VI, 600–602). Wordsworth is then rewarded by just such a moment. On the gloomy downward track, through a scene of "woods decaying," buffeting winds, "torrents shooting," muttering rocks, "drizzling crags," and a "raving stream" (VI, 625–633), he suddenly perceives "the invisible world." All the unlikely hostile features of the landscape are to him

> . . . like the workings of one mind, the features
> Of the same face, blossoms upon one tree;
> Characters of the great Apocalypse,
> The types and symbols of Eternity,
> The first, and last, and midst, and without end.
> (VI, 636–640)

The similes are insistent in the sense that there is no apparent visual correspondence between the actual scene, a terrifying fragmented wilderness, and the unitary, organic vision of one mind, one face, one tree. The fullness of the rhetoric, with its increasing abstraction ("Apocalypse," "Eternity") and its conflation of ideas (person superimposed on tree, time sequence jumbled), suggests that Wordsworth is not only celebrating the synthesizing power of creative imagination but also striving to assert its autonomy from the physical world.

The ascent of Mt. Snowdon, by repeating many of the features of the journey through the Simplon Pass, becomes proof once again of the individual's ability to climb to the heights. Temporally displaced, this episode from the poet's early adulthood functions as a final climax in a book which organizes itself as a series of climaxes. The initial mood is related to the feeling of disappointment at the Simplon Pass. The evening is unpromising ("Wan, dull, and glaring, with a dripping fog" [XIV, 12]), and the travelers are pensive and sunk in "private thoughts" (XIV, 18). But here the scene Wordsworth stumbles upon is apparently hospitable to the imagination; the moon's illumination produces a "flash" of insight, and the mist signifies the "invisible world" toward which the poet yearns:

> For instantly a light upon the turf
> Fell like a flash, and lo! as I looked up,
> The moon hung naked in a firmament
> Of azure without cloud, and at my feet
> Rested a silent sea of hoary mist.
>   (XIV, 38–42)

What follows is a discourse on the scene as "the emblem of a mind/That feeds upon infinity" (XIV, 70–71). But Wordsworth's exegesis of his chosen symbols departs widely from the original terms of moon and mist, again, as in the Simplon Pass episode, implying the mind's freedom from mere facts. Describing the poetic faculty of "higher minds," he applauds the fact that "They from their native selves can send abroad/Kindred mutations" (XIV, 93–94) in a way that rivals nature. When he asserts that "they build up greatest things/From least suggestions" (XIV, 101–102), he is at the same moment demonstrating the process. The language becomes heightened in a way reminiscent of the alpine revelation, with references to the transcending of time ("till Time shall be no more") and to "Deity" (XIV, 111–112). Again there is a turning away from the actual scene in nature toward philosophic abstraction and discursive eloquence.

If Wordsworth has in this instance once again achieved the sublime, it may be asked what is the effect of this repetition, and indeed of all the repetitions of The Prelude. As Harold Bloom remarks, "For Wordsworth there is always a precise extent and a *howness*, to the mind's mastery. . . ."[1] Each case is the same insofar as the creative faculty remains a constant, or at least a constant potential, but each is different in terms of how the mind is stimulated to its imaginative potential, which works "but in alliance with the works/Which it beholds" (II, 259–260).

In a sense, Wordsworth's compulsion to record many interactions with many landscapes becomes a testimony to the inherent power and beauty of nature, which continually evokes the fullest possible response of the poet, again and again, in every phase of the poet's life. Conversely, and more importantly, the repeated encounters constitute a proof of the poet's unfailing powers. As the poem progresses, Wordsworth increasingly presents himself as independent of the visible scene, using it primarily as something to transcend or transfigure as he proves once again that he has the power to do so. Thus every "spot of time" is an individual victory wrested from the merely visible. It is only by an accumulation of such victories that Wordsworth can persuade the reader, and perhaps himself, of humankind's spiritual capacity for interaction with and dominion over nature.

B.S.

[1] Harold Bloom, *The Ringers in the Tower: Studies in Romantic Tradition*, University of Chicago Press, Chicago, 1971, p. 46.

SUGGESTED READINGS

Abrams, M. H. (ed.), *Wordsworth: A Collection of Critical Essays* (1972).
Bloom, Harold, *The Visionary Company: A Reading of English Romantic Poetry* (1971).
Hartman, Geoffrey, *Wordsworth's Poetry, 1787–1814* (1964).
Woodring, Carl, *Wordsworth* (1965).

SAMUEL TAYLOR COLERIDGE

C H R O N O L O G Y

1772   Born at Ottery, St. Mary, Devonshire. Son of the parish vicar John Coleridge and Ann Bowdon Coleridge.

1775   Enters Dame Key's Reading School.

1778   Begins study at the Henry VIII Free Grammar School, headed by his father. Reads widely and deeply in literature and philosophy.

1782   Enters Christ's Hospital School; by his account, his years there are cheerless and bleak. Meets Charles Lamb, later a poet and essayist, a longtime friend.

1791   Enters Jesus College, Cambridge University. He is a fine scholar but improvident and debt-ridden.

1793   Forced to leave school by debts, enlists under the false name of Silas Tomkyn Comberback in the Light Dragoons. Is a laughable failure as a soldier.

1794   With the help of his brother, is discharged from the army and returns to Cambridge; leaves soon after without a degree, however. On a visit to Oxford, meets the poet Robert Southey. Together they conceive a scheme for a democratic society to be founded on the banks of the Susquehanna River in America. By the next year, this idea of "Pantisocracy" collapses.

1795   Moves to Bristol, where he delivers public lectures on literature and politics. Marries Sarah Fricker; meets William Wordsworth.

1796   Publishes *Poems on Various Subjects*. Also briefly edits periodical *The Watch-man*, which soon folds. Around this time begins to take laudanum, an opium-derived drug, to relieve the pain of neuralgia; addiction to opium will plague him through most of his remaining years.

1797   Known as Coleridge's *annus mirabilis*: his year of greatest creativity. Writes *The Rime of the Ancient Mariner*, his masterpiece, along with the unfinished *Christabel* and the dream-inspired "Kubla Khan."

1798   With Wordsworth, publishes *Lyrical Ballads*, first great work of English romanticism; it contains the *Ancient Mariner* and three other poems by Coleridge. Travels to Germany with Wordsworth and his sister.

1799   Studies at University of Gottingen until July, then returns to England and tours the Lake District with the Wordsworths. Meets and falls in love with Sara Hutchinson, Wordsworth's sister-in-law.

1800   Translates *Wallenstein* by the German poet and playwright Schiller.

1801   Health deteriorating. Second edition of *Lyrical Ballads* published, with Wordsworth's famous "Preface."

1802   Writes "Dejection: An Ode," his greatest lyric poem.

1803   Tours Scotland with the Wordsworths.

1804   In poor health, travels to Malta in hope of a cure.

1806   Returns to England; separates from his wife.

1808   Delivers lectures on poetry at the Royal Institute in London.

1809   Begins periodical *The Friend*, with contributions by Wordsworth; it lasts only a year.

1810   Quarrels with Wordsworth; they are estranged. Moves in with the family of friend John Morgan. Begins work on an ambitious philosophical work to be called *Logosophia*; like many of Coleridge's works, it is never completed.

1811–
1812   Delivers lectures on English poets, including famous lectures on Shakespeare. Reconciled with Wordsworth.

1813   Play *Remorse* performed at the Drury Lane Theatre.

1816   His health again declining, Coleridge takes up residence with physician James Gilman at Highgate. Gilman treats him with great sympathy and intelligence; his literary productivity increases as a result. Publishes volume of poetry including *Christabel* and "Kubla Khan."

1817   Publishes *Biographia Literaria*, brilliant though sketchy work combining philosophical and literary remarks, including famous discussion of the poetry of Wordsworth.

1818–
1819
Lectures on literature and philosophy. Enters last period of his life, in which he writes little poetry but entertains visitors with brilliant and abstruse literary and philosophical conversation.

1825
Publishes philosophical work *Aids to Reflection*. Named royal associate of the Royal Society of Literature.

1828
Publishes pamphlet *On the Constitution of Church and State*; it indicates that he, like Wordsworth, has moved steadily to the right politically during his later years.

1834
Death of Coleridge.

ESSAY QUESTIONS WITH ANSWERS

"Kubla Khan"

4.1 Discuss the unity of the poem, giving special attention to the strands of imagery which connect its two parts.

Answer Although the poem consists of three verse paragraphs, a natural structural division seems to occur after the first two paragraphs, which describe Kubla Khan's pleasure dome and Alph the sacred river. The last paragraph, which records the poet's vision of "a damsel with a dulcimer" and his yearning for prophetic power, seems on the surface to be an unrelated fragment. At the beginning of this paragraph, the "damsel" suddenly appears, with no overt connection with the narrative of the first part of the poem.

However, while lacking narrative logic, the damsel's appearance has a symbolic logic related to the latent theme of the poem. Like Kubla Khan, who has decreed a "stately pleasure dome" in Xanadu, the damsel creates her own sacred realm by "singing of Mount Abora" (line 40), which, according to tradition, is the site of the earthly paradise. Both emperor and singer, then, are types of the poet, who decrees a holy place through the magical power of language: "I would build that dome in air,/That sunny dome! those caves of ice!/And all who heard should see them there" (lines 46–48).

Emperor, damsel, and poet are all creators, each generating an order independent of nature. Thus Kubla creates, through an act of will and by imperial fiat, an image of static perfection. The dome is a perfect hemisphere or half circle, the walls constitute another precisely measured circle ("twice five miles of fertile ground/With walls and towers were girdled round" [lines 6–7], and the sacred ground thus demarcated is sunny and fruitful, a perfect paradise. Kubla's decree supersedes the world of nature. Against the "caverns measureless to man" (line 4) he measures out his "twice five miles," and against the "sunless sea" (line 5) he pits his "sunny pleasure dome" (line 36). His art is a human answer to a nature that is inhuman, cold, and dark.

60

Nature's own answer to the art of Kubla Khan appears in the next verse paragraph, describing the origin and course of "Alph, the sacred river" (line 3). Nature here is "savage," "holy and enchanted" (line 14), animated and animistic. The earth is alive, and the fountain is forced out of the chasm with something like birth throes:

> And from this chasm, with ceaseless turmoil seething,
> As if this earth in fast thick pants were breathing,
> A mighty fountain momently was forced:
> > (lines 17–19)

However, the frenzied power of nature does not produce chaos; rather, it yields an image of order within an unfolding vital process. The allusion to dance is significant, for dance offers aesthetic design in the context of a plastic, moving, temporal art. Choreographic pattern both manifests itself in time and transcends time. Thus the chasm with its dancing rocks creates the river each moment and for all moments: "And 'mid these dancing rocks at once and ever/It flung up momently the sacred river" (lines 23–24). It would seem that nature with its active and ongoing creation constitutes a threat to the static perfection of Kubla Khan's art. The tumult of the ocean where the river empties is linked with the tumult of "ancestral voices prophesying war" (line 30). The reference to coming upheaval and destruction implies the transience of the dome and of any art "decreed" by humankind.

The description of the shadow of the pleasure dome floating "midway on the waves" (line 32) suggests a merging of art and nature. The dome is no longer fixed and static but "floating"; the reflection in the water is "at once and ever" (line 23), both a transitory optical phenomenon and an eternal vision. The "mingled measure/From the fountain and the caves" (lines 33–34) implies a kind of synesthesia or fusion of sense impressions; sound merges with sight, just as the art of the dome merges with the medium of nature in its shadow suspended in the waves. There is a paradoxical quality to this blending or merging of two disparate realms: "It was a miracle of rare device,/A sunny pleasure dome with caves of ice!" (lines 35–36). As heat is wedded to cold (sun and ice), so "miracle," a given to be wondered at, is fused with "device," a thing willed, devised, contrived. The floating dome is both a magical manifestation, nature's gift, and an autonomous creation devised by Kubla Khan.

The last verse paragraph, the second part of the poem, offers another image of the relationship between art and nature, with the poet strongly asserting the autonomy and permanence of art. As we have seen, the damsel with a dulcimer is linked with Kubla Khan and the poet as an artist or originator. Her "singing of Mount Abora" represents the creative process both in its association with primal joy (it produces "delight," just as Kubla Khan's dome is devoted to "pleasure") and in its magical effect. Both the dome and the song, artifacts themselves, have the power to stimulate the creative imagination, stirring the poet to ecstasy and prophetic frenzy. Although the damsel's inspirational power is stated conditionally ("Could I revive within me/Her symphony and song" [lines 42–43]), the poet does in fact call up the vision and revive the song. The whole of "Kubla Khan" is the "music loud and long" with which the poet builds his "dome in air," his verbal artifact that makes "that sunny dome! those caves of ice!" palpable to the reader. The poet's art, deriving from dream, vision, and memory, is independent of nature; it is an art of incantation and "decree" rather than perception or imitation.

The final image, one of the poet as magician, seer, and bacchic celebrant inspired by a sacred ritual of ingestion, suggests an occult and mysterious access of creative power. The poet seems to incorporate within himself some of the wildness, fierceness, and vitality which characterize nature and the chasm's ceaseless creation of the river "at once and ever." Like the "sacred river" and the "holy and enchanted" place, the poet is a sacred object: "Weave a circle round him thrice,/And close your eyes with holy dread" (lines 51–52). His "flashing" eyes are subtly related to the dome and the caves, which glitter with sunlight and with ice, and his "floating" hair links him to the floating dome, which is both ephemeral and timeless. As artist and magician, miracle maker and rare deviser, the poet appropriates the raw power of nature to confer life and being on the forms of his imagination. His poem, the "dome in air" built "with music loud and long," is like Kubla Khan's "stately pleasure dome" in its ability to supersede nature; it is a fixed, self-contained "device" with aspirations to eternity.

4.2 Discuss the relationship between the prose introduction and the poem itself.

Answer In the introduction, Coleridge describes the circumstances in which "Kubla Khan" was conceived. After taking an "anodyne" prescribed for an indisposition, he fell asleep over his book (*Purchas's Pilgrimage*, a history of the far east) and had a dream which, on awaking, he wrote down. This account of the origins of the composition implies a particular view of the poetic imagination and the creative process. Coleridge's direct transcription of a dream suggests his belief in the occult powers of the human mind to transfigure known experience and animate the world with entirely new forms. The poet is not primarily either an artisan or an observer of the natural world but a seer who receives inspiration or prophetic power from a realm beyond the natural. The poetry that springs from this supernatural agency is akin to magic in its power to make palpable what has been only imagined.

By emphasizing that the poem was "given to him," Coleridge is not only stating a theory of inspiration but touching on the question of his own troubled creativity. His ambivalent sense of dependence on an external agent (in this instance a drug) is implied by his partial denigration of "Kubla Khan" as a "fragment" and a "psychological curiosity." His long-standing intention, never fulfilled, "to finish for himself what had been originally, as it were, given to him" is part of Coleridge's continual unsuccessful effort to locate creative power within himself by an act of conscious will. At the same time, he is clearly attracted to the notion of passive inspiration, with the poet waiting for an infusion of "joy" or mental power from outside. The struggle between the desire for conscious control and the longing for magical inspiration is evident in much of Coleridge's writing, both in poetry and in criticism.

Two passages from the introduction have special relevance to the poem. In the first of these, Coleridge refers to having "composed . . . from two to three hundred lines; if that indeed can be called composition in which all the images rose up before him [the author] as *things*, with a parallel production of the correspondent expressions, without any sensation or consciousness of effort." This emphasis on the tangibility and solidity of the poet's mental images relates to the lines in the poem describing the power of poetry to render real an imaginary vision:

> That with music loud and long,
> I would build that dome in air,
> That sunny dome! those caves of ice!
> And all who heard should see them there,
> And all should cry, Beware! Beware!
>
> (lines 45–49)

Like Coleridge in his drug-inspired trance, the poet is a vehicle or vessel for the vision he produces. The creations of both are magical; they need only record, or incant, what spontaneously arises within them to "build" something entirely original and astonishingly real.

In a second passage, Coleridge regrets his inability to recall portions of his dream. Quoting from an earlier poem of his entitled "The Picture; or, the Lover's Resolution," he compares the vanishing of his vision to the shattering of a reflection in a pool of water:

> Then all the charm
> Is broken—all that phantom world so fair
> Vanishes, and a thousand circlets spread,
> And each misshape[s] the other. . . .
> . . . .
> And soon the fragments dim of lovely forms
> Come trembling back, unite, and now once more
> The pool becomes a mirror.
> (lines 91–94; 98–100)

This reuniting of fragments to restore the integrity of the pool, turning it into a mirror, is connected with the image in "Kubla Khan" of the "dome of pleasure" floating "midway on the waves." Although in the introduction Coleridge's point seems to be that the fragments are irrecoverable and the unity and coherence of his dream forever lost, in the poem the river is a true mirror, and the vision is conveyed whole.

The repeated emphasis in the introduction on the fragmentary quality of "Kubla Khan" and the apparent discontinuities of the poem itself raise the question of the poem's completeness. But Coleridge's publication of the work, despite his own disclaimers about its inadequacy, suggests that in some sense, even to him, it had the status of a finished artifact. The poem itself is unified by a single, continuous theme and by its coherent imagery; furthermore, it is connected with other poems by Coleridge dealing with the imaginative process (for example, "The Eolian Harp" and "Dejection: An Ode"). Thus, "Kubla Khan" can properly be treated as a self-contained, complete work of art. Indeed, Coleridge offers, within the poem and in the language of poetry, an enduring image of art. In the introduction Coleridge describes his own struggle for imaginative unity, a struggle which he feels is unsuccessful; in the poem he presents, despite his tentativeness and self-doubt, the unity itself.

The Rime of the Ancient Mariner

4.3 Discuss the moral symbolism of the poem and its connection to the poem's theme.

Answer   The poem offers an explicit "moral" in the Mariner's farewell words to the Wedding Guest:

> He prayeth best, who loveth best
> All things both great and small;
> For the dear God who loveth us,
> He made and loveth all.
>   (lines 614–617)

This homily is reinforced by Coleridge's marginal gloss, which explains that the Mariner's role is "to teach, by his own example, love and reverence to all things that God made and loveth." He is thus presented as a reformed sinner, preaching a doctrine of charity to the Wedding Guest, who is moved and chastened by the Mariner's tale ("A sadder and a wiser man,/He rose the morrow morn" [lines 624–625]).

Certain earlier moments in the poem contribute to a heavily moralistic effect. The marginal glosses especially provide a running didactic commentary on the Mariner's story: "The ancient Mariner inhospitably killeth the pious bird of good omen"; "And the Albatross begins to be avenged"; "By the light of the Moon he beholdeth God's creatures of the great calm"; "He blesseth them in his heart"; "By grace of the Holy Mother, the ancient Mariner is refreshed with rain"; "The Mariner awakes, and his penance begins anew"; "The curse is finally expiated"; "The ancient Mariner earnestly entreateth the Hermit to shrieve him; and the penance of life falls on him." These explanatory statements suggest a Christian allegory involving the pilgrimage of an Everyman through sin, retribution, and penance to a kind of provisional redemption. This redemption is apparently dependent on repeated confession as a sign of the Mariner's continual renewal of spiritual recognition.

The poem itself, however, does not invite such simple equations as "Mariner equals Everyman," "Albatross equals Christ," and so on. The *Rime* is richer in connotation than such equations would suggest, and Coleridge seems to have regretted including the overtly moralistic passages, coming to see them as false to his central concept. Answering an objection from a reader that the poem lacked a moral, he said that on the contrary "the poem had too much. . . . It ought to have had no more moral than the *Arabian Nights'* tale of the merchant's sitting down to eat dates by the side of a well and throwing the shells aside, and lo! a genie starts up and says he *must* kill the aforesaid merchant because one of the date shells had, it seems, put out the eye of the genie's son" (*Table Talk* [May 31, 1830]).

By his own account, then, Coleridge meant the Mariner's act to be sudden, inexplicable, and casual rather than malignant or willful. In the poem, the Mariner narrates the event in an abrupt, disconnected manner which suggests that the action itself was disconnected and "causeless." When the Wedding Guest questions the Mariner's sudden agitation, the Mariner answers with a bald assertion:

> "God save thee, ancient Mariner!
> From the fiends, that plague thee thus!—
> Why look'st thou so?"—With my crossbow
> I shot the ALBATROSS.
>   (lines 79–82)

The Mariner fails to provide an explanation of motive here. Again, later, at the crucial moment when his view of the water snakes changes from that of "a thousand thousand slimy things" (line 238) to "O happy living things! no tongue/ Their beauty might declare" (lines 282–283), the spiritual change seems inexplicable. The final "moral" ("He prayeth best, who loveth best" [line 614]) represents in a sense another failure to explain in its reduction of the poem's complex significance to a simple adage. The Mariner's compulsive narration of physical details and his striking omission of any meaningful attempt at interpretation suggest a kind of enthrallment. He is possessed by a supernatural vision which he can recount but cannot elucidate. When he blesses, he is "unaware"; when he preaches, he is superficial and naive. He is like a vessel for something beyond himself, incapable of interpreting his own experience.

Despite the Mariner's limitations as a narrator, his experience remains deeply meaningful. As an ordinary person gripped by strange events and stranger visions, he represents the potency of God's grace, which can alter the individual's relation to the world. What the Mariner speaks of, albeit somewhat tritely, is love ("A spring of love gushed from my heart" [line 284] and "For the dear God who loveth us,/He made and loveth all" [lines 616–617]), a love that is at least implicitly Christian. This love has the power to transfigure existence, to animate it and render it coherent. The individual is bound to the phenomenal world not simply by transient sensations and perceptions but by a supernatural infusion, proceeding from divine will, which awakens a deeper consciousness. The description of the water snakes swimming in the moonlight which precedes the Mariner's sudden ability to pray suggests something beyond a prevailing mood or trick of perception. The moon, for Coleridge as for many other romantic poets, symbolizes a magical or supernatural radiance which attends, and arouses, imaginative excitement. The special significance of the moon is suggested by the unusually elaborate marginal note describing it:

> In his loneliness and fixedness he yearneth towards the journeying Moon, and the stars that still sojourn, yet still move onward; and everywhere the blue sky belongs to them, and is their appointed rest, and their native country and their own natural homes, which they enter unannounced, as lords that are certainly expected and yet there is a silent joy at their arrival.

The Mariner, then, wants the world to belong to him as the sky belongs to the stars; he wants to feel at home in nature, to move through it and to experience the silent joy of arrival. In the poem, the radiance and movement of the night sky are transferred to the water snakes, which move, rear, coil, and swim, shedding an "elfish light," "hoary flakes," and "a flash of golden fire." In the Mariner's mind, for the moment inspired by God's grace, nature is alive and glowing, with the moon, stars, and creatures of the deep connected and unified in a single vision. In contrast to this vision of connection and oneness, the Mariner's original crime had been profoundly discontinuous, implying a view of the albatross as an isolated thing, separate from and alien to himself. The sense of inclusiveness, continuity, and connection, of a world bathed in a single radiant medium, is the mark of grace, the "one life" as perceived by every sensitive, vital being. The Mariner's naive statement at the end of the poem about loving "all creatures," for "God made and loveth all," is an acknowledgment of the comprehensiveness and coherence of the creative vision conferred by God. God frees the Mariner from the curse of guilt by an act of divine will, just as the rain pours from heaven into the "silly" ("blessed" or "happy") buckets on the deck (lines 297–300). The Mariner is literally a vessel for God's grace; his obtuseness and naiveté constitute a way of emphasizing the miraculous quality of grace, which can arouse even a limited consciousness to a sense of love.

The supernatural apparatus of the poem is connected to the theme of the quickening of consciousness which is God's gift. It functions as a metaphor for the animation and plenitude of the world as imaginatively perceived. Thus, the Latin epigraph of the poem (adapted by Coleridge from Thomas Burnet, *Archaeologiae philosophicae* [1692]) alludes to a populous universe of "invisible natures" and, while acknowledging humankind's ignorance of these natures, stresses that "it is helpful sometimes to contemplate in the mind, as on a tablet, the image of a greater and better world, lest the intellect, habituated to the petty things of daily life, narrow itself and sink wholly into trivial thoughts." The Mariner's reports of supernatural visions—death and life-in-death playing dice on the skeleton ship, the dead crewmembers animated by angelic spirits, the conversation of two polar spirits—suggest that despite a certain obtuseness and literalness in his narration, he can at times see the invisible world, strangely alive with hidden significance. As a vessel of God's will, he is afforded glimpses of something beyond the merely physical.

The weather, too, is a sign of the Mariner's state of grace, constituting a symbolic index of his relationship to nature. The opening descriptions of the wind, the albatross, the roaring ice, and the glimmering moonshine suggest a world alive with imaginative possibility, just as the "hot and copper sky," "bloody Sun," "painted ocean," and "slimy sea" of the terrible calm imply a dead world, enlivened by "nor breath nor motion." The albatross is above all a natural being, perceived primarily as alive, or "quick." One of the underlying themes of the poem is the contrast between the quick and the dead, between imagination and mere perception. This polarity is dependent on the spiritual condition of the beholder, for it is only God's grace that allows the Mariner to perceive nature as significant and vital. Thus the Mariner is truly animated, inspirited and inspired, when he sees the water snakes flashing in the moonlight.

The conclusion of the poem, with its pat didacticism, fails to embrace the thematic implications of the whole. The theme of imaginative perception, which derives from the mysterious operation of grace, transcends the narrow categories of conventional morality, just as the Mariner's extraordinary tale outstrips his capacities as a rather ordinary teller. The inadequacy of the Mariner's final formulation emphasizes the mystery. Although he seems only partially aware of the significance of his experience, his glimpse of a coherent world, divinely illumined, is his mark of grace.

4.4   The *Rime* is in some ways a "naive" narrative, using the short stanzas, simple prosody, and predictable images of the ballad form. Discuss the effect of this simple narrative style.

Answer   The general effect of the "naive" narrative is to produce an atmosphere reminiscent of folktales and fables. The central story of sin and redemption is common to much folklore, and the supernatural elements are like those found in many fabulous tales and legends. The emphatic sermonizing of the Mariner's tale suggests the style of naive allegory, again a feature typical of popular storytelling. This admonitory quality is particularly associated with the ballad form, and the *Rime* ends, like many ballads, with an explicit moral:

> He prayeth best, who loveth best
> All things both great and small;
> For the dear God who loveth us,
> He made and loveth all.
>   (lines 614–617)

The Mariner's strange journey becomes an ethical exemplum, an admonition not only to the Wedding Guest ("A sadder and a wiser man,/He rose the morrow morn") but to every reader.

Coleridge's use of ballad prosody (short lines, alternating tetrameter with trimeter, and an *abab* rhyme scheme) produces a musical verse which mesmerizes the reader as well as the Wedding Guest. But apart from the songlike quality which it has in common with many ballads, the *Rime* is generally quite different in effect from medieval exemplars of the form. Within the inherently repetitive structure of the ballad stanza, Coleridge heightens the hypnotic effect by frequent use of verbal repetition. Single words, phrases, and whole lines are reiterated verbatim, usually in an exclamatory way. For example, the emphatic repetitions in the Mariner's description of the sudden calm which paralyzes the ship after his slaying of the albatross convey his own sense of paralysis and horror:

> Day after day, day after day
> We stuck, nor breath nor motion;
> As idle as a painted ship
> Upon a painted ocean.
>
> Water, water, everywhere,
> And all the boards did shrink;
> Water, water, everywhere,
> Nor any drop to drink.
>   (lines 115–122)

The Mariner's tale is spellbinding in the sense of casting a spell; he binds his listener not only "with his glittering eye" (line 13) but by reliving and thus transferring his strange experience through the hypnotic medium of words. The verbal repetitions suggest the stress of compulsion, for it is only by obsessively naming his sensations and visions that the Mariner can exorcise them. There is at times a mechanical quality to the recitation, as though the narrator himself were under a spell. The generally repetitive diction also suggests the Mariner's alienation from the physical world. His language is somehow blocked, the con-stricted word choice suggesting his emotional constriction.

The simplicity of the imagery, although again partly attributable to the oral tradition of ballads, contributes to the "automatic" tone of the narrative. Many of the similes function like epithets, sketching basic sensations and sights in an unimaginative, subdued fashion. Thus, the sails "sigh like sedge" or make a noise "like of a hidden brook," and the ice is "as green as emerald." Only in the description of the sea snakes does the imagery grow more complicated, in order to signal the Mariner's new perception at the climactic moment before the breaking of the spell:

> Beyond the shadow of the ship,
> I watched the water snakes:
> They moved in tracks of shining white,
> And when they reared, the elfish light
> Fell off in hoary flakes.
>
> Within the shadow of the ship
> I watched their rich attire:
> Blue, glossy green, and velvet black,
> They coiled and swam; and every track
> Was a flash of golden fire.
>
> (lines 272–281)

The specificity of the language implies the Mariner's new relationship to nature, his sudden closeness to, and ability to see, the universe of living things. The water snakes are no longer "slimy things" (line 125) but "happy living things" (line 282), unspeakably beautiful. This vivid description is very different from the constricted, naive style which dominates the poem.

The prevailing naiveté of the poetic style creates a sense of strangeness. The narrator is both casting a spell and locked in a spell, and his language is for the most part incantatory and obsessive. The strangeness of the narrative derives, then, from the contrast between this flat, somewhat literal style and the su-pernatural events reported. At the same time, the style itself has a certain strangeness, with its hypnotic, driven diction and unvarying rhythms.

"Dejection: An Ode"

4.5 In Chapter XIII of *Biographia Literaria* on "the imagination, or esemplastic power," Coleridge makes a distinction between the "primary imagination" and the "secondary imagination":

The primary I hold to be the living power and prime agent of all human perception, and as a repetition in the finite mind of the eternal act of creation in the infinite I AM. The secondary I consider as an echo of the former, coexisting with the conscious will, yet still as identical with the primary in the *kind* of its agency, and differing only in *degree*, and in the *mode* of its operation. It dissolves, diffuses, dissipates, in order to recreate; or where this process is rendered impossible, yet still, at all events, it struggles to idealize and to unify. It is essentially *vital*, even as all objects (*as* objects) are essentially fixed and dead.

Relate this theory to Coleridge's "Dejection: An Ode."

Answer   In this passage, Coleridge differentiates sense perception from the creative and integrative faculty which "struggles to idealize and to unify." Thus the primary imagination, common to all people, corresponds to the act of seeing or hearing and is a sign of human existence, the finite mind's assertion of "I AM." In somewhat obscure language, Coleridge defines the secondary imagination as an "echo" of the primary, implying that it is somehow dependent on sense perception; however, this second faculty is a more active function of the perceiving mind, "coexisting with the conscious will," which "dissolves, diffuses, dissipates in order to recreate."

In general, Coleridge discusses the difference between the two modes of imagination as a contrast between passive and active. The primary imagination takes in the world of objects but leaves those objects unchanged, "essentially fixed and dead," while the secondary imagination disintegrates the world of appearances in order to reconstruct them and make them live.

In "Dejection: An Ode" the poet repeatedly makes a distinction between the passive reception of an "inanimate cold world" and the act of creative will which vitalizes nature, engendering "a new Earth and a new Heaven." The activity of the secondary imagination is called, in the poem, "Joy," while the state in which the primary imagination is in ascendance is implicitly linked to the dejection of the title. In stanza 2, Coleridge illustrates the primary mode, beginning with a description of his profound depression ("A grief without a pang, void, dark, and drear,/A stifled, drowsy, unimpassioned grief " [lines 21–22]) and moving on to a precise visual description of the world perceived as so many sense impressions. Gazing at the western sky in the calm before the storm, Coleridge catalogues the sights which strike his eye: the thin clouds, the crescent moon, the scattered stars, and the tinted horizon. These perceptions, representing the activity of the primary imagination, suggest that it is in the main a physical process, similar in function to Blake's "vegetable eye." But Coleridge insists that merely seeing these objects is not enough: "I see them all so excellently fair,/I see, not feel, how beautiful they are!" (lines 37–38). The absence of creative joy, of what he later calls "my shaping spirit of Imagination" (6, 86, meaning stanza 6, line 86), makes him impotent to transform or enliven this world of objects:

> It were a vain endeavor,
>   Though I should gaze forever
> On that green light that lingers in the west:
> I may not hope from outward forms to win
> The passion and the life, whose fountains are within.
>
>   (3, 42–46)

The "Aeolian lute" in stanza 1 is connected with the impotence and passivity of the primary imagination. (An Aeolian lute is a harp with strings stretched over a rectangular sounding box, placed in an opened window so that it produces musical chords when played on by the breeze. It was a common household object in the early nineteenth century and often was used in romantic poetry as an image of the mind responding to the natural world.) The allusion to "the dull sobbing draft, that moans and rakes/Upon the strings" (lines 6–7) suggests that the poet is himself just such a harp, visited by the elements and plucked upon by the wind, without any force or energy of his own. In contrast, the discussion of Joy in stanza 5 implies that the secondary imagination is itself elemental, compounded of air and water, simultaneously as tangible as rain and as intangible as light or vapor. It is the source of all "that charms or ear or sight," the origin of "all melodies" and "all colors." It is "this light, this glory, this fair luminous mist,/This beautiful and beauty-making power" (lines 62–63); it is "cloud at once and shower," "the spirit and the power" (lines 66–67). The world perceived imaginatively or "joyfully" is neither cold nor dead but born again into "a new Earth and a new Heaven" (line 69).

When Coleridge returns to the lute in stanza 7, it seems that his identification is less with the harp than with the wind that plays upon it. The wind, like "Joy, the luminous cloud" (line 71), is an elemental power that vitalizes the world, imbuing it with motion and sound. On the one hand, Coleridge has the answer to his grim wish, expressed in stanza 1, that the wind "might startle this dull pain, and make it move and live!" (line 20); the "sobbing draft" has become "a scream/Of agony by torture lengthened out" (lines 97–98), and Coleridge, like the lute, helplessly responds to an external power. At the same time, the poet is not solely a responsive instrument, answering the storm, but is himself a maker of storms. Poet and wind merge in the description of the latter as an impassioned actor, "perfect in all tragic sounds!" and a "mighty poet, e'en to frenzy bold!" (lines 108–109). The poem is a dramatic performance, a record of frenzy and boldness in confronting the poet's own imaginative loss and failure.

Although the emphasis throughout most of the poem is on the suspension of imagination and the oppression of Joy by sudden visitations of grief, stanza 7 appears to present a catharsis or release. The breaking of the storm animates both the scene and the poet. The wind does not so much cause an imaginative renewal (it "long has raved unnoticed" [line 97]) as signal or accompany it. Coleridge himself is a "Mad lutanist" (line 104), once again in possession of the image-making power. "What tell'st thou now about?" (line 110) Coleridge asks the wind, and immediately he has his own answer: " 'Tis of the rushing of an host in rout," and "It tells another tale, with sounds less deep and loud!/A tale of less affright,/And tempered with delight" (lines 111; 117–119). The world is no longer static, silent, and dead but alive with meanings which the poet, gifted with secondary imagination, bestows.

Though ostensibly Coleridge has lost his way, like the little child "upon a lonesome wild" sobbing for her mother (lines 121–125), and though Joy is apparently wholly transferred to another (the "Lady" to whom the poem is addressed), stanza 7 suggests that the poet has at least momentarily recovered his creativity. The reference to the little child lost, the "tender lay" which Coleridge hears in the moaning of the wind, is significant: Coleridge is like the child not only in that he is lost but in that he is "not far from home" (line 123). He is near to "what nature gave me at my birth,/My shaping spirit of Imagination" (lines 85–86).

"Dejection: An Ode" documents that "struggle to idealize and to unify" which Coleridge attributes to the secondary imagination. As he records his sense of suspended will and imaginative impotence, he at the same time covertly attempts to summon up the "sweet and potent voice" of Joy. Despite his insistence that this voice is sent "from the soul itself . . . of its own birth" (lines 56–57), something given rather than willed, the whole poem is an invocation of that power, a willing of the wind to rise and the storm to break. The ode both calls forth the "secondary imagination" and witnesses its coming.

4.6 Compare the ideas on poetic imagination in Coleridge's "Dejection: An Ode" with those expressed in Wordsworth's "Ode: Intimations of Immortality from Recollections of Early Childhood."

Answer That the themes of the two poems are related is a consequence of the fact that Coleridge began composing his ode immediately after hearing the opening stanzas of Wordsworth's. Although Coleridge revised the poem extensively in the next six months, the concerns expressed in the original verse letter to Sara Hutchinson, dated April 4, 1802, survive in the final version.

The poem is both an inquiry into the origins of creative joy and a description of imaginative loss and emptiness. Coleridge considers the secondary imagination, the power of Joy, to be inexplicable, a "given" which emanates from the soul itself. No plan "by abstruse research to steal/From my own nature all the natural man" (line 89–90) can regenerate "what nature gave me at my birth,/ My shaping spirit of Imagination" (lines 84–85). Indeed, in Coleridge's view, intellect "infects" him, and his soul is strangled by "habit" and "reality's dark dream" (lines 92, 93, 95). The whole of stanza 6 sketches the journey from "joy" and "dreams of happiness" to the "afflictions" of his current life. There is no explicit resolution of the crisis he presents; although stanza 7 dramatizes a reawakening of creative power, Coleridge never clearly acknowledges that Joy can be recovered. He wholly transfers it to the "Lady":

> Joy lift her spirit, joy attune her voice;
> To her may all things live, from pole to pole,
> Their life the eddying of her living soul!
> (8, 134–136)

By locating the source of imaginative power within the soul, Coleridge denies the effectiveness of the external world to stimulate joy. "O Lady! we receive but what we give,/And in our life alone does Nature live" (lines 47–48). Joy, like its contrary, dejection, is a visitation; but dejection is a kind of robbery or theft, while joy is a gift "that ne'er was given,/Save to the pure, and in their purest hour" (lines 64–65).

Coleridge's handling of the theme of imagination is similar to Wordsworth's in the "Immortality" ode in that both poets emphasize the mysterious gift of creative joy and express sorrow at its loss. However, Wordsworth suggests a developmental scheme: as children we come "trailing clouds of glory" (line 64), but the light of joy grows dim with the passage of time until "at length the Man perceives it die away,/And fade into the light of common day" (lines 76–77). Wordsworth's firm connection between joy (or "light") and childhood allows him the consolations of nostalgia. He empathizes with the delight of "Thou Child of Joy," treating him almost as an intercessor, one who reminds him of his original divine spark and recalls him to the love of nature. He also places more emphasis on the comfort which maturity can bring, as thought and memory play over the natural scene and compensate, in part, for the loss of the imaginative radiance which once flooded his vision:

> Though nothing can bring back the hour
> Of splendor in the grass, of glory in the flower;
>   We will grieve not, rather find
>   Strength in what remains behind;
>   In the primal sympathy
>   Which having been must ever be;
>   In the soothing thoughts that spring
>   Out of human suffering;
>   In the faith that looks through death,
> In years that bring the philosophic mind.
>   (10, 178–187)

For Coleridge, however, who treats imaginative loss more as a robbery than a natural process, there is no "primal sympathy" or "philosophic mind"; rather, he unsuccessfully struggles by "abstruse research to steal" what once was his and is haunted by "viper thoughts . . ./Reality's dark dream!" (lines 89, 94–95).

Wordsworth has the further solace of turning once again to nature, as he does in the final stanza of the "Immortality" ode. He does not so rigorously confine the origins of joy to the perceiver so that the world is without influence. Where Coleridge says that "in our life alone does Nature live," Wordsworth turns to "ye Fountains, Meadows, Hills, and Groves" and, denying any separation, asserts "yet in my heart of hearts I feel your might" (lines 188, 190). For Coleridge, the light seems to have irrevocably failed, leaving behind an "inanimate cold world" (line 51), while to Wordsworth "the meanest flower that blows can give/Thoughts that do often lie too deep for tears" (lines 203–204).

4.7 What is the function of the Lady in "Dejection: An Ode"?

Answer The apostrophe of the Lady (lines 25, 47, 59, 64, 67, 139) gives the ode a dramatic quality. Rather than reflecting in solitude, Coleridge is ostensibly talking to someone, explaining and confessing. In sucessive drafts of the poem, the unseen auditor was called "Sara" (Sara Hutchinson), "William" (William Wordsworth) and "Edmond" before Coleridge settled on the neutral appellation "Lady." The implication of these revisions is that the hearer's roles are more important than his or her particular identity. The roles seem to be those of intercessor, surrogate, and heir. In stanzas 4 and 5, the lady is closely associated with Joy, that power of the soul, both a light and a voice, which regenerates nature:

> Joy, Lady! is the spirit and the power,
> Which wedding Nature to us gives in dower
> A new Earth and new Heaven
>
> (5, 67–69)

The Lady is "pure of heart!" (line 59) and thus intimately acquainted with "this strong music in the soul. . . This light, this glory, this fair luminous mist" (lines 60, 62). In her exceptional virtue she is possessed of the radiance which Coleridge can no longer find. Although the poet never explicitly asks her to intercede for him, she has a saintlike quality as one through whom he can regain access to Joy. Through her he can call up, or at least remember, "a new Earth and new Heaven."

At the same time, the Lady is like Wordsworth's sister in "Tintern Abbey." In the latter poem, Wordsworth's "dearest Friend,/My dear, dear Friend" (lines 115–116) becomes a surrogate for the poet; her "wild ecstasies" recall his own youthful experience of nature, and the "sober pleasure" of her "after years" will repeat his mature experience. He lives again through her and, by mixing memory and anticipation, deepens the significance of the current moment. Coleridge likewise calls the Lady "friend devoutest of my choice" and treats her experience as an extension of his own. He need hardly explain to her "the sweet and potent voice" of the soul or the joy that animates the world since she is living witness of what he has known. It is noteworthy that both poets introduce their "friends" after a reference to a failure or decay of their "genial spirits," for the surrogates are somehow linked to the ideas of inner power and vitality. Wordsworth says that even should nature fail to provide him with a moral center, he will not "suffer my genial spirits to decay:/For thou art with me" (lines 113–114). For Wordsworth, his sister is a consolation and a guide; her life heightens and clarifies his own.

For Coleridge, the inner decay has already occurred, apparently without hope of reversal. "My genial spirits fail;/And what can these avail/To lift the smothering weight from off my breast?" (lines 37–40). Nature cannot help him, and the reference to the Lady in line 47 suggests that she is not a guide or teacher but rather a disciple or heir: "O Lady! we receive but what we give,/

And in our life alone does Nature live" (lines 47–48). The closing benediction in stanza 8 confirms the lady's role as heir, one to whom Coleridge passes on the legacy of joy while he himself is resigned to loss and sorrow.

> Visit her, gentle Sleep! with wings of healing,
> . . . .
> Joy lift her spirit, joy attune her voice;
> To her may all things live, from pole to pole,
> Their life the eddying of her living soul!
> (lines 128; 134–136)

If to him the world lacks "the passion and the life, whose fountains are within" (line 46), to her "all things live," animated by "her living soul."

Despite the Lady's somewhat different function from Wordsworth's "Friend," the effect is similar. Although Coleridge is not explicit about the resolution of his crisis, the language of the poem's closing suggests that his friend too brings a renewal of hope and vitality. The ode's progress from "unimpassioned grief " to its final word, "rejoice," suggests that Coleridge has, over his own protestations, achieved a release of some kind from the "smothering weight" of dejection. He has also found the means to create a poem even in lamenting his creative impotence; the poem, like the storm, is a "mountain birth," a brief but highly charged performance. If not Joy, then the animating influence of the Lady has "attuned" his voice to write it.

B.S.

SUGGESTED READINGS

Abrams, M. H., *The Mirror and the Lamp* (1953).
Bloom, Harold, *The Visionary Company: A Reading of English Romantic Poetry* (1971).
Coburn, Kathleen (ed.), *Coleridge: A Collection of Critical Essays* (1967).
House, Humphry, *Coleridge* (1953).
Taylor, Anya, *Magic and English Romanticism* (1979).

GEORGE GORDON, LORD BYRON

C H R O N O L O G Y

1788	Born in London. Son of a notorious rake, John Byron (known as "Mad Jack") and Catherine Gordon. Byron's uncle is William, fifth Lord Byron (known as the "Wicked Lord" for his dissolute ways).
1791	Death of John Byron, in poverty.
1798	While attending Aberdeen Grammar School, receives news of death of William Byron, making him sixth Lord Byron. Goes with his mother to the family estate at Newstead; is sent to study at Dr. Glennie's school at Dulwich.
1801	Enters Harrow, a British public school (private boarding school).
1805	Enters Trinity College, Cambridge University. Gains reputation as a spendthrift; quickly dissipates inherited fortune.
1806	Self-publishes a book of poems, *Fugitive Pieces*.
1807	Publishes another book of poems, *Hours of Idleness*. It is criticized severely by the *Edinburgh Review*. By this time has run up debts of £12,000.
1808	Receives M.A. from Cambridge. Returns to Newstead, where he lives a life of idleness and carousing.
1809	Assumes seat in the House of Lords, having attained his majority. Publishes satirical poem *English Bards and Scotch Reviewers* in retaliation for the attack

on him by the *Edinburgh Review*. Leaves England for a tour of Europe and the middle east.

1810–
1811   Travels through Portugal, Spain, Italy, Greece, and other countries; swims the Hellespont in imitation of the Greek romantic hero Leander. Engages in romantic affairs with both men and women. Works on long narrative and satiric poem *Childe Harold*. Returns to England ill and impoverished.

1812   In an attempt to raise much-needed cash, publishes Cantos I and II of *Childe Harold*. They are greeted with acclaim, and Byron is lionized by the fashionable world. He has an affair with Lady Caroline Lamb. Makes his first speech in Parliament, a plea for leniency for the framebreakers (rioters attacking automation of the textile industry).

1813   Publishes *The Corsair*; it sells 10,000 copies in one day. Byron remains poor, however, because of unfavorable publishing contracts. Begins an affair with his half sister, Augusta Leigh.

1814   Birth of Augusta's daughter, Elizabeth, possibly Byron's child.

1815   Marries Annabella Milbanke; she bears daughter Ada. Their marriage is unhappy; debt collectors pursue them, and Byron drinks heavily and takes laudanum (opium-derived drug).

1816   Byron sends his wife and daughter to live with her parents. Travels through Europe. In Switzerland, meets Percy Shelley, Mary Godwin, and Claire Clairmont, with whom he has an affair. At work on poem *Manfred*; publishes Canto III of *Childe Harold* and *The Prisoner of Chillon*. Settles in Venice.

1817   Publishes *Manfred*. At work on many lyric poems and on his memoirs, which he gives to friend George Moore and which are subsequently lost. Arranges the sale of the family estate at Newstead, which relieves his financial burdens. Arranges better publishing terms and soon is earning £6000 a year by his writing. Daughter Allegra born to Claire Clairmont.

1818   Publishes *Beppo* and Canto IV of *Childe Harold*. Begins work on his masterpiece, the mock-epic satire *Don Juan*. Daughter Allegra is sent to him in Italy; he puts her in care of friends.

1819   Begins an affair with Teresa, Countess Guiccioli, a young noblewoman married to an old man. With the count's acquiescence, Byron will follow her around Italy for the next four years. Publishes *Mazeppa* and Cantos I and II of *Don Juan*. Late in the year is ill with a fever.

1820   Active in the secret Carbonari movement, seeking to overthrow Austrian rule in Italy. Begins work on play *Cain* and on *The Vision of Judgment*, an attack on poet laureate Robert Southey.

1821   Publishes Cantos III and IV of *Don Juan* as well as *Cain* and some lesser
         plays. In the suppression of the Carbonari, Teresa's family, along with other
         liberals, are exiled to Pisa; Byron follows her.

1822   To Genoa in train of Teresa. At work on *Don Juan*. Death of daughter
         Allegra; death of Shelley in accident while sailing the yacht he had received
         as a gift from Byon.

1823   Publishes Cantos VI through XIV of *Don Juan*. Is enlisted by the Greek
         Committee in London to work on behalf of revolutionaries seeking to free
         Greece from Turkish rule. Sails to Greece.

1824   Spends last four months of life organizing the Greek rebellion; is an able
         leader and a skilled orator. Also donates huge sums of money to the cause.
         Is increasingly ill, however, and dies of a fever at Missolonghi in April.
         Body returned to England; refused burial at Westminster Abbey; interred
         in family vault at Hucknall Torkard Church. Cantos XV and XVI of *Don
         Juan* published.

ESSAY QUESTIONS WITH ANSWERS

"She Walks in Beauty"

5.1 Analyze the imagery of the lyric.

Answer   The lyric employs basically conventional imagery, although it does depart from the traditional picture of the lady as fair and bright, associated with the splendors of daylight, in its comparison of the mistress to the night. This mistress, like Shakespeare's, is "nothing like the sun."

Apart from the slight paradoxical tension of the first line, however, the distinctive quality of the poem derives not from any departure from the norm but rather from a graceful elaboration of the conventions of compliment. Avoiding trite or obvious similes, Byron employs instead an extended metaphor which conveys the idea of a subdued and subtle radiance. The mistress is "like the night/Of cloudless climes and starry skies" (lines 1–2), not pitch dark but glimmering with a diffused light. Like a portrait in chiaroscuro, her face is modeled through an interplay of light and shadow, and her dusky beauty makes daylight seem garish:

> And all that's best of dark and bright
> Meet in her aspect and her eyes:
> Thus mellowed to that tender light
> Which heaven to gaudy day denies.
> (lines 3–6)

Imagery drawn from painting continues as the poet discusses the shades, rays, and tints that compose the mistress's particular radiance.

The whole poem is marked by a kind of nonchalant ease that places it within the central tradition of the English love lyric. The smoothly flowing lines, the simple rhymes, and the fresh handling of the imagery of light and dark contribute to the impression of elegant and unlabored compliment. Although the poet suggests that the lady's grace is "nameless," that is, beyond the power of words to express, he in fact "names" the grace through his subtle use of metaphor and simile.

"Darkness"

5.2 The poem is in essence Byron's vision of the apocalypse, or end of the universe. What are the philosophical and psychological implications of this vision?

Answer Byron's vision assumes an intense reality from the opening line: "I had a dream, which was not all a dream." The poet thus insists on the ambiguous status of his nightmare, implying that the mind's images represent another order of reality and reveal an underlying truth.

The truth which the poem reveals is both philosophical and psychological. Philosophically, the poem is a statement of absolute nihilism; Byron seems to be saying that beneath the surface of society and civilization, beneath all the appearances of the world, there exists a formless chaos of appetite and self-destructive passion. Thus, social institutions and social bonds appear in the poem as perverted mockeries. The blazing hearth is replaced by "blazing homes" (line 14), feasting becomes "a meal . . . bought/With blood" (lines 39–40), and an altar becomes a heap of "holy things/For an unholy usage" (lines 59–60). Light—the emblem of warmth, life, reason, intellect, and love—becomes a transient flicker created by the self-consuming, self-destructive acts of humankind.

In a sense, the poem is like an admonitory sermon, cataloguing the horrors for sinners of the Day of Judgment. However, the unemphatic, matter-of-fact style is the antithesis of the persuasive rhetoric associated with sermons. Instead of an admonition or argument, "Darkness" constitutes a bleak description of a dying world. The conjunction of a neutral reportorial style with a nightmare vision gives the poem a surrealistic, allegorical quality. The poem reads like a parable, but the meaning is elusive. If this is a picture of hell, it is a hell on earth, rendered realistically and exhaustively.

The narrator's description, while rhetorically subdued, nonetheless conveys a definite emotional texture. The "dream" the narrator recounts is profoundly melancholic and despairing. In its imagery of violence, isolation, madness, and cannibalism, the poem documents a process of dehumanization, focusing obsessively on the catastrophic rending of individual and social connections. Thus the psychological landscape is as dark as the physical one, projecting a sense of radical alienation and deprivation, with all order perverted and all values eroded. The studied impersonality of the style only intensifies the impression of psychological fragmentation. It is as though the narrator were morally catatonic, reciting a catalogue of horrors in a flat and affectless monotone.

5.3   There are two anecdotes in the poem, one concerning a dog and his master, the other about two enemies who meet before an altar. What is the significance of these stories?

Answer   In the catalogue of horrors which constitutes the poem, these incidents stand out for two reasons. First, they offer narrative interest. Instead of merely itemizing or naming catastrophes, Byron singles out specific figures in the bleak landscape as characters in a drama. Moreover, these individual dramas hold out the promise of personal salvation or heroism in the midst of chaos. The faithful dog standing watch over his dead master represents heroic virtue, and the two enemies who meet in the flickering light of the altar symbolize the possibility of some form of communion. However, both episodes end the same way, with a laconic "he died" (line 54) and "they died" (line 67). The numbing flatness and finality of the rhetoric prevails over the slight suggestion of suspense and drama which the two anecdotes provide.

Indeed, Byron's handling of these episodes dramatizes not heroism or communion but the inevitable succumbing of all living creatures to the general annihilation. The dog, who "sought out no food" (line 51), dies of hunger, and the enemies die "even of their mutual hideousness . . ./Unknowing who he was upon whose brow/Famine had written Fiend" (lines 67–69). The irony of these stories—the futility of the dog's being "faithful to a corse" (line 48) and the enemies' ignorance of each other's identity—suggests the leveling power of darkness. Every human feeling, be it loyalty or hatred, becomes an absurdity at the world's end, in a universe of utter blackness.

5.4   It is possible to criticize "Darkness" for its repetitive style and diction; the poem may be seen as both boring and slightly ridiculous because of its excessive morbidity. Can it be defended against these criticisms?

Answer   Byron's rhetorical strategy in "Darkness" is intentional. The use of catalogue and the accumulation of images of conflagration and death contribute to the obsessive tone of the poem and the poet's intensely nihilistic vision. Each item becomes an illustration of the overriding theme: ". . . no love was left;/All earth was but one thought—and that was death" (lines 41–42). The blank verse, with its flat, conversational rhythms, does not poeticize or embellish the horrible vacuum which is the poem's subject.

The most consciously "poetic" moment comes at the very end of the poem in the personification of "Darkness." This selective use of figurative adornment is powerful, for in the final image the blunt recital of facts has its necessary denouement. What has been happening recurrently in the poem, the fitful dying of flickers of flame and gleams of light, happens conclusively in the last lines:

> And the clouds perished; Darkness had no need
> Of aid from them—She was the Universe.
>   (lines 81–82)

The syntax of these lines suggests that Darkness is not merely a passive force, a physical by-product of the death of the sun. "She" is an active agent, who swallows up and overwhelms the whole world. The clipped assertion "She was the Universe," still in keeping with the factual style of the whole poem, nonetheless implies some kind of victory or domination. In this climactic vision, the usual terms are reversed: Instead of describing darkness as the absence or extinction of light, as he did earlier in the poem, Byron portrays "her" as a positive presence, asserting hegemony over the entire cosmos and actively possessing it. If throughout the poem the insistent, detailed, claustrophobic language creates a feeling of nightmare, the last line is particularly nightmarish, turning a passive physical event into an illogical and terrifying apparition.

Childe Harold's Pilgrimage

5.5   Discuss the Byronic hero as he appears in the persons of Harold and Napoleon.

Answer   In *Childe Harold*, Byron offers a new image of the hero and a distinctive concept of existence, developing these ideas through self-portraiture, fictional creation, and historical analysis. Byron's vision of the hero is unconventional in that it includes anti-heroic features and an exaggerated sensibility which goes beyond the classical restraint of the traditional epic protagonist. Byron's hero is in the first place a fallen man, haunted by a dark past and by his own sinful excesses. As the narrator says of Childe Harold, "Worse than adversity the Childe befell;/He felt the fullness of satiety" (I, 4, meaning Canto I, stanza 4). A mixture of ennui and what we might call existential anguish sends the hero abroad into the world as an outlaw and exile. In all his travels the Byronic pilgrim remains alienated from the world of humankind, indulging in melancholy and dark despair. The dark and brooding nature of Childe Harold is essential to Byron's definition of heroism, for it is his intense and dramatic inner life that sets the Byronic hero apart from, and above, the common herd. Free from the constraining rules and conventions of civilized society, Harold can let his true passions emerge in response to the sights he experiences in his pilgrimage.

All the characteristics which Childe Harold possesses belong equally to the bard. In fact, the hero and the narrator seem at many points in the poem to merge into one consciousness. If the bard seeks to "fling/Forgetfulness around me" (III, 4), Harold, "he of the breast which fain would no more feel" (III, 8), seeks a similar oblivion. The narrator describes not only the hero's life but his own as embittered and ruined. Thus the bard recounts that "my springs of life were poisoned" and that time has taught him only to "feed on bitter fruits without accusing Fate" (III, 7). Of Harold, the bard says that his cup of life "had been quaffed too quickly, and he found/The dregs were wormwood"; despite all Harold's efforts, "still round him clung invisibly a chain/Which galled forever" (III, 9). The long passage addressed to Napoleon (III, 36–51), apparently spoken by the bard, is forcibly put into Harold's mouth as Byron suddenly treats the elaborate apostrophe as his hero's interior monologue: "Thus Harold inly said, and passed along" (III, 52). In Cantos III and IV, first-person narration dominates, and in the closing address to the reader at the end of Canto IV ("Ye! who have traced the Pilgrim to the scene/Which is his last . . ./Farewell! with *him* alone may rest the pain,/If such there were—with *you*, the moral of his strain!" [IV, 186]) the Pilgrim is no longer clearly Harold but rather the narrator who has been describing the pilgrimage.

Both Harold and the "I" of the poem are implied self-portraits of Byron. The sense of sin, isolation, melancholy, defiance, and emotional richness identifies both figures as extraordinarily sensitive men. Both Harold and the bard are embarked on journeys of self-creation, living out lives which are faithful to every fluctuation of feeling and sensation.

The image of Napoleon is related to the bard-Harold hero in his separateness from the masses and in the extreme nature of his passions and desires. He also represents some of the more conventionally heroic features of the Byronic ideal: the daring and imagination which sway the multitudes, the martial valor which creates empires, and the endurance and bravado in the face of ultimate defeat.

The Byronic hero, then, is a deeply ambivalent figure, both damned and blessed by virtue of the same characteristics. Possessing a kind of genius which is close to madness, he is an overreacher, driven by fantasies more vivid than reality and fated to disappointment:

> . . . there is a fire
> And motion of the soul, which will not dwell
> In its own narrow being, but aspire
> Beyond the fitting medium of desire;
> And, but once kindled, quenchless evermore,
> Preys upon high adventure, nor can tire
> Of ought but rest; a fever at the core
> Fatal to him who bears, to all who ever bore.
>   (III, 42)

This image of a self-destructive wanderer seeking the summits of experience has a Faustian splendor which caught the imagination of Byron's contemporaries and contributed a new facet to the romantic movement. The Byronic hero represents part of the celebration of inner vision and emotional experience which distinguishes romanticism.

5.6 Analyze the poet's handling of the themes of nature and childhood. How does Byron's approach to these themes compare with Wordsworth's?

Answer In parts of Cantos III and IV of *Childe Harold*, Byron's subject and style are similar to Wordsworth's. The passages on Lake Leman, the night sky, and the tempest in Canto III and on the ocean in Canto IV all suggest the solace that the narrator, alienated from the society of people, finds in nature. Byron turns to Lake Leman in somewhat the same mood as Wordsworth turns in imagination to the Wye in "Tintern Abbey," in order to revive and renew his spirit. The lake "woos" Byron like a lover (III, 68) and, as source of the Rhone, the "nursing lake/Which feeds it as a mother" (III, 71), it is also presented as maternal and nurturing. Nature is thus portrayed as an active influence on the life of the poet and a vital partner in the enterprise of discovering a sense of connection and meaning. Paradoxically, the poet experiences an escape from the loneliness he feels in the company of people in a solitary confrontation with nature, merging with the scene around him:

> I live not in myself, but I become
> Portion of that around me;
>
> (III, 72)

Later, the poet wonders:

> Are not the mountains, waves, and skies a part
> Of me and of my soul, as I of them?
>
> (III, 75)

The description of the lake at night, in the moment before the tempest bursts, has some of the charged intensity of Wordsworth's "spots of time." In the preternatural stillness before the storm, Byron half perceives and half creates a "mighty world":

> All heaven and earth are still. From the high host
> Of stars to the lulled lake and mountain coast,
> All is concentered in a life intense,
> Where not a beam, nor air, nor leaf is lost,
> But hath a part of being, and a sense
> Of that which is of all Creator and defense.
>
> Then stirs the feeling infinite, so felt
> In solitude, where we are *least* alone;
>
> (III, 89–90)

Byron's closing apostrophe of the ocean (Canto IV), which he describes as "boundless, endless, and sublime—/The image of Eternity—the throne/Of the Invisible" (stanza 183), bears a resemblance to Wordsworth's description of the moon lighting up a sea of mist as "the emblem of a mind/That feeds upon infinity" (*The Prelude* [Book XIV, lines 70–71]). In each case, there is a similar tendency to "build up greatest things/From least suggestions" (*The Prelude* [Book XIV, lines 101–102]). Both poets project a yearning for the infinite upon the forms that meet their eyes, and both transfigure the physical scene by an act of creative imagination.

In addition, Byron's attitude toward childhood to some extent reflects Wordsworth's celebration of the innocent perceptions of infancy. For example, the kinship the poet feels with the ocean has its origins in childhood memories of spontaneous and fearless pleasure:

> For I was as it were a child of thee,
> And trusted to thy billows far and near
> And laid my hand upon thy mane—as I do here.
> (IV, 184)

Even the misanthropic Childe Harold feels an innate sympathy with infancy as part of his generalized yearning for a lost golden age of innocence and natural affection.

> And he had learned to love—I know not why,
> . . . .
> The helpless looks of blooming infancy,
> Even in its earliest nurture;
> (III, 54)

However, Byron differs from Wordsworth in several important ways. First, the Wordsworthian meditation on nature is only one of the postures Byron adopts in the lengthy chronicle of Childe Harold's pilgrimage. Nature is Wordsworth's great theme, and humankind's interaction with the living universe is, for him, the sole source, actual or potential, of illumination, significance, and happiness. In Byron's *Childe Harold*, alienation is the chief theme, and the isolated hero's strenuous attempts to respond to and understand his experiences constitute the main action. Thus the reading of nature is only one of a number of attempts the poet makes to find a sustaining faith and a healing sense of connection. The apostrophe of Napoleon (III, 37–41) is an act of sympathetic identification with another "quick bosom" suffering a "fever at the core." The description of Venice (IV, 1–4) is a reflection on its eternal glory, bestowed by history and preserved in people's imaginations. The apostrophes of "Ada" (III, 1) and "my daughter" (III, 115) express a yearning for a kind of immortality as both parent and poet ("My voice shall with thy future visions blend,/And reach into thy heart—when mine is cold—/A token and a tone even from thy father's mold" [III, 115]). Finally, the allusions to "one fond breast" and "one soft breast" (III, 53, 55), which refer most probably to Byron's half sister Augusta Leigh, invoke the ideal of a pure, undying love in contrast to the sullied, transient bonds existing among the common herd. Thus Byron does not, like

Wordsworth, turn and turn again to nature, finding spiritual renewal and abiding wonder in its wealth and vitality. He searches everywhere, in the history of humanity and places and in personal relationships, as well as in nature, for significance and continuity.

Furthermore, even within the passages devoted to description of the natural world, Byron's technique is to dramatize and embellish nature rather than embody it through sensory impressions. Although Wordsworth, too, embroiders on the physical scene before him, using concrete particulars as a trigger for relatively abstract reflection, he almost always begins with a sensitive record of exact images and sensations. In *Childe Harold*, on the other hand, there is often an immediate flight from specific description into imaginative storytelling or analogy. Like Harold, who peoples the stars on which he gazes "with beings bright" (III, 14), Byron scarcely pauses to record what he sees before he "peoples" or transforms it. Thus he selects inherently dramatic phenomena—a tempest, the ocean—and reads into them a "genius" or spirit similar to that of his hero. He embroiders on the visual scene of the Rhone's divided cliffs by developing a fanciful tale of separated lovers and amplifies his description of the ocean's "yeast of waves" with allusions to the Armada, Trafalgar, and stories of war and conquest.

The excitation of Byron's descriptions accords with the narrator's general posture of intense sensitivity and yearning. He is open to every scene and every image which offers itself, but at the same time he is compelled to strive for something beyond the merely natural. He not only seeks communion with nature but "preys upon high adventure," constantly aspiring "beyond the fitting medium of desire" (III, 42).

5.7   Comment on Byron's use of archaic diction, apostrophe, exclamations, rhetorical questions, and listing in *Childe Harold's Pilgrimage*.

Answer   The archaic diction appearing in the earliest lines of the poem is in imitation of Spenser's *Faerie Queene*. By making this allusion to the great Renaissance romance, Byron lends his "romaunt" the flavor of an earlier period of romantic chivalry and adventure. Childe Harold's pilgrimage thus gains some of the epic scope of the Spenserian legend while at the same time standing in ironic contrast to it. Childe Harold is no Red Cross Knight in search of holiness but an alienated person in search of self. Lacking the central faith or creed that consecrates a given spot as a shrine or holy place, he embarks on a "pilgrimage" that is aimless and erratic. Holiness is nowhere or, in another sense, anywhere, something stumbled upon over and over again rather than attained in one climactic encounter. Childe Harold is thus more knight-errant than pilgrim, one of the "wanderers o'er Eternity/Whose bark drives on and on, and anchored ne'er shall be" (III, 70).

If the archaic diction of the title, subtitle, and opening verses is designed to recall the breadth and grandeur of Renaissance epic, its rapid disappearance, after just a few stanzas in Canto I, shows Byron in the act of substituting a modern form of epic adventure that rivals the moral and spiritual sojourns of classical and Renaissance forms. The older literary forms, evoking an epoch characterized by a belief in providential order and Christian values, are inadequate to chart the emotional and spiritual vagaries of a modern exile. While retaining the Spenserian stanza, with its spacious narrative flow, Byron creates his own dramatic rhetoric, exclamatory and urgent, to convey the restless fluctuations of Childe Harold's moods and yearnings.

A prominent feature of this rhetoric is apostrophe—direct address to an absent person or an insentient thing—which is used to establish a personal relationship between the narrator and the people, places, and things he witnesses. Sometimes the mode of address is conventional, for example, in the invocation of the muse which opens Byron's epic romance. More often, however, Byron transforms the convention of direct address into something more. As he uses it, apostrophe is not verbal decoration but the central activity of the bard-hero. The calling up of various figures and objects represents the exile's constant yearning for a feeling of connection. The narrator not only speaks to but identifies with the object addressed, attempting to merge himself with the "other," whoever or whatever it may be. Thus the apostrophe of Napoleon (Canto III) becomes an encomiastic address to a superior being, the Byronic hero, who in many ways reflects the bard's own temperament as one of the "quick bosoms" and "unquiet things" aspiring beyond the common mob. Byron's invocation of his estranged daughter blends into prayer and benediction (Canto III) as he yearns to "reach into thy heart" and attain a kind of immortality through his child. The addresses to Lake Leman, the stars, the tempest, and the ocean (Canto IV) represent an attempt to become one with them. The soft murmuring of Lake Leman is like a "sister's voice" (line 804) urging him to seek solitude and quiet; the stars, the "poetry of heaven," inspire a wish to "claim a kindred with you" (line 829); to night he says, "Let me be/A sharer in thy fierce and far delight—/A portion of the tempest and of thee!" (lines 870–872). He likewise draws close to the ocean, "the image of Eternity," "for I was as it were a child of thee,/And trusted to thy billows far and near,/And laid my hand upon thy

mane—as I do here" (lines 1653–1656). In each instance, Byron moves spir-
itually close to his object, not only speaking to it but communing with it and
often claiming a literal relationship as brother, kindred, child.

The final apostrophe, the address to the reader, reinforces the theme of
spiritual communion which has been latent throughout the epic. The poet ends
with a kind of bequest to the reader, the imaginative legacy contained within
the story of "the Pilgrim":

> Farewell! with *him* alone may rest the pain,
> If such there were—with *you*, the moral of his strain!
>   (IV, 186)

Byron moves close to the reader, becoming a martyr or intercessor through the
gift of himself and his story.

Byron's use of exclamations and rhetorical questions also contributes to the
intimate tone of the poem by offering a dramatic rendering of speech which
conveys qualities of excitement, wonder, and emotional intensity. Often these
rhetorical features coincide with moments of direct address, when a sudden
illumination or heightened mood overwhelms the narrator. Thus the excited
series of questions in Canto III, stanza 75 ("Are not the mountains, waves, and
skies a part/Of me and of my soul, as I of them?") suggest the narrator's awakening
to nature's awesome influence and his sense of inspired commitment, perhaps
intermixed with a hint of doubt, to the world of natural sympathy as against
worldly cynicism. Similarly, the exclamations in Canto III, stanza 92 ("The sky
is changed!—and such a change! Oh night") constitute a kind of emotional
fireworks in answer to the fireworks of the tempest. Finally, the many broken
phrases and exclamations in Canto III, stanzas 115–118, addressed to Ada ("My
daughter! with thy name this song begun—"), imitate the rhythms of a voice
breaking with emotion, a man uttering his deepest feelings in short, resonant
cadences. Taken together, the exclamations and questions create a breathless
rhetoric of excitation, a fitting medium for Byron's pilgrimage of the emotions.

Another prominent feature of the language of the poem is extensive lists of
places and things, often presented without conjunctions or sometimes with too
many, in a kind of hurried outpouring. Both the length of the itemizations and
the treatment of syntactic connectives produce the effect of a jumble, giving
the impression that the narrator is so overcome by what he is witnessing that
he can neither separate nor classify the objects but merely name them one after
another. In some instances Byron conventionally lists foreign or historic places
in a kind of traveler's itinerary ("Assyria, Greece, Rome, Carthage, what are

they?" [IV, 182]). At other moments he presents a breathless accumulation of natural wonders or spiritual sensations. For example, in depicting the abundant riches of nature at Lake Leman, Byron uses a long list to convey the fullness and variety of the scene:

> Sky—mountains—river—winds—lake—lightnings! ye,
> With night, and clouds, and thunder, and a soul
> To make these felt and feeling
>
> (III, 96)

Similarly, Byron, by the very act of naming his inner sensations and yearnings, reproduces the sense of emotional overflow which the scene arouses:

> . . . —Could I wreak
> My thoughts upon expression, and thus throw
> Soul, heart, mind, passions, feelings, strong or weak,
> All that I would have sought, and all I seek,
> Bear, know, feel—and yet breathe—into *one* word
> And that one word were lightning, I would speak;
>
> (III, 97)

Such a list enacts on a rhetorical level the theme of endless yearning, of struggling on and on for unity and coherence. By recording a welter of sensations and impressions the bard seeks to "name" his life and thus to discover its meaning. The very naming creates a sense of plenitude and heightened significance. The lists thus become an act of invocation in which the narrator calls on both the outer universe and his inner world to validate his experience and lend it meaning and richness. At the same time the headlong rush of items suggests confusion and disorientation, as though in the midst of plenty there is no unity, no "*one* word." Byron uses lists to convey, in one instant, hope and despair, wonder and doubt. Having called on "Sky—mountains—river—winds—lake—lightnings!" and drawn close to the grandeur of the physical world, Byron must ultimately recognize the separateness of humanity from nature. He asks, "But where of ye, oh tempests! is the goal?/Are ye like those within the human breast?/Or do ye find at length, like eagles, some high nest?" (III, 96). The longing to speak "*one* word" of lightning is followed by a sense of impotent inarticulateness: "But as it is, I live and die unheard,/With a most voiceless thought, sheathing it as a sword" (III, 97).

Don Juan

5.8   What is the relationship among the episodes of Donna Julia, Haidée, and the ghost story in *Don Juan*?

Answer   The three episodes form part of a picaresque narrative structure involving Don Juan's sexual misadventures. The Donna Julia story portrays Don Juan's first sexual encounter in terms of bedroom farce, with the cuckolded husband discovering the lovers after a series of comic mishaps. The story of Haidée is an idyllic interlude of innocent passion destroyed by parental opposition. The ghost story is a satire on gothic horror tales and English society women. Broadly speaking, Byron's narrative is reminiscent of a picaresque novel like *Tom Jones*, in which a sexually naive hero bumbles into liaisons with a number of women in the course of wide-ranging travels. The difference between Byron's mock-epic and the typical novel is that in the latter the hero gains important knowledge through his experiences, while in *Don Juan* the narrator does not undergo any significant change. Don Juan does not so much develop as persist, acting out his single role as sexual innocent, and sometimes victim, again and again.

Just as the hero's recurrent scrapes with women provide a unified thread of action, so the narrator's ongoing discussion of love, sex, and marriage lends the disparate incidents thematic coherence. The narrator's voice is a unifying force which places events, interpreting what each reveals about love.

In the Donna Julia episode (Canto I), the final remarks on love are expressed in the lady's passionate letter of farewell to Don Juan, after Don Alfonso has discovered them and she is to be sent off to a convent:

> "Man's love is of man's life a thing apart,
>   'Tis woman's whole existence; man may range
> The court, camp, church, the vessel, and the mart;
> . . . .
> Men have all these resources, we but one,
> To love again, and be again undone."
>
>   (I, 194)

Byron does not leave the reader with this lament but goes on, a few stanzas later, to detail the physical particulars of Donna Julia's letter:

This note was written upon gilt-edged paper
With a neat little crow-quill, slight and new;
. . . .
The motto, cut upon a white cornelian;
The wax was superfine, its hue vermilion.

(I, 198)

This tactic of digressing from the romantic passions of the principals to other topics—stationery, English newspapers, the climate, Wordsworth, the rules of rhetoric—is a pervasive feature of the epic as a whole and is particularly obtrusive in Canto I, where Byron is at pains to establish a satiric voice. The net effect is to undercut the passions in favor of a broadly comic view of Don Juan's sexual initiation and subsequent embarrassments.

The Haidée story (Cantos II-IV) is somewhat different despite the continuing presence of the satiric persona. The narrator seems more fully engaged in this story of shipwreck and Edenic love, treating Don Juan and Haidée as though they were, at least in part, types of Adam and Eve before the fall. Despite the comic animadversions on piracy, food, marriage, and so on, the tone on the whole is darker than that of Canto I. Haidée's death is a far more wrenching and tragic conclusion than Donna Julia's confinement in a convent, and the tone at the end of Canto IV is somber and austere. Byron heightens the effect of tragedy by focusing on Haidée's unborn child who died with her.

She died, but not alone; she held within
A second principle of life, which might
Have dawned a fair and sinless child of sin;
But closed its little being without light,
And went down to the grave unborn, wherein
Blossom and bough lie withered with one blight;
In vain the dews of Heaven descend above
The bleeding flower and blasted fruit of love.

(IV, 70)

The tone is most variable in Canto XVI, just as the narrative materials in that canto are the most heterogeneous. The account of Don Juan's sexual flirtations with a trio of society women and the tale of the Black Friar who haunts the Amundeville estate barely make a coherent story, so frequently is the narrative interrupted by the author's comments on social accomplishments, superstition, connoisseurship, gothic architecture, and local politics. However, the narrator lightly touches on the underlying theme of his epic in stanzas 107 through 109, describing the resurgence of love kindled in Juan's breast by Aurora Raby:

> The love of higher things and better days;
> The unbounded hope, and heavenly ignorance
> Of what is called the world, and the world's ways;
> The moment when we gather from a glance
> More joy than from all future pride or praise
> (XVI, 108)

There follows a lament for the inevitable transience of love, coupled with a comic appreciation of its value ("but though thou hast played us many tricks,/ Still we respect thee, 'Alma Venus Genetrix!' " [XVI, 109]). Finally, Juan, "full of sentiments, sublime as billows," betakes him to his midnight "pillows" (XVI, 110). This passage links Canto XVI to the earlier episodes by stressing Don Juan's emotional life and his passionate attachment to womankind as personified by Venus.

Nostalgia for and mockery of romantic love are characteristic of *Don Juan* as a whole. In this mock-epic Byron seems to be reworking the obsessive yearning of Childe Harold in a comic fashion, with Don Juan's specifically sexual involvements substituting for Harold's more diffuse desires for soul-satisfying encounters. *Don Juan* is not only a grab bag of disconnected anecdotes and essays but also a coherent story of an extended quest for fulfillment. Although the narrator is sometimes cynical toward this quest, he can be sympathetic and affectionate as well. The episodes of Donna Julia, Haidée, and the ghost story, even though the last is an ostensible "mystery," are really love stories. The worldly skepticism Byron claims for the narrator ("the sad truth which hovers o'er my desk/Turns what was once romantic to burlesque" [IV, 3]) is not the whole truth; just as the desire to burlesque excess and contradiction manifests itself in deflationary and digressive commentary, so the romantic impulse expresses itself in stanzas describing the throes of passion.

5.9 Characterize the narrator of the poem. How does the poet's persona contribute to the satiric effect?

Answer Despite the narrator's opening lament, "I want a hero" (I, 1), he is in a sense the hero of his own epic. The "I" of the persona constantly intrudes on the story he is telling; his views, problems, quirks, and preferences create an ongoing autobiography which overshadows Don Juan's adventures. This persona wears a series of different masks. For example, in the opening canto, he displays himself as a fussy, avuncular bachelor, interfering in the domestic affairs of Donna Inez and Don José and informing the audience of his personal opinions on education, literature, women, the law, and other topics. His bumbling naïveté is only a pretense, however, for at the same time he offers a knowing though deadpan perspective on the events he describes. At times he underscores his sophisticated outlook by directly punctuating the action with pungent asides and deflationary parentheses. For example, Byron ends a stanza describing Juan's moody meditations after meeting Donna Julia with an earthy, realistic judgment on his "longings sublime, and aspirations high": "If *you* think 'twas philosophy that this did,/I can't help thinking puberty assisted" (I, 93).

Another mask of the persona is a comic version of the Byronic hero, the melancholy romantic man of feeling. Toward the end of Canto I, he parodies romantic emotion, lamenting his lost youth (though he is only 30) and saying adieu to affairs of the heart. By exaggerating his age and preparing to take up the "good old-gentlemanly vice" of avarice, he satirizes the world-weariness of a Childe Harold. At the beginning of Canto IV, he emphasizes an adult perspective which transforms melancholy cynicism into comic satire:

> And the sad truth which hovers o'er my desk
> Turns what was once romantic to burlesque.
> (IV, 3)

Throughout we are aware of the narrator as a writer, endlessly embroiled in the act of composition. He discusses his structural design ("My poem's epic" [I, 200]), names his literary antecedents and contemporaries, self-consciously comments on his rhetorical techniques, and scrambles to keep up with his story, almost like a Tristram Shandy. As a writer, the narrator often pretends to be a bumbling novice not in full control of his materials. For example:

> I don't pretend that I quite understand
> My own meaning when I would be *very* fine;
> But the fact is that I have nothing planned,
> Unless it were to be a moment merry,
> A novel word in my vocabulary.
> (IV, 5)

Beneath the surface, however, his plan "to be a moment merry" is the artful strategy of an expert satirist who pokes fun at various targets while appearing to be nothing more than an idle bystander seeking innocent amusement. Thus in a passage on the meaning of life, the narrator's pretended befuddlement serves as a means of satirizing abstract philosophy and bringing the reader back to the realm of practical judgment, all in the spirit of a genial game:

> Few mortals know what end they would be at,
>   But whether glory, power, or love, or treasure,
> The path is through perplexing ways, and when
> The goal is gained, we die, you know—and then—
>
> What then?—I do not know, no more do you—
> And so good night.—Return we to our story:
>   (I, 133–134)

The ultimate effect of the narrator's voice is to provide a comic sense of distance which contributes to the success of the satire. The double entendres, digressions, and self-reflexive commentary undercut the narrative and help create a discrepancy between the heroic ideals of conventional epic and the down-to-earth realism of *Don Juan*.

5.10 *Don Juan*, one of the longest satires in the English language, employs an arsenal of rhetorical figures to create its ironic effect, including epithet, epigram, hyperbole, understatement, circumlocution, condensation, zeugma, and catalogue. Analyze the comic effect of these figures, giving an example of each.

Answer Some of the figures Byron uses, especially epithet and epigram, have the effect of pinning the satiric object with a telling phrase. Others work more obliquely, creating comic discrepancy by exaggerating the literal subject (hyperbole, circumlocution) or by diminishing it (understatement, colloquialism). Zeugma and catalogue are further means of producing incongruity, by means of the insertion of unexpected or inappropriate items into the syntax of a statement.

Epithets, or vividly descriptive adjectival phrases, provide a method of condensed caricature. For example, Haidée's stern and villainous father is transformed into a comic swaggerer by the label "her piratical papa" (III, 13). The affected duchess of Fitz-Fulke is reduced to a ridiculous bundle of contradictions by the epithet "her gracious, graceful, graceless Grace" (XVI, 49).

Epigrams are frequent throughout the poem; in fact, almost every final couplet at the end of a stanza constitutes one. Byron strikes off vivid images or telling generalizations in pointed phrases which temporarily halt the narrative flow. Many of the epigrams have the quality of brief definitions, such as the following:

> For instance—passion in a lover is glorious,
> But in a husband is pronounced uxorious.
>
> (III, 6)

> What men call gallantry, and gods adultery,
> Is much more common where the climate's sultry.
>
> (I, 63)

Sometimes they have the colloquial, concise quality of a well-told joke:

> Think you, if Laura had been Petrarch's wife,
> He would have written sonnets all his life?
>
> (III, 8)

The epigrams often offer generalizations about human nature. Thus the lines "In her first passion woman loves her lover,/In all the others all she loves is love" (III, 3) constitute a neat maxim on feminine psychology.

Figures involving inflation and deflation—hyperbole, circumlocution, understatement, and colloquialisms—are part of Byron's general strategy of creating a multileveled satire. The constant movement from high to low diction undercuts the lofty pretensions of both people and language. The following stanza is only one among many in which exaggerated, "poetical" circumlocution gives way to an understated, colloquial clincher:

> And she bent o'er him, and he lay beneath,
>   Hushed as the babe upon his mother's breast,
> Drooped as the willow when no winds can breathe,
>   Lulled like the depth of ocean when at rest,
> Fair as the crowning rose of the whole wreath,
>   Soft as the callow cygnet in its nest;
> In short, he was a very pretty fellow,
> Although his woes had turned him rather yellow.
>
> (II, 148)

Here the satire is directed against both elaborate language (exemplified by the series of decorative phrases) and the elaborate posturing of romantic love. Throughout the poem a major part of Byron's attack is directed toward the elevated conventions of the epic, with understatement and idioms being two of his chief weapons for deflating the heroic style. Thus the opening fragment of the entire epic invokes not only the muse but "hock and soda water," and the bow to classical convention at the beginning of Canto III is reduced to an airy "Hail, Muse! et cetera."

Zeugma and catalogue are other stylistic techniques useful for producing an effect of incongruity and ironic discrepancy. For example, the following passage on the influence of the moon pairs a lofty ideal with a humble physical fact:

> Great thoughts we catch from thence (besides a cold
> Sometimes, unless my feelings rather err);
>   (XVI, 14)

This use of zeugma treats abstract philosophy ("great thoughts") as the equivalent of physical discomfort ("a cold"), with the humor increased by the use of a single verb "catch" governing both high and low objects. Similarly, lists containing both the sublime and the ridiculous have the effect of cutting the heroic down to size. For example, in urging the salutary effects of hock and soda water in human life, the narrator jumbles mundane events with heroic experiences:

> Nor Burgundy in all its sunset glow,
> After long travel, ennui, love, or slaughter,
> Vie with that draught of hock and soda water.
>   (II, 180)

The seriousness of the epic protagonist's arduous sojourns as well as the sincerity of his ardor, are compromised by the allusions to boredom and random bloodshed; the whole of the second line could be read as a laconically comic summary of *The Odyssey*, evoked by Byron only to be deflated.

All these rhetorical techniques constitute means of exposing the absurdity of human vices and follies. By means of direct description (the figures of generalization and definition), distortion and caricature (the figures of exaggeration and understatement), and startling syntactic conjunctions (the figures of zeugma and listing), Byron unmasks hypocrisy and pretension.

5.11   There are many ways to categorize *Don Juan*—as a satire, a mock-epic, an anatomy, or a picaresque romance. Analyze the various generic cues within the poem and discuss their net effect.

Answer   One of the proposed derivations of the word "satire" links it with *satura*, which is Latin for a "mixed dish" or "potpourri." Byron's work has some of the quality of a culinary hodgepodge, with a variety of motifs and strategies contributing to the finished (or in this case unfinished) product. As the Latin derivation suggests, satire depends in part on a multigeneric strategy in that no single genre can be allowed to prevail intact and thus achieve a privileged status, for the purpose of satire is to unmask and expose all settled convictions and conventions. Thus it is characteristic of satire to offer a jumble of conflicting or competing genres, with one set of norms implicitly criticizing another.

Don Juan aggressively announces its own formlessness, with the narrator consistently underscoring his wanderings from the story line:

> But let me to my story: I must own,
>   If I have any fault, it is digression—
> Leaving my people to proceed alone,
>   While I soliloquize beyond expression;
>   (III, 96)

The fact that the epic, whose completion was interrupted by Byron's death, ends on a cavalier punchline (the mystery of the ghost is solved with the unmasking of "the phantom of her frolic Grace—Fitz-Fulke!" [XVI, 123]) is true to the spirit of a work which owes allegiance to no one literary genre or structure.

Of the genres which go into Byron's "mixed dish," mock-epic and picaresque romance contribute to the meandering narrative line. The naive hero traveling from place to place, pursuing forbidden experiences, is like a comic Odysseus— or a Don Quixote, Tom Jones, or Childe Harold—embarked on an epic pilgrimage of adventure. The mock-epic fuses with picaresque romance, for the adventures in the poem are all amorous, and Don Juan, like the conventional picaro (rogue), has a knack for getting into and out of scrapes. Making his escape from irascible husbands and fathers (Cantos I-IV) and falling into the clutches of a lascivious society dame (Canto XVI) are typical of his unlucky escapades.

The essayistic commentary of the epic, on the other hand, offers an attack on the generic cues provided by the narrative portions. Taken together, the digressions constitute a kind of anatomy or dissection of the world, all-inclusive and rambling. This commentary subverts the coherence and authority of the narrative itself by bringing in all sorts of material foreign to the conventions of epic and picaresque romance. Whenever Byron departs from his story to reflect on climate, theology, politics, men, women, marriage, food and drink, education, or economics, he is adding to that other "structure" in his work, the satiric analysis of human life. At the same time, *Don Juan* has the quality of an anthology of literary kinds, with Byron offering overt allusions to epic, picaresque, gothic horror, travelogue, and critical essay as he toys with each of these forms. Through allusion and critical commentary he creates the sense of a literary pilgrimage through assorted styles and strategies. He further enhances the aspect of pastiche or collage by peppering his text with foreign languages, special idioms, jargon, and quotations, producing a patchwork effect, as though he were making up *Don Juan* out of the shreds and patches of other languages, cultures, and literary works.

Partly because of the heterogeneous materials which contribute to Byron's satiric epic, the work has a mood of exhilarated freedom and rebelliousness. It is anticonventional in its subversive refusal to respect form, logic, coherence, and precedent. The formlessness of *Don Juan* is in a sense a manifesto, linked with one of Byron's enduring themes: the importance of individual expression as opposed to the deadly weight of conformity and tradition. Anticipating James Joyce, Byron seems conscious that there is no escape from linguistic convention or rhetorical stratagem; the only freedom possible lies in exploiting all available genres and styles and so wresting a kind of personal victory, and an idiosyncratic voice, from their comic collisions.

B.S.

SUGGESTED READINGS

Marchand, Leslie, *Byron: A Biography* (1957).
Rutherford, Andrew, *Byron: A Critical Study* (1961).
West, Paul, *Byron: The Spoiler's Art* (1960).

PERCY BYSSHE SHELLEY

C H R O N O L O G Y

<table>
<tr>
<td>1792</td>
<td>Born at Field Place, Sussex. Son of Timothy Shelley and Elizabeth Pilford Shelley. The family are minor country gentry with a modest fortune acquired by trade.</td>
</tr>
<tr>
<td>1798</td>
<td>Begins schooling under the instruction of the local clergyman, the Reverend Evan Edwards.</td>
</tr>
<tr>
<td>1802</td>
<td>Enters Syon House Academy at Isleworth, near London.</td>
</tr>
<tr>
<td>1804</td>
<td>Enters Eton, leading English public school (private boarding school). Has begun writing; before leaving Eton will have written many poems as well as two novels. Shows special interest in science, not then included in the curriculum of the classical education.</td>
</tr>
<tr>
<td>1808</td>
<td>Corresponds with cousin Harriet Grove; they are briefly engaged but break it off by 1810.</td>
</tr>
<tr>
<td>1810</td>
<td>Earliest publications: Zastrozzi and Original Poetry by Victor and Cazire. Enters University College at Oxford; meets Thomas Jefferson Hogg.</td>
</tr>
<tr>
<td>1811</td>
<td>Meets Harriet Westbrook. With his friend Hogg, writes and publishes The Necessity of Atheism, a tract arguing in favor of what today would be called agnosticism. In an act of youthful folly, they send copies to the heads of all Oxford colleges—clergymen all. Shelley and Hogg are expelled as a result. Shelley elopes with Harriet Westbrook (she is 16 years old); they marry in Edinburgh and then move to Ireland.</td>
</tr>
</table>

1812   Active in Irish politics in Dublin. Publishes political tracts *Address to the Irish People, Proposals for an Association,* and *A Declaration of Rights.* Travels to Wales and Devon; goes to London and meets radical leader William Godwin. At work on political-satiric poem *Queen Mab.*

1813   Daughter Ianthe born to Harriet. *Queen Mab* published. Shelley in Wales, Ireland, and London. Meets Godwin's daughter Mary Wollstonecraft Godwin; her mother is Mary Wollstonecraft, author of early feminist work *A Vindication of the Rights of Women.*

1814   Publishes *A Refutation of Deism.* Begins affair with Mary Godwin; they secretly leave for the Continent, taking with them Claire Clairmont, Mary's half sister. Son Charles born to Harriet.

1815   After death of Shelley's grandfather, he begins to receive annual income of £1000, which removes threat of poverty; he settles one-fifth of the income on Harriet. Mary bears a child, who dies within two weeks. They move to a cottage near Windsor.

1816   Birth of son William to Mary. Shelley, Mary, and Claire visit Switzerland; they meet Lord Byron, already a famous poet, with whom Claire has an affair. Shelley publishes *Alastor,* writes "Mont Blanc" and the "Hymn to Intellectual Beauty." Harriet dies by drowning (perhaps a suicide); Shelley marries Mary.

1817   Shelleys settle at Marlow; enjoy friendship with Hogg and with Leigh Hunt (editor and critic). Birth of daughter Clara; also of Allegra, Claire's daughter by Byron. *Laon and Cythna* published; later revised as *The Revolt of Islam.*

1818   Travels to Italy with Mary and Claire; they send Allegra to Byron, who is living in Venice. At work on play *Prometheus Unbound,* whose Act I setting is suggested by the Shelleys' passage of the Alps. Death of Clara.

1819   In Naples, Rome, and Florence. Death of William; birth of son Percy Florence. Writes voluminously: *The Cenci, The Mask of Anarchy,* the "Ode to the West Wind," and "Peter Bell the Third," a satirical attack on the political conservatism of Wordsworth's old age. Also completes *Prometheus Unbound* and writes political tract *A Philosophical View of Reform.* Shelleys adopt an Italian baby; it dies within a year.

1820   Writes "Ode to Liberty," "To a Skylark," "The Witch of Atlas," other poems; also *Swellfoot the Tyrant,* a political skit.

1821   Meets Emilia Viviani, Italian girl; writes *Epipsychidion* based on his idealization of her beauty. Death of John Keats; Shelley writes his elegy on Keats, *Adonais.* In response to an article by Peacock attacking modern poetry, writes essay "A Defense of Poetry." Visits Byron.

1822   Writes "The Triumph of Life"; works on "Charles I" (unfinished). Death
            of Allegra Byron. Mary suffers a miscarriage; she is ill and lonely, especially
            since Shelley has developed a strong attraction to Jane Williams, wife of a
            friend. Shelley receives yacht, the *Don Juan*, as a gift from Byron; sailing
            it from Leghorn to San Terenzo, he has an accident and drowns. His body
            is cremated on the beach at Leghorn; the ashes are later buried at Rome.

ESSAY QUESTIONS WITH ANSWERS

"Ozymandias"

6.1 Most of the poem is a direct quotation of the words of the "traveller from an antique land," who in turn quotes the inscription on the base of the shattered statue. Discuss the significance of the use of quotation in the poem.

Answer The effect of quotation in "Ozymandias" is paradoxical. On the one hand, it conveys a sense of historical and factual authenticity as the "witness" reports his experiences in a distant land; on the other hand, it creates an aura of mystery, for the traveler, like Coleridge's ancient mariner, is a nameless figure returned from a foreign country with a strange and marvelous tale to tell. As first the traveler, then the poet, and finally the reader receive the message on the statue, the process of historical transmission is enacted. The difficulty of reading the past rightly is suggested by the emphasis on the distancing powers of time (the "antique" land, the statue wrecked by history) and space (the faraway setting, the "boundless" sands). History begins to have the quality of legend or fable as past events become "storied."

The fact that the language of the poem is relatively prosaic is also a product of the rhetorical strategy of quotation. In contrast to many of his other lyrics, Shelley is here not constructing a mythology but rather examining the ironic relationship between myth and fact. History makes its own ironic comment on the story of Ozymandias, for the statue designed to make him into a legend is itself half buried in the sands of time.

6.2 Discuss dramatic irony in the poem.

Answer After one line which establishes the narrative frame, the lyric develops into an extended description of the scene in the desert. The drama of the episode is heightened by the piecemeal imagery as the traveler begins with, literally, fragments of the tableau. The traveler's eye focuses first on the looming, enigmatic columns of stone. The more elaborate description of the statue's "shattered visage" (line 4) then suggests the image of a conqueror. The inscription ("My name is Ozymandias" [line 10]) constitutes the last piece of the puzzle; it provides the only specific identification offered by the poem. Already irony is at work, for the loud proclamation of Ozymandias's omnipotence comes after we have seen the remnants of his ruined majesty. But the irony is further compounded as the traveler surveys "the lone and level sands" (line 14) which reduce Ozymandias to a speck on the horizon.

These ironic juxtapositions are underscored verbally, for the "words" of Ozymandias echo eerily in the surrounding emptiness:

> My name is Ozymandias, King of Kings,
> Look on my Works, ye Mighty, and despair!
> Nothing beside remains.
>
> (lines 10–12)

The "works" have disappeared back into the desert, Ozymandias himself is nothing more than a "colossal Wreck" (line 13), and the claim to empire has become an absurd, empty boast. In retrospect, it seems that the ironic perspective of the traveler who surveys the shattered idol is shared even by the sculptor who was originally commissioned to glorify Ozymandias. In his handiwork the sculptor mocked the "passions . . . stamped on those lifeless things" (lines 6–7), even as the king's "heart" fed on a passion for infinite power (lines 7–8). What survives are not, clearly, the "lifeless things," the physical man or his material monuments, but the "passions" themselves. All these ironies in the poem breed a final irony. The only enduring monument the tyrants of the past leave to future generations is a record of their hubris and, what they never intended, a memento mori, or a reminder of the death they sought to avoid.

6.3   How is the poem constructed?

Answer   Although its rhyme scheme is somewhat irregular, "Ozymandias" has the general structure of an Italian sonnet, with the major logical division occurring between octave and sestet. The octave presents the fragmentary evidence of the ancient ruin, the sestet its specific significance. The sestet consists of two triplets, the first proclaiming the message on the pedestal and the second describing the eloquent emptiness of the scene. In terms of narrative structure, the poem consists of a story within a story within a story. Ozymandias's tale is contained within the traveler's, and the traveler's story is contained within the narrator's. These multiple narratives suggest that the past is like a legacy passed from hand to hand, a message conveyed from Ozymandias to the traveler to the poet and, finally, to the reader.

The rhyme scheme of the poem (*abab, acdc, ede, fef,* with several slant rhymes) formally reinforces both the turns in the thought from description to quotation and back to description and the underlying theme of the interweaving of past and present. The cross-linkings in the rhyme constitute an acoustic interweaving: the *a* rhyme ("land"/"sand") is carried over into the second quatrain ("command"), the *d* rhyme of the second quatrain ("things") is carried over into the first triplet of the sestet ("kings"), and the *e* rhyme of the first triplet ("appear"/"despair," a slant rhyme) is carried into the second triplet ("bare"). The result is a closely textured pattern without sharp breaks, with the ideas unfolding harmoniously as the traveler tells his story. The organic interconnections of the rhyme words work against any clear distinction among the "voices" of the poem. The "I" offers his one line, then the traveler picks up the story, then Ozymandias speaks his piece, and finally the traveler concludes, each voice rhyming with its predecessor. Unlike a closed couplet, the final triplet gives an impression of openness, as though the rhymes, and the story, could continue to expand. Instead of offering a final conclusive word, the poem subsides into silence: "Round the decay/Of that colossal Wreck, boundless and bare/The lone and level sands stretch far away." The rhyme structure thus becomes a metaphor for historical transmission, enacting its own acoustic "legacy" and suggesting the echoing effect of the past as it impinges on the present.

"Ode to the West Wind"

6.4 Discuss the strategy of invocation, comparing its use in "Ode to the West Wind" with that in "To a Skylark."

Answer Both poems are in a sense long apostrophes to an external agent of inspiration. In "Ode to the West Wind," the poet literally prays for "inspiration" (in Latin, *inspirare* means "to breathe in"), wishing to draw in the "breath of Autumn's being" (line 1). The first three sections are extended addresses to the west wind, each ending with the words "O, hear!" Thus the poet is a supplicant, begging the potent force of nature to heed his cry. In the fourth section, the prayer becomes more specific as the narrator yearns for liberation through a passive yielding to the power of the wind: "Oh! lift me as a wave, a leaf, a cloud!" (line 53). Finally, in the fifth section, the poet's prayer becomes a wish for total identification and fusion with the wind: "Be thou, Spirit fierce,/ My spirit! Be thou me, impetuous one!" (lines 61–62). This symbolic connection between the poet and the force of nature is elaborated in terms of agent and vehicle, with the wind "driving" and "scattering" the poet's thoughts and words through the universe. Thus the poet is an instrument on which the wind plays, a prophet inspired by a higher power.

Shelley's image of the wind playing upon the poet as upon an instrument ("Make me thy lyre" [line 57]) frequently appears in the works of other romantic poets as well. Coleridge's conversation poem "The Eolian Harp," dramatizing the quickening power of the wind as it "plucks" the poet's soul, and the first line of Wordsworth's long poem The Prelude ("Oh there is a blessing in this gentle breeze" [Book I, line 1]) are two instances of this romantic convention. Among the romantics the classical notion of poetic inspiration is naturalized, with prophetic power conferred on the passive, waiting vessel by the vital infusion of the breath of the wind. The aeolian harp—an actual musical instrument popular in the nineteenth century, whose music was produced by the wind—was a natural symbol of this relationship.

In "To a Skylark" the poet again addresses an aspect of nature, this time a bird. At once he "dematerializes" the literal bird, making it as spiritual and symbolic a presence as the wind becomes in "Ode to the West Wind":

> Hail to thee, blithe Spirit!
> Bird thou never wert—
> (lines 1–2)

The bird's song, like the breath of the wind, represents the force of inspiration for which the poet longs. Much of "To a Skylark" is devoted to a series of elaborate comparisons between the invisible outpouring of the skylark's melody and other natural phenomena: the "aerial hue" of the unseen glowworm or the sweet scent of the hidden rose. These similes for the skylark, like the lengthy epithets describing the west wind, suggest the potent and magical influence of nature's inspiration.

Aside from the first line of the poem, there are only two other instances of direct address in "To a Skylark," beginning "Teach us" (line 61) and "Teach me" (line 101). The most significant moment of prayer comes at the very end, in the last stanza, where the poet seeks to learn the bird's "gladness" so that he may utter an inspired ("mad") harmony for the world to hear (lines 101–105). The emphasis here on the idea of teaching is very different from the fused identification the poet desires in "Ode to the West Wind." Instead of union and a prophetic inspiration, the poet develops the concept of transmission: the "secret" of song is a legacy from bird to poet and from poet to world. "Ode to the West Wind" insists on a symbolic merging between inner self and outer world, while "Skylark" observes the inevitable separateness of humanity from nature, dramatizing instead the longing to approach and "learn" nature's un-selfconscious expressive power.

6.5 The "Ode to the West Wind" contains many images drawn from nature. How does Shelley integrate these natural images into his vision of humanity and the universe?

Answer The images in the poem are interconnected according to the scheme of the elements, with air, water, and earth as the dominant motifs. More specifically, air (the west wind) animates earth, heaven, sea, and finally humanity with a vital power of regeneration. In fact, a myth of regeneration underlies the whole poem as Shelley moves from the chaos of the autumnal scene to a closing prophecy, or at least a hope, of new life: "If Winter comes, can Spring be far behind?" (line 70).

The opening section describes the effects of wind on the landscape, treating the autumnal blast as a metaphor for death and pestilence and only hinting at the possibility of a future revitalization. The allusion to "thine azure sister of the Spring" (line 9) and the epithet "Destroyer and Preserver" (line 14) suggest the ambivalent significance of this wild and hectic phase of the seasonal cycle.

Shelley elaborates on the idea of chaos in the two succeeding sections. In section II, he describes the tempest brewing in the heavens, again emphasizing the theme of death in the image of the vaulted sepulcher of the sky. In section III, the underwater scene is described metaphorically as an autumnal landscape like that in section I, with the trees of the sea denuded of their foliage like those of the land. In fact, images of trees run throughout the poem, from the literal falling of leaves in the first section, to the "tangled boughs of Heaven and Ocean" (line 17) in the second, to the "sapless foliage" (line 40) underwater in the third, to the poet's references to himself as a "dead leaf" (line 43) and an autumnal forest in sections IV and V. In these descriptions of the force of nature, the poet is a supplicant, powerless and beseeching. His longing to "pant beneath thy power" (line 45), to "share the impulse of thy strength" (line 46), or, as in his childhood, to be "the comrade of thy wanderings" (line 49) attests to a feeling of impotence, alienation, and loss. The suggestion is that poet and nature are out of phase and that the poem represents a striving to overcome the resulting sense of isolation and emptiness.

If nature is presented throughout most of the poem as "other," an external force, in the final section the poet claims this "other" for his own. All the images of the poem fuse in the closing movement as Shelley locates a natural landscape within himself. Praying to the wind to "inspire" him, to fill him with its own prophetic knowledge and promise, he says, "Oh! lift me as a wave, a leaf, a cloud!" (line 53). In recapitulating the dominant images of the ode, Shelley insists on the essential harmony existing between humanity and nature, with all living things participating in the oneness of the universe.

The theme of regeneration provides the climax of the poem in section V:

> Drive my dead thoughts over the universe
> Like withered leaves to quicken a new birth!
> (lines 63–64)

The vegetative, seasonal, and human cycles merge and combine in this vision of new life and springtime awakening. There is a quasi-religious quality to the vision, with its implicit reference to winter crucifixion ("I fall upon the thorns of life! I bleed!" [line 54]) and springtime resurrection ("new birth" [line 64]). However, Shelley's vivid images of earth, sky, and water place the poem firmly in the world of nature. The role of the poet is especially significant in Shelley's vision of an animated universe, for his is the voice of the prophetic seer whose incantation endows the word with meaning.

Adonais

6.6 Where is the climax of the poem?

Answer   The climax of the poem begins with the lines "Peace, peace! he is not dead, he doth not sleep—" (39, 1, meaning stanza 39, line 1) and continues through stanza 44, which describes the apotheosis of the dead poet, Keats. This section of the elegy marks the decisive shift from the mood of lament which dominates the opening ("I weep for Adonais—he is dead!") to the joyous recognition of Adonais's eternal life.

In the conventional Christian elegy, the climax is always a revelation of the soul's salvation; the center of the poem thus restates the central tenet of Christian theology, that we "die to live." In *Adonais*, Shelley offers a variation on this theme, describing the spirit's immortality in terms of a natural religion. The dead soul, instead of rising up to heaven, diffuses itself everywhere in the living world below:

> He is made one with Nature: . . .
>
> . . . .
> He is a presence to be felt and known
> In darkness and in light, from herb and stone
>   (42, 370; 373–374)

The preeminent Christian elegy, Milton's *Lycidas*, exploits some of the same pagan and pastoral motifs Shelley draws on in *Adonais*. For example, after death Lycidas becomes a "genius of the shore" (line 183), merging with the natural world even as he "rises" above it ("So Lycidas sunk low, but mounted high,/ Through the dear might of him that walked the waves,/. . ./In the blest kingdoms meek of joy and love" [lines 172–173; 177]). Thus Shelley's emphasis on a pantheistic nature inhabited by spiritual "geniuses" and gods has a precedent in the residual paganism of Christian elegy. However, Shelley's avoidance of any specifically Christian allusion (such as Milton's "through the dear might of him that walked the waves") sets "Adonais" apart from the convention. Shelley presents nature as an animistic realm of being, imbued with the vitality of a spiritual "One," rather than simply as a metaphor for the soul's immortality. Thus the poem's paganism is central rather than a merely symbolic gesture.

The spiritual quickening of nature is connected with the dead poet's utterances. Thus it is Adonais's "voice" that survives in nature:

> . . . there is heard
> His voice in all her music, from the moan
> Of thunder, to the song of night's sweet bird;
>   (42, 310–313)

The communion with nature in death is the epitome of the romantic poet's struggle, in life, to merge with the vital forces of the universe. Thus Keats's odes, celebrating the identification between subject and object, humanity and nature, are one precedent for his apotheosis in *Adonais*: "He is a portion of the loveliness/Which once he made more lovely" (44, 379–380).

These stanzas constitute both the philosophical and the emotional heart of the poem. The elegy is structured on affective rather than narrative sequences, first evoking a mournful response by means of images and tableaux and then eliciting an epiphanic joy by shifting the refrain (from "O weep for Adonais—he is dead!" [stanza 3] to "He lives, he wakes—'tis Death is dead, not he;/Mourn not for Adonais" [stanza 41]). The whole climactic section of the poem heightens the sense of joy by emphasizing the participation of the dead poet in the life of nature.

6.7 In stanza 52, Shelley alludes to a Neoplatonic conception of the universe. Comment on the Neoplatonism found here and elsewhere in the poem.

Answer Shelley expresses his sense of a spiritual presence presiding over the universe in terms of the Neoplatonic image of a unitary source of light. This light, which is a metaphor for essential being or the "One," emanates from above, filtering down to the mundane realm of shadows and colors. The notion of a prism which stains, bends, shatters, refracts, and "transfuses" the pure, heavenly light into the illusory images of the world suggests that the world is a fragmented and shadowy imitation of the "One." In stanza 52, this recognition of the inferior nature of mortal life becomes a longing for death: ". . . Die,/If thou wouldst be with that which thou dost seek!" (lines 464–465).

Earlier, in the climactic section of the elegy (stanzas 39–44), the allusions to Neoplatonism contribute to the shift from sorrow to joy. According to the Neoplatonic doctrine of ideas or "forms," a realm of unseen essences exists above the realm of sense, endowing the physical world with spiritual significance. In Shelley's treatment, Adonais himself becomes a kind of essence or "idea," animating the material world and lending it an aspect of formal beauty. The dead poet is associated with a pervasive "Power" and with "the one Spirit's plastic stress" which "sweeps through the dull dense world" (43, 381–382). He thus participates in the eternal life of the divine Forms which impress on dead matter an elemental beauty, imbuing it with light. The image of the "one Spirit" overcoming dull matter and "bursting in its beauty and its might/From trees and beasts and men into Heaven's light" (43, 386–387) turns a loss into a gain as Keats "doth bear/His part" (lines 380–381) in the loveliness of a nature endowed with visionary significance.

There is some ambiguity in the imagery, indicating the poet's ambivalence about succumbing to the "plastic stress" of the spiritual "One." The "light" explodes and the "fire" consumes so that spiritual apotheosis is at the same time

an annihilation. Nonetheless, as the poem moves to its conclusion, the recognition of the Neoplatonic ideal becomes a positive longing for death. In stanza
54, for example, the poet formally invokes the "One" ("That Light . . . That
Beauty") as the seductive end of his desires: "The fire for which all thirst; now
beams on me,/Consuming the last clouds of cold mortality" (lines 485–486).
Thus Shelley uses Neoplatonism in a way similar to the Christian paradox of
life in death, so that death becomes a movement from dark to light, cold to
heat. There is, however, no hint of a Christian God or of such concepts as sin,
sacrifice, or atonement. Shelley's paganism is austere, and his consolations are
metaphoric, aesthetic, and philosophical rather than religious.

6.8 Analyze the poet's relationship to Adonais.

Answer In stanzas 31 through 34, Shelley gives a portrait of himself as a
mourner at Adonais's tomb, presenting himself as a martyr sharing the poet's
fate already suffered by the "slain" Keats. Alluding to himself as a "frail Form"
(line 271), "a pardlike Spirit" (line 280), and "a dying lamp, a falling shower,/
A breaking billow" (lines 284–285), he suggests that he himself is dying, fading
away into pure spirit. In stanza 33, Shelley dresses himself in the attributes of
mourning and in stanza 34, he indicates his sympathetic identification with the
dead poet describing himself as one "who in another's fate now wept his own"
(line 300). The highly charged emotionalism of the passage suggests not only
Shelley's empathy with Keats but his sense of his own martyrdom. The references
to Actaeon, the hunter turned into a deer and pursued by his own hounds, are
followed by the allusion to a mark on his brow "which was like Cain's or
Christ's—Oh! that it should be so!" (lines 305–306). By identifying himself
with the slain Adonais, Shelley attempts to transform himself, like Keats, into
an emblem of the poet's fate. The poet, regardless of individual personality and
circumstances, is marked, doomed to suffer in the world because of his intense
spirituality.

At the end of the poem, the identification between the two poets becomes
complete. Shelley treats Keats as a kind of alter ego who has gone before to
prepare the way for his own death. The voice of Adonais is a seductive call for
a "reunion" with his other self:

> 'Tis Adonais calls! oh, hasten thither,
> No more let Life divide what Death can join together.
>   (53, 476–477)

In the final stanza, Shelley eerily prefigures his own actual death by drowning, describing his spirit as a bark "driven/Far from the shore" (lines 488–489). In the midst of the tempest, Adonais becomes the polestar, guiding his ship toward death:

> Whilst burning through the inmost veil of Heaven,
> The soul of Adonais, like a star,
> Beacons from the abode where the Eternal are.
> (55, 493–495)

The poet is driven toward the spiritual self-realization which only death can confer.

B.S.

SUGGESTED READINGS

Bloom, Harold, *Shelley's Mythmaking* (1959).
Reiman, David, *Percy Bysshe Shelley* (1969).
Ridenour, George M. (ed.), *Shelley* (1965).
Wasserman, Earl, *Shelley: A Critical Reading* (1971).

JOHN KEATS

C H R O N O L O G Y

1795   Born in London. Son of Thomas Keats, manager of an inn, and Frances Keats. His modest social status will provoke some malicious mockery by snobbish reviewers during his brief literary career.

1803   Enters the Clarke School at Enfield, ten miles north of London. Meets Cowden Clarke, son of the headmaster there, who will introduce him to poetry.

1804   Death of Keats's father in a riding accident, leaving four small children. His widow remarries; the children go to live with their grandparents.

1805   Death of Keats's grandfather; his mother becomes embroiled in a lawsuit over his will with her mother. Keats and his grandmother move with the other children to Edmonton.

1806   Keats's mother and stepfather separate.

1808   Keats's mother returns to her children. Soon after, she becomes seriously ill.

1810   After a long illness, through which Keats nursed her, Keats's mother dies of tuberculosis. His grandmother sets up a trust fund for the children. However, the sum involved is not great, and Keats and the other children remain in highly straitened circumstances for years to come. Keats leaves school and becomes an apprentice to Thomas Hammond, a surgeon and apothecary (pharmacist).

1813	Keats first reads the poetry of Edmund Spenser; he is captivated by it and sets to work writing his own poems, including an "Imitation of Spenser."
1815	Enters Guy's Hospital in London to study medicine; proves an apt student.
1816	Is quickly promoted to dresser (assistant surgeon) at Guy's Hospital and later receives an apothecary's license. This promises an escape from poverty, but Keats decides to abandon medicine after a series of events launch him firmly on a literary career. In May, first poem, "O Solitude!" published in the *Examiner*; writes "Sleep and Poetry," and sonnet "On First Looking into Chapman's Homer"; meets Shelley; is praised in an article, "Young Poets," by Leigh Hunt.
1817	Publishes first book, *Poems*; it is well reviewed but sells little. Moves to Hampstead. At work on *Endymion*. Makes famous literary-critical comments in letters written in November and December. Meets Wordsworth but does not like him.
1818	Brother Tom falls ill with tuberculosis; Keats nurses him. Publishes *Endymion*; it is attacked in several papers, and Keats is scornfully dismissed as a member of Leigh Hunt's "Cockney School" of poetry. He is unperturbed. Meets Fanny Brawne. Writes "Isabella, or the Pot of Basil," based on a story from Boccaccio; also begins *Hyperion*.
1819	Writes most of his greatest poetry at this time. Works on *Hyperion*, narrative poem *Lamia*, play *Otho the Great*; writes *The Eve of St. Agnes* and the odes ("To Psyche," "On Indolence," "To a Nightingale," "On a Grecian Urn," "To Melancholy," and "To Autumn"). Becomes engaged to Fanny Brawne, although his poverty precludes marriage. Is ill.
1820	Illness progresses; he is nursed by Fanny Brawne and her mother. Volume containing *Lamia* and other poems is published. Keats travels to Italy in hopes of curing his tuberculosis, but the strain of the voyage worsens his condition.
1821	Death of Keats, in Rome. He is buried in the Protestant Cemetery there, under the epitaph he requested: "Here lies one whose name was writ in water." Shelley publishes his beautiful elegy for Keats, *Adonais*.

ESSAY QUESTIONS WITH ANSWERS

"On First Looking into Chapman's Homer"

7.1 As the title suggests, the occasion of this sonnet was Keats's first reading of a translation of Homer by the Elizabethan poet George Chapman. On first looking into Keats's sonnet, however, readers may feel that they are reading a travel poem rather than a poem about books, for Chapman's translation of Homer receives no specific description. Why are details about Chapman's Homer omitted, and why does Keats choose instead to use the imagery of physical exploration?

Answer Although the title refers to a specific literary work, Chapman's Homer, the subject of the poem is the experience of discovery and vision. The specific attributes of Chapman's translation of Homer as opposed to those of other translations are secondary to the purpose of the poem, which is to capture in fourteen lines the sensation produced in Keats by the work. The poem ends with the specific image of Cortez gazing in amazement at the sight of the Pacific because this is a physical analogue for the exhilaration and breathless sense of discovery Keats experienced in reading Chapman.

That climactic image is prepared for in the octave of the sonnet. The basic analogy between reading poetry and exploring is established in the first line: "Much have I travell'd in the realms of gold." The metaphor "realms of gold" immediately connotes the power, majesty, and rhetorical splendor of poetry. The poet says that he has read some of the best, most elevated poetry and that in addition he has been told of one particular poetic kingdom, Homer's, which he has not encountered directly. It is only when he refers to Chapman's speaking "out loud and bold" (line 8) that the poet introduces the occasion of the poem itself, and at this point, the metaphors of discovery supersede the metaphors of exploration. He presents first a general analogy for his sense of discovery upon reading Chapman's Homer: he feels like a stargazer who discovers a new planet. The last four lines introduce a new analogy, this time providing, through a specific allusion, a particular scene of discovery. The picture of Cortez standing on the mountaintop gazing out to sea and, specifically, the focus on visual imagery ("eagle eyes," "star'd at," "look'd at") convey an almost dizzying sensation of prospect and vision. Upon reading Chapman's Homer, Keats experienced such a feeling of exhilaration and expansiveness.

Keats exploits the formal division of the Italian sonnet form to reinforce the rhetorical progression of the metaphors. After eight lines which establish the general analogy between reading poetry and exploring the world, Keats focuses on the specific discovery at the heart of the poem. The colon at the end of line 8 contributes to this emphasis by suggesting that the whole poem has been preparing for the image presented in the sestet. As the focus and tempo intensify in the sestet, metaphor is replaced by simile. In the final section, the speaker tries to convey what his experience felt like. This step into a more explicit acknowledgment of the metaphoric process corresponds with the sense that the experience was so amazing that it may elude the powers of language; after all, Cortez and his men are almost dumbfounded at the spectacle.

During his short career, Keats wrote other poems about his feelings upon encountering objects of art: "On Seeing the Elgin Marbles" and "Ode on a Grecian Urn" are two notable examples. "On First Looking into Chapman's Homer" is an earlier and, it seems, less ambivalent treatment of discovery than those other examples, for although the poet is stunned by his experience, he conveys none of the pain and dejection described in "On Seeing the Elgin Marbles" or the frustration described in "Grecian Urn." The optimism Keats feels upon reading great poetry seems comparable to that which he feels at the prospect of writing great poetry, a theme he treats in "Sleep and Poetry." In this poem, as in "Chapman's Homer," the imagery of exploration conveys hope and expectancy: Keats refers to the different types of poems he will write as "countries that I see/In long perspective." The connotations of conquest are also significant, since they suggest that Keats sees art as a way of dominating and controlling the world of experience.

"Ode on a Grecian Urn"

7.2 Why does the poet say in stanza 1 that the urn "canst thus express/A flowery tale more sweetly than our rhyme"?

Answer In contemplating the Grecian urn, the poet is struck by its permanence and silence; it is an art object that represents human action frozen in mute gesture for all time. Although made by a specific Greek artisan (its "real" parent), it is nevertheless a timeless object, a "child" adopted and loved through the ages but not engendered or understood in any one epoch.

The contrast established in stanza 1 between poetry and the urn as types of art objects depends on the urn's special liberation from temporality. Unlike the urn, a poem has a temporal dimension; it moves in time and depends for its existence on being spoken or read. The word "thus" in line 3 seems to refer to the urn's special link to eternity and stillness: Because the urn has this relationship to time, it is privileged in a way that poetry is not.

"Heard melodies are sweet, but those unheard/Are sweeter" (lines 11–12), the poet says in stanza 2, extending the contrast between art that exists only in time and in reality and the urn, which represents eternity and potential. The antiquity and classic quality of the urn shroud it in mystery and divest it of all purely topical interest. For the purposes of this poem at least, the urn is depicted as more tantalizing and inviting to the imagination than other art forms. Instead of the "heard" melody of, for example, the nightingale in "Ode to a Nightingale," the "unheard" melodies piped on the silent friezes of the Grecian urn stimulate the poet to contemplate time and eternity, life and art.

7.3   "Ode on a Grecian Urn" is an apostrophe to an inanimate object. How does this rhetorical device function in the poem?

Answer   In response to the inviting silence of the friezes on the Grecian urn, the speaker offers his own voice; he addresses the urn directly, attempting to fill in the blanks of its story. What is most striking about the apostrophe in the poem is the heavy use of interrogation, especially in stanzas 1 and 4.

The poet addresses the urn in these stanzas in order to ask it questions about the tale it tells. The pictures on the urn portray the pastoral ideal, with male and female figures gamboling through beautiful rustic landscapes and pagan ritual being piously observed. But the poet is curious to know more about these silent gestures. He wants to know what exactly is being represented. Who are these figures and what motivates their actions?

By stanza 4 the questions become longer as the poet makes suggestions about the possibilities of the story that clearly exceed the boundaries of what is actually depicted. For example, he conjectures about the town that is "emptied" of the folk represented in the friezes. He has begun, that is, to conjecture about something that is not represented on the urn rather than something that is. He seems to want to extend the limits of the art object beyond what it offers.

In stanza 5, a further change in the speaker's apostrophizing signals his growing frustration with the silence and stillness of the urn. If he began the poem by praising these very attributes, at the end of stanza 4 and beginning of stanza 5 he characterizes the urn as "teasing" rather than inviting. "Cold Pastoral!" he says in his address to the urn, and in this apostrophe he distances himself from the object that he began by anthropomorphizing in familial terms ("bride of quietness," "fosterchild"). Perhaps even more revelatory of this distancing is the apostrophe in the first line of stanza 5, "O Attic shape," for in this mode of address the urn loses all its "human" qualities; it becomes a mere "shape," an object for contemplation. Although the speaker goes on to call the urn a "friend to man," he has realized the distance between life frozen in art and life as a process. Perhaps Keats is suggesting that the real "sacrifice" which is enacted is a sacrifice of time-bound human experience for the sake of art.

7.4 In the ode, the speaker begins to establish a contrast between life as it is represented on the urn and life as it is lived. What is the nature of this contrast, and where does it surface in the poem?

Answer Stanza 3 is the focus for the contrast between life and art in the poem. The speaker continues the joyful exclamations of stanza 2; the life on the urn, he declares, neither alters nor decays. The experience of love, for example, is never sated in fulfillment, for the Greek artisan has caught it at the moment before the actual expression of passion. All is excited, forever unwearied anticipation. As in other versions of Arcadia, in the pastoral world of the urn one finds eternal spring. But as the poet continues his encomium of the joys of the immortal life of art, he becomes aware of its distance from the life of process and passion he finds in the real world. The picture of life he paints in lines 28 through 30 is one of cloying satiation and sorrow; this is a love that takes its toll on the lover, not a love of promise sustained forever.

The often debated, difficult lines which end stanza 5, " 'Beauty is truth, truth beauty,'—that is all/Ye know on earth, and all ye need to know," are relevant to the contrast between the urn's truth and the truth of life. After addressing the urn as "Cold Pastoral!" and accusing it of teasing us "out of thought," the speaker goes on to call it "a friend to man" that offers humanity a piece of aphoristic wisdom. But despite the rather neat formulation attributed to the urn, the poem as a whole presents an ambiguous picture of the relationship between life and art. The urn's truth and beauty are indissolubly linked, partly because it is undying and permanent, free from decay and time. This perception of permanence and beauty constitutes one kind of truth, but it is questionable whether it is sufficient as a guide for our lives on earth. The urn tells an important "story," but not the only one. In "Ode on Melancholy," for example, Keats himself shows a different, more mixed image of truth and beauty, for in that poem he shows us a beauty that depends on death and change rather than on being immune from it.

"Ode on Melancholy"

7.5 In contrast to the graceful apostrophe that begins "Ode on a Grecian Urn" and the heavy, slow-paced lament in the opening lines of "Ode to a Nightingale," the "Ode on Melancholy" begins abruptly with a negative command: "No, no, go not to Lethe." What effect is achieved by this opening?

Answer The abruptness of the opening lines suggests that the poem begins in the midst of an already raging debate, as if the speaker were responding to a series of previous statements and arguments. In fact, "Ode on Melancholy" begins in a sense where "Ode to a Nightingale" leaves off. The final question of "Nightingale," "Do I wake or sleep?" is answered with an almost defiant affirmation of wakefulness: the speaker here refuses to sink "Lethe-wards" or to drown his anguish in forgetfulness. Though the "Ode on Melancholy" is not literally a sequel to the "Ode to a Nightingale," we can better understand both poems by examining them as stages in a debate occurring within the poet.

The speaker of "Melancholy" warns against the courting of death and oblivion that was so tempting to the speaker of the earlier ode. "Many a time/I have been half in love with easeful Death,/Call'd him soft names in many a mused rhyme," the speaker of "Nightingale" confesses (stanza 6). In "Melancholy," however, the speaker renounces death worship ("Make not your rosary of yew-berries" [line 5]) and refuses the "high requiem" of the immortal nightingale. His anguish is a part of experience that, he believes, should not be obliterated from existence. He disparages the anodynes welcomed by the speaker of the earlier ode.

Yet if "Ode on Melancholy" in a sense renounces the solutions offered in "Ode to a Nightingale," in other ways it extends the themes raised in the earlier poem. The abruptness of the opening line suggests that a certain dialogue about life and art continues in this ode, and indeed, the relationship of creativity to pain and death is explored in both odes. The paradoxical mixture of pain and happiness the speaker feels in "Ode to a Nightingale" becomes the subject of "Ode on Melancholy." His conclusion is that only pain can enhance pleasure and that only the knowledge of death creates beauty.

7.6 In "Ode on Melancholy," unlike "Ode on a Grecian Urn" and "Ode to a Nightingale," no controlling symbolic object provides the meditative impulse of the poem. The speaker contemplates the feeling of melancholy, but it is not until the final stanza that melancholy is personified as the goddess Melancholy. Yet despite the absence of any central symbolic object, a dominant metaphor does figure in the poem, most prominently in stanza 1. What is this metaphor and how does it operate?

Answer The dominant metaphor in the first stanza is one of religious ritual. The speaker warns against participation in a false, suicidal ritual that would allow an escape from sorrow and pain. He decries the poisonous kiss of the nightshade plant, a false benedictory gesture toward the pale sufferer. "Make not your rosary of yew-berries," the speaker says, again urging against a ritual worship of "easeful death," perhaps like that to which the speaker of "Ode to a Nightingale" is prone. Finally, the poet refers to "sorrow's mysteries," using the word "mysteries" in the sense of religious rites; again, the image is one of false, secret, hypnotic rituals that seek to dull the experience of sorrow.

In contrast to the false death worship described in stanza 1 is the proposed worship of the goddess Melancholy in stanza 3. This religion is meant to be the opposite of an opiate; it represents a search for intense experience rather than an escape from it. The experience the poet seeks, however, is difficult to describe, for it combines what we usually regard as pleasure and pain. "Aching Pleasure" turns "to Poison while the bee-mouth sips," and April showers that somehow bring rejuvenation paradoxically bring death as well ("April shroud"). The poet seems to be saying that beauty and death are inextricably linked because nature's beauty depends on its transience. Delight, beauty, and love are all tinged with, even heightened by, sorrow because they must die. He who is initiated into the shrine of "veil'd Melancholy" bursts "Joy's grape against his palate fine"; paradoxically, those sensitive enough to experience melancholy taste exquisite joy at the same moment that they experience joy's destruction. The poem ends on this strange note of exaltation tinged with a heightened consciousness of mortality.

K.L.

The Eve of St. Agnes

7.7 How does the imagery of the poem contribute to its theme?

Answer Keats develops the central theme through a series of contrasts which suggest the antithetical extremes involved in human love: carnal desire versus spiritual striving, real experience versus fantasy, self-expression versus repression. The oppositions between heat and cold, red and white, music and silence, feasting and fasting, and waking and sleeping delineate ambivalent impulses which are finally reconciled when the lovers unite. The complex imagery illustrates the ways in which religious feeling, while in many respects an obstacle to the fulfillment of carnal passion, becomes absorbed into the experience of sexual love.

The opening stanzas introduce the forms of religious experience in terms of the ascetic withdrawal of the Beadsman, who, responsible for the salvation of all the souls in the house, is praying in the chapel on St. Agnes's Eve. Here spiritual striving is associated with physical discomfort (the night is "bitter chill," the Beadsman is "meagre, barefoot, wan," and the sculptured knights "ache in icy hoods and mails" [lines 1, 12, 18]); with silence (the statues pray "in dumb orat'ries" [line 16]); and with self-denial (the Beadsman resists the tempting sound of music to do "harsh penance on St. Agnes' Eve" [line 23]). The chambers where the revelry is beginning stand in immediate contrast to the chapel; the chambers are glowing, filled with music, and enlivened by movement, as opposed to the chapel with its darkness, silence, and stillness. In the guestrooms, even the "carv'd angels" seem to participate in the preparations (they are "eager-eyed . . . With hair blown back" [lines 34, 36]), while the "sculptured dead" of the chapel "seem to freeze,/Emprisoned in black, purgatorial rails" (lines 14–15).

The superstitious aspect of religion, like the ascetic, is opposed to sensuous experience, but the effect is akin to a bargain. The believer agrees to withdraw from the world and deny the flesh in order to achieve fulfillment of a wish. Thus Madeline, the believer in St. Agnes, has repressed her passions and yearnings; instead of seeking fulfillment in the real world, she relies on the hope of a pseudo-religious miracle. The tale of the old dames, with which she is so preoccupied, requires certain ceremonies of self-denial—fasting and the rejection of all sensations and distractions—before the promised vision can be achieved. The vision itself ("And soft adorings from their loves receive/Upon the honey'd middle of the night" [lines 48–49]) suggests a sort of sexual fantasy, which is confused with religious revelation. At the dance, Madeline is withdrawn from

real experience, deaf to the music, blind to the sights, "all amort,/Save to St.
Agnes" (lines 70–71). She is lost in anticipation of a false promise, in contrast
to Porphyro, who comes across the moors in active pursuit of fulfillment.

That the magic Madeline relies on is false is revealed in the exchange
between Porphyro and old Angela. Angela tells the suitor that "my lady fair
the conjuror plays/This very night: good angels her deceive!/But let me laugh
awhile" (lines 124–126). Porphyro thinks of Madeline's hopes as "cold" en-
chantments and of Madeline herself as "asleep in lap of legends old" (lines 134–
135). The midnight charm under which Madeline lies is an "iced stream" (line
283) which must be melted. Throughout the poem, coldness seems to signify
frozen purity, asceticism, and withdrawal from life. As the bearer of human
passion and the agent of release, Porphyro is always described in terms of heat:
he is "burning Porphyro" (line 159), "with heart on fire/For Madeline" (lines
75–76). A similar polarity exists between the whiteness and pallor connected
with the St. Agnes charm (the virgins must "couch supine their beauties, lily
white" [line 52], and Madeline, when she retires, sleeps "in blanchéd linen"
[line 262]) and the red of passion. When Porphyro thinks of the scheme by
which he hopes to win his love, his brow flushes and there is "purple riot" in
his heart. The thought itself is like a "full-blown rose" (lines 136–138), in
contrast to the spellbound Madeline, who later sleeps "as though a rose should
shut, and be a bud again" (line 243). All these contrasts—between cold and
hot, white and red, constriction and opening—illustrate the opposition of two
states of being. The opposition is not between good and evil but between two
partial conditions which must be integrated to achieve a mature love. Porphyro's
passion must be disciplined by the sanctity of spiritual love lest he become the
"cruel man and impious" (line 140) that Angela fears he is, and Madeline's
disembodied yearnings must take on flesh lest she, like "a tongueless nightingale . . . die, heart-stifled, in her dell" (lines 206–207).

Thus, the image of Madeline kneeling in prayer at the casement, transformed
into an angelic creature by the colored light shining through the panes, chastens
Porphyro, almost quelling his passion. But the stolen sight of the ceremony of
undressing revives him. The image is one of virginal promise, with the description suggesting a breathtaking slowness (she unclasps her jewels "one by one,"
and her dress slips down "by degrees") and a delicate sensuality (the images are
of warmth, fragrance, and quiet rustling). Madeline herself "dreams awake"
(line 232), immune to reality. Her sleep, in which she is protected and shut
up from emotional and sensuous experience, is only an intensification of her
numb waking state.

Porphyro arouses Madeline from her dream world by tempting the senses of taste (the feast) and hearing (the lute song). Once awake, Madeline continues to reject reality. Her dream, it would seem, was one of passion and fulfillment: she pants and moans as she wakes up, and she speaks to Porphyro in "voluptuous accents" (line 317). The vision is preferable to the real Porphyro, who has adopted the pose of a courtly lover, kneeling frozen, silent, and worshipful beside her bed. But when Porphyro arises, "ethereal, flush'd, and like a throbbing star" (line 318), to resume his identity as active lover, the distinction between the dream and reality disappears ("Into her dream he melted" [line 320]). At this moment, fantasy, carnal passion, and spiritual longing merge.

The lovers' fairy-tale escape from the wicked warriors of the castle is also paradoxically an escape into reality. One of the thematic implications of the escape is that the stirrings and desires of Porphyro and Madeline represent a transient enchantment, an adolescent rite of passage. Porphyro's flushes and throbbings and Madeline's tremblings and moans are the fitful impulses of a confused longing which becomes love through the enactment of the ritual in Madeline's chamber on St. Agnes's Eve. Porphyro need no longer be a voyeur or a worshiper, and Madeline need no longer be a dreamer or an icon. Their midnight meeting has the effect of a sacramental consummation. They complete their journey into the real world, away from the enthralled, sleeping castle, in a "flaw-blown sleet" (line 325), that is, in real weather very different from the still, moonlit climate of St. Agnes's Eve.

B.S.

SUGGESTED READINGS

Bate, W. J., *John Keats* (1963).
Ridley, M. R., *Keats' Craftsmanship* (1933).
Rollins, Hyder E., *Letters of John Keats* (1958).
Vendler, Helen, *The Odes of John Keats* (1983).
Wasserman, Earl R., *The Finer Tone: Keats' Major Poems* (1953).

Part Two

VICTORIAN POETRY AND PROSE

T I M E L I N E

The Age

1801:   Preface to *Lyrical Ballads*

1804:   Napoleon named emperor of France; war throughout Europe

1810:   George III insane; the Regency

1815:   Napoleon's final defeat at Waterloo

1820:   Accession of George IV

1825:   First English railway opened

1830:   Death of George IV; accession of William IV

1832:   Passage of Reform Bill

1837:   Death of William IV; accession of Queen Victoria

1845:   Great Famine in Ireland

1848:   Revolutions in France, Italy, Austria; publication of *Communist Manifesto*

1854:   Outbreak of Crimean War

1859:   Publication of Darwin's *Origin of Species*

1860:   Outbreak of American Civil War

1865:   Assassination of Lincoln

1876:   Invention of the telephone

1886:   Publication in English of Marx's *Capital*

1887:   Golden Jubilee of Queen Victoria

1895:   Invention of motion picture camera

1900:   Publication of Freud's *Interpretation of Dreams*

The Authors

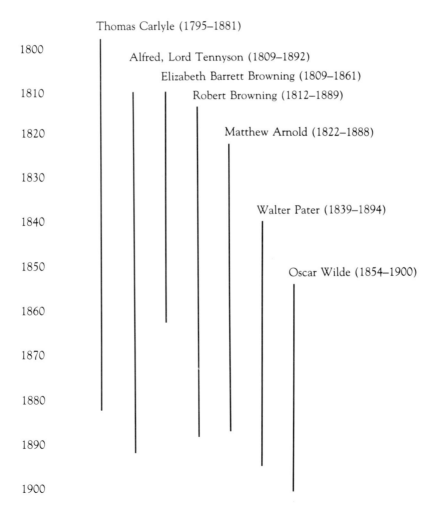

Thomas Carlyle (1795–1881)

1800

Alfred, Lord Tennyson (1809–1892)

Elizabeth Barrett Browning (1809–1861)

1810   Robert Browning (1812–1889)

1820   Matthew Arnold (1822–1888)

1830

1840   Walter Pater (1839–1894)

1850   Oscar Wilde (1854–1900)

1860

1870

1880

1890

1900

THOMAS CARLYLE

C H R O N O L O G Y

1795	Born the oldest of nine children in Ecclefechan, Scotland, of poor Calvinists who teach him frugality, hard work, and discipline. His father, recognizing Thomas's unusual ability, gives him a good education.
1809	After finishing Annan Grammar School, he walks ninety miles to enter Edinburgh University, planning to prepare for the ministry.
1814	Leaves Edinburgh University without a degree to teach mathematics at Annan Academy and other grammar schools. Reads German literature and philosophy voraciously.
1818–1822	Undergoes spiritual crisis. Abandoning the Christian faith, he experiences a conversion to a belief in a secular order of the universe.
1823–1824	His first important work, "The Life of Schiller," appears in the *London Magazine*. For the rest of his life he will support himself on his writings.
1824	His translation of Schiller's *Wilhelm Meister* appears in the *London Magazine*.
1826	Marries Jane Baillie Welsh, the clever daughter of a doctor. A popular, socially prominent woman with many suitors, she shocks her family and friends by marrying a peasant's son.
1828	Moves to a farm at Craigenputtock to cut down expenses and continue writing for periodicals.
1829	Publishes "Signs of the Times" in the *Edinburgh Review*, an assessment of the spirit of the age.

1831   Writes but cannot find publisher for *Sartor Resartus,* his spiritual autobiography in unique form—part novel, part essay, and part autobiography; it is partially published in *Fraser's Magazine.* It expounds "Clothes Philosophy," distinguishing between appearance and reality. Carlyle publishes "Characteristics" in the *Edinburgh Review;* it contains in embryo all his later religious and philosophical ideas. Meets John Stuart Mill, the intellectual and essayist who opposed the utilitarianism of Jeremy Bentham.

1832   Ralph Waldo Emerson, influential American thinker and writer, visits Carlyle at Craigenputtock.

1834   Moves to London to work on *The French Revolution.*

1835   Completes first volume of *The French Revolution* and gives the manuscript to John Stuart Mill to read. Mill's servant uses it to start a fire, destroying it and all the notes. Carlyle tries to hide the enormity of his loss from Mill.

1836   Emerson arranges to have *Sartor Resartus* published in America.

1837   Completes and publishes both volumes of *The French Revolution,* a great popular success which warns England of the dangers of tolerating social injustice.

1838   Publishes *Sartor Resartus* in England.

1840–
1845   Delivers a series of important lectures, among them "Heroes and Hero Worship" (1840), "Chartism" (1840), and "Past and Present" (1843).

1845   Publishes his edition of *The Letters and Speeches of Oliver Cromwell.*

1850   Publishes *Latter Day Pamphlets.*

1858–
1865   Writes *The History of Friedrich II of Prussia, Called Frederick the Great.*

1866   Returns to Scotland in triumph to deliver the inaugural address as lord rector of Edinburgh University, an especially satisfying celebration for his wife, who lived just long enough to see her husband enjoy the world renown she had always believed he would earn. The marriage was difficult for her; Carlyle was irascible, demanding, temperamental, and sick with various stomach ailments all his life. After Jane Welsh Carlyle dies, Thomas finds and edits her diary, which reveals his own lack of understanding of her. He grieves over the loss and for the remaining fifteen years of his life writes very little.

1874   Accepts the Prussian Order of Merit from Bismarck but refuses an English baronetcy from Disraeli.

1881   Dies and is buried near his family in Ecclefechan churchyard.

ESSAY QUESTIONS WITH ANSWERS

Sartor Resartus

8.1 What is the meaning of the title *Sartor Resartus?*

Answer The Latin phrase *sartor resartus* literally means "the tailor retailored." The title refers first to the central metaphor used by the book's hero, the imaginary Professor Teufelsdröckh, in his history of clothing, in which he compares the institutions and ideas of society to pieces of clothing as outward signs or emblems of the spirit of society. Artists, politicians, and the clergy are all "tailors" in this sense—makers of clothing or of symbols. In his autobiography and "Clothes Philosophy," Professor Teufelsdröckh hopes to "retailor" outmoded institutions, such as the Christian church, which he finds to be out of keeping with the spirit of the age.

Teufelsdröckh is himself symbolically "retailored" in Part II of *Sartor Resartus,* which describes his conversion experience, his passage from the "Centre of Indifference" to the "Everlasting Yea." The Professor's experience leaves him feeling reborn, as if he had shed one body for another. Teufelsdröckh is remade; in a spiritual sense, he is retailored.

Finally, the title applies to the work of the fictitious English editor who finds Teufelsdröckh's autobiographical fragments and stitches them together for his English audience with his own commentary. He is a tailor retailoring the German professor's metaphysics, just as Carlyle, the English prophet, is attempting to unite German metaphysics with British skepticism in his own philosophy.

The symbolic meanings of the title indicate the scope of Carlyle's philosophical reformism. Although his tones are apocalyptic, his central metaphor suggests that he wishes to reshape society's existing institutions and ideas rather than destroy them or return to primitivism in hopes of circumventing the complex problems of a sophisticated society. Everywhere Carlyle calls for a retailoring; nowhere does he advocate walking naked.

8.2 How is the style of *Sartor Resartus* related to its theme?

Answer The voice and diction in *Sartor Resartus* reflect Carlyle's major themes. The often strident, evangelical tone of the Professor reveals Carlyle's subject: the current crisis. To quote Shakespeare, Carlyle believes that "the times are out of joint" and that he, as a prophet and sage, must alert the people to the crisis they face. In the hyperbolic language and declamatory voice of the Professor, Carlyle appeals to the emotions rather than to reason. Like a preacher, he exhorts us to recognize and reject the evil and temptation that surround us in modern times:

> All kindreds and peoples and nations dashed together, and shifted and shovelled into heaps, that they might ferment there, and in time unite. The Birth-pangs of Democracy, wherewith convulsed Europe was groaning in cries that reached Heaven, could not escape me. ("Centre of Indifference")

Carlyle's extensive use of metaphor also corresponds to his basic ideas concerning language and meaning. Carlyle believes that language has become worn and clichéd. Like the other elements of society's "clothing," it has suffered from wear and tear in the marketplace. By creating new metaphors with which to express his ideas, Carlyle attempts to revitalize language even as he decries its abuse.

The use of metaphor and symbol also reflects Carlyle's basic sense of the mystery of existence and the hidden nature of truth. The professor says, "So spiritual (*geistig*) is our whole daily life: all that we do springs out of Mystery, Spirit, invisible Force; only like a little Cloud-image, or Armida's Palace, air-built, does the Actual body itself forth from the great mystic Deep" ("Centre of Indifference"). Plain-speaking, denotative language conveys only the surface of things; for Carlyle, figurative language is better able to get at the inner meaning of truth. The English editor laments the fact that the Professor speaks in "figures" rather than using plain diction. He quotes the Professor asking how, in these "profane times," the mystery of life, the "unspeakable," can be expressed. The Professor's answer is that obscure figures express the mysteries of the soul which could never be captured in the common language.

8.3 What was Carlyle's relationship to the romantic writers of the previous generation?

Answer   Carlyle's belief in social change and in the possibility of literature's effecting change is a basic romantic notion. His stance as writer-prophet harks back to the visionary strain in romantics such as Shelley and Blake, who believed that writing could change things and reveal, as Shelley wrote in his "Defence of Poetry," "the laws according to which present things ought to be ordered" as well as "the future in the present."

For Carlyle, as for Shelley, the role of prophet makes the poet or writer responsible to society rather than an escapist. But while accepting the romantic legacy of the role of poet-prophet, Carlyle criticized the romantic poets, especially Byron, for their withdrawal from society. Although a "seer" and a revolutionary, Carlyle showed himself to be a Victorian and a Calvinist in his emphasis on work and on the necessity of translating private melancholy into action for public benefit. In Byron especially, Carlyle thought he recognized an irresponsible pursuit of melancholy and self-pity, and even in Shelley he criticized the poet's "inarticulate wail."

Finally, Carlyle's theory of "Natural Supernaturalism" explained by the Professor in Part III of *Sartor Resartus* recalls the romantics' belief in the mystery of ordinary things. For the romantics, as for Carlyle, the task of the writer is to reinvest humble matter with the sense of the divine and to make familiar things unfamiliar. Carlyle inherited these views from Wordsworth and Coleridge; all three writers believed that nature was a manifestation of the divine and that the writer must perceive and express this relationship.

K.L.

SUGGESTED READINGS

Campbell, Ian, *Thomas Carlyle* (1974).
La Valley, Albert J., *Carlyle and the Idea of the Modern* (1968).
Le Quesne, A. Laurence, *Carlyle* (1982).
Levine, George, *The Boundaries of Fiction: Carlyle, Macaulay, Newman* (1968).

ALFRED, LORD TENNYSON

C H R O N O L O G Y

1809   Born at Somersby, Lincolnshire. Son of the Reverend George Tennyson, rector of the parish, and Elizabeth Fytche Tennyson.

1815   Enters Louth Grammar School.

1820   Leaves school; after this time is educated at home by his father.

1824   Father experiences a physical and mental breakdown which causes the whole family to suffer both emotionally and financially. By this date Tennyson is a prolific writer, having produced an epic poem, a play, and many shorter works.

1827   Enters Trinity College, Cambridge University. Publishes anonymously *Poems by Two Brothers*, written in collaboration with his older brother, Charles; it receives little attention.

1828   Meets Arthur Hallam at Cambridge, with whom he will have an intense friendship.

1829   Joins the Apostles, a literary-intellectual group at Cambridge; Hallam also a member. Wins the Chancellor's Gold Medal for a poem, *Timbuctoo*.

1830   Visits the Continent with Hallam. Publishes, under his own name, *Poems, Chiefly Lyrical*; it receives mixed reviews. (As he will throughout his career, Tennyson reacts with extreme dismay to all unfavorable comments.)

1831	Death of Tennyson's father. Tennyson leaves Cambridge without a degree. Hallam is engaged to be married to Tennyson's sister Emily.
1832	Tours Germany with Hallam. Publishes *Poems*, a volume including "The Lady of Shalott" and "The Lotos-Eaters."
1833	Hallam dies of a ruptured blood vessel. Tennyson falls into a profound depression; according to many, he never fully recovers from this blow. Probably begins work on his masterpiece, *In Memoriam*, soon after.
1836	Charles Tennyson marries Louisa Sellwood; Alfred falls in love with Louisa's sister Emily. They become engaged some time in the next two years.
1840	The Tennyson family has become increasingly straitened since the death of the poet's father; to trim expenses, they move to Tunbridge Wells. Tennyson's engagement is broken off; his health is poor. He decides to invest his small inheritance in a scheme (pyroglyphs) for making wood-carving machinery.
1842	Publishes two volumes of *Poems*.
1843	The pyroglyphs scheme fails; Tennyson is virtually bankrupted. He spends part of the year in the hospital.
1845	Friends who admire Tennyson's poetic gifts arrange for him to receive a government pension of £200 a year; this lifts him out of poverty. He is at work on *In Memoriam*, *The Princess*, and *The Idylls of the King*.
1847	Publishes *The Princess*.
1848	Visits Ireland and Cornwall, studying British antiquities as material for the *Idylls*.
1850	*In Memoriam*, a long philosophical-elegaic poem inspired by Hallam's death, is published anonymously. Tennyson's income now permits him to marry Emily Sellwood; by all accounts, their marriage is a happy one. On the death of Wordsworth, Tennyson is appointed poet laureate.
1851	Visits Italy.
1852	Writes "Ode on the Death of the Duke of Wellington," one of the few fine poems written by a laureate in commemoration of a public event.
1853	Settles with family at Farringford in the Isle of Wight.
1855	Publishes *Maud*.
1859	Publishes first stories from the *Idylls of the King*, a collection of verse narratives based on Arthurian legends.

1862	Meets Queen Victoria; is granted permission to dedicate the *Idylls* to Prince Albert, her consort, who had died the year before.
1864	Publishes *Enoch Arden*, which sells 60,000 copies; the height of Tennyson's popularity. Italian nationalist leader Garibaldi visits Tennyson at Farringford.
1865	Tennyson is offered a baronetcy, which he declines.
1872	Publishes an edition of his *Works* which includes virtually all of the *Idylls of the King* (one tale, "Balin and Balan," follows two years later).
1875	Publishes play *Queen Mary*, which Tennyson hoped would be the first of a great series of tragedies drawn from English history. Though several of these plays were written and some were produced, they proved unpopular and are usually viewed as lacking dramatic merit.
1876–1884	Publishes several plays: *Harold, The Falcon, The Cup, The Promise of Mary,* and *Becket.* Accepts a peerage in 1884.
1885	Publishes *Tiresias and Other Poems.*
1886	Publishes *Locksley Hall Sixty Years After,* a poem attacking the Victorian-era civilization with which Tennyson himself is often identified.
1889	Publishes *Demeter and Other Poems,* including "Crossing the Bar."
1892	Death of Tennyson. Buried in Poets' Corner at Westminster Abbey.

ESSAY QUESTIONS WITH ANSWERS

"Ulysses"

9.1 The poem is a dramatic monologue representing the musings of a solitary mind. What techniques does Tennyson employ to characterize the speaker?

Answer One of Tennyson's methods of conveying the personality of Ulysses is his use of a blank verse soliloquy as the form of the poem. The Shakespearean tradition of tragic soliloquy immediately charges the form with significance, leading the reader to expect a psychological revelation of inner doubts and longings. The poet capitalizes on the inherent drama of the soliloquy by choosing a turning point in Ulysses's life when, as an old man, he decides to resume his travels. In the natural movement of the unrhymed lines and the repetitive phrasings, Tennyson exhibits the musings of a sensitive, solitary mind. This is how nineteenth-century readers viewed Shakespeare's soliloquies as well.

We know by the form itself that Ulysses is a man of great stature grappling with the meaning of his existence, but the speaker particularizes his condition through a series of self-definitions. Using epithet, adjective, and simple assertion, Ulysses redefines himself at this crossroads of his life. He refers to himself as "our idle King" and "this grey spirit" while at the same time identifying himself with "men that strove with Gods" and "heroic hearts." Thus he establishes his dilemma: he is a hero grown old, a man past his prime. Furthermore, he uses a series of equations to analyze his essential character. For example, the lines beginning with "I am become a name" suggest the Ulysses of the past, the self that has become a legendary being. However, the sense of a glorious legend is undermined by the connotation of emptiness or hollowness that being merely a "name" suggests. Again, in the line "I am a part of all that I have met," Ulysses emphasizes the solidity of his past achievements: the public self, the finished product of all his experiences. The poignancy of Ulysses's situation derives from the collision of his past greatness with his present condition: "You and I are old." His resolution is expressed as a revitalization in the closing lines. He begins with simple acceptance and moves on to a vow to extend his personal horizons:

>One equal temper of heroic hearts,
>Made weak by time and fate, but strong in will
>To strive, to seek, to find, and not to yield.
>
> (lines 68–70)

A final rhetorical means Tennyson uses in his dramatic monologue is the speaker's comparison between himself and his son Telemachus. After describing Telemachus as prudent and sober, "centered in the sphere/Of common duties" he closes the section with a contrast: "He works his work, I mine." The implication is that Ulysses is imprudent, one who strives beyond the tame duties of civic life. Thus, Telemachus becomes the means of emphasizing both the speaker's limitations and his virtues. Restless within the confines of day-to-day obligations, Ulysses maintains his heroic wanderlust, his appetite for high adventure.

9.2 Comment on Tennyson's use of the following poetic devices: (a) meter, (b) repetition, (c) metaphor, and (d) direct address.

Answer   The meter of the verse is smooth, with the steady beat of the iambic pentameter line progressing through the poem without interruption. Unrhymed and containing very few end-stopped lines, the poetry creates an almost proselike effect, with the thought extending across the rhythmic structure and developing a pattern of its own. The few lines that are end-stopped achieve a special status, isolated from the fluent surface as pointed, self-contained units. These lines usually contain syntactically separate half lines, following a strong caesura which marks the end of the previous thought:

>. . . Vexed the dim sea. I am become a name;
>
> (line 11)
>. . . When I am gone. He works his work, I mine.
>
> (line 43)
>. . . Free hearts, free foreheads—you and I are old;
>
> (line 49)

These phrases become key moments of recognition in Ulysses's dramatic monologue.

Another skillful manipulation of rhythmic properties occurs in the lines "The long day wanes; the slow moon climbs; the deep/moans round. . . ." The substitution of spondees for iambs slows the verse, dramatizing the ideas of a lengthening twilight and the sea's plangent cry.

Tennyson uses repeated words and phrases in a variety of ways: to create rhetorical rhythms, to emphasize antitheses, to provide poetic intensification, and to produce paradox. The lines "All times I have enjoyed/Greatly, have suffered greatly" are grandly oratorical, insisting on the idea of the "greatness" of Ulysses's experiences through the repetition of the adverb. Similarly, the phrase "Forever and forever" in line 21 acts as an intensifier, a means of emphasizing the limitless longings of Ulysses for a limitless horizon. Emphasis coupled with paradox is produced by the repetition of "life" and "little" in the following lines:

> As though to breathe were life! Life piled on life
> Were all too little, and of one to me
> Little remains;
> (lines 23–25)

Tennyson plays with the ideas of duration and brevity in this complicated interweaving of reiterated words. Finally, the schematic repetition of "It may be" in "It may be that the gulfs will wash us down;/It may be we shall touch the Happy Isles" (lines 62–63) creates a seesaw effect, weighing the two alternatives in equal balance and suggesting the hero's indifference to fate. Thus, in "Ulysses," repetition is a way of enriching connotation.

The poem contains a central metaphor:

> Yet all experience is an arch wherethrough
> Gleams that untraveled world whose margin fades
> Forever and forever when I move.
> (lines 19–21)

In a sense it constitutes the basic idea of the poem, that is, the relationship between the adventuring individual and the individual's experience of life. Posing the image of a perspective frame which constantly opens out into new vistas, Tennyson suggests the constant beckoning of the future, the lure of the unknown.

Ulysses's monologue is largely interior, following the conventions of soliloquy in being primarily addressed to himself. However, in the closing section of the poem, Ulysses addresses his loyal followers directly: "My mariners,/Souls that have toiled, and wrought, and thought with me—/. . . you and I are old" (lines 45–49). Here Ulysses begins to move toward a return to the world of action, the world of "men that strove with Gods" (line 153). By calling on his men ("Come, my friends" [line 156]) Ulysses reconfirms his faith that "some work of noble note may yet be done" (line 52). A sense of fellowship and solidarity gained through shared experience is part of the hero's definition of himself. In the closing lines, he identifies himself and his men as one:

> . . . that which we are, we are,
> One equal temper of heroic hearts,
> (lines 67–68).

In Memoriam A. H. H.

9.3 The structure of the poem rests on certain "nodal points" that create a pattern of recurrence and development. Identify these points and analyze their significance.

Answer Tennyson uses the calendar as an organizing principle for *In Memoriam*. In a poem that is loosely based on reflection, meditation, and memory, the specific account of the anniversaries of Hallam's birth and death, as well as the descriptions of succeeding Christmases, provide a narrative strand. The seasonal cycle is delineated through the recurrence of the anniversaries of Hallam's death in September and birth in February, with Christmas coming in between. In the Christmas sections (sections 28, 78, 104), the poet documents the tension between the joy of the day and his inner despair. From the first Christmas to the third, the poet makes some progress toward reconciling himself to the loss of his friend. In section 30, describing the first Christmas after Hallam's death, he starkly compares the "obligatory" gaiety of the occasion with the genuine grief he experiences:

> We gamboled, making vain pretense
> Of gladness, with an awful sense
> Of one mute Shadow watching all.

Though the section ends with a conventional acknowledgment of Christ's power of renewal ("Rise, happy morn"), the whole suggests a struggle with depression.

In section 78, which describes the second Christmas, the prevailing mood is calmer and more accepting. But characteristically Tennyson fights against his own acceptance, feeling angry that time, by robbing him of his anguish, robs him of his friend:

> Who showed a token of distress?
> No single tear, no mark of pain—

> O sorrow, then can sorrow wane?
> O grief, can grief be changed to less?

In section 106, the process of reconciliation seems complete. The whole section is a Christmas carol, an invocation of Christ's influence in the future ("Ring in the Christ that is to be"). In addition to drawing on a traditional form and traditional language to show his renewed hope, Tennyson alludes to a personal process of acceptance. The lines "The year is dying in the night;/ Ring out, wild bells, and let him die" and "The year is going, let him go" allude not only to the passage of time but to the death of Hallam.

The anniversaries of Hallam's birth and death serve a similar function, marking a progression toward tranquility. The early sections of the poem describing the funeral ship bearing the remains of the dead are colored with melancholy and despair. The first anniversary of the death (section 72) uses weather as an emotional symbol, with Tennyson inviting the already wild day to further chaos as an appropriate symbol for his anguish:

> And up thy vault with roaring sound
> Climb thy thick noon, disastrous day;
> Touch thy dull goal of joyless gray,
> And hide thy shame beneath the ground.

Weather is also an important element of the birthday description. Section 107 begins with an intentional ambiguity; the line "It is the day when he was born" immediately follows the Christmas carol in section 106, thus fusing Hallam with Christ. The wintry February landscape is here paradoxical in that the harsh environment is hostile to the ritual of remembrance. Shutting out nature's cold indifference, Tennyson creates a warm interior scene as a symbol for the power of human memory and love:

> We keep the day. With festal cheer,
> With books and music, surely we
> Will drink to him, whate'er he be,
> And sing the songs he loved to hear.

9.4 In Memoriam embodies both Tennyson's crisis of doubt and his statement of faith. As T. S. Eliot wrote, "Its faith is a poor thing, but its doubt is a very intense experience." One of the ways Tennyson dramatizes his doubt is through images of science and nature. Isolate some of these images and discuss their philosophical relevance.

Answer   Essentially, Tennyson expresses his doubt by presenting God and nature as antagonistic. All the evidence of the senses, the poet feels, points to a blind materialism, a ceaseless process of struggle and change without meaning or providential design. In two key parts of the poem (sections 50–56 and 118–124), the poet presents his own battle to penetrate the appearance of mechanistic chaos and discover his faith in God.

The view of human experience as absurd and brutish is expressed through imagery of insect life in section 50. Praying to his dead friend to act as an intercessor and mitigate his despair, he says

> Be near me when my faith is dry,
>   And men the flies of latter spring,
>   That lay their eggs, and sting and sing
> And weave their petty cells and die.

Tennyson vacillates between this black vision of empty cycles of life and death and a faint hope that "not a worm is cloven in vain" (section 54), that a providential pattern informs every physical event. Nature, colored by the Darwinian conceptions of natural selection and evolutionary process, "lends . . . evil dreams" of random chance. Humankind, nature's "last work, who seemed so fair," may be nothing, so much chaff "blown about the desert dust," and nature itself appears as a bloodstained animal, "red in tooth and claw," shrieking against God's creed (sections 55–56).

In the later sections devoted to this scientific view of nature, the poet combats the idea of random evolution and mere scientific process. Life is not just matter, "idle ore"; people are not "wholly brain;/Magnetic mockeries," not "only cunning casts in clay." Moving beyond body and intellect, Tennyson is able to find a kind of faith. Though the physical landscape may melt and "nothing stands," humanity's essence endures: "But in my spirit I will dwell/ And dream my dream, and hold it true" (section 123).

Tennyson's dream is founded not on reason but on faith. He rejects the "reasonable" proof of God's existence, the eighteenth-century deistic arguments that infer God from the design of nature:

> I found Him not in world or sun,
>   Or eagle's wing, or insect's eye,

> Nor through the questions men may try,
> The petty cobwebs we have spun.

Furthermore, Tennyson responds to the doubting voice that says "believe no more" with the heart's answer "I have felt" (section 124). The closing image of the section—the hands of God reaching down through darkness to mold humanity—recalls Michelangelo's *Creation of Adam*, suggesting as well the paternal image of a father reaching for his child.

By finding his own solution to the conflict between science and faith, Tennyson "earns" the optimistic conclusion of the poem. He has recreated a universality of meaning and a vision of unity through his subjective experience.

B.S. and L.R.

SUGGESTED READINGS

Jump, J. D. (ed.), *Tennyson: The Critical Heritage* (1967).
Killham, J. (ed.), *Critical Essays on the Poetry of Tennyson* (1964).
Steane, J. B., *Tennyson* (1966).

ELIZABETH BARRETT BROWNING

C H R O N O L O G Y

1806	Born Elizabeth Barrett Moulton-Barrett at Coxhoe Hall, County Durham. Daughter of Edward Moulton-Barrett, a country gentleman, and Mary Graham Clarke Moulton-Barrett; fourth of twelve children.
1809	Family moves to Hope End, a country estate in Herefordshire. Within the next three to five years, Elizabeth begins writing poems.
1818	Date of a brief diary, still surviving, which presents an interesting record of Elizabeth's early development. Probable date of *The Battle of Marathon*, a narrative poem.
1820	Elizabeth's father has *Battle of Marathon* printed for her; this is indicative of family's support for her literary endeavors.
1821	Is ill; takes opium by medical prescription, leading to a lifelong habit.
1825	First published poem, "The Rose and Zephyr," in *Literary Gazette*.
1826	Publication of first volume of poems, *An Essay on Mind*, anonymous; no critical notice is taken.
1828	Death of mother. Engaged in study of classical literature under guidance of scholar H.S. Boyd.
1832	Declining family fortunes force move to more modest home in Sidmouth, Devonshire.

1833   Publication of *Prometheus Bound*, translation from Greek playwright Aeschylus; like her first book, it is anonymous, and it receives no notice.

1835   Family moves to a house at Gloucester Place in London.

1837   Family settles at 50 Wimpole Street in London. Elizabeth's first major illness: burst blood vessel affecting lungs. Beginning of long period of invalidism.

1838   Publication of *The Seraphim and Other Poems* under Elizabeth's own name; it receives long, mainly favorable reviews and sells well. Beginning of her successful literary career. Though confined by illness, she communicates with prominent members of the literary world by correspondence, including Wordsworth, Carlyle, and Edgar Allan Poe. Moves to seaside town of Torquay for her health, accompanied by different family members at varying times; her favorite brother, Edward ("Bro"), is her primary companion. Death of uncle; his legacy leaves Elizabeth financially secure.

1840   "Bro" drowns in Babbacombe Bay off Torquay; profound blow to Elizabeth. She writes "De Profundis," expressing grief over his death; it is published posthumously. Also writes "Queen Annelida and False Arcite" for a modernized edition of poetry by Chaucer and "The Cry of the Children," a poem attacking child labor.

1841   Still an invalid; returns to live in family home in London. Writes book reviews, articles, and translations.

1842   Publication of "The Cry of the Children." It is very popular and helps bring about movement for regulation of child labor.

1844   Publication of two-volume edition of *Poems*; American edition published with an introduction by Poe.

1845   After receiving complimentary letter from poet Robert Browning, then virtually unknown, she is visited by him at Wimpole Street home. Next day, he writes her a declaration of love. Her parents will not consent to marriage, however; father opposes marriage by any of his children. Elizabeth begins work on sequence of love poems, *Sonnets from the Portuguese* (not translations; so named from Robert Browning's pet name for her, "the Portuguese").

1846   Robert Browning and Elizabeth secretly wed in London. They leave England and travel through France and Italy, finally settling in Florence. The move proves beneficial for Elizabeth's health, and the marriage is an exceptionally happy one.

1848   Elizabeth becomes involved in cause of Italian political unity; many of her later poems will deal with this theme. Her approach to politics is basically romantic and unrealistic, however.

1849   Birth of son, Robert Barrett-Browning ("Pen").

1850   Publication of new two-volume edition of *Poems*, including the *Sonnets from the Portuguese*. Elizabeth mentioned in literary journal *The Athenaeum* as the leading candidate to succeed Wordsworth as poet laureate, indicative of her high reputation at that time. (Tennyson received the post, however.)

1851   Publication of *Casa Guidi Windows*, work on Italy including political reflections. Health improved enough to permit travel; during the 1850s the Brownings visit England, France, and other cities in Italy while maintaining their home in Florence.

1857   Death of father; he was never reconciled to Elizabeth or her marriage. Publication of *Aurora Leigh*, described as a "novel in verse." Highly popular work, it is critically acclaimed and, in some quarters, attacked on moral grounds for its sympathetic treatment of a woman as independent, an artist, and an unmarried mother.

1860   Publication of *Poems Before Congress*, a collection of poems on political themes; it is unpopular. Health in decline.

1861   Death of Elizabeth Browning at Florence. Buried in the Protestant Cemetery there.

1862   Posthumous publication of *Last Poems*, including "De Profundis" (written in 1840). Later, her juvenilia, other poems, and correspondence will be published as well.

ESSAY QUESTIONS WITH ANSWERS

Sonnet 43, Sonnets from the Portuguese

10.1   Discuss the rhetorical strategy of the poem, commenting on its connection with the theme.

Answer   The chief rhetorical figure of the poem is catalogue, which attempts to measure love by listing each shade of the lover's feelings toward the object of desire. Beginning with the question "How do I love thee?" the poet answers by enumeration: "Let me count the ways." The repetition of "I love thee" contributes to the effect of accumulation. The attempt to define love by measuring it is made explicit in the lines "I love thee to the depth and breadth and height/My soul can reach. . . ."

The second important figure in the sonnet is hyperbole, which goes beyond the limits of mathematical measurement to suggest a heightened and ethereal passion. Thus, the soul that seeks to embrace love is overreaching itself, stretching "for the ends of Being and ideal Grace." Not only is every nuance of existence bound up in love ("the breath,/Smiles, tears, of all my life!"), but love continues for all eternity ("and, if God choose,/I shall but love thee better after death").

In addition, Browning employs quiet images to round out her definition of love. The references to daily needs, childhood griefs and faith, and religious yearnings give substance to an emotion which is the measure of all her experience.

The emphasis on summation throughout is, in a sense, paradoxical. The "how" of love escapes quantification, yet Browning's breathless catalogue conveys something of its variousness and richness. In the last line, the poet stresses the ultimate mysteriousness of a passion which extends beyond the grave.

10.2   To what extent can this poem be defended against charges of sentimentality?

Answer   This love sonnet is immediately open to the charges of sentimentality and cliché. The amount of hyperbole and repetition can be seen as mannered and excessive, while such lines as "I love thee freely, as men strive for Right;/I love thee purely, as they turn from Praise" can be faulted for relying too heavily on abstraction.

At the same time, however, the general use of the technique of enumeration and the poem's range of imagery, extending from passionate hyperbole to simple metaphor, give the poem its unique texture and feeling. Browning's sonnet, a personal paean to her husband, has a freshness and sincerity of tone that makes it appealing.

In general, then, the poem has merit, though perhaps not the startling drama of a song by Donne or the lyrical beauty of a sonnet by Shakespeare.

B.S. and L.R.

SUGGESTED READINGS

Hayter, Althea, *Elizabeth Barrett Browning* (1965).
Taplin, Gardner B., *The Life of Elizabeth Barrett Browning* (1957).

ROBERT BROWNING

C H R O N O L O G Y

1812	Born in Camberwell, a suburb of London. Son of a clerk at the Bank of England. Family are religious dissenters (that is, not members of the Church of England). Robert's parents dote on him, resulting in a tendency to remain somewhat immature throughout his life.
1820	Begins education as a weekly boarder at a school in Peckham.
1826	Begins writing poetry under the influence of the works of Shelley. Receives private tutoring at home in French, Italian, Latin, and Greek.
1828	Spends one semester at London University, where he toys with atheism. Returns home, where he will remain until into his thirties, studying, writing, and publishing (at his father's expense) his early poetic works.
1833	First published work, the autobiographical *Pauline, A Fragment of a Confession*. Printed anonymously, it has virtually no sales. Begins work on *Sordello*.
1834	Travels across Europe to Saint Petersburg, Russia, and home.
1835	Publishes *Paracelsus*; it is praised in literary circles. Browning begins friendships with such figures as Carlyle, poet and critic W. S. Landor, and others.
1837	*Strafford*, first of a series of unsuccessful plays, is produced and published.
1838	First visit to Italy.
1840	Publishes *Sordello*, a long narrative poem demonstrating Browning's first use of his most characteristic form, the dramatic monologue. Though not very

difficult to read by modern standards, it was widely derided as "unintelligible" and "meaningless," establishing Browning's reputation for the rest of his career as an obscure poet.

1841   Begins publishing a series of books under the general title *Bells and Pomegranates*; they include mainly plays. Publishes *Pippa Passes*.

1842   Publishes collection of poems called *Dramatic Lyrics*, including notably "My Last Duchess."

1843–
1844   Production of three more plays, all now little read. Second visit to Italy.

1845   Writes letter to poet Elizabeth Barrett praising her work. Visits her and subsequently declares his love. Her parents oppose their marriage, however. Publication of *Dramatic Romances and Lyrics*.

1846   Publication of *A Soul's Tragedy*, concluding the *Bells and Pomegranates* series. Secretly weds Elizabeth Barrett. They visit France and settle in Florence, Italy, where they will live very happily for fifteen years. Her inherited income and book earnings are their main income, since Robert is still little known at this time.

1849   Birth of son, Robert Barrett-Browning ("Pen").

1850   Publishes *Christmas Eve and Easter Day*.

1851–
1852   Makes visits to Paris and London; friendship with literary and artistic figures of the day, including Dante Gabriel Rossetti, Charles Kingsley, Tennyson.

1855   Publishes two-volume collection of poems, *Men and Women*; it contains most of the poems considered his best, including "Fra Lippo Lippi" and "Andrea del Sarto."

1861   Death of Elizabeth Barrett Browning; Browning moves to London with son "Pen."

1864   Publishes *Dramatis Personae*.

1868   Publishes *The Ring and the Book*, a long narrative poem based on an Italian story of greed, deception, and murder. A popular success in its day, it is now little read. Following this work, Browning's poetic talent enters a long period of decline, although he will publish many more books.

1869   Browning proposes marriage to Lady Ashburton; he is rejected. This proposal, often seen as an example of Browning's propensity for social climbing, will remain an embarrassment to him in society as well as a cause of personal shame over infidelity to his wife's memory.

1871–1887	Publishes over a dozen volumes of poetry during this period, all almost forgotten now. They include narrative poems such as *Red-Cotton Nightcap Country* and the two collections of *Dramatic Idyls*, verse plays such as *The Inn Album*, and translations from Greek such as *The Agamemnon* of Aeschylus. Browning is now a famous and popular poet and a fixture of society; his tendency to vanity is satisfied by adulation from a circle of admirers.
1880	Dr. F. J. Furnivall and others establish the Browning Society in London, devoted to studying the works and idolizing the man.
1889	Publishes *Asolando*, his last collection of poems, and an edition of his complete works. Dies in Venice of bronchitis; is buried in Poets' Corner of Westminster Abbey.

ESSAY QUESTIONS WITH ANSWERS

"My Last Duchess"

11.1   The poem is a dramatic monologue which hints at a complicated story behind the speaker's description of his first wife's portrait. Characterize the persona and the situation.

Answer   The poem consists of a speech delivered by the duke of Ferrara to the count of Tyrol's emissary. The duke describes his dead wife and alludes to the arrangements for a second marriage. Though the poem is ostensibly a portrait of the first duchess, it reveals far more about the duke. The colloquially ingratiating style suggests a host performing the rites of hospitality. He calls the agent "sir" and invites the agent to admire one of his prized possessions: "I call/ That piece a wonder, now: . . ./Will't please you sit and look at her?" (lines 2–5). However, something strange begins to happen behind the polite facade, for his description of the duchess becomes, in fact, a diatribe on her failings. Beginning with an artist's appreciation of "the spot of joy" on her cheek, he coldly appraises her personality. The "joy" is, for the duke, the sign of her undiscriminating affection and her failure to be bound solely to him. In his view, she was ungrateful, too impressionable, and flighty. There is even the suggestion that she prostituted herself by being so freely responsive to others.

In attempting to expose the flaws of his wife, the duke exposes himself. His criticisms of the duchess are ironic, for the qualities he disparages are generally accepted as virtues. Her modest blush at the painter's compliments, her appreciation of a servant's gifts, her delight in sunsets and even in animals all suggest a woman of breeding, kindness, and sensitivity. The irony deepens as the duke's criticisms become nearly savage. When he imagines confronting her with her sins, he uses the language of a perfectionist and an aesthete: " 'Just this/Or that in you disgusts me; here you miss,/Or there exceed the mark' " (lines 37–39). This strand of aesthetic evaluation is the defining quality of the duke's personality. He appraises his wife as though she were an *objet d'art*, a thing which he possessed. He takes pleasure in the fact that she is now transfixed on the wall like a collector's item. He has stilled her vital qualities and made her into a showpiece; he has captured her in a way he was unable to do in life.

> . . . I gave commands;
> Then all smiles stopped together. There she stands
> As if alive. . . .
>
> (lines 44–45)

Connected with this theme of aesthetic valuation are the motifs of pride, power, and money. The duke is a man who will not stoop, who gives commands, who possesses "a nine-hundred-years-old name," and who has plans for a second marriage that center on the dowry. The central contrast in the poem is between the generosity of the duchess and the possessiveness of the duke. In the last lines, the duke points casually to yet another object in his gallery of "things": the Neptune struck in bronze, "thought a rarity." This reference underscores the fact that he is essentially a connoisseur.

Browning uses the dramatic monologue as a mirror for the speaker's innermost thoughts. Because the speaker is narrow and mean, the entire piece is colored by dramatic irony, with the reader constantly aware of the persona's false pretenses, hollow values, and profound cruelty. There is an admonitory, almost menacing quality to the speech, for the duke is at least partly outlining what he expects of his next duchess.

11.2　Discuss the special features of Browning's use of rhymed iambic pentameter. How do meter, rhythm, and syntax contribute to the total effect of the poem?

Answer　Although the poem consists of rhymed couplets, the rhyme is largely obscured because of the pervasive enjambment. This technique of running the sense of a statement across the end of a line into the next makes syntax take precedence over meter in the rhythm of the poem. Rather than stressing the use of couplets, Browning presents the more fluid, unpredictable musings of extemporaneous speech. Thus, the rhymed iambic pentameter lines approach the free movement of blank verse, which is the traditional mode for dramatic monologue.

However, despite the suppression of the chiming quality of rhyme, the poem retains the steady rhythmic pulsations of regular meter. The iambic pattern informs certain sections of the poem to create rhetorical "periods," or long sentences built up in measured phrases. The rhymes, though unstressed, add to the sense of measured formality. For example, in the list of the duchess's pleasures (lines 25–31), the poet exploits the smooth ripples of the pentameter line to construct a polished portrait:

> . . . My favor at her breast,
> The dropping of the daylight in the West,
> The bough of cherries some officious fool
> Broke in the orchard for her, the white mule
> She rode with round the terrace—all and each
> Would draw from her alike the approving speech,
> Or blush, at least
>
> (lines 25–31)

At the same time, Browning uses syntax to break up the seamless metrical surface, with asides, questions, and exclamations creating staccato rhythms within the larger flow. In lines 31 through 33 ("She thanked men—good! but thanked/Somehow—I know not how—as if she ranked/My gift"), the poet reproduces the colloquial pattern of everyday speech. The stops and pauses suggested by dashes, exclamation points, parentheses, and question marks constitute a kind of syncopation to the alternating stresses of the meter.

In this poem, remarkably lacking in metaphor, the burden of meaning rests on literal statement and mode of speech. Of course, the dramatic situation gives resonance to what the duke says, while the way he says it—his mode of speaking—betrays him. The insinuating rhythms suggest his facile public persona, while the qualifying asides and abrupt breaks imply a savage emotion beneath the surface.

"Fra Lippo Lippi"

11.3 Discuss Browning's conception of art and aesthetics as revealed through the character of Fra Lippo Lippi. How does he convey his ideas on these themes?

Answer The historical Fra Lippo Lippi lived during the flowering of early Renaissance painting, that moment when the techniques for creating perspective space, three-dimensional human figures, and other effects of verisimilitude came within the artist's grasp. Thus, Renaissance art represented a sharp break with the more stylized sacred art of the middle ages.

Browning uses the character of Fra Lippo Lippi to express his own aesthetic creed of naturalism. By making Fra Lippo Lippi an earthy, rebellious character, resistant to the authority of church and state, Browning immediately subverts the conventional idea of the devout painter of holy images. The monk is motivated not by spiritual promptings but by the urges of his own flesh: ". . . zooks, sir, flesh and blood,/That's all I'm made of!" (lines 60–61). Not only his bawdy forays into the nightlife of Florence but also his paintings are products of his celebration of the senses. Even his "vocation" as a monk is no more than a search for a "mouthful of bread" and a bargain exchanging "pride and greed" for "the good bellyful. . . . And day-long blessed idleness beside" (lines 97, 103–105).

This portrait of the artist as cynic is part of Browning's attack on what he saw as the hypocrisies of society. The Prior's disdainful advice to "Rub all out!" and the crowds of worshipers defacing one of his paintings in a frenzy of "piety" are two instances in which the artist is misunderstood and abused, on the one hand by the political powers of society and on the other hand by the masses. The shocking language and behavior of the monk are his response to the boorishness of those around him: "And I do these wild things in sheer despite" (line 251).

The theory of aesthetics presented by Browning is a natural extension of the character of the speaker of the poem. Although Fra Lippo Lippi agrees with the traditional view of art as morally instructive, saying that he seeks to "interpret God to all of you!" (line 311), he disagrees with the means proposed by the Prior for accomplishing that end. The Prior wants him to paint "the souls of men" (line 183), to resort to an iconography of symbol, allegory, and metaphor to render the realm of spiritual ideals. In contrast, Fra Lippo Lippi, the man of "flesh and blood" wants to express "the value and significance of flesh," (line 268), to imitate the wonder and beauty of God's creation in recognizably human images. This theory of verisimilitude does not constitute a rejection of art's function as moral teacher; in a sense, it extends the sphere of art into subtler regions of recognition and response. Art is not mere catechism or hagiography ("Why, for this/What need of art at all?" [lines 319–320]) but a living representation of God's works which evokes love, admiration, and gratitude.

11.4   In the closing section of the poem, Fra Lippo Lippi describes his project for a *Sacra Conversazione* (a picture of the Virgin and Child surrounded by saints). What is the significance of this final vision?

Answer   The closing of the poem constitutes the complicated intersection of all Fra Lippo Lippi's motives, ambitions, and theories. Retracting his "idle word/Spoke in a huff by a poor monk" (lines 336–337), the painter promises an altarpiece as penance ("to make amends"). The work is described in oddly ambivalent language. The "bowery flowery angel brood" with "white faces, sweet/As puff on puff of grated orris-root" (lines 349–351) suggest both pristine beauty and a slightly saccharine style of art. He throws in the necessary holy personages in an offhand manner ("of course a saint or two") and plans to include a self-portrait ("who but Lippo! I!— . . . I, in this presence, this pure company!" [lines 363–368]). While his attitude is in part cynical and self-deflationary, as when he describes himself as an adulterer playing "hot cockles" in the midst of a sacred assembly, he also seriously suggests that his art will intercede for him and win him forgiveness:

> And so all's saved for me, and for the church
> A pretty picture gained.
>
> (lines 388–389)

This is Fra Lippo Lippi's compromise with the world: to combine realistic observation with idealized beauty and to please the church while slyly playing a game of his own.

11.5 Why does the poem end with the word "zooks?"

Answer "Zooks" is a shortened version of "gadzooks," an expletive perhaps meaning "God's truth." In addition to its appearance in the last line, Fra Lippo Lippi uses the oath on three other occasions in the course of the poem, always in company with some truism or idiomatic expression. Mild swearing is, of course, in keeping with Fra Lippo Lippi's character as an earthy realist and constitutes part of his generally expostulatory, bawdy, colloquial diction. In resorting to the language of ordinary speech, the monk claims kinship with the cullions in the patrol guard, the sportive ladies of the night, and the festive celebrants implied by the snatches of street song interspersed in the poem. In every idiom, adage, and exclamation he announces his attachment to the real world of common sense and common experience, as opposed to the cloistered life of a monk "shut within my mew." His style of expression is thus related to his aesthetic theory, which defines art as the realistic representation of "flesh and blood," of "simple beauty," which is "about the best thing God invents."

The epithet "zooks," then, is in a sense thematic. Fra Lippo Lippi is searching for God's truth in his own way, by celebrating the life of the senses rather than through the Prior's catechisms, the Medicis' commissions, or the masses' idolatry.

His art represents the truth by representing God's visible creations "just as they are, careless what comes of it":

> God's works—paint any one, and count it crime
> To let a truth slip.

(lines 294–295)

It is thus no accident that the poem concludes with "Zooks!" for the word suggests both the painter's character and his artistic philosophy.

"The Householder"

11.6   Discuss the meaning of "the house."

Answer   The poem opens with the poet sitting in his house in a state of fatigue and melancholy. With the knock at the door, the scene abandons reality, and a visionary confrontation occurs between the poet and "She." The visitor is a phantasm, a ghost, and the "house" begins to take on the metaphoric connotation of the poet's body.

In the second stanza, Browning elaborates on the physical attributes of the house as symbol for the body. The house is old, its " 'every crumbling brick embrowned with sin and shame!' " It is also a haunted house, where temptations and torments in the shape of devils besiege the lodger within. The metaphor becomes explicit in the description of the building's collapse: " 'Till, crash, comes down the carcass in a heap!' " Finally, in stanza 3, the allusions to "street sounds, window sights" and to "flapping door and echoing roof" convey the daily monotony and emptiness experienced by the poet's soul, which inhabits the house.

By representing the soul's anguish through the concrete imagery of bricks, doors, roofs, and windows, Browning dramatizes subjective experience. There is also irony in the image of the householder, for the implications of orderliness, practicality, decency, and comfort suggested by the word "householder" are subverted by the frantic and cluttered mind of the melancholic speaker.

11.7   Who are "She" and "I"? What is the meaning of the dialogue?

Answer   "I" is the dramatized self of the poet, and "She" is his dead wife. They face each other almost as adversaries, with his despairing outbursts countered by the refrain of her more moderate urgings. This visionary confrontation is apparently a recurrent one, with the self and the phantasm meeting to debate on the value of life in moments of revelation and reconciliation: "Half a pang and all a rapture, there again were we!—"

The brief statements made by the wife at the end of each stanza restrain the fluid outpourings of the husband both by their mere presence as "final word" and by their content. In stanza 2, he paints a lurid picture of his degeneracy and speaks of his desire to flee life immediately; she argues for "decency" or patience. In stanza 3, he bewails the trials of temporal life "down here"; she answers with a complaint of her own: " 'And was I so better off up there?' quoth She."

Despite its emotionally charged mysteriousness, this back-and-forth debate has in part the effect of a domestic spat, with the practical, hardheaded wife getting in the last word.

However, the effect changes in the last stanza, where the speaker urgently longs for death (" 'Help and get it over!' "). He even composes his own obituary, using prosaic language which suggests that nothing in his life matters; who he is and when he died become obscure facts (" *'Lies M, or N,' " " 'year the so and so'* "). His epitaph consists of jingling maxims, again with a reductive effect. In answer, "She" offers not a wifely reminder but a defiantly romantic cry: " 'I end with—Love is all and Death is naught!' " By concluding with the idea of the transcendent power of love, Browning moves the poem out of the realm of the ironic and self-deflating into a sphere of passionate lyricism.

B.S. and L.R.

SUGGESTED READINGS

Drew, P. (ed.), *Robert Browning: A Collection of Critical Essays* (1966).

Langbaum, R., *The Poetry of Experience: The Dramatic Monologue in Modern Literary Tradition* (1957).

Litzinger, B., and K. L. Knickerbocker (eds.), *The Browning Critics* (1965).

MATTHEW ARNOLD

C H R O N O L O G Y

1822	Born at Laleham on the upper Thames. Son of Thomas Arnold, a young clergyman who will soon become an eminent historian, a renowned educator, and a leading light in the Broad Church movement of the Church of England.
1828	Moves to Rugby School, where his father, who became headmaster in 1827, becomes famous as an educational reformer. When Matthew attends Rugby, he responds to the moral force of his father's mind with a mixture of acceptance and rebellion.
1833	His father builds a summer cottage in the Lake Country, where Matthew makes friends with neighbors Dorothy and William Wordsworth.
1842	His father dies.
1844	Takes second honors at Balliol College, Oxford. His Rugby friends, who had expected him to take first honors, consider this a disaster.
1844	Takes post as classical undermaster (that is, assistant teacher) at Rugby School for one year.
1846	Redeems himself in eyes of his friends by election to a one-year fellowship at Oriel College, Oxford.
1847	Gets appointment to post of private secretary to Lord Landsdowne, a liberal peer.
1849	Publishes first volume of verse, *The Strayed Reveller and Other Poems*.

1851	Marries Frances Lucy Wightman, daughter of an eminent judge. To support his marital responsibilities, reluctantly takes post as inspector of schools, a position he holds for thirty-five years.
1852	Publishes second volume of verse, *Empedocles on Etna, and Other Poems.* Both volumes are eventually withdrawn from circulation.
1853	Publishes *Poems* with his famous "preface," Arnold's first important critical essay, in which he introduces the principle that a major consideration of criticism must be the work's effect on the emotional and moral health of the reader and the nation. This principle becomes the foundation of his subsequent criticism.
1855	Publishes *Poems, Second Series.* Poems are suffused with melancholy and nostalgia and sense of loss.
1857	Becomes professor of poetry at Oxford, a post he holds for ten years. During these years, he publishes several books of literary criticism, among them *On Translating Homer* (1861), *Essays in Criticism* (1865), and *On the Study of Celtic Literature* (1867).
1861	His boyhood friend, poet Arthur Hugh Clough, dies at age forty-two; subject of Arnold's elegy, "Thyrsis."
1865	Publishes *Essays in Criticism.* Includes the essay "The Function of Criticism at the Present Time," in which he describes the mission of criticism as "to try to know the best that is known and thought in the world."
1867	Resigns chair at Oxford and, practically speaking, gives up poetic career. Widens his interests to include social and religious criticism.
1869	Publishes *Culture and Anarchy,* the central statement by which he became known as "the apostle of culture." He sums up the ideal of the civilized mind in the phrase "sweetness and light," suggesting insight, openness, and reasonableness.
1871	Publishes *Friendship's Garland,* which further broadens his social criticism of the unenlightened middle classes.
1873	Publishes *Literature and Dogma,* the first of four major studies of the Bible and the Church of England.
1879	Publishes the essay "Wordsworth" as the preface to *The Poems of Wordsworth.* Thus returns to his beginnings in literary criticism.
1883	First tour of America, for which he prepares three lectures: "Literature and Science," "Emerson," and "Numbers." Although reaction is mixed, his trip on the whole is a success.

1886   Second tour of America. Poor health forces him to retire from his school post.

1888   Dies of a heart attack. He is buried at Laleham beside his three sons, whose early deaths had darkened his life.

ESSAY QUESTIONS WITH ANSWERS

"The Buried Life"

12.1   Is "The Buried Life" a love poem?

Answer   In the poem, the speaker and his lover are engaging in light banter when he suddenly tries to pierce through the superficial surface of their interaction to the real feelings beneath. In the final section of the poem (lines 77–98), he says that only love can unlock the prison of the heart, that only love can give a person's life a sense of purpose. Thus both the situation and the conclusion would support the idea that "The Buried Life" is a love poem.

However, it is not clear how the speaker moves from his original malaise over his interaction with his lover to the serenity of the metaphoric landscape that ends the poem. The speaker still addresses his lover, but the talk of love has grown more general: "When a beloved hand is laid in ours," he says, "Our eyes can in another's eyes read clear." This rather abstract statement is followed by further generalizing; from the second person plural ("we," "our"), the speaker passes to the more aloof third person singular: "A man becomes aware of his life's flow. . . ." The proposed "solution" to the speaker's malaise is indeed love, but the speaker retreats from his particular romantic situation even as he argues for the power of love. Ultimately, the poem's most powerful image is the "buried stream" within the self rather than even the "beloved hand" and "loved voice" of the lover. Love, important in its own right, seems even more significant as a possible avenue of liberation for a person, the only means by which one may know oneself.

12.2   The metaphoric structure of the poem depends on a series of contrasts. Discuss the use of these contrasts.

Answer   The structure of the poem hinges on the contrast between the kind of social knowledge mentioned at the beginning and the deeper, more difficult knowledge described at the end. Rather impatiently, the speaker says at the beginning, "Yes, yes, we know that we can jest,/We know, we know that we can smile!" (lines 4–5). He goes on: "I knew the mass of men concealed their thoughts . . . I knew they lived and moved/Tricked in disguise" (lines 16–17, 20–21). This first kind of knowledge is detached; it is perspicacious enough to see through the facades of others, but it does not yet recognize the universality of the alienation of the self. The middle of the poem mediates between this kind of knowledge and that other kind which ends the poem. The speaker refers to his desire "to know/Whence our lives come and where they go" (lines 53–54). At the end of the poem, he envisions this knowledge which is at once less definable and more penetrating: "And what we mean, we say, and what we would, we know/A man becomes aware of his life's flow" (lines 87–88); "and then he thinks he knows/The hills where his life rose,/And the sea where it goes" (lines 96–98). The knowledge here is more elusive and difficult. The speaker, in fact, can offer only a metaphoric landscape for this kind of truth; he cannot really tell us of what this knowledge consists.

Similarly, the sights and sounds of the poem have a binary structure. The image of the "blind uncertainty of our lives" contrasts with the final vision at the end of the poem when "the eyes sink inward" and the metaphoric pastoral landscape is "seen." The fake "eloquence" of social interaction gives way first to the "loved voice" of the lover and, finally, to the "winding murmur" of "life's flow." The "world-deafened ear" can now truly hear the inner voice; the eyes that had missed the buried stream can now penetrate to the wellspring of the self. By means of these contrasting images in the middle of the poem, Arnold tries to capture a sense of the revelation of one's inner life.

12.3

> But often, in the world's most crowded streets,
> But often, in the din of strife,
> There rises an unspeakable desire
> After the knowledge of our buried life;
>
> (lines 45–48)

The feeling described in these lines is reminiscent of Wordsworth's "Tintern Abbey." How is Arnold's speaker both like and unlike Wordsworth's?

Answer   The particular lines from "Tintern Abbey" evoked by Arnold are:

> But oft, in lonely rooms, and 'mid the din
> Of towns and cities, I have owed to them
> In hours of weariness, sensations sweet,
> Felt in the blood, and felt along the heart;
>
> . . . .
>
> With tranquil restoration—feelings too
> Of unremembered pleasure.
>
> (lines 25–31)

Of course, a similar experience occurs in the two poems: a mental separation from the bustling and enervating urban world that surrounds the speaker. In "Tintern Abbey," the speaker recollects the sweet pleasures and calm of the country; in "The Buried Life," he feels a desire to penetrate beneath the veil of civilization and go back to the origins of his own feelings, although no particular scene is remembered.

The final scene evoked in "The Buried Life"—"The hills where his life rose/ And the sea where it goes"—is a pastoral metaphor representing the speaker's discovery of his roots and true nature. In a poem by Wordsworth, those "hills" would be more specific (like the "steep and lofty cliffs" of Monmouthshire in "Tintern Abbey") and literal. The Wordsworthian landscape in Arnold's poem is a metaphor for the knowledge he seeks rather than an actual physical place that leads to a certain awareness or revelation.

The sense of a debt to Wordsworth in "The Buried Life" is not surprising, since Arnold considered Wordsworth the third greatest among English poets, surpassed only by Shakespeare and Milton. In "Wordsworth," an introduction to a volume of Wordsworth's poems, Arnold praises his predecessor for "the extraordinary power with which Wordsworth feels the joy offered to us in nature." In "The Buried Life," Arnold builds on this Wordsworthian joy in nature by using the pastoral imagery to represent the joy of psychological and emotional discovery.

"The Function of Criticism at the Present Time"

12.4   Which of the following statements about the purpose of criticism most accurately paraphrases Arnold's sentiments on the subject?

1. Criticism prepares the way for creative invention.
2. Criticism locates and preserves value.
3. The critical faculty is as valuable as the creative faculty.
4. Criticism seeks to preserve the purity of literature by treating it as separate from the society that produces it.

Answer Statements 1 and 2 accurately paraphrase Arnold's notion of the function of criticism: Criticism helps readers discover the fresh ideas of a particular age or period, consolidates these ideas, and so inspires a new burst of creativity. In describing criticism as "preparing the way" for creativity, statement 1 accurately captures the sequential dimension of Arnold's argument, for he does indeed argue that an age of good criticism must precede an age of great literature. Criticism creates an "intellectual situation of which the creative power can profitably avail itself"; it makes "the best ideas prevail." Its function, then, is to identify these ideas and present them to society.

It is evident from this description that Arnold both subordinates the critical faculty to the creative and relates it very closely to the characteristics of society at a given time. Thus, statements 3 and 4 do not accurately paraphrase Arnold's ideas in the essay.

The objection to statement 3, however, must be carefully defined, for Arnold in no way dismisses the importance of criticism. In fact, he begins the essay by mentioning that he has been accused of emphasizing too strongly the importance of criticism, and, indeed, the entire essay argues for its significance. Arnold also suggests that criticism can itself be a creative activity (a point made by many twentieth-century literary critics as well), but he does not pursue this implication. The main thrust of the argument is that criticism derives its significance from preparing the way for literature. Ultimately, the functional significance of criticism turns on the question of how much great literature succeeds it. Unlike a twentieth-century critic such as Geoffrey Hartman in *Criticism in the Wilderness*, Arnold does not emphasize either the independent value or the literary nature of criticism but rather its usefulness to literature, as it is conventionally understood.

Obviously, the close relationship that Arnold describes between the intellectual and cultural situation of a given age and the literature it produces negates the idea of the purity and autonomy of literature. In fact, Arnold relies heavily on the concept of the *Zeitgeist*, or spirit of the age. Whether he refers expressly to an author or literary work (as in *On Translating Homer*) or to culture itself (as in *Culture and Anarchy*), he is concerned with the broad outlines of culture and the way in which it supports humanistic values, as embodied in "the best that is known and thought in the world."

12.5   As a critic of culture as well as literature, Arnold is fond of posing dichotomies, or sets of oppositions. In "The Function of Criticism," he contrasts French culture and British culture. What are the major contrasts that Arnold cites between the two cultures?

Answer   According to Arnold, the major opposition between French culture and British culture is between philosophical and practical tendencies of mind. The French cultural tradition is philosophical and intellectual; the British is practical and utilitarian. Arnold's essay is meant to describe the contemporary situation of British letters to the British public, and one of his points is that the English can learn much from the intellectual tradition of the French. Arnold's Francophilia, or love of the French, occasioned much angry criticism among the British public, for he seemed to them almost un-English in his sympathies.

Arnold believed that the French Revolution was the most important event of recent history and that despite the unfortunate political turn it took, it had been motivated by an enthusiasm for "pure reason": "In spite of the extravagant direction given to this enthusiasm, in spite of the crimes and follies in which it lost itself, the French Revolution derives from the force, truth, and universality of the ideas which it took for its law, and from the passion with which it could inspire a multitude for these ideas, a unique and still living power." This, he suggests, would be impossible in modern England, where ideas are treated suspiciously and political pragmatism governs every movement or action.

Finally, the dichotomy between the French philosophical tradition and the English pragmatic tradition leads to one of Arnold's main points about the value of criticism: English pragmatism is inimical to good criticism because it does not allow for the free play of the mind. Criticism, Arnold writes, "must obey an instinct prompting it to try to know the best that is known and thought in the world, irrespectively of practice, politics, and everything of the kind . . . this is an instinct for which there is, I think, little original sympathy in the practical English nature." Criticism, in Arnold's view, must be "disinterested," that is, aloof from "the practical view of things." Thus the term "disinterested" in Arnold's vocabulary is not synonymous with "detached"; on the contrary, it implies a tremendous commitment to pursuing one's ideas without being restrained by political allegiances or purely practical concerns.

12.6 What opinion of the middle classes and bourgeois life in England is expressed in the essay?

Answer Arnold draws on the biblical story of the Philistines, the tribe that fought against the people of Israel, to underscore the unenlightened mentality of the British middle classes. In Arnold's view, the evils of the middle classes, or Philistines, include complacency, insularity, and materialism. For Arnold, all three evils are related. Satisfied with the status quo and daily comforts, the British middle classes do not seek out quality and value. For Arnold, the "best" in life includes culture outside England; the classics of Homer and Aeschylus, for example, can serve as "touchstones" or models of excellence. But the Philistine middle classes are concerned with expediency rather than ultimate value. They have no interest in developing a system of values that extends beyond the parochial.

It is no accident that Arnold draws on biblical imagery to make his point about the middle classes, for the entire essay has a note of urgency that recalls the role of the prophet issuing a warning. Arnold is appealing to other intelligent people to fight the misguided and leveling impulses of the masses. For Arnold, the study of literature is a humanizing influence in an age when traditional religious belief is waning. He ends the essay with another figure from the Bible by saying that criticism is "in the wilderness," only gesturing toward the promised land. In more solemn and certainly less emotional tones than his predecessor, Carlyle, Arnold nevertheless assumes the mantle of the prophet, warning his people of the danger of their ways, hoping to show them at least a glimpse of the promised land.

K.L.

SUGGESTED READINGS

Buckler, William E., *On the Poetry of Matthew Arnold: Essays in Critical Reconstruction* (1982).
Culler, A. Dwight, *Imaginative Reason: The Poetry of Matthew Arnold* (1966).
DeLaura, David J., *Hebrew and Hellene in Victorian England* (1969).
Trilling, Lionel, *Matthew Arnold* (1949).

WALTER PATER

C H R O N O L O G Y

1839   Born at Shadwell in East London, second son of Dr. Richard Glode Pater and Maria Hill Pater. His father dies while Walter is very young, and the family moves to Enfield.

1853   Enters King's School, Canterbury, where the shy, sensitive, meditative boy shows complete indifference to outdoor games. He aspires to become a clergyman.

1858   Enters Queen's College, Oxford.

1862   Takes a second in classics and abandons his plan to take orders. Instead, he reads with private pupils in the High Street, Oxford, among them C. C. Shadwell, who becomes his closest friend and later provost of Oriel.

1864   Receives a fellowship at Brasenose College, Oxford, and goes into residence there.

1865   Takes M.A. degree. Visits Italy with Shadwell and is powerfully influenced by the Renaissance art of Ravenna, Pisa, and Florence. Gradually loses his belief in the Christian religion.

1866   Publishes his first essay, on Coleridge's philosophy, in the *Westminster Review*.

1867   Publishes essay on Winckelmann in the *Westminster Review*. Otto Jahn's *Life of Winckelmann* profoundly changes his thinking from the abstract idealism of Ruskin to more concrete reflections on beauty.

| 1869–
1870 | Publishes several essays in larger periodicals, especially the *Fortnightly Review*, on Leonardo, Botticelli, Pico della Mirandola, and Michelangelo. |

| 1869 | Takes a house at 2 Broadmore Road, where his two sisters come to live, although he keeps his Brasenose rooms. Associates with members of the Pre-Raphaelite brotherhood, especially the poet Swinburne. |

| 1871–
1878 | Publishes essays on Wordsworth, Charles Lamb, and romanticism. Delivers lectures which appear posthumously as *Greek Studies*. Writes several other studies, including a semiautobiographical piece entitled *The Child in the House*. |

| 1873 | Publishes his first book, *Studies in the History of the Renaissance*, which sets a new trend in art criticism—impressionistic criticism, which focuses on the effect of the work of art on the viewer. |

| 1880 | Resigns his tutorship at Brasenose, though not his fellowship, to devote more time to writing. |

| 1885 | Publishes his "most valuable legacy to literature," *Marius the Epicurean*, a romance written to illustrate through elaborate sentences with delicate shadings the perfection of prose style and the ideal of the aesthetic life. |

| 1885–
1887 | Writes several reviews, essays, and portraits for *The Guardian*, *The Athenaeum*, and the *Pall Mall Gazette*. |

| 1887 | Publishes volume of *Imaginary Portraits*, philosophic descriptions of characters carefully set in their environment. |

| 1889 | Publishes *Appreciations, with an Essay on Style*, a collection of his miscellaneous writings and an essay on his theory of composition. |

| 1893 | Publishes *Plato and Platonism*, highly stylized college lectures designed to introduce Plato and clarify Plato's historical position. Moves back to a house in Oxford at 64 St. Giles. |

| 1894 | Receives honorary LL.D. from University of Glasgow. Falls ill of rheumatic fever and dies rather suddenly at Oxford. Buried in cemetery of St. Giles at Oxford. |

ESSAY QUESTIONS WITH ANSWERS

The Renaissance

13.1   At the beginning of his "Preface" to *The Renaissance*, Pater endorses Matthew Arnold's definition of the aim of criticism, which is "to see the object as it really is." How does Pater use and modify Arnold's idea?

Answer   Although Pater begins his "Preface" with Arnold's description of the aim of criticism, he subtly qualifies Arnold's idea by shifting the emphasis from the object to the viewer's impression of the object. To determine the nature of the object, in Pater's view, one must analyze its impact on oneself, the viewer. Pater asks, What kind of impression does it produce? "What is this song or picture . . . *to me*[emphasis added]?" Thus Pater stresses the affective nature of the work of art and the subjective nature of criticism. He concentrates on the interaction of object and viewer, the beauty in the object producing pleasure in the viewer. For both Arnold and Pater, seeing the object as it really is involves using powers of discernment and discrimination. But whereas Arnold tends to use the vocabulary of ethical judgment (the "best," "the greatest") and to compare each work of art with the classic "touchstones" of the past, Pater uses the vocabulary of aesthetics and feelings (the "beautiful," the "intense") to stress the uniqueness of the aesthetic object.

However, though Pater's focus on the viewer and the viewer's impressions produces a more subjective criticism than Arnold's, it does not sanction carelessness or self-indulgence on the part of the critic. For Pater, the validity of criticism lies in the scrupulousness with which critics analyze their own impressions. Pater draws an analogy between the analysis of the virtues of an object of art and the chemical analysis of a substance. Just as the chemist must isolate the elements that make up a compound, the critic must attempt to isolate the exact sources of his or her impressions of a work of art and the conditions which produce them.

Pater and Arnold attempted to liberate criticism from both orthodoxy and pragmatism. For both, seeing the object as it really is involves the ability to detach oneself from preconceived principles as well as from utilitarian needs. Both critics believed in the integrity of art and its independence from the demands of religious authority as well as those of the marketplace.

13.2   How does the "Conclusion" of *The Renaissance* anticipate the aesthetic principles and practices of modern writers?

Answer   Pater's definition of success in life—"to burn always with this hard, gemlike flame, to maintain this ecstasy"—and his attempt to separate art from traditional morality paved the way, most immediately, for the life and art of Oscar Wilde. (Wilde once told W. B. Yeats that he never traveled anywhere without a copy of *The Renaissance*.) Seeking to translate Pater's descriptions of emotional and intellectual intensity into physical experience, Wilde tried to experience ecstasy through various types of physical stimuli. In the preface to his fable *The Picture of Dorian Gray*, Wilde maintained that art could not be inherently moral or immoral but merely well or badly created, a distinction anticipated by Pater's focus on style and sensibility.

More generally, Pater's stress on the play of consciousness, the instability of experience, and the importance of the single moment anticipate certain modernist tendencies, reflected in, for example, the stream of impressions traced in Joyce's *A Portrait of the Artist as a Young Man* and Woolf's *To the Lighthouse*. Woolf's famous description of life and its representation in modern fiction seems quite Pateresque: Life is "a luminous halo, a semi-transparent envelope surrounding us from the beginning of consciousness to the end" ("Modern Fiction"). The fleeting quality of experience and the sense of flickering impressions in her novels are also reminiscent of Pater. In *To the Lighthouse*, for example, she presents single moments of significance, such as the moment of harmony around the dinner table, that are, as Pater describes them in *The Renaissance*, "gone while we try to apprehend" them.

Thus, Pater's inner-directed, impressionistic criticism anticipated and in some cases influenced the direction of subsequent literature. Signaling the end of Victorian "earnestness," Pater's emphasis on the purely aesthetic value of art led the way for some of the significant trends of modernism.

K.L.

SUGGESTED READINGS

Child, Ruth, *The Aesthetic of Walter Pater* (1940).
Crinkley, Richmond, *Walter Pater: Humanist* (1970).
DeLaura, D. J., *Hebrew and Hellene in Victorian England* (1969).
McKenzie, Gordon, *The Literary Character of Walter Pater* (1967).
Monsman, Gerald Cornelius, *Walter Pater's Art of Autobiography* (1980).

OSCAR WILDE

C H R O N O L O G Y

1854	Born in Dublin. Son of Sir William Wilde, a leading oculist and ear surgeon who founded the first eye and ear hospital in Great Britain, and Jane Francesca Elgee Wilde, a writer.
1864	Enters the Portora Royal School at Enniskillen.
1871	Enters Trinity College, Dublin.
1874– 1879	Attends Magdalen College, Oxford, where he vacillates between the moralism of Ruskin and the aestheticism of Pater. He is also torn between Roman Catholicism and Freemasonry and between heterosexuality and homosexuality. Distinguishes himself for scholarship and for eccentric behavior and dress. His witty conversation and affected aestheticism single him out for ridicule.
1878	Wins Newdigate Prize for his poem *Ravenna*.
1881	Publishes his first volume of verse, *Poems*. His affectations in dress and manners are satirized in Gilbert and Sullivan's comic opera *Patience*.
1882	Scores great personal success in lecture tour of the United States. Produces in New York his first play, *Vera*; it is unsuccessful.
1883– 1884	Extends his success in lecture tour of the United Kingdom. Writes his second unsuccessful play, *The Duchess of Padua*.
1884	Marries Constance Lloyd, a woman of means, the daughter of a Dublin

barrister. Takes a house in Chelsea, an artistic section of London, where he makes friends with James McNeill Whistler and other artists.

1887–   Edits *Woman's World*, a popular magazine.
1889

1888   Publishes *The Happy Prince and Other Tales*, a collection of original fairy tales.

1889   Publishes essay on Shakespeare's sonnets in *Blackwood's Magazine*, "The Portrait of Mr. W.H.," which puts forth the theory that many of the sonnets are addressed to a man. "The Decay of Lying" appears in *The Nineteenth Century*.

1890   Serializes *The Picture of Dorian Gray* in *Lippincott's Magazine*.

1891   Publishes several essays and three books exhibiting his far-ranging interests: *Intentions*, an important collection of dialogues containing Wilde's aesthetic philosophy; *Lord Arthur Savile's Crime, and Other Stories*, a collection of short stories; and *The Picture of Dorian Gray*, his only novel. The novel arouses a storm of controversy over its morality. Publishes another collection of stories, *A House of Pomegranates*. Produces *The Duchess of Padua*. Begins his ruinous friendship with Lord Alfred Douglas, third son of the ninth marquess of Queensberry.

1892   Enjoys great popular success for his production of *Lady Windermere's Fan* at the St. James's Theatre. Writes (in French) *Salomé*, but sees it denied a license for production because of an old law forbidding theatrical depiction of biblical characters.

1893   Produces another success with *A Woman of No Importance*, a play whose witty, epigrammatic dialogue transcends a conventional plot. Publishes *Lady Windermere's Fan*. Publishes *Salomé* in French.

1894   Renowned actress Sarah Bernhardt puts on *Salomé* in Paris. Wilde publishes *Salomé* in English translation. Writes *The Importance of Being Earnest*.

1895   Puts on *An Ideal Husband* at the Haymarket Theatre and *The Importance of Being Earnest* at the St. James's Theatre, his last and greatest play. This is the height of his dramatic success; both plays are popular and critical hits. Infatuated with the egocentric young Douglas, Wilde flaunts the friendship in public, causing Lord Douglas's father to publicly criticize him. Wilde sues for libel, then abandons the case. However, incriminating evidence brought out in cross-examination leads to arrest of Wilde for homosexual offenses. After a hung jury on his first trial, the second jury finds Wilde guilty of homosexuality; the sentence is two years at hard labor. Suffers bankruptcy, vilification in press, humiliation.

1897   In prison, writes *De Profundis*, a moving description of his spiritual progress through suffering to religious insight, in the form of a letter to Lord Alfred Douglas; published in part in 1905 and in full in 1962. On release from prison, goes in exile to the Continent under the alias of Sebastian Melmoth.

1898   Publishes his best known poem, *The Ballad of Reading Gaol*. Also publishes two letters on prison reform. His wife dies.

1900   After being baptized into the Roman Catholic Church, he dies of cerebral meningitis at the Hotel D'Alsace. He is buried at Bagneaux.

ESSAY QUESTIONS WITH ANSWERS

The Picture of Dorian Gray

14.1   What is the relationship between Dorian and his portrait?

Answer   Dorian's portrait first reveals to him his own beauty. Along with Lord Henry's compliments, the portrait awakens Dorian's narcissism, and he begins to worship himself. This self-love leads Dorian to make his Faustian bargain, offering to sell his soul if only the picture will age rather than his face and body. Dorian's narcissism leads him to want to separate himself from his experience; it is the picture that provides "a diary of [his] life from day to day" (Chap. XIII). In one of his letters, Wilde wrote that "to reject one's own experiences is to arrest one's own development" (*Letters of Oscar Wilde* [1962], p. 469). Dorian's unchanging appearance suggests this fixity in his development, just as the hidden portrait reflects his attempt to divorce himself from his past.

Dorian first notices a change in the portrait after he cruelly rejects Sibyl Vane; he then begins to interpret the portrait as the "visible symbol of the degradation of sin," the "ever-present sign of the ruin men brought upon their souls" (Chap. VIII). From a reflection of the "unspotted" image of the innocent Dorian, the portrait now becomes a record of Dorian's sins. It provides a picture of his degraded soul. But the portrait can also be viewed as a reflection of Dorian's self-loathing. Rather than an objective sign of his actual degradation, it may be regarded as Dorian's mental picture of himself. Dorian's self-love thus leads ultimately to self-loathing, a change the picture records. His attack on the portrait expresses this self-loathing and becomes an act of suicide.

14.2   Discuss the role of Lord Henry in the novel.

Answer   Lord Henry is the detached, cynical critic who expresses some of Wilde's opinions in *Intentions*, his only book of criticism. Whereas Basil is the romantic artist whose touchstone is sincerity, Henry, like Wilde, praises artifice.

The more insincere a person is, Lord Henry proclaims, "the more purely intellectual" will be that person's ideas; they will not be colored by "either his wants, his desires, or his prejudices" (Chap. I). Henry is Prince Paradox to Dorian's Prince Charming, and although his love of paradox makes him sound like one of the witty conversationalists in Wilde's social comedies, his view of the relation between art and artifice is to be taken seriously. Henry's very detachment allows him to survive where, in contrast, the artist and the beautiful young hedonist both die.

Lord Henry is also the critic as artist, an observer of human nature who sees Dorian Gray as "his own creation." Whereas Basil worships Dorian as his subject and muse, Henry views him as his material, a "work of art," a living masterpiece. Henry presents an alternative to the type of artist Basil represents; he is a sculptor of human personality rather than a painter of worshipful portraits.

Henry is also the spokesman for an attack on Victorian earnestness and morality. He expresses Wilde's belief in the perniciousness of repression and public morality. He preaches a new hedonism as opposed to the old morality. He is thus the artist as critic, a self-appointed anatomist of society's hypocrisies and foibles. Like Gilbert in "The Critic as Artist," a fictional dialogue in *Intentions*, Henry believes that creativity is antiauthoritarian and true art subversive. "The books that the world calls immoral," he says, "are books that show the world its own shame" (Chap. XIX).

And yet Lord Henry miscalculates in the novel, for it is clear that he would be totally surprised to learn of Dorian's crime. When Dorian asks, "What would you say, Henry, if I told you that I had murdered Basil?" (Chap. XIX), Henry tells him that he is incapable of crime. It seems that Henry's detachment finally renders him incapable of understanding the magnitude of Dorian's sin. He can preach the philosophy of hedonism but cannot understand Dorian's final step into criminality.

K.L.

SUGGESTED READINGS

Chamberlin, J. E., *Ripe Was the Drowsy Hour: The Age of Oscar Wilde* (1977).
Shewan, Rodney, *Oscar Wilde: Art and Egotism* (1977).
Ellmann, Richard, *Oscar Wilde: A Collection of Critical Essays* (1969).

Part Three

THE VICTORIAN NOVEL

T I M E L I N E

The Age

1810: George III insane; the Regency

1815: Napoleon's final defeat at Waterloo

1820: Accession of George IV

1825: First English railway opened

1830: Death of George IV; accession of William IV

1832: Passage of Reform Bill

1837: Death of William IV; accession of Queen Victoria

1845: Great Famine in Ireland

1848: Revolutions in France, Italy, Austria; publication of *Communist Manifesto*

1854: *Outbreak of Crimean War*

1859: Publication of Darwin's *Origin of Species*

1860: Outbreak of American Civil War

1865: Assassination of Lincoln

1876: Invention of the telephone

1886: Publication in English of Marx's *Capital*

1887: Golden Jubilee of Queen Victoria

1895: Invention of motion picture camera

1900: Publication of Freud's *Interpretation of Dreams*

1901: Death of Victoria; accession of Edward VII

1903: Wright brothers' flight at Kitty Hawk

1905: Einstein's theory of relativity

1910: Death of Edward VII; accession of George V

The Authors

William Makepeace Thackeray (1811–1863)

Charles Dickens (1812–1870)

Anthony Trollope (1815–1882)

Charlotte Brontë (1816–1855)

1810

Emily Brontë (1818–1848)

George Eliot (1818–1880)

1820

1830

Samuel Butler (1835–1902)

1840

1850

1860

1870

1870

1880

1890

1900

1910

WILLIAM MAKEPEACE THACKERAY

C H R O N O L O G Y

1811	Born in Calcutta, India, the only son of Richmond Thackeray, an East India Company administrator, and Anne Becher Thackeray, the daughter of distinguished civil servants in India.
1816	His father dies, and William is sent home to England to live with his aunt, Mrs. Ritchie. His mother soon remarries.
1817	Attends school in Chiswick Mall; is unhappy there.
1822–1828	Attends the famous Charterhouse School at Smithfield, whose tyrannical headmaster, Dr. Russell, will be depicted in *Pendennis*. Distinguishes himself as a comic versifier and caricaturist.
1828	Under tutelage of his stepfather at Larkbeare House near Ottery St. Mary, Devonshire, prepares for entrance to Cambridge.
1829–1830	Enters Trinity College, Cambridge; enjoys friendships with Tennyson, R. Monckton Milnes (Lord Houghton), Edward Fitzgerald, and W. H. Thompson (later master of Trinity). Leaves Cambridge without a degree; travels on Continent, where he meets Goethe and is presented at the German court.
1831–1833	Studies law at Middle Temple, London, but gives it up on coming of age and inheriting £20,000 from his father's estate. Buys the *National Standard*, a newspaper, and goes to Paris as its correspondent. However, it fails.

1834–1835	Studies art in Paris and becomes a caricaturist. Contributes to *Fraser's Magazine*.
1836	Unsuccessfully applies to illustrate *Pickwick Papers* for Dickens. Stepfather buys a newspaper, *The Constitutional*, and hires him as Paris correspondent. This newspaper also fails. Marries a penniless Irish girl, Isabella Gethen Creagh Shawe, daughter of Colonel Matthew Shawe. Speculates and gambles away his inheritance.
1837	Returns to London and establishes himself as a literary "hack." Contributes to *The Times*, *Fraser's Magazine*, *The New Monthly Magazine*, and *Punch* under pseudonyms.
1840	Thackeray's wife goes insane and is cared for by country friends in Essex. She survives her husband by thirty years. His two daughters go to live with his grandmother in Paris.
1842	Visits Ireland and stays with the novelist Lever.
1843	Publishes *The Irish Sketchbook*, the first work to appear under his own name.
1844	Through a friend's influence, obtains passage to the far east.
1846	Publishes *From Cornhill to Cairo*, impressions of his trip. Establishes a home for his daughters, his grandmother, and himself at 13 Young Street in Kensington. Becomes emotionally attached to Cambridge friend's wife, Mrs. Henry Brookfield.
1847–1848	Serializes *Vanity Fair* (published 1848), his greatest achievement and one of the outstanding novels of the period.
1848	Publishes *The Book of Snobs*, a collection of portraits that appeared in *Punch*.
1848–1850	Publishes *The History of Pendennis*, developing the line of the historical novel, the first of a trilogy in which Arthur Pendennis (Pen) grows up.
1851	Breaks off his relationship with Mrs. Brookfield at her husband's insistence, an emotional trauma second only to his wife's insanity.
1852	Publishes *The History of Henry Esmond* (three volumes), a formally structured historical novel which is not well received.
1852–1853	Makes a lecture tour of the United States on "The English Humorists of the 18th Century."
1853–1855	Publishes *The Newcomes*, a sequel to *The History of Pendennis*, which Pen narrates.

1855–   Second lecture tour of the United States on "The Four Georges." Publishes
1857   *The Rose and the Ring*, his Christmas book, and *Miscellanies* (four volumes),
           a collection of his best early writings.

1857–   Publishes *The Virginians*, sequel to *Henry Esmond*; *The Adventures of Philip
1862   on His Way Through the World*, the last of his Arthur Pendennis trilogy;
           and *Lovel the Widower*, his last complete novel.

1860–   Founds and edits the *Cornhill Magazine*, which is exceptionally successful.
1862

1863   Dies on Christmas Eve in his new home at Palace Gardens of a cerebral
           hemorrage. Leaves an unfinished novel, *Denis Duval*. Buried at Kensal
           Green.

ESSAY QUESTIONS WITH ANSWERS

Vanity Fair

15.1 Compare and contrast the characters of Amelia Sedley and Becky Sharp. What are their positions in the moral scheme of the novel?

Answer Ostensibly, the contrast between the two women is a simple one between good and evil, with Amelia the much sinned against saint and Becky the soulless schemer. However, Thackeray's treatment of the two is far more complex than this simple judgment would suggest.

In characterizing Amelia, Thackeray from the beginning takes pains to establish her as a noble, kind, and delicate paragon of womanhood. His descriptions of her tend to be full of pathos. Amelia is beloved by all at Miss Pinkerton's, generous to her friend Rebecca, loving and submissive to her childhood sweetheart George, and devoted to her parents and her son. She stands apart from the vain, malicious ladies of Vanity Fair—Thackeray's central metaphor for society—in the strength of her attachments and the quiet humility of her manner. It is a measure of her trusting nature that she is so easily victimized by the careless George, by the entire Osborne family, and by Becky as well.

However, Thackeray's portrait of "poor Amelia" is deeply colored by irony. All her virtuous actions may be interpreted as symptoms of a self-conscious desire for martyrdom, an obsession with a romantic ideal that distorts all her relationships. Amelia's unhappy lot, originating in her refusal to see the weakness of George Osborne, is a self-created misery which she perpetuates by idolizing her dead husband. And her adoration of her son turns the boy into a self-indulgent replica of his father.

The fact that William Dobbin, the one undeniably good character in the novel, loves Amelia cuts two ways. On the one hand, it suggests Amelia's extraordinary virtue and gentility in contrast to the ranks of fraudulent, designing women who inhabit the world of *Vanity Fair*. On the other hand, it becomes apparent in the course of the novel that Amelia is unworthy of Dobbin's un-wavering loyalty, a point Thackeray makes explicit in the denouement. William himself realizes, "No, you are not worthy of the love I have devoted to you," while the narrator comments a few lines later:

> He had placed himself at her feet for so long that the poor little woman had been accustomed to trample upon him. She didn't wish to marry him, but she wished to give him nothing, but that he should give her all. (Chap. 66)

The epithet so frequently applied to Amelia, "poor little woman," has here a definitely ironic ring. Throughout the book, Thackeray betrays ambivalence toward Amelia. He tenderly defends her as a pitiful little creature and at the same time draws attention to her excessive emotionalism and willful self-flag-ellation. In the end, Amelia's actions speak louder than Thackeray's words, demonstrating the self-interest and self-love that lie behind her humility.

In his portrait of Becky, Thackeray seems less divided. He sets out to draw a "bad woman," disloyal to friends and constantly seeking her own advantage. From the beginning, his comments on her orphaned status and her exclusion from society are sharply satirical. This "poor" woman is not poor at all. Her personal advantages include a quick wit, a sharp mind, physical attractiveness, and immense vitality. However, Thackeray undercuts the impressiveness of this female artillery by showing Becky's manipulative use of her abilities. Each of her virtues becomes a seductive wile, a persuasive ploy by which she seeks to win a place in society. In some instances, her striving for position leads her to be unnatural and even cruel, as in her cavalier neglect of both Rawdons. By lying to her husband and discarding her son she becomes the reverse of ideal womanhood, a faithless, heartless siren.

Still, Thackeray does not simply present Becky as a caricature of vice. Partly, she is redeemed by the entire context of *Vanity Fair*; in a world of fortune hunters, deceivers, and hypocrites, she is superior in her skill at playing the game as well as in her honest acknowledgment that it is a game. She is also capable of generosity when it does not hinder the pursuit of her self-interest. One of her last actions is to bring Dobbin and Amelia together by puncturing Amelia's foolish illusions about George.

Thus, Thackeray transcends both simple satire and simple sentimentality in his portraits of Becky and Amelia. Using gray tones as well as stark black and white, he presents us with rounded characters in whom we can believe while still placing them within a definite moral scheme.

15.2   Discuss the treatment of history in the novel.

Answer   The notion of history in *Vanity Fair* is a complicated one. Set during the Napoleonic wars, the novel is certainly tied to, as well as being a product of, its historical period.

The battle of Waterloo (June 15, 1815) is the centerpiece of the novel, the moment at which the frivolous social world of Thackeray's fiction comes into collision with the "real" world of historical action. Thackeray's treatment of this heroic chapter in the military annals of Great Britain is ironic, for his characters go to war as though to a party. In fact, Thackeray gives the duchess of Richmond's ball more emphasis than the battle itself, which occurs "offstage." The most minute details of Becky's amorous intrigues and Amelia's disappointments are recorded, while George Osborne's death receives only a single line. Thus, the vanities of Vanity Fair are emphasized by the somber background of war and death. Empires may hang in the balance, but Jos Sedley must dine.

However, apart from this ironic perspective supplied by the background of historical action, the main emphasis of the novel is not on public events but on private lives. Histories personal, ancestral, and fictitious fill the pages of *Vanity Fair*. On one level, each character creates his or her own life story in the course of the novel, and all the changes registered over time—for example, the elder Sedleys' growing bitterness, Rawdon's increasing goodness, and Dobbin's disillusionment—constitute case histories of personalities in flux. On another level, ancestral lineage is a major "historical" theme of the novel; in a society in which status is determined by birth, the bloodlines of the aristocratic Steynes, Crawleys, Bareacres, and Southdowns carry immense prestige despite the characters' individual failings and vices. Finally, there are the fictitious histories, those stories circulated by parvenus and upstarts seeking to gain admittance to the fair. These invented social biographies include the elder Osborne's pretensions to nobility in borrowing a coat of arms from the unrelated Osbornes of the aristocracy and Becky's many versions of her past.

Thus, Thackeray accomplishes in this novel the interweaving of public history with individual case histories. Despite the elaborately drawn backgrounds, the author's true interests lie with certain segments of society and the psychology of his cast of characters.

15.3   Discuss the nature of the narrative voice in *Vanity Fair* and its effect on the novel as a whole.

Answer "Thackeray," as represented by the chatty, opinionated narrator, is a constant presence in the world of *Vanity Fair*. The dramatic events of the novel are filtered through the perspective of this intrusive bystander so that the reader is never left in doubt about the significance of the tale. Thus, one of the effects of the narrative persona is to emphasize the importance of moral judgment and discernment, the faculties of perception which puncture the veils of vanity and illusion to reveal the emptiness and vice beneath.

Many of the satiric comments in the novel generalize from a specific event in the plot to human nature as a whole. In a sense, Thackeray employs argument as a frame for his fiction, using the story to prove his moral case against Vanity Fair. For example, Chapter 36 ("How to Live Well on Nothing a Year"), devoted ostensibly to the grand lifestyle of Captain and Mrs. Crawdon in Paris and London, begins with an essay on the profligacy of the middle class. Offering a personal anecdote about his acquaintance with the high-living Jenkinses, "Thackeray" draws the reader into an acknowledgment that the world abounds with similar instances of hypocrisy: "Many a glass of wine have we all of us drunk, I have very little doubt, hob-and-nobbing with the hospitable giver, and wondering how the deuce he paid for it." One of the main themes of the following chapter is the exploitation of Raggles, the Crawleys' landlord on Curzon Street, by the conniving Crawleys. This is the explanation of how the Crawleys live so well "on nothing a year," and Thackeray's satire turns bitter in the remark "yet somebody must pay even for gentlemen who live on nothing a year—and so it was this unlucky Raggles was made the representative of Colonel Crawley's defective capital" (Chap. 37). In both of these examples, the narrator is alerting the reader to the victims of the Crawleys' game as well as passing a moral (though somewhat ironic) judgment on the poor tradesman and landlord.

A further effect of the narrative commentary is to puncture the illusion of "realism" by means of the constant emphasis on the act of writing. For example, early in the novel, Thackeray apologizes for the dullness of his narrative ("I know that the tune I am piping is a very mild one") and boasts of his ability to render the love affair between Joseph Sedley and Becky in a variety of rhetorical styles ("we might have treated this subject in the genteel, or in the romantic, or in the facetious manner" [Chap. 6]). This stress on the writer's choice among alternatives keeps the readers aware that they are reading a fiction invented by the author to entertain, persuade, and educate. We are never allowed to forget that, as the novelist, Thackeray knows all and controls all. As he reminds his readers in the last line of the book, he is chief stage manager of this drama:

Come, children, let us shut up the box and the puppets, for our play is
played out. (Chap. 67)

A final aspect of the authorial interference in the novel is the somewhat
odd appearance of the novelist as a quasi-character, poking his head on stage
and claiming a minor role in the proceedings. Thus, he claims that at Pum-
pernickel he "first saw Colonel Dobbin and his party" and says of Amelia that
"it was because it was predestined that I was to write this particular lady's memoirs
that I remarked her" (Chap. 62). This strategy has a number of contradictory
effects. First, it puts forth the familiar claim of the novelist that he is an
eyewitness and thus lends an air of reality to the fiction. At the same time, it
undermines the realism of the narrative by playing on the idea of authorial
intrusion; having the author literally materialize on the stage raises questions
for the readers as to the source and reliability of their knowledge.

Throughout, Thackeray's presence has the effect of juxtaposing the teller
with the tale. In this kind of fiction, the story cannot stand alone because what
happens is at every point clearly manipulated and conditioned by the genial,
ironic, indignant, and playful personality of the writer.

15.4   In the description of Vanity Fair in *Pilgrim's Progress*, Bunyan presents
an allegory of the futility of worldliness and sin in the illusory wares displayed
by the hawkers and tradesmen. Discuss some of the varieties of social vice
exhibited in Thackeray's fair.

Answer   Thackeray's *Vanity Fair* is populated with characters representing
all of the seven deadly sins. Vanity or pride motivates nearly every character
in the book, and greed and envy are almost equally pervasive. The sins of
gluttony and sloth are personified by Joseph Sedley, wrath by the elder Mr.
Osborne, and lust by Lord Steye and, to a lesser extent, old Sir Pitt.

Most figures in the novel may be readily identified by a dominant obsession
or vice. Thus Miss Crawley, old Sir Pitt, the Bareacres, Lady Sheepshanks, Lord
Steyne, Mrs. Bute, and a host of others are caricatures, broadly sketched to
illustrate a moral point. Miss Crawley is a Volpone-like cynic, tantalizing her
dependents with the promise of an inheritance; old Sir Pitt is a degenerate miser;
the Bareacres are social snobs; Lady Sheepshanks is a religious and medical
fanatic; Lord Steyne is a lecherous hypocrite; and Mrs. Bute is a falsely humble
do-gooder. The effect of these portraits is on the one hand topical, constituting

a gallery of social types exhibited for public notice, and on the other hand allegorical, suggesting a parade of the seven deadly sins.

Despite the pervasive social comedy, Vanity Fair simultaneously projects a serious moral dimension. Just as the title of the book emphasizes the theme of vanity (that is, emptiness, futility, and self-love), so these lives enact it. Thackeray devotes the final lines of the book to a reflection on the inevitable illusions and follies of mortal life:

> Ah! Vanitas, vanitatum! Which of us is happy in this world? Which of us has his desire? or, having it, is satisfied? (Chap. 67)

The melancholy tone of this passage is central to Thackeray's philosophy, more so than the comic byplay or indignant satire that sometimes characterizes his treatment of individual characters. Like Bunyan, Thackeray is concerned with opening the eyes of the reader to the essential emptiness of worldly existence.

As the most fully rounded character in the book, Becky Sharp illustrates Thackeray's idea of the futility of human endeavor with special vividness. After all her strenuous efforts to achieve status and security, she ends up compromised both socially and morally. Despite her charm, intelligence, vitality, and ambition, she never finally "arrives." Becky's defeat may be read both as a moral comeuppance for her particular vices and, at the same time, a realistic image of the disappointing outcome of any life or any ambition. Our last glimpse of Becky, at a literal fair, suggests that she will go on buying and selling, making one bargain after another.

L.R.

SUGGESTED READINGS

Ray, Gordon, *The Uses of Adversity* (1955).
Tillotson, G., and D. Hawes (eds.), *Thackeray: The Critical Heritage* (1968).
Van Ghent, Dorothy, *Form and Function in the English Novel* (1953).

CHARLES DICKENS

C H R O N O L O G Y

1812 Born in Portsmouth, the second of eight children, to John Dickens, a clerk in the naval pay office famed for his storytelling ability, and Elizabeth Barrow Dickens, the daughter of a naval lieutenant. Part of the insecure lower middle class, the family moves to London and then to Chatham during Charles's early childhood. His mother tutors the sickly Charles at home.

1821 Charles receives further instruction from Mr. Giles, the son of the Dickenses' next-door neighbor.

1822 The family moves back to London, where Charles's father drifts into debt and his mother tries to open a school in their home, to which, however, no one comes.

1824 His father is imprisoned for debt in the Marshalsea, where the family lodges with him. Charles gets a job in a blacking warehouse (where shoe polish is manufactured). His social humiliation—his sense that he has become a "little labouring hind" with no hope of further education or advancement—is enhanced when he is set to label bottles in a window, where curious onlookers can observe him at work.

1825–
1827 A legacy releases John Dickens from prison, and he receives a pension from the navy. Improved family circumstances permit Charles to attend Wellington House Academy.

1827–
1828 Works as a law clerk at Lincoln's Inn and Gray's Inn.

1828–1833	Learns shorthand and reports first court proceedings, then parliamentary debates for *The True Sun* and *The Mirror of Parliament*. Falls violently in love with Maria Beadnell, a banker's daughter, but is rejected because of his poor prospects.
1833	His first published sketch appears in *The Monthly Magazine*, signed "Boz," his brother's nickname, based on a family joke.
1834	Continues his work as a stenographer on the staff of *The Morning Chronicle*.
1836	Anecdotal vignettes of London life and manners are collected in *Sketches by Boz*, illustrated by George Cruikshank. Marries Catherine Hogarth, daughter of an engraver and journalist, but is at least equally attached to her younger sister, Mary.
1837	After coming to live with Charles and Catherine Dickens, Mary Hogarth dies. Dickens is devastated by her death, which is usually thought to have inspired the death of Little Nell in *The Old Curiosity Shop*.
1836–1837	Hired to supply a narrative text for a series of sporting illustrations by Robert Seymour. When Seymour commits suicide, Dickens persuades the skeptical publishers to continue the commercially feeble serial, and Hablot K. Browne ("Phiz") is hired as an illustrator. As *The Pickwick Papers*, the monthly publication becomes an unexpected success and skyrockets Dickens from obscure poverty to fame and fortune.
1837–1839	Publishes *Oliver Twist*, with its nightmare vision of the London underworld and its implicit plea for reform of workhouses. Edits *Bentley's Miscellany*, a popular magazine, in which *Oliver Twist* first appears.
1838–1839	*Nicholas Nickleby* reinforces the success of Dickens's first two novels, reverting to the looser, more episodic form of *The Pickwick Papers*. Dickens's characteristic combination of comic vision and indignation at social abuses and injustice is by now well established; so is the publication of his novels in monthly parts, although his next two novels will appear as part of a weekly serial.
1841	*Barnaby Rudge* (Dickens's first historical novel, based on the anti-Catholic riots of the 1780s) and *The Old Curiosity Shop* appear as parts of the serial *Master Humphrey's Clock* (which is less a separate periodical than a frame story enclosing the two novels). Although the flight of Little Nell and her grandfather from city to country provides a panorama of nineteenth-century England, the character of Little Nell herself creates a sentimental sensation; her death is responsible for much of the novel's immediate popular impact (as well as its notoriety for later generations of critics).

1842	Georgina Hogarth, another of Catherine's younger sisters, comes to live with the Dickenses and help care for the children. (She stays on even after Catherine leaves in 1858.) Dickens tours America and, resentful of publishers who have pirated his works, begins a campaign for international copyright. He is received with uncritical adulation, which, however, turns to hostility when he writes *American Notes* and *Martin Chuzzlewit* after returning to England.
1843	Publishes *A Christmas Carol* shortly before Christmas; it sells over 6000 copies on the first day.
1843– 1844	Publishes *Martin Chuzzlewit*. Dickens sees its thematic unity as an artistic advance—it is the first of his novels for which he writes a detailed advance plan—but the public responds coolly to its satirical tone, less genial than that of his earlier novels. The hero's excursion across the Atlantic to America has generally been interpreted as an attempt to boost sales, and it is again related to the novel's thematic concerns.
1844	Takes his large family and settles in Genoa, partly from motives of economy. Publishes *The Chimes*, a New Year's tale and, after *A Christmas Carol*, his second most popular seasonal story.
1845	Returns with his family to London and becomes, for three weeks, editor of *The Daily News*. Goes to Lausanne, Switzerland.
1846	Settles again in London and takes an uncharacteristic rest from writing.
1846– 1848	Publishes *Dombey and Son*.
1849– 1850	Publishes *David Copperfield*, an autobiographical narrative of a writer's development. Like *Dombey and Son*, it shows new artistic assurance.
1852– 1853	Publishes *Bleak House*, in which the abuses of chancery become a metaphor for the general inequities of Victorian society. Like Dickens's other late novels, its power and coherence depend less on a narrative than on an increasingly poetic and symbolic vision.
1854	Publishes *Hard Times*, attacking capitalist industrial organization and the dehumanized educational system which he sees as its corollary.
1855– 1857	Publishes *Little Dorrit*, in which the Marshalsea prison and the already defunct system of debtors' prisons become symbols of the social and psychological imprisonment of nineteenth-century England.
1858	Separates from his wife, Catherine. Georgina and the younger children stay with him, although Catherine takes their oldest son. Dickens's readers are

shocked both by the separation and by his explanation in print that the couple had lived together for twenty-two years and had ten children without having genuinely loved each other. Eventually, in the 1860s, a young actress, Ellen Ternan, becomes Dickens's mistress.

1859	Publishes *A Tale of Two Cities*, a historical romance. Assumes editorship of the magazine *All the Year Round* (his second venture in the 1850s, after the earlier *Household Words*).
1860–1861	Publishes *Great Expectations*.
1864–1865	Publishes *Our Mutual Friend*, his last complete novel.
1865	Suffers a minor paralytic stroke.
1867–1868	Returns to the United States for a final reading tour, which is very successful despite his earlier satiric writings about Americans.
1868	Begins but never finishes *The Mystery of Edwin Drood*.
1870	Dies at his home, Gad's Hill. Buried in Poets' Corner in Westminster Abbey.

ESSAY QUESTIONS WITH ANSWERS

Great Expectations

16.1   *Great Expectations* is a *Bildungsroman*, that is, a novel about growing up. Its hero, Pip, tells his own story through the use of first-person narration. Discuss the character of Pip, including the effect of the use of first-person narration.

Answer   Pip introduces himself to the reader as a very young child, wandering in the graveyard where his parents are buried. In the opening section of the novel, Pip is for the most part a sympathetic figure; an orphan brought up "by hand" by a sadistic older sister, he is primarily a victim who must constantly struggle to survive in the cruel, incomprehensible world of adults. The shifts in perspective associated with Pip's first dramatic encounter with Magwitch, when the convict literally turns him upside down, suggest the distorted child's-eye view of the universe Pip carries with him into maturity.

In fact, the whole unhappy course of Pip's later life is determined by adult whims or fancies which cause him to lose his moral and intellectual balance. The chief instances of this syndrome are Miss Havishman's manipulation of him as Estella's plaything and Provis's transformation of him into a "gentleman." The exposure to Satis House and Estella and later the bequest of "great expectations" encourage Pip to live in a world of illusion.

However, Pip is more than the pathetic victim of external forces and stratagems. From the beginning, it is clear that there is a weakness in his character, a narcissism which makes him quick to forget the homely virtues and truths represented by Joe Gargery and Biddy. His wish to cast off his true friends suggests his self-aggrandizing pride; he rejects the concrete pleasures of the forge for the inflated emptiness of his "expectations." Thus, in the second stage of Pip's development, his obsession with Estella and with his own imagined role as her intended shut out both the genuine claim Joe and Biddy have on him and the possibility of a realistic and meaningful life for himself. His life is a waiting game given over to fantasy and endless anticipation.

Still, Pip's rejection of Joe as a social embarrassment in Part II is counter-balanced by his generous backing of Herbert Pocket's expectations. This be-nevolent relationship anticipates the moral regeneration of Part II, when, with his false self-image shattered, Pip begins to grope toward true emotional maturity. Despite his abhorrence of Magwitch, he stands by him, protecting the life of the man who gave him his own life as a gentleman. Despite his recognition of Miss Havisham's deceit, he is kind to her in her madness and refuses to take the conscience money she offers him. Despite his own bitter disappointment, he keeps Estella's best interests at heart, urging her to accept a worthier man than Bentley Drummle as her husband. Finally, he recognizes the true value of Joe's and Biddy's friendship and love, exchanging "portable property" for the more genuine riches of fellow feeling.

Throughout the novel, Pip displays a mixture of qualities; he is capable of both warm affection and the most unfeeling cruelty. In general, he moves from relative innocence to base self-absorption and finally to true self-recognition. Dickens retains the reader's sympathies for Pip, even· at Pip's worst moments, through a narrative device which may be called moral retrospective. Thus the Pip who speaks to the reader is, from the outset, the mature adult who has already passed through the refining fires of experience described in the novel. At every point, he is able to judge and interpret his own activities in the light of his later, greater wisdom. In a sense, there are two Pips, one who acts and suffers and another who can stand back and assess.

One instance of this type of moral judgment occurs when Pip, after an emotional interview with Joe in town, goes to Miss Havisham's, where he sees Estella for the first time as an adult. Caught up in his infatuation, he neglects to make his intended visit to Joe. The chapter concludes:

Ah me! I thought those were high and great emotions. But I never thought there was anything low and small in my keeping away from Joe, because I knew she would be contemptuous of him. It was but a day gone, and Joe had brought the tears into my eyes; they had soon dried, God forgive me! soon dried. (Chap. 29)

Thus, the first-person narration draws the reader into an identification with Pip, flawed though he may be. The book has a confessional quality; it is a kind of moral fable told by a young man who has sinned, done penance, and matured in the process.

16.2   There are many unforgettable characters in *Great Expectations*, including minor ones such as Wemmick, Mr. Pumblechook, Mr. Wopsle, the Pocket family, and Bentley Drummle. Examine Dickens's techniques of delineating subsidiary characters and discuss their function in the novel.

Answer   To bring his crowded canvas to life, Dickens uses the art of caricature, broadly sketching the outlines of the minor figures by means of a variety of descriptive techniques. Perhaps the chief techniques are naming and, to a lesser extent, epithet. Using names that are idiosyncratic and aurally evocative, Dickens in a single stroke suggests both the prevailing traits and the physical appearance of characters.

For example, the name "Pumblechook" evokes, in itself, the portrait of a large, overbearing man who mumbles, fumbles, pummels, chokes, and shakes. The self-importance of this pretended benefactor is implied in his polysyllabic, consonantal name. Similarly, the idea of whimsicality is suggested in the name "Wemmick," the name "Wopsle" calls to mind foppishness and foolishness, and the "Pockets" constitute a whole family of absentminded, nearly useless accessories, much like decorative pockets on a garment. (The names of the major characters, too, point out both physical attributes and psychological tendencies. "Miss Havisham" contains the word "sham"; "Estella" represents the cold, unreachable star; "Jaggers" symbolizes the cutting edge of legal manipulation; and "Pip" suggests baby talk and "pipsqueak.")

Epithets, too, play an important role in defining characters. Thus, Bentley Drummle is characterized not only by his name, with its connotations of humdrum and dumb, but by Jagger's evocative description of him as the "Spider." Epithets also distinguish between the two Wemmicks. The Walworth Wemmick is a man of simple domestic life, while the Little Britain Wemmick is a man of sharp business acumen.

Dickens also uses other techniques to pinpoint his characters' obsessions and habits. Repeated physical gestures become a kind of shorthand for the whole person, for example, Mr. Pocket's habit of lifting himself up by the hair and Mr. Pumblechook's mechanical handshakes. Verbal tag lines also identify character through repetition: Mr. Wemmick's preoccupation with "portable property" and Joe's introductory "What I meantersay" underline the former's dry common sense and the latter's poignant wish to express his feelings. Props, too, serve to characterize their possessors, with Miss Havisham's dreadful bridal array; Mr. Wemmick's castle, moat, and cannon; Mr. Jaggers's death masks; and Magwitch's file constituting expressive extensions of the characters themselves.

Though the minor characters are minor precisely because they sound only a single note and so lack the complexities of the central characters, Dickens individualizes his entire cast through his use of these descriptive techniques.

16.3 The plot of *Great Expectations* is highly melodramatic; it is littered with buried secrets and interwoven pasts and is punctuated by coincidences and climactic revelations. Discuss Dickens's conception of life as presented in this narrative.

Answer Dickens's plot displays his virtuoso skill in fashioning links among the lives of his characters. Miss Havisham and Magwitch both share Jaggers as their lawyer, a circumstance which leads Pip to believe that the powerful heiress rather than the degenerate convict is the source of his "great expectations." Compeyson is both Miss Havisham's former lover and Magwitch's partner in crime. Magwitch is not only Pip's benefactor but Estella's father; Molly is not only Jagger's serving woman but Estella's mother. The list could go on, extending to Orlick and Wopsle (who pop up in a variety of unlikely places) and the Pocket family (who have connections with both Miss Havisham and Pip).

This interweaving of lives creates a sense of some kind of order or pattern in experience. In his use of coincidence, Dickens points to fate as an agent in human affairs that imbues even the most seemingly random meeting with significance. The implication seems to be that life has a meaning, that even chance experiences can be part of the process of creating a moral existence founded on self-understanding. Dickens's conception of fate furthermore contains an element of psychological determinism, with the passions of individuals helping to shape the design of existence. Miss Havisham's bitter hatred, Magwitch's gratitude mixed with his obsessive desire to "own" a gentleman, Estella's conditioned heartlessness, and Pip's narcissism and ambition all contribute to the patterned unfolding of Pip's story.

The sense that life is forged out of significant links, moments of time which create a progression shaped by destiny, appears in Pip's reflection early in the novel, following his first visit to Satis House:

That was a memorable day to me, for it made great changes in me. But it is the same with any life. Imagine one selected day struck out of it, and think how different its course would have been. Pause you who read this, and think for a moment of the long chain of iron or gold, of thorns or flowers, that would never have bound you, but for the formation of the first link on one memorable day. (Chap. 9)

The interplay between external event and inner response which informs the patterns of life is emphasized through the plot's reliance on fateful turning points and dramatic revelations. The melodramatic plot as a whole suggests the possibility of inner growth as the hero meets the truth of his situation in a series of climactic interviews. Thus, Dickens depicts order and meaning developing out of the characters' ability to interpret and understand the pattern of the events of their lives.

16.4 *Great Expectations* has two endings, one Dickens's original version, the other written on the advice of his friend Bulwer-Lytton, who suggested that Dickens's first ending would be unsatisfactory to the novelist's large reading public. Which ending is better? Why?

Answer Dickens's original ending seems more appropriate to the tone which pervades *Great Expectations*. Like many of Dickens's later works, the novel paints a somber view of life as a series of fateful steps which cannot be retraced. The early love that Pip feels for Estella grows out of his narcissistic yearnings rather than a genuine sympathy of minds. Given his failure to understand Estella's character as fashioned by Miss Havisham, he is fated to disappointment and misery. The baseless nature of his passion means that he has lost her before he ever tries to win her. Thus, the conclusion of the novel is in keeping with the hard lesson of Pip's life: If one lives on appearances, on "expectations," one drains reality of all substance.

This theme of expectations is central to the book; Pip is trapped by his illusions for the first two-thirds of the novel and, in his relationship with Estella, is willfully self-destructive. The fact that we see Pip's slow development beyond this impasse makes Estella's similar reformation, so rapidly summarized in the final paragraphs of the book, believable. However, to assume that they can now live "happily ever after" would violate the major premises of the book: that some mistakes are irrevocable and that most gains in life come in the form of deeper understanding rather than material rewards. Thus, in the last line of the first ending of *Great Expectations*, Dickens fittingly places his emphasis on the mature understanding that both Pip and Estella have achieved through suffering:

> I was very glad afterwards to have had the interview; for, in her face and in her voice, and in her touch, she gave me the assurance that suffering had been stronger than Miss Havisham's teaching, and had given her a heart to understand what my heart used to be. (Chap. 59)

Yet it can be argued that the second ending is superior to the first in terms of providing a true resolution to the romantic tension in the novel. From the opening chapters, Pip is obsessed with Estella as the symbol of all his aspirations and longings. That he should win her in the end may seem a fitting consequence of the long learning process he undergoes in the novel. He cannot possess her when both are bound by the distorted code of Satis House. However, both Pip and Estella free themselves from narcissistic illusions through their harsh experiences of living. They are "re-formed" so that they match perfectly in the end.

Furthermore, there is evidence in the novel to suggest that Dickens may have always planned a happy conclusion for the pair, for at several points he indicates Estella's appreciation of Pip as different from her assorted "victims." The most striking of these passages occurs at the assembly ball at Richmond, when Pip questions her about her entrapment of Bentley Drummle: "Do you deceive and entrap him, Estella?" "Yes, and many others—all of them but you" (Chap. 38).

It might be argued that the second ending is inflated, romantic, and unrealistic. That both Estella and Pip happen by the ruins of Satis House on the same night after a lapse of eleven years is highly coincidental. However, throughout the book, Dickens has been playing with the theme of coincidence, those chance occurrences which shape a life. This final, seemingly random meeting completes a hidden design buried beneath the somber events of Pip's life. The union with Estella is not a part of Miss Havisham's manipulative vengeance but a true intersection of two lives which have, at last, through the processes of time and experience, come together.

A case can be made, then, for either ending. In both, Pip appears as a mature adult who has insight into himself and Estella. This quality of sympathetic, mutual understanding permeates both versions.

However, despite certain tonal and even verbal similarities, the two scenes remain widely different. The very full descriptive rendering of a romantic tête-à-tête in a secluded moonlit garden suggests a more optimistic view of life's possibilities than the terse postscript recounting a random meeting on a city street, which implies that happy endings are hard to come by. Bulwer-Lytton's advice to Dickens was based primarily on the Victorian public's demand for happy endings. It would be easy to say that Dickens merely succumbed to commercial pressure, but he did it with such artistry that the revised ending can be seen as an integral part of the fabric of the novel.

The revised ending relies heavily on atmospheric detail. In describing the ruined building, the silvery moonlight, and the new ivy growing out of old stoves, Dickens evokes a sense of the relationship between past and present. Furthermore, the scene dramatizes the two kinds of recognitions which occur: the physical presence and the emotional apprehension of change. All these factors contribute to the fullness and fitness of this conclusion.

In contrast, the original ending is far more prosaic and somber in tone. Dickens summarizes the major events in Estella's life and condenses the final scene to a single significant line of dialogue. Through this very different rhetorical technique, he achieves a similar sense of proper closure. There is the same sense of change, but the effect is one of restraint and irrevocable loss.

A reader may prefer one ending or the other on the basis of personal taste and temperament. However, from a critical point of view, it must be conceded that this is a rare instance in which almost opposite endings for a book have equal artistic merit.

Hard Times

16.5   There are three distinct "worlds" in Hard Times, each associated with a particular setting and group of characters. Identify each of these worlds. Which of them, if any, does Dickens seem to view as the ideal society?

Answer   Hard Times can be seen as a universe which holds within its bounds three well-defined views of the world. The first is represented by the Gradgrind school of utilitarianism, the second by the dissatisfaction of the workers in Coketown, and the third by the theory of fancy advocated by Sleary.

The flaws in the Gradgrind view of the world are obvious from the opening chapter. The as yet unidentified advocate of a "factual" view of life speaks in a schoolroom pictured as a vault. The speaker himself is dry and inflexible, with eyes that are cellared in two black caves. The introduction of young Tom, the repressed Louisa, and the entire Gradgrind household reveals to the reader the malignant results of the utilitarian system. Mrs. Gradgrind, too, is at least half dead at the beginning of the novel.

Mr. Bounderby and Mrs. Sparsit add still another dimension to this world of hard "facts." The "bully of humility" and his personal Uriah Heep suggest its falseness and cruelty. Upon perceiving Bounderby's interest in Louisa, the reader is almost forced to cringe for her predicament.

The world of the workers of Coketown intersects the world of hard facts, but there are subtle differences between the two. The workers do not seem as emotionally repressed as the young Gradgrinds. Stephen Blackpool and his fellow "hands" are bound by a form of repression which is symptomatic of an industrial society, and their mournful condition has a sound arithmetic and economic basis. The problems in Coketown reflect the problems of the entire working class.

The antithesis to both the utilitarian world and the industrial world can be found in the world of Sleary's circus. Towards the end of Chapter 6, Sleary astounds Gradgrind and Bounderby with his philosophy that "people must be amuthed." His theory of fancy provides the novel with its counternote and completes the fact versus fancy motif which dominates the novel. But a close study of the text will show that this world, too, has its drawbacks. Sleary is plagued by asthma, Cupid is only half a man, and Sissy's father, unable to cope with his failure as a clown, deserts his daughter. Despite Sissy's protestations to the contrary, her father has fled from what clearly appears to be the rigors of circus life. Though Cupid correctly sees that Thomas Gradgrind is walking on a figurative "tight-jeff," Cupid's compound performs nightly on a literal rope. This is not to suggest that Dickens does not find the world of fancy far more attractive than the world of fact, but there is another alternative: a mixture of the best features of both fact and fancy. This is the solution at which Sissy Jupe appears to arrive. Though she is raised in the circus community, she honors her father's wish that she pursue an education, not an apprenticeship. Ultimately, she leaves Sleary's community and joins the Gradgrind household, thus combining her two lifestyles.

16.6 Discuss the relationship between Stephen Blackpool and Louisa Gradgrind.

Answer   Stephen Blackpool and Louisa Gradgrind, the doomed "heroes" of the novel, are both victims of their circumstances. Stephen, Dickens's model of the industrial worker, is clearly a martyr to the injustices of that system. He is preyed upon by both the utilitarian and the economic-industrial universe and is obvious in his unsuccessful attempt to obtain a divorce. For Stephen there is "no way out."

Louisa is, in a sense, the upper-class counterpart to Blackpool. Both are sacrificed to the system. Both are misunderstood by their masters. Stephen is aware of this instinctive bond and addresses himself to Louisa while in Bounderby's house. Louisa, in turn, recognizes Stephen's plight and later says to Rachel:

> Then by the prejudices of his own class, and by the prejudices of the other, he is sacrificed alike? Are the two so deeply separated in this town, that there is no place whatever for an honest workman between them? (Book II, Chap. 6)

Moreover, Louisa shares Stephen's role as an outsider. Estranged from her own world, she retreats into herself. Helped by Tom, James Harthouse discovers Louisa's unrest and encourages her to reveal her inner self to him. But because Harthouse's maneuvers are calculated, the bonds he creates between them are artificial.

Ultimately, both Stephen and Louisa must be sacrificed to the universe of *Hard Times*. Following Louisa's marriage to Bounderby, young Tom observes, "Time's Up," and it is precisely the notion of time as an instrument of punishment that works to seal both Stephen's fate and Louisa's. The major realizations of the characters are arrived at when it is, simply, too late. Stephen must descend into the Old Hell shaft in order to be able to reemerge as a martyr to the masses of Coketown. Louisa, though allowed to escape from Bounderby's evil, may neither marry nor bear children, thus enduring a kind of figurative death.

16.7   In an article called "Lancashire Witchcraft" published February 4, 1854, Dickens wrote:

> Mighty indeed are the dealings of these cotton monarchs. Complicated are their transactions; numberless the interests they affect; and far away

and strange the lands they give vitality to, the mouths they feed, the forms they clothe.

Given this view of the industrial magnate, discuss Dickens's attitude toward industrialism.

Answer   Dickens expresses mixed feelings about industrialism and industrial revolt. Though he is opposed to the injustices of the masters of labor represented by Bounderby in *Hard Times*, he also sees trade unions as a threat to individuality. This becomes clear in his portrayal of Stephen Blackpool. Blackpool is a member of the oppressed class and is subjected to Bounderby's unfair treatment of the workers, yet he refuses to go along with the strike because of a mysterious pledge he once made to Rachel. Even after she releases him from that pledge, Stephen remains unwilling to break his promise. In an effort to give credence to this refusal, Dickens paints a very unflattering picture of the strike leader, the outside agitator, Slackbridge. The rhetoric used by Slackbridge is similar to that used by Thomas Grandgrind in the opening chapter and becomes, in that sense, the gospel of the striking workers:

> Oh my friends, the down-trodden operatives of Coketown! Oh my friends
> and fellow country-men, the slaves of an ironhanded and a grinding
> despotism! Oh my friends and fellow-sufferers, and fellow-workmen, and
> fellow-men! (Book 2, Chap. 4)

Though his sentiment is avowedly proworker, Slackbridge becomes, for Dickens, as much an exploiter of the working classes as Bounderby. And since both the Slackbridges and the Bounderbys of the world fail to solve the problems created by industrialization, Dickens attempts to save the proletariat through his characterization of Stephen.

Stephen can be seen to represent Dickens's personal view of industrialism. In that view, the problems of the economic system are not a direct result of that system but are caused instead by a moral failure in the masters; they must learn, simply, to be kinder and more fair to the workers. As Stephen tells Bounderby:

> Sir, I canna, wi' my little learning an my common way, tell the genelman
> what will better aw this—though some working man o' this town could,
> above my powers—but I can tell him what I know will never do't. The
> strong hand will never do't. Victory and triumph will never do't. (Book
> 2, Chap. 5)

It is clear, then, that the system lacks morality, precisely that antiutilitarian morality which is fundamental to *Hard Times*. The radicalism in the novel calls not merely for economic changes but for the more permanent changes that Dickens advocates throughout all his novels, changes in people themselves.

L.R.

SUGGESTED READINGS

Butt, Jay, and K. Tillotson, *Dickens at Work* (1957).
Johnson, Edgar, *Charles Dickens: His Tragedy and Triumph* (1952).
Marcus, Steven, *Dickens from Pickwick to Dombey* (1965).
Miller, J. Hillis, *Charles Dickens: The World of His Novels* (1958).

ANTHONY TROLLOPE

C H R O N O L O G Y

1815	Born in Bloomsbury, London, the fourth son of Thomas Anthony Trollope, an irascible chancery lawyer from New College, Oxford, and Frances Milton Trollope, a highly successful novelist and writer of travel books.
1816	Family moves to a country house called Julians near Harrow, on inheritance expectations from Thomas's uncle which never materialize. Thomas's temper alienates clients until his business drops off almost to nothing.
1822	Becomes a day boy at Harrow School, where life is a daily "purgatory." He is the dunce of the class, slovenly in dress and physically dirty. The headmaster flogs him often.
1825	Transfers to Arthur Drury's private school at Sunbury, where he is unjustly blamed for some minor misdemeanor.
1827	Goes to his father's old school, Winchester, where his older brother, Thomas, as prefect, continues the mistreatment. His mother goes to America with socialite Frances Wright and painter Auguste Hervieu to build a bazaar in Cincinnati for the sale of English goods. The bazaar, an architectural horror, is built, but the business fails, precipitating the financial ruin of the family.
1830	Returns to Harrow in the spring because of low finances. A large, uncouth, ill-clad boy, he feels like an unhappy outcast among the aristocrats. His schoolmates taunt him for his poverty; his tutor takes him on without a fee but embarrasses him by telling everyone about this.

1832	His mother, Frances, supports the family with publication of her popular book *Domestic Manners of the Americans*, a satiric novel widely disliked in America.
1834	Unable to win a university scholarship, Trollope moves with his family to Bruges, Belgium, and becomes an usher in a school, hoping to learn enough French and German to accept a promised commission in the Austrian cavalry.
1834–1841	Becomes a junior clerk in the general post office, London, at £90 a year. Lonely years with few friends; gains reputation for insubordination. His father dies in Bruges (1835); his older brother, Henry, and his younger sister, Emily, die there the following year.
1841–1845	Transfers to Banagher, Ireland, as deputy postal surveyor, and finds a freer, happier outdoor life in fox hunting. Begins writing novels. Marries Rose Heseltine, daughter of a Rotherham bank manager (1844).
1845–1859	Transfers to Mallow, Ireland, with a promotion; then goes on postal missions to the west of England in 1851, to Belfast in 1853, to Donnybrook near Dublin in 1854, and to Egypt, Scotland, and the West Indies in 1858–1859. Settles at Waltham Cross near London as surveyor general of the post office at £800 a year.
1847–1848	Publishes his first novel, *The Macdermots of Ballycloran*, in which he tries to discover the real reasons for Irish discontent, and *The Kellys and the O'Kellys*, another political novel. Neither does well.
1855–1867	Publishes his most universally popular books, the six novels known as the Barset chronicles, set in the imaginary county of Barset: *The Warden* (1855), first in the series, a psychological study of the warden in a hospital for old men; *Barchester Towers* (1857); *Doctor Thorne* (1858), a depiction of a social caste system based on landed property; *Framley Parsonage* (1861), serialized first in Thackeray's *Cornhill Magazine*; *The Small House at Allington* (1864), the least successful of the Barset novels; and *The Last Chronicle of Barset* (1867), longest and most panoramic in scope, unique for the nearly tragic stature of its most memorable character, Mr. Crawley, the scholarly and desperately poor curate of a poor parish. During this period, Trollope writes very methodically 1000 words an hour every morning from 5:30 to 8:30 before going to work at the post office.
1865–1880	Publishes a second series of novels, the political novels, less witty and humorous but more difficult and complex than the Barset series. These novels, covering the lives of the Plantagenet Palliser family, include *Can You Forgive Her?* (1865), *Phineas Finn* (1869), *Ralph the Heir* (1871), *The*

Eustace Diamonds (1873), *Phineas Redux* (1874), *The Prime Minister* (1876), and *The Duke's Children* (1880). They depict the inner political workings of the House of Commons, the political clubs, and the social entertainments of the great political hostesses.

1868   Resigns from the civil service and stands as the Liberal party candidate for Beverley in the House of Commons.

1869–   Last and in some ways most intriguing phase of his writing career. Publishes
1883   twenty-three more novels, generally psychological and political, his autobiography, and other miscellaneous writings. Among the more significant novels are *He Knew He Was Right* (1869), a sophisticated portrayal of a rich man's jealous obsession with his innocent wife, and *The Eustace Diamonds* (1873), a sensitive study of the effect of money on sexual relationships.

1875   Travels to Australia to visit his second son, who is a sheep rancher there.

1882   After years of depression and seclusion in a Sussex village, dies in London, stricken by paralysis at an evening party at his brother-in-law's. He is buried in Kensal Green Cemetery.

1883   *Autobiography* is published posthumously, along with two novels: *The Landleaguers* and *Mr. Scarborough's Family.*

ESSAY QUESTIONS WITH ANSWERS

The Warden

17.1 Despite its being set in a small ecclesiastical community, *The Warden* is in many ways as political a novel as any in Trollope's parliamentary series. Discuss the political undercurrents in *The Warden*.

Answer *The Warden* is concerned with the most fundamental of political issues, power. The small clerical community at Barchester has a clearly defined pecking order, with Archdeacon Grantly acting as a dictator over not only the minor canons but even his father, the bishop. For Grantly, both the church's power and his own are at stake in the contest over Hiram's Hospital. John Bold's apparently disinterested crusade on behalf of the pensioners (or "bedesmen") masks an equally self-aggrandizing ambition. Although both Grantly and Bold are above motives of personal gain, the stake for each is the sense of victory and power.

This desire for power characterizes a host of lesser characters as well. Mrs. Grantly's blunt scoldings in the bedroom represent the exercise of her wifely prerogative in the domestic "dictatorship" at Plumstead Episcopi. The mild Eleanor Harding exerts her own powers to alter John Bold's schemes against her father. And the infighting among the twelve old men at the hospital constitutes a political campaign for power between the rebel forces of Abel Handy and the conservative party of Bunce.

More broadly, the entire world of *The Warden* is founded on the political machinations of power-hungry men and institutions. For example, Tom Towers of *The Jupiter* embodies the tremendous influence and propagandizing tendencies of the popular press. Personally ignorant of the inhabitants of Barset, he viciously smears the Warden's name, ostensibly in the interests of justice but actually to gratify his own pride. "It is probable," Trollope says, "that Tom Towers considered himself the most powerful man in Europe; and so he walked on from day to day, studiously striving to look a man, but knowing within his breast that he was a god" (Chap. 14).

Another institution which comes under Trollope's scrutiny is the law, as symbolized by the attorney general Sir Abraham Haphazard. The Warden's moral dilemma, which forms the core of the book—his confusion between his duty to the church and his duty to the poor—entirely escapes Sir Abraham's attention: "It was very clear that to Sir Abraham, the justice of the old men's claim or the justice of Mr. Harding's defense were ideas that had never presented themselves. . . . Success was his objective, and he was generally successful" (Chap. 8). The other lawyers brought into the case—Finney on the one side, Cox and Cummington on the other—are depicted as self-serving, small-minded men, concerned, like Sir Abraham, only with victory.

It is significant that each of these political crusaders, from Dr. Grantly down to Abel Handy, has his own inflated rhetorical style for describing his view of the situation. The eloquent, often pompous language of the combatants suggests a political arena in which orators rise for debate. In contrast, the Reverend Septimus Harding is almost inarticulate, playing his imaginary cello rather than offering lofty sentiments. As an apolitical character in a highly political world, he is doomed to become the pawn of his peers.

17.2 As the narrator, Trollope often wears the mask of a personal friend and guide to the reader. Select several narrative intrusions in the novel and analyze their effect on *The Warden* as a whole.

Answer Trollope's presence as the teller of the tale is highly visible at many points in the novel. He freely uses the first person in presenting his views of the characters and their actions and just as freely digresses from the story to offer small essays on journalism, law, religion, politics, art, literature, and human nature. His intrusions take several characteristic forms: the autobiographical aside, which suggests his personal relationship with and definite opinions about the characters; the direct address to the reader, which suggests his personal relationship with the audience; and the mock-heroic passage, which suggests his affectionately satiric attitude toward social life and institutions. Through these interruptions of the narrative, Trollope reaches out to the reader, inviting identification with his own judgments on and attitudes toward the fictional world of the novel.

An example of this autobiographical intrusion occurs in Chapter 8, "Plumstead Episcopi," where Trollope as narrator elaborates on his own reactions to the household. After a lengthy and pointed description of its members and its daily fare, he underlines his distaste for the establishment with a direct statement: "And yet I have never found the rectory a pleasant place. . . ." In the next paragraph, the use of the first person is frequent as the narrator catalogues the history of his unpleasant relations with the Grantly children. In this way, the narrator weaves himself into the fiction he is creating, heightening its verisimilitude by making himself an eyewitness.

The second kind of aside involves the novelist confiding the problems of his craft to the reader. Writing of Eleanor's plan to beseech Bold on bended knee, he pauses to comment on his audience's probable reaction to the coming episode: "And now I own I have fears for my heroine; not as to the upshot of her mission— . . . but as to the amount of sympathy she may receive from those of her own sex." (Chap. 11) This blends into a discussion of female readers and finally a direct address to them: "Dear ladies, you are right as to your appreciation of the circumstances, but very wrong as to Miss Harding's character" (Chap. 11). As the all-knowing author who pronounces on what will happen to Eleanor and what is in her mind, Trollope is playing with the idea of fictional illusion. He creates the impression of a real woman with an independent life and at the same time partially undercuts the reality of his creation by emphasizing his own role as the author.

A third kind of intrusion is the exclamatory, inflated, mock-heroic set piece describing an event such as the Warden's tea party or an institution such as the newspaper *The Jupiter*. Here the narrator puts a screen of rhetoric between the reader and the scene being described, pointedly suggesting the discrepancy between reality and illusion. In Chapter 14, "Mount Olympus," Trollope pauses after his epic eulogy of the newspaper to remark, "There are those who doubt the *Jupiter*. They live and breathe the upper air, walking here unscathed, though scorned,—men, born of British mothers and nursed on English milk, who scruple not to say that Mount Olympus has its price, that Tom Towers can be bought for gold!" A passage such as this conveys in a witty and biting manner the author's view of Towers as a fraud and hypocrite.

All the authorial intrusions exert a centrifugal pull on the narrative, since they do not contribute directly to the unfolding story. However, they do clearly communicate a view of the fictional world and strengthen the reader's relationship to that world. Thus, Trollope's created persona as narrator is not merely the medium of the novel but part of its message as well.

17.3   One of the dominant themes of *The Warden* is love: between parent and child, between man and woman, and between the individual and humankind. Comment on Trollope's handling of this theme.

Answer   Trollope handles the theme of love in *The Warden* in two ways: He satirizes marital and romantic love, and he celebrates filial and fraternal love. The chief instance of satire occurs in the treatment of the relationship between Dr. and Mrs. Grantly, in which the autocratic husband receives the blunt advice of his apparently submissive wife in the privacy of their bedroom. This antiromantic view of marriage is one means Trollope uses in exposing the archdeacon's inflated pretensions. Similarly, the author's tongue-in-cheek presentation of the courtship between Eleanor Harding and John Bold makes Bold's radical ideals seem insubstantial and self-aggrandizing. What is at issue in the lovers' conference over the fate of the Warden and Hiram's Hospital is, in fact, a kiss and a pledge.

The treatment of the parent-child relationship is very different; Trollope paints the filial tie as the most tender and meaningful of bonds. In Chapter 10, "Tribulation," he emphasizes the mutual tears and embraces of Reverend Harding and Eleanor as they comfort each other in the midst of their crisis: "Mr. Harding could not well speak now, for the warm tears were running down his cheeks like rain in May, but he held his child close to his heart, and squeezed her hands as a lover might, and she kissed his forehead and his wet cheeks, and lay upon his bosom, and comforted him as a woman only can do."

The tenderness between father and daughter in this scene is almost sexual, and it suggests a kind of swooning into will-less passion. It is against the world of power and of mean, egotistical motives that these instances of love are portrayed.

Domestic values and the bonds of love are demonstrated in the initial relationship between the Warden and the twelve bedesmen of Hiram's Hospital. An almost fraternal order exists among these men, with Harding as the cohesive force which binds the brethren together. The telling scene in which the Warden plays his cello before the assembled group symbolizes the harmony prevailing at the hospital before the self-righteous, zealous interference of John Bold. In insisting on an abstract notion of justice, Bold destroys the concrete reality of love which envelops the Warden and his men.

The pathos which emerges at certain moments in the novel represents a shift from the generally prevalent satirical tone. In presenting ideal images of love, Trollope mitigates the skepticism of *The Warden* as a whole. If good and evil are often inextricable, and human nature is regrettably imperfect, nonetheless there are connections which survive unsullied. Harding's attachments to his daughter and his friend the bishop provide him with some compensation for the cruelty of his encounter with the loveless world of lawyers and journalists.

17.4 There are three major characters in *The Warden*: Septimus Harding, John Bold, and Theophilus Grantly. Each man represents a distinct point of view on the moral dilemma of the Warden's sinecure. Analyze this triad, commenting on their individual characteristics and their relationships with each other.

Answer The novel begins almost as a character study, with the opening chapters devoted to rounded sketches of the three men whose actions and reactions constitute the slender plot. The first chapter, "Hiram's Hospital," delineates the personality and history of the Warden himself. Harding is a man eminently suited to his post at the hospital. He is peace-loving, kindly, unworldly, and generous as well as indolent, impractical, and weak. His virtues contribute to his important role as father and mentor of the pensioners, while his failings make him a ready pawn for Grantly and an easy target for Bold. The inner conflict between the Warden's personal kindness and his confused sense of what is right is exploited by the stronger men who surround him. Caught between his duty to the church and his duty to the poor, he takes refuge in music, playing on an imaginary cello as he miserably debates his moral dilemma with his peers and advisers.

Chief among his advisers is Dr. Grantly, the archdeacon of Barchester, who is also the bishop's son and the Warden's son-in-law. Trollope paints Grantly in vivid colors as a tower of self-righteousness, devoid of the internal conflicts which both weaken and humanize the Warden. "His great fault," Trollope explains, "is an overbearing assurance of the virtues and claims of his order, and his great foible is an equally strong confidence in the dignity of his own manner and the eloquency of his own words" (Chap. 2). In his dominant role in the parish, Grantly is part villain, part comic caricature. Insensitive to the moral qualms of the Warden, he concentrates on expediency, defending the rights of the church and insisting on the subtleties of the law.

In contrast, John Bold is obsessed with morality. Incapable of assessing the human complexities of the problem, including the values of tradition and personal relationship, he insists on an abstract idea of justice. Though his views are opposite to Grantly's, he is allied to his enemy in temperament, for he, too, is self-righteous and zealous. Trollope combines admiration with criticism in his assessment of "the Barchester Reformer" to create a three-dimensional portrait:

> Bold is thoroughly sincere in his patriotic endeavors to mend mankind,
> . . . but I fear that he is too much imbued with the idea that he has a
> special mission for reforming. It would be well if one so young had a
> little more diffidence himself, and more trust in the honest purposes of
> others—(Chap. 2)

Each of the three protagonists of *The Warden* demonstrates many shadings
and ambiguities of character. None is entirely a hero, none a black-dyed villain.
Interestingly, the man seemingly least likely to assume a heroic stance is the
one who does. In resigning his post, the Warden makes a personal moral choice
which has nothing to do with Grantly's sense of divine right and Bold's zeal for
social justice. But even this choice is not without irony, for in being true to
himself the Warden abandons the bedesmen to the impersonal administration
of indifferent officials.

L.R.

SUGGESTED READINGS

Cockshut, A. O., *Anthony Trollope: A Critical Study* (1955).
Praz, Mario, "Anthony Trollope," in *The Hero in Eclipse in Victorian Fiction* (1956).
Sadleir, Michael, *Trollope: A Commentary* (1961).

CHARLOTTE BRONTË

C H R O N O L O G Y

1816	Born at Thornton, Yorkshire, the third daughter of Patrick Brontë, a poor Irishman who, aided by Wesleyan Methodists, had attended St. John's College, Cambridge, and become curate at Thornton, and Maria Branwell Brontë.
1820	Patrick Brontë becomes rector of Haworth and moves his family there.
1821	Maria Brontë dies of cancer; her sister, Elizabeth Branwell, moves in with the family.
1824	Patrick Brontë sends his two oldest daughters, Elizabeth and Maria, to school at Wakefield, then transfers them to the Clergy Daughters' School at Cowan Bridge, Lancashire. Charlotte and Emily join them at this infamous school portrayed in *Jane Eyre*. Elizabeth and Maria sicken and go home to die of consumption.
1825–1831	Charlotte and Emily return home. To amuse themselves, they invent the imaginary Kingdom of Angria, about which they write thousands of pages in miniature books with tiny writing. Their brother, Branwell (born 1817), and their youngest sister, Anne (born 1820), join them in the elaboration of these romantic sagas, which occupy the girls well into their twenties. These writings serve as the girls' writing apprenticeship, in which they work out many of the characters, dramatic conflicts, and themes that later appear in their novels.

1831	Charlotte attends Miss Wooler's school at Roe Head, near Huddersfield. Becomes friend of Mary Taylor and Ellen Nussey.
1832	Returns home to teach her sisters. All four study, write, and play together.
1835	Returns to Roe Head as a teacher to make money for her family, especially for Branwell, who wants to study art.
1838	Resigns her position and goes home to Haworth.
1839	Rejects marriage proposal from the Reverend Henry Nussey, Ellen's brother, and also proposal from another young clergyman.
1842–1843	Charlotte and Emily go to Brussels to study French and German at the Pensionnat Heger. Both return home when their aunt, Miss Branwell, dies and leaves each niece and nephew a small sum. Charlotte goes back to Brussels alone but is lonely and depressed. She forms an attachment to Constantin Heger, the head of the school, whose stimulating and sophisticated mind appeals to her. He injures her feelings when he apparently mistakes her devotion for love. Madame Heger's jealousy forces her to leave.
1844	Tries to start a school at the Haworth parsonage, but no pupils come.
1845	Branwell is fired as tutor for making love to his employer's wife; he spends three years at home drinking, taking drugs, and otherwise indulging himself until he dies of his excesses.
1846	Charlotte, Emily, and Anne publish at their own expense a joint volume of *Poems by Currer, Ellis, and Acton Bell*, using pseudonyms to avoid prejudice against women poets. They sell only two copies. Charlotte's novel *The Professor* is turned down by publishers Smith, Elder, and Co. She begins *Jane Eyre* while taking care of her father after an eye operation in Manchester.
1847	Publishes *Jane Eyre*, an impassioned portrait of an intelligent and sensitive woman. It is an immediate success.
1848	Double tragedy: deaths of Branwell and Emily. Anne catches consumption (tuberculosis) from Emily. Charlotte interrupts her work on new novel, *Shirley*, to nurse Anne.
1849	Anne dies of consumption. Charlotte completes *Shirley*, a regional novel with sharp, incisive portraits of local color and a shrewd feminism.
1841	Travels to London three times as guest of her publisher; meets Thackeray; sits for a portrait by Richmond. Travels to the Lake Country, to Scotland, and to Manchester, where she visits Elizabeth Gaskell, her future biographer. Turns down another proposal, this time from James Taylor, a member of her publishing house.

1853   Publishes *Villette*, a novel set in Brussels.

1854   Marries her fourth suitor, Arthur Bell Nichols, her father's curate, who does not share her intellectual interests but who makes her happy. They honeymoon in Ireland and then return to Haworth. Begins but does not finish a novel, *Emma*.

1855   Dies in pregnancy and is buried beside her mother, brother, and four sisters at the Haworth parsonage, which has now become a place of pilgrimage and a Brontë museum.

1857   Her previously rejected novel *The Professor* is published posthumously; it is another novel based on her Brussels experience.

ESSAY QUESTIONS WITH ANSWERS

Jane Eyre

18.1 *Jane Eyre* is a *Bildungsroman*, documenting a young woman's growth to maturity. An important part of Jane's education is the development of her sense of spiritual mission. Discuss the varieties of religious belief that Jane encounters and show how these influence her development.

Answer In almost every episode of the novel, Jane encounters individuals who formally espouse religious doctrines. All contribute to the shaping of Jane's personal code of belief and, in a larger sense, her character. In most cases, Jane sharpens and defines her own views against the opposing philosophies of harsh or misguided zealots.

The most negative of Jane's religious experiences is her cruel indoctrination by Mr. Brocklehurst. In their first interview at Gateshead Hall, he threatens her with the fate of naughty girls, "a pitful of fire" where the wicked burn forever. At Lowood, his fire-and-brimstone theology underlies the institutionalized sadism and cruel discipline of the charity school. The viciousness of his religion is made apparent in Jane's exposure as a "liar." Relying on Mrs. Reed's word alone, Brocklehurst defames Jane publicly, delivering a sermon on the sin of deceit with an unwarranted, self-righteous wrath. He is equally fanatical on the questions of burnt porridge and curls, insisting on the benefits of self-abnegation while his frivolous, vain, and gorgeously clad daughters stand piously by, silently testifying to the family's hypocrisy.

But it is also at Lowood that Jane first encounters true spirituality and goodness in the person of her schoolmate Helen Burns. Martyrlike, Helen patiently suffers the unjust chastisement and scorn of her teachers, thus tempering Jane's excessively passionate nature and teaching her the values of patience and forgiveness. If Helen lacks Jane's fire and independence, she offers a beneficial example of restraint and passivity.

At climactic moments later in the narrative, Jane behaves in accordance with Helen Burns's truly Christian teachings. When most tempted to give way to passion or wrath, she refuses. For example, when Aunt Reed confesses on her deathbed to withholding Jane's rightful legacy, Jane generously displays Christian mercy, saying that "you have my full and free forgiveness: ask now for God's; and be at peace" (Volume II, Chap. VI). Even more striking is Jane's forgiveness of Rochester for concealing his marriage. When she leaves him, it is not in bitterness or to punish him but only to adhere to her own sense of right and resist the temptations of the flesh. She will not commit a sin; she refuses to compromise herself and become another Celine Varens.

By the time Jane arrives at Moar House, she is a fully developed person, no longer serving an apprenticeship to the ideas of others. Thus, when she meets St. John Rivers, she is able to withstand his missionary zeal. Although he shares Jane's qualities of self-sacrifice, martyrlike self-denial, and ascetic spirituality, he is less yielding, less passionate, and less loving than she. He forces himself to resist the claims of his heart and body, rejecting the affection of Rosamund Oliver because of a rigid adherence to what he perceives as his Christian vocation. His offer of marriage to Jane is prompted not by love but by a sense of her fitness as his partner in religious service; it also represents an attempt to force her soul to bow to his domination. With Jane, however, no conflict exists between the claims of human and divine love. She finally arrives at a union with Rochester which is both passionate and spiritual.

18.2 An influential critic has suggested that one of the dominant image patterns in *Jane Eyre* involves the four traditional elements—earth, air, fire and water—which appear in descriptions of landscape, place, weather, and seasonal cycles. Analyze the significance of "atmosphere" in the novel.

Answer   Brontë uses the traditional connotations of the elements and seasons to create a pervasive emotional symbolism which projects Jane's feelings onto the outside world. By dubbing her heroine with a name that puns on "air," the author is playing with the idea of elemental characters and passions. Jane Eyre, like the wind, is a wanderer; she is a spiritual, ethereal being whom Rochester instinctively associates with the world of fairies and elves. Her "opposite" in this elemental scheme is St. John Rivers, whose name suggests water. He has a dampening, frigid influence on Jane's passionate nature; he is not only water but ice. Although Rochester's name is not symbolic, he is repeatedly associated with the element earth. He has the "thorniness" of the trees at Thornfield, and his face is described as having the strength and hardness of rocky granite. The last element, fire, is not associated with a single character. Rather, it is embodied in the fierce passions of sexual love and madness which trigger the crises in the novel.

Not only characters but weather and seasons are assimilated into the symbolic scheme of the novel. For example, every one of Jane's journeys to a new "situation"—to Lowood, Thornfield, Moor House, and Ferndean—occurs in wet, wintry weather, with the hostile and inclement atmosphere emphasizing the heroine's isolation and vulnerability. Springtime weather is used in equally suggestive fashion, always carrying with it the promise of hope, renewal, and happiness. The coming of spring at Lowood signifies Jane's adjustment to the school and her growing maturity. The season itself is described in the metaphor of a young girl awakening to life: "And now vegetation matured with vigour; Lowood shook loose its tresses; it became all green and flowery" (Chap. 9).

Another instance of the association between seasons and human emotions occurs in the scene on Midsummer Night in which Rochester proposes marriage to Jane. Brontë exploits the romantic symbolism of a burgeoning landscape to suggest the climactic moment of courtship: The orchard where the pair meet is "Eden-like," a secret garden illuminated by moonlight and perfumed with the "incense" of flowers (Chap. 23). But the change in the weather immediately after the proposal scene signals the coming expulsion from paradise. Not only rain (water) and wind (air) but fire, in the form of lightning, descends on the lovers, and the splitting of the rooted chestnut tree augurs the fall of Thornfield and its master as well as the separation of Jane from Rochester.

The extent to which Brontë draws on the vocabulary of weather, seasons, and elements to dramatize the emotional significance of events may be seen most vividly in Jane's reflections after the disastrous revelation of the existence of Rochester's first wife. To describe her desolation, Brontë resorts to an elaborate metaphor:

A Christmas frost had come at midsummer; a white December storm had whirled over June; ice glazed the ripe apples, drifts crushed the blowing roses; on hay-field and corn-field lay a frozen shroud; lanes which last night blushed full of flowers, to-day were pathless with untrodden snow; and the woods, which twelve hours since waved leafy and fragrant as groves between the tropics, now spread waste, wild, and white as pine forests in wintry Norway. (Chap. 26)

Brontë here accumulates all the possible connotations of season and climate to convey the cold, obliterating, deathlike impact of Rochester's betrayal, which necessitates Jane's expulsion from the Eden of Thornfield.

As a gothic novel, *Jane Eyre* is never far from the realms of romance, allegory, and myth. The use of symbolic descriptions of landscape and weather reinforces the sense that the story means far more than its surface incidents suggest, existing on a deeper level of semiconscious passions and spiritual strivings which can be expressed only indirectly.

18.3   Charlotte Brontë was one of the first women novelists to employ the theme of the "independent" woman. Throughout the novel, Jane Eyre is seen as a woman struggling against social strictures to define herself on her own terms. How is the female sensibility expressed in the novel?

Answer   As it is generally thought of today, the gothic novel is essentially reactionary in its view of women. The romantic myth of the innocent young girl finding sexual fulfillment in the arms of a dark, saturnine stranger exploits sexual stereotypes. In a sense, the relationship between the man and the woman involves a struggle for power, and the conventional "happy ending" consists of the young girl's swooning submission to her lord and master.

Some of these elements may be found in *Jane Eyre*. Certainly there is the stock dark, brooding hero and the vulnerable young heroine whose passion for each other must overcome obstacles before it can be consummated. The sexual tension which imbues most gothic novels of today is present in the cat-and-mouse dialogue between the ill-fated lovers as well as in the tragic circumstances which separate them.

However, Jane Eyre differs from the conventional heroines of the modern gothics in a number of important respects. Though there is a strain of masochism and self-martyrdom in Jane, Brontë emphasizes her strong individuality. The author apprises the reader of Jane's distinctiveness by emphasizing the fact that she is plain. In a sense, her plainness is the badge of her extraordinary character. Unlike the beautiful women in the novel, who are almost uniformly hollow and superficial, Jane has substance, depth, and intelligence. This rejection of the stereotype is elaborated at many points in the novel where instead of self-indulgence and vulnerability Jane exhibits practicality, self-discipline, and independence. She also possesses a restless ambition and energy of a kind traditionally associated with men. In a passage which reads almost like a manifesto, Jane says:

> Women are supposed to be very calm generally: but women feel just as men feel; they need exercise for their faculties and a field for their efforts as much as their brothers do; they suffer from too rigid a restraint, too absolute a stagnation, precisely as men would suffer; and it is narrow-minded in their more privileged fellow-creatures to say that they ought to confine themselves to making puddings and knitting stockings, to playing on the piano and embroidering bags. (Chap. 12)

This claim to a fundamental kinship with men is enacted in her relationship with Rochester. Their attraction, though unmistakably sexual, also constitutes a meeting of minds and spirits. In the marriage proposal scene, when Rochester allows her to believe that he is going to marry Blanche Ingram, Jane makes her own claim on him by asserting the likeness of their tempers: "I am not talking to you now through the medium of custom, conventionalities, nor even of mortal flesh—it is my spirit that addresses your spirit; just as if both had passed through the grave, and we stood at God's feet, equal,—as we are!" (Chap. 23).

In his proposal, Rochester finally acknowledges the truth of her words: " 'My bride is here!' he said, again drawing me to him, 'because my equal is here, and my likeness. Jane, will you marry me?' " (Chap. 23).

Jane's words are not idle, for even after their engagement, she insists on her independence, almost resenting the financial support which her fiancé has to offer. She does not want to be "dressed like a doll," to be one of his possessions, like his former mistress Celine Varens.

When Jane returns to him at the end of the novel, she is no longer in a dependent position. She has money of her own and is no longer indebted to Rochester for employment; nor is he the self-sufficient, haughty master of former days. Their marriage, then, is of the most "liberated" kind, in which husband and wife are partners in every thought and action.

In her handling of the "women's theme," Brontë is not antiromantic but anticonventional. She preserves the traditional social values of love and marriage but gives them new psychological resonance by characterizing her heroine fully as a living and independent person.

18.4   Many of the narrative developments in *Jane Eyre* involve a struggle between master and victim or oppressor and martyr. Discuss the treatment of this theme in the book.

Answer   In myth and romance, psychological undercurrents are often very close to the surface. Although on one level *Jane Eyre* reads like a fairy tale, on another it reads like a nightmare. Jane Eyre can be seen not only as a romantic ingenue but as a masochist and a martyr, one who takes pleasure in enslavement. Rochester is not only the perfect Byronic hero but the symbolically castrated victim of Jane's unacknowledged sexual aggression.

Jane is cast in the role of victim beginning with her childhood, when her chief tormentors include John Reed, Mrs. Reed, and Mr. Brocklehurst. She continually attempts to stand up for her rights; however, she comes away from these early experiences with a conviction of her own helplessness, as suggested by the incident of the Red Room, into which, despite her terror, she is thrust back by Mrs. Reed. Furthermore, she learns the religious lessons of humility and self-denial through the example of the devout Helen Burns. These self-images as victim and religious martyr color the later events of her life.

Jane's commitment to a life of self-denial is evident even in her decision to escape the constraints of Lowood for adventures in the larger world outside. Rather than seeking her own excitement, pleasure, and freedom, Jane intends only to devote herself to others. Anything else she considers self-indulgent fantasy: "But servitude! That must be a matter of fact. Any one may serve: I have served here 8 years; now all I want is to serve elsewhere" (Chap. 10).

The relationship with Rochester, in itself full of possibilities for romantic pleasure, is likewise metamorphosed into a form of bondage and suffering. Rochester contributes to Jane's natural propensity for self-flagellation by teasing her with his pretended affection for Blanche Ingram. To school herself in humility, Jane draws two portraits, one entitled "Blanche, an accomplished lady of rank," and the other her self-portrait, "a Governess, disconnected, poor, and plain." Even when Rochester finally proposes marriage, the scene develops as a vicious game of cat and mouse as he maintains the fiction of his intention to marry Blanche until Jane is driven to a tortured confession of her own feelings.

In her sojourn with St. John Rivers after the blighting of her hopes at Thornfield, she accepts her cousin's harsh spiritual tutelage as a means of disciplining the passionate longings she still retains for Rochester. She goes so far as to agree to accompany St. John on his missionary service in India, although a part of her recoils from his severity and coldness:

> By straining to satisfy St. John till my sinews ache, I *shall* satisfy him—
> to the finest central point and farthest outward circle of his expectations.
> If I *do* go with him—if I *do* make the sacrifice he urges, I will make it

absolutely: I will throw all on the altar—heart, vitals, the entire victim. (Chap. 34)

Of course, in the end it is not Jane who is immolated on a sacrificial altar, but Rochester, mutilated in the burning of Thornfield. The roles of master and victim are thus reversed, with Jane becoming guide and caretaker of her blinded—metaphorically castrated—lover. In the denouement, Jane is able to combine the servitude which she consciously desires with the subtle pleasures of domination and independence, the desire for which she has always repressed.

Obviously, *Jane Eyre* is not a psychiatric case history, nor is it a transcription of Charlotte Brontë's fantasy life; it is a product of literary art, and its power as a work of art is not explained or diminished by the presence of recognizable psychological symbols and patterns of behavior. But recognizing their presence can help us understand the novel and some of its deep-seated emotional force.

L.R.

SUGGESTED READINGS

Craik, W. A., *The Brontë Novels* (1968).

Heilman, Robert B., "Charlotte Brontë, Reason, and the Moon," *Nineteenth Century Fiction* (1960).

Tillotson, Kathleen, *Novels of the Eighteen-Forties* (1967).

EMILY BRONTË

C H R O N O L O G Y

1818	Born at Thornton, Yorkshire, the fifth child of Patrick Brontë, a poor Irishman, and Maria Branwell Brontë.
1821	Maria Brontë dies of cancer, and Emily's aunt, Elizabeth Branwell, moves in with the family.
1824	Emily and Charlotte join their older sisters, Elizabeth and Maria, at the Clergy Daughters' School at Cowan Bridge, Lancashire.
1825– 1831	After the deaths of her two older sisters, Emily returns home to learn and play with Charlotte, Branwell, and Anne. They invent the imaginary Kingdom of Angria, about which they write many books. Emily fills the books with her own responses to local life.
1831	After Charlotte goes to Miss Wooler's school at Roe Head, Emily and Anne start a rival Kingdom of Gondal, for which Emily writes many dramatic poems and stories. None of the Gondal prose has survived, but for Emily, these stories were the training school for her genius.
1835	When Charlotte returns to Roe Head as a teacher, Emily accompanies her as a student; she soon grows ill and returns home.
1838	Accepts teaching position at Miss Hatchett's school at Law Hill near Halifax but returns home after six months.
1842	Accompanies Charlotte to Brussels to sharpen her skill in French and to

learn German at the Pensionnat Heger. Returns to Haworth in October for her aunt Elizabeth's funeral and stays there to keep house.

1846   Publishes joint volume with Charlotte and Anne, *Poems by Currer, Ellis, and Acton Bell*.

1847   Publishes *Wuthering Heights*, an immediate popular success. Not until the 1930s does Emily begin to receive critical recognition for the structural innovations, psychological depth, and cosmic symbolism of her masterpiece.

1848   After three years of excessive indulgence in alcohol and drugs, Branwell dies on September 24. Emily takes ill at his funeral, refuses all medical aid, and dies on December 19. She is buried beside her brother, mother, and other sisters at Haworth parsonage.

ESSAY QUESTIONS WITH ANSWERS

Wuthering Heights

19.1 The central story of *Wuthering Heights* is told by two relatively peripheral characters: Mr. Lockwood, the tenant at Thrushcross Grange, and Nelly Dean, the old family retainer. Why does Brontë choose these particular narrators? What effect does this choice have on the tale?

Answer The choice of peripheral characters as narrators creates a perspective frame around the tragic melodrama played out by the protagonists of the novel. Both Nelly Dean and Mr. Lockwood serve the function of intermediaries who stand midway between the reader and the book's chief characters. They thus provide an avenue into the novel's almost mythic tale of incest and revenge, reacting as they do with an ordinary spectator's curiosity and horror to the strange doings at Wuthering Heights. Nelly Dean's prudential wisdom, moral disapproval, and cautionary advice suggest the futile efforts of a village gossip or busybody to intervene in the fateful course of events. Similarly, Mr. Lockwood's primness and propriety, his stereotyped attitudes and romantic ideas, represent a visitor's stock reactions to a world of alien emotions. Both characters give the credibility of the mundane to events which are incredible and bizarre. Precisely because we can believe in them as characters, we can believe in what they have to tell us.

The viewpoint of the reader does not remain identical to that of Nelly and Mr. Lockwood, however. Their perspectives are confined by their limited roles, and neither is capable of imaginative sympathy with the passionate lives of Heathcliff and Catherine. Therefore, their interpretations of events are suspect. When Nelly calls Heathcliff a devil or misinterprets Catherine's illness as pure hysteria, and when Lockwood fears that the younger Cathy is tainted by the shrewishness of her mother, their judgments have an ironic quality, expressing more about the narrators than about the tragic lovers. In fact, Brontë uses her emotionally and mentally limited narrators to endow Heathcliff and Catherine

Earnshaw with greater stature, causing them to loom majestically over the small minds that attempt to explain them.

A final technical consideration in Brontë's choice of narrators is the time scheme of the book. Two generations are encompassed in the novel, and the heroine dies halfway through. Only Nelly Dean is present from the beginning of the story to its end, and thus she is the natural heir to the tale, as the survivor who has witnessed all. The sense we have of *Wuthering Heights* as folklore, as a tale of events long past surviving only through oral transmission, derives from Nelly's roll as witness and messenger. If Heathcliff and Catherine were to speak in their own voices, the quality of mystery and legend thus created might be lost.

19.2 Catherine Earnshaw dies almost exactly at the midpoint of the novel. Does this render everything that follows anticlimactic?

Answer At least two reactions to this question are possible. In one view, the second generation's tale is only a diluted version of that of the first. Cathy Linton and Hareton Earnshaw make poor surrogates for the first Cathy and the demonic Heathcliff, while Linton Heathcliff is a laughable caricature of Edgar Linton. The inevitable comparisons with the originals create a sense of attenuation. Even the major events of the second half—the secret courtship of Cathy and Linton, Cathy's imprisonment, Edgar's death, and the blossoming love between Hareton and Cathy—lack the raw mythic power of the love between the gypsy foundling and his stepsister. Thus, the second-generation saga seems gratuitous, a pointless spinning out of incidents to fill the time until Heathcliff rejoins his lost love. The feeling of emptiness also derives in part from the relative absence of Heathcliff from this story. Only on the three occasions when he speaks directly to Nelly of his private torments—after Cathy's death, after Edgar's death, and just before his own death—does the narrative regain its intensity. The "secret" story of Catherine's constantly haunting him is the real story of the rest of the novel, but it is displaced by the activities of the younger set and in any case does not require hundreds of pages to be told.

On the other hand, the second half of *Wuthering Heights* may be seen as a natural extension of the first, contributing to the structure and meaning of the novel by means of rhythmic and thematic repetition. The recurrence of names, intertwined and rearranged, emphasizes the intertwined destinies of the two households at Wuthering Heights and Thrushcross Grange and the incestuous connections between them; in this novel of family romance, a stepsister and stepbrother marry a brother and sister, and two sets of first cousins marry. Thus, the names Cathy, Linton, Earnshaw, Heathcliff, and Hareton run through the book like a musical motif. Not only do names survive the passage of time, personalities recur, and events are reenacted. For example, Hareton is heir to the savagery of Heathcliff and shares with him the role of outcast and prodigal. Likewise, the "courtly" love of Linton Heathcliff for Cathy Linton reenacts Edgar Linton's courtship of Catherine Earnshaw.

The whole second movement of the novel may also be seen as representing Heathcliff's conscious attempt to control destiny by wreaking revenge on the Lintons for robbing him of his love. He uses his son as an instrument of revenge against the daughter who "killed" the original Cathy and tries to mock the dead Hindley by making Hareton into a subhuman drudge.

Furthermore, the evidence that time passes and life does go on is important as a backdrop for the supernatural passions of the protagonists. Catherine survives her own death as the ghost who appears in Lockwood's dream and haunts Heathcliff's imagination. While Nelly Dean prattles on about the comings and goings of her young mistress, Heathcliff remains obsessed with the invisible realm of pure spirit, pure soul. The second half of the novel allows the reader to feel the powerful undercurrent of passion which draws Heathcliff, finally, to a grave beside that of his beloved.

19.3   Emily Brontë fashions her narrative out of a variety of materials, including elements drawn from the ghost story, the family romance, the revenge drama, the fairy tale, and the gothic novel. Discuss the traces of these genres as they appear in *Wuthering Heights* and explain their significance.

Answer   The plot of *Wuthering Heights* depends in part on the conventions of the eighteenth-century gothic novel as first developed by Horace Walpole, William Beckford, and Ann Radcliffe. These conventions include an eerie atmosphere, a haunted house, a familial curse, mysterious characters, and episodes involving madness and violence. The title immediately associates the novel with this genre, with the word "Wuthering" referring to the tumultuous and stormy emotional "climate" of the story. The action of *Wuthering Heights* suggests the working out of a familial curse or stigma, as Hindley's alcoholic degeneracy, Heathcliff's inexplicable rages, and Catherine's hysteria all represent the dark effects of their tormented childhood.

Furthermore, Heathcliff literally curses himself, begging that he be haunted by Catherine beyond the grave. This bargain with the forces of darkness extends its influence through the second generation as Heathcliff plays out his obsessions through his son, niece, and nephew.

The suggestion of a cursed past links this novel to the conventions of the family romance as well. This literary tradition derives from Greek mythology, particularly the Oedipus legend, and involves the sin of incest and the punishment of the gods. Although no literal incest occurs in the story, the passionate attachment between Catherine and Heathcliff and Hindley's role as vengeful father figure link *Wuthering Heights* to the primal, Oedipal myth of family life. The attenuated repetition of this theme in the next generation, in the love between cousins, may represent a civilized resolution of the theme of forbidden love.

Myth blends into fairy tale in the motifs of cruel lord, gypsy foundling, willful princess, and interfering servant in *Wuthering Heights*. In addition, the metaphoric significance of Wuthering Heights as a castle or fortress in which the "princess" Cathy is imprisoned by the forces of evil derives from folklore and legend. In the second half, the action assumes the shape of a revenge drama like those written for Elizabethan and Jacobean audiences by John Webster, John Marston, and even Shakespeare (*Hamlet*): The avenger feigning madness in order to further his violent ends is a typical revenge drama motif. Heathcliff is, in a sense, the chief agent of the forces of evil, half devil and half avenging spirit.

Heathcliff thus reinforces the sense of the supernatural pervading the plot. *Wuthering Heights* has very much the aspect of a ghost story recounted by the fire on a wintry night as the hearers huddle against the cold. The first event of the novel is Lockwood's eerie account of the night he spent at Wuthering Heights, with the ghost of Catherine scratching at the casement to be let in. Almost the last event of the novel is the village boy's report of seeing two mysterious figures wandering the moors in all types of weather. Throughout the book, Heathcliff's passionate yearning to rejoin the other half of his soul and his literal descent into Catherine's grave suggest parallels with tales of terror and the supernatural.

All these narrative influences combine to make *Wuthering Heights* an unconventional novel. As the novel form developed through the eighteenth and nineteenth centuries, realism in describing life and human social relations was one of its characteristic, though by no means invariable, features. By drawing on a subgenre such as the gothic novel and also exploiting conventions from numerous nonnovelistic forms of storytelling, Brontë shifted the novel from the realm of realism to that of allegory. In describing the distorted lives and passions of *Wuthering Heights*, she creates a cosmic arena in which good and evil clash and souls play out their darkest desires.

19.4

Heathcliff is no more ethically relevant than is flood or earthquake or whirlwind. It is as impossible to speak of him in terms of "sin" and "guilt" as it is to speak in this way of the natural elements or the creatures of the animal world.

> (Dorothy Van Ghent,
> *The English Novel: Form and Function*)

We continue to sympathize with Heathcliff, even after his marriage with Isabella, because Emily Brontë convinces us that what Heathcliff stands for is morally superior to what the Lintons stand for. This is, it must be insisted, not a case of some mysterious emotional power with which Heathcliff is charged. The emotion behind his denunciation of Edgar is *moral* emotion.

> (Arnold Kettle,
> *The Victorian Novel*, edited by Ian Watt)

Heathcliff, indeed, stands unredeemed; never once swerving in his arrow-straight course to perdition, from the time when "the little black-haired, swarthy thing, as dark as if it came from the Devil," was first unrolled out of the bundle and set on its feet in the farm-house kitchen, to the hour when Nelly Dean found the grim, stalwart corpse laid on its back in the panel-enclosed bed, with wide-gazing eyes that seemed to sneer at her attempt to close them, and parted lips and sharp white teeth that sneered too.

> (Charlotte Brontë,
> "Editor's Preface" to the new edition of
> *Wuthering Heights*)

These critics take different views on the subject of Heathcliff's nature. Evaluate the "hero" of *Wuthering Heights*. Is he moral, immoral, or amoral?

Answer   The range of critical responses to Heathcliff suggests the moral ambivalence of his character, in which cruelty coexists with personal magnetism.

Only Charlotte Brontë sees him as utterly evil, citing the language in the novel that associates Heathcliff with the devil and a fallen human being. Her interpretation is, in part, an apology directed to the Victorian reader, who was accustomed to novels where social decorum and Christian ethics molded both character and action. Standing outside conventional morality, Heathcliff would seem the very incarnation of evil to a God-fearing soul such as Nelly Dean or to a proper Victorian. Many of his actions have a sadistic quality; he treats his wife Isabella, his son Linton, his nephew Hareton, and his niece Cathy as so many pawns in his scheme for power and revenge. He is also violent in his encounters with others, physically abusing Isabella and even setting the dogs on the ingenuous Lockwood.

However, Charlotte Brontë's description of Heathcliff ignores her sister's enlisting of the reader's sympathy for the character by means of a number of artistic devices. Arnold Kettle isolates one aspect of Heathcliff's sympathetic side when he alludes to his "moral superiority." Kettle is not defining Heathcliff as a traditional moralist like an Edgar Linton or a Nelly Dean but as a free spirit whose personal code both condemns and transcends the petty ethics of ordinary people. Calling Heathcliff's morality Blakean, Kettle connects his demonic nature with his sympathetic role as the novel's energizing force. Like William Blake, Heathcliff has no use for the social hypocrisies of "pity" or "humanity," which in Wuthering Heights take the form of Edgar's dutiful nursing of Catherine or Nelly Dean's ideas about propriety. Propriety—the obligations of marriage, mannerly conduct to strangers, indebtedness to family—means nothing to Heathcliff, who is bound up with the life of the spirit and soul in his urgent love of Cathy.

Thus, Heathcliff appears to tower over the whining Edgar, the deluded Isabella, and the limited Nelly Dean. Emily Brontë also manipulates events in order to maintain the reader's sympathy for Heathcliff. His early history of mistreatment by Hindley, followed by Catherine's apparent rejection of him, prepares the reader to understand his later vengeful behavior. Furthermore, at key moments in the narrative, notably after Catherine's death and then after Edgar's, Heathcliff confesses his innermost feelings of grief and loss to Nelly Dean, thus evoking our compassion. Finally, the severe judgments on his behavior are filtered through Nelly Dean's myopic and prejudiced viewpoint. Thus, when he rescues Hareton from a probably fatal fall, Nelly interprets this good deed as one that Heathcliff regrets. Her general view of him as the devil's offspring is constantly suspect; we realize that it may be no more than the uncomprehending fear of a small-minded observer.

Van Ghent's description of Heathcliff as an elemental spirit existing outside conventional morality—that is, as amoral rather than immoral—is perhaps the most accurate view, for it accommodates both the negative and the positive aspects of his character. His vitality is like a force of nature, capable of excessive violence and at the same time passionate emotion. Like the moors themselves or the changeable weather on the heights, he is a vivid natural presence, a phenomenon that charges the universe of the novel with significance.

L.R.

SUGGESTED READINGS

Goodridge, F., *Emily Brontë: Wuthering Heights* (1964).
Leavis, F. R., and G. D. Leavis, *Lectures in America* (1969).
Van Ghent, Dorothy, *Form and Function in the English Novel* (1961).
Watt, Ian (ed.), *The Victorian Novel* (1971).

GEORGE ELIOT

C H R O N O L O G Y

1819   Born Mary Ann Evans, the third child of Robert Evans's second wife, Christiana, at Arbury Farm in Chilvers Coton, Warwickshire. Robert Evans, the agent for the Francis Newdigate estates in Derbyshire and Warwickshire, is renowned for great physical strength, integrity, and business skill.

1828–
1832   Boards at Miss Wallington's school at Nuneaton, where the principal governess, Maria Lewis, greatly influences her with a strong evangelical piety.

1832   Enters school at Coventry, where her religious ardor grows more fervent. She shows exceptional talent for music, French, and Italian.

1836–
1841   After her mother dies, Mary Ann manages her father's household with executive skill. Studies German, Italian, Latin, and Greek.

1841   When her brother, Isaac, takes over father's business at Griff, she moves with her father to Coventry and meets the Charles Bray family and the Hennell family, freethinkers and skeptics who greatly influence her break from religious orthodoxy.

1844–
1846   Translates D. F. Strauss's *Das Leben Jesu*, a historical and rationalist examination of Christ's life, and publishes it anonymously.

1849   Her father dies, leaving her a small income of £100 a year for life.

1851   Settles in London as a free-lance writer. Lives with the John Chapman family until Chapman's jealous wife and mistress (the governess) force her back to Coventry.

1852–
1854
Returns to London as an editorial assistant to John Chapman, who has recently become editor of the *Westminster Review*. Does all the editorial drudgery and writes reviews, mainly of philosophical books. Meets many brilliant and eminent thinkers, including Herbert Spencer, whose book *Social Statistics* (1851) Chapman had published the year before. The two become very close, but Spencer avoids marriage and instead introduces her to George Henry Lewes, a versatile journalist whose wife had had two sons with Lewes's best friend. (Because Lewes had acknowledged the sons, he could not get a divorce.) Lewes and Mary Ann Evans become intimate friends, consulting on articles together and attending operas and plays.

1854
Evans publishes her translation of Feuerbach's *Essence of Christianity*, the only book ever to appear under her own name. She and Lewes announce their union to their friends and leave for Germany. Ostracized, they lead a difficult life. Though short on funds, Lewes nevertheless continues to support his wife and her children. Recognizing Mary Ann Evans's genius for fiction, Lewes persuades her to write a story about her childhood. He becomes her mentor and supporter, carefully helping her fulfill her talents.

1857
Evans publishes "The Sad Fortunes of the Rev. Amos Barton" in *Blackwood's Magazine*, and then, serially, "Mr. Gilfil's Love-Story" and "Janet's Repentance."

1858
Blackwood's publishes all three of Evans's stories in book form as *Scenes of Clerical Life*, under the pseudonym George Eliot.

1859
Publishes *Adam Bede*, her first full-length novel, a country story based on an incident told her by her aunt. Distinctive in its unique combination of deep human feeling and rigorous morality.

1860
Publishes *The Mill on the Floss*, another country story, which brings the English novel to a new height of psychological subtlety in its analysis of Maggie Tulliver's complex motivations.

1861
Publishes *Silas Marner*, the story of a miserly weaver who replaces his lost gold with a child.

1862
Deserts her old publisher, Blackwood's, to accept an offer of £10,000 from the *Cornhill Magazine* to publish serially *Romola*, a historical romance on Savonarola. For aesthetic reasons she disagrees with the publisher over the number of installments and accepts instead £7000.

1863
Now financially well off, she and Lewes move to the Priory in Regent's Park and set up a brilliant literary salon.

1866
Publishes *Felix Holt the Radical*, set in the year of the Reform Bill, 1832.

1872   Publishes *Middlemarch*, her generally acknowledged masterpiece.

1876   Publishes *Daniel Deronda*, her last novel. Some critics consider the incisive
            character analysis of Gwendolyn Harleth her greatest achievement.

1878   At Regent's Park, George Lewes dies suddenly of a heart attack. She mourns
            him greatly and devotes herself to finishing his uncompleted work, *Problems
            of Life and Mind* (1879). Founds the George Henry Lewes Studentship in
            Physiology at Cambridge.

1880   Lonely and needing support, Eliot marries at age 61 her dear friend and
            financial adviser, John Walter Cross, age 40. After a seven-month wedding
            trip to Italy, they return to her house in Chelsea. Later that year, she dies
            suddenly of pneumonia and is buried at Highgate Cemetery.

ESSAY QUESTIONS WITH ANSWERS

The Mill on the Floss

20.1 At one point in *The Mill on the Floss*, George Eliot asserts that "character is destiny" (Book 6, Chap. 6). By contrast, Freud, the founder of psychoanalysis, asserted that "anatomy is destiny." Discuss Maggie Tulliver's destiny in light of these two statements.

Answer In *The Mill on the Floss*, Eliot charts Maggie's fate as she develops from early childhood into maturity, attempting to give her story a tragic resonance by emphasizing its inevitability. This inevitability arises both from her personality and from her circumstances as a woman, in a sense, from her "character" and her "anatomy." Her whole experience of life is colored by that anatomy—by the fact that she is a woman—as well as by her subjective individuality, which makes her a particular kind of woman.

In the early phase of the novel, we see Maggie's passionate and intellectual nature hampered by her gender. She is criticized for her failure to be a perfect young lady like her cousin Lucy Deane; her brown skin, unruly hair, and disheveled clothes meet with the cold disapproval of her aunts and her mother. She is also rejected as a tagalong little sister by the brother she worships. Even her intellectual gifts, because they fall outside of what is considered proper to her sex, elicit no encouragement or praise. Tom's schoolmaster, Mr. Stelling, casually discounts women as "quick and shallow" (II, 1, meaning Book II, Chap. 1), while even Maggie's father, who admires her, can only lament, "It's a pity but what she'd been the lad—she'd ha' been a match for the lawyers, *she* would" (I, 3).

Rejected at every turn, Maggie is thrown back upon herself. In childhood, she vents her despair and anger on the fetish in the worm-eaten attic; in adolescence, she schools herself to renunciation and self-discipline by reading the spiritual exercises of Thomas à Kempis; and in adult life, she repeatedly pleads for Tom's forgiveness and struggles against her yearning to be loved and admired. Her acceptance of suffering, which borders on masochism, is the by-

255

product not only of her individual temperament but of her position as a woman, especially a gifted woman, in a man's world.

The importance of Maggie's womanhood in her continual struggle for self-mastery is particularly evident in the second half of the novel. As Maggie grows into a physically beautiful woman, the narrator shifts the focus from her intellectuality to the passionate promptings of her nature. Maggie's love for Philip represents, in part, an attempt to cling to the safety of childish affection and intellectual friendship. Indeed, Philip's deformity is in a certain sense a comfort to Maggie, for it aids her in banishing sexual feeling by evoking pity instead. By contrast, her relationship with Stephen is primarily one of sexual feeling, with the emphasis all on looks, slight touches, and inarticulate murmurings. In a final effort to renounce this "great temptation," she flies back to her brother Tom. The return home is, on one level, a flight back to the innocence of childhood, and on another, an attempt to recapture the original, almost incestuous passion for her brother. Their death together in the flood, locked in an embrace, is the ambiguous symbol of Maggie's ultimate fulfillment as a woman.

What happens to Maggie Tulliver is the enactment of her deepest tendencies as both an individual and a woman. Eliot suggests a polarity between the sexes, with Tom's unyielding, principled, judgmental character the symbol of masculinity and Maggie's sensitive, compassionate, self-conflicting nature the symbol of femininity. A modern feminist might say that not anatomy but social strictures inhibit and frustrate Maggie, whose "masculine" strength of mind requires only the freedom of a public arena. A Freudian psychologist might say that her divided consciousness is a sign of individual neurosis, her erotic and egocentric desires conflicting with her sense of duty and obligation. In a sense, however, both Freud and Eliot would agree that Maggie's tragic fate is psychological, not social. It is the provincial view of the proper role of women that drives Maggie to the outskirts of "good" society; it is her own inner promptings that drive her back into the fateful, drowning embrace of her brother.

20.2   Maggie's biography provides the basic structure of *The Mill on the Floss*. However, Eliot also uses myth, fairy tale, and thematic repetition to give the book inner coherence and significance. Discuss.

Answer   One of the myths underlying Eliot's novel is that of the golden age, connected with the memory of childhood as a period of pastoral bliss and innocence. In the early scenes, Maggie continually imagines an idyllic union with her brother. In reality, their moments of joy are only fleeting, as when she catches the fish in the Round Pool and so wins Tom's approval or when she shares cake with him in a ritual of reconciliation. However, despite the more frequent experience of painful rejection by her aunts, her brother, and her mother, she retains a sense of childish joy and wonder in the people and things which signify home to her. The mill on the Floss is, for her, the origin of her being, an earthly paradise despite its imperfections.

Maggie's innocence is destroyed by her father's failure; Mr. Tulliver's financial losses and illness signal the end of all her security and happiness. Eliot closes Volume I with a description of Tom and Maggie as exiles from paradise: "They had entered the thorny wilderness, and the golden gates of their childhood had forever closed behind them" (II, 7). This feeling of exile pervades Maggie's adolescence.

Flight is another form of separation that recurs at different points in the narrative. Exile and flight are in opposition; the sense of loss associated with growing up contrasts with the desire to mature and leave home. The act of running away is characteristic of Maggie from early childhood, for example, when she seeks solitude in the attic of the mill while running away to become queen of the gypsies. Even her pleasure in books and fantasy as she imagines a life filled with love and understanding is a form of flight. In every case, the flight ends with a return to the mill and to Tom in a continual effort to recapture the lost innocence of childhood, her golden age.

As a *Bildungsroman* concerned with Maggie's education and growth, the novel also incorporates a fairy-tale pattern of metamorphosis, recalling the story of the ugly duckling which turned into a beautiful swan. All the references to Maggie's unfortunate brown skin, tangled mane of hair, and gypsy appearance suggest that she is the black sheep of her family, suspect and somehow alien. In adulthood, however, her dark-eyed, majestic beauty is the sign of her unique worth, the special quality which distinguishes her from ordinary pretty women like Lucy Deane and the Dodson women in general. With her metamorphosis, Maggie becomes magnetically attractive, capturing the imagination of the spiritual Philip Waken and becoming involved in a mutual passion with Stephen Guest. But despite her magical transformation, there is no fairy-tale ending for Maggie; her nature is far too complex for that. She is torn by family loyalty and the desire to renounce personal joy and love.

Eliot also elaborates the story's significance by means of the recurrent image of water. On one level, Eliot uses references to drowning and to floods simply to foreshadow the novel's end. On a deeper level, the Floss symbolizes unconscious currents of feeling: Maggie literally drifts away with Stephen on a tide of sensual longing and drowns in the love of her beloved brother. Finally, the river takes on some of the traditional mythic meanings of water. The flood is Noah's flood—God's vengeance on a sinful society—and at the same time a baptismal purification for Tom and Maggie. The death which comes to them through the medium of water is like a return to paradise, to the complete merging of the "boy and girl" of the golden past.

Although the texture of the book is in the main realistic, recording the life of a young woman at a particular time and a particular place, the elements of myth and symbol help universalize the story.

20.3   Eliot devotes much space in *The Mill on the Floss* to descriptions of apparently peripheral characters, especially Maggie's aunts and uncles. What is their function in the book?

Answer   The Dodson women and their husbands are extremely important in establishing the social background against which Maggie's personal tragedy takes place. In various ways, they bring into the novel the themes of family, sexual role, property, and worldly success. The conversations about plate, linen, and china carried on in such excruciating detail by Mrs. Glegg, Mrs. Pullet, Mrs. Tulliver, and Mrs. Deane signify the materialistic obsession of genteel provincial society. The related concerns with keeping things in the family, doing things according to ritual, and maintaining the Dodson honor in society suggest a preoccupation with empty family pride rather than the bonds of genuine affection. In this context, Maggie is singular, for her every action is linked to her inner emotional life rather than to set ideas of decorum. Mrs. Moss is Maggie's true kin in the sense that she is deeply loyal and loving, although her lot, unlike Maggie's, is that of a conventional woman devoted entirely to child-bearing and menial labor. There is no woman in the book with whom Maggie can meet on grounds of equality other than her cousin Lucy Deane, who, despite her ordinary intellect, has some of the sympathy and warmth of the rebellious Maggie.

Another theme suggested by the familial relationships in the novel is that of money. Mr. Deane, who has "pulled himself up by his bootstraps" to become wealthy, is the only man in the Dodson clan with any authority. Mr. Tulliver's loudmouthed irascibility ends in a symbolic emasculation when he loses his contest with Waken and, in consequence, his property. Tom establishes his own manhood by allying himself with his financially successful and prudent uncle, Deane. In the sexual polarity Eliot establishes, financial realism is a masculine virtue while illusion is a sign of feminine weakness.

Marital relationships among the aunts and uncles further strengthen the sense of a sexual polarity, an inherent opposition between men and women. Mr. Glegg is henpecked by his irritable, dissatisfied wife, while Mr. Pullet takes refuge from his wife's hypochondria in his lozenges. In the Tulliver family, the father prides himself on his wife's stupidity. Maggie's attachments differ from the older generation's precisely in that they are romantic, filled with youthful idealism and mutual fervor. With Philip, her romance is intellectual, based on a shared enthusiasm for books, music, and ideas. With Stephen, it is passionate and sensual, a charged exchange of half-expressed thoughts and feelings. It is inevitable that in a society otherwise made up of stereotyped relationships, Maggie's bond with Stephen will be doomed to disaster.

Only by juxtaposing Maggie with the other, more ordinary characters in the novel can Eliot suggest her unconventional nature and reinforce the sense of individual tragedy in what befalls her. Unable to content herself with feminine trivia, find relief in a masculine world of duty and work, or find a place in the narrow society of St. Ogg's, she is once more driven back into her divided self, finding release only in death.

Middlemarch

20.4 Discuss the use of melodrama in Middlemarch.

Answer In a novel remarkable for its realistic texture and psychological subtlety, the plot of Middlemarch is oddly skewed toward improbable coincidences, dark secrets, and bizarre revelations. An old man writes a will forbidding his young wife to marry his own young cousin on pain of forfeiting her inheritance; an eminent banker who has achieved his wealth and status through fraudulent means assists in the death of his blackmailer; an old man, tantalizing a young nephew with the promise of a legacy, scandalizes his family by leaving his property to a bastard son; and a young doctor is implicated in the murder of his patient by innocently accepting a loan from the man who allows the patient to die. In part, Eliot "inherited" such machinations from the popular fiction of the eighteenth and early nineteenth century. While they provide the immediate pleasures of suspense and romantic exaggeration, they are also convenient novelistic tools for portraying human greed, jealousy, and vanity. It is for their psychological reverberations rather than their crude drama that Eliot exploits these narrative motifs.

For example, the inheritance scheme provides insight into character. Peter Featherstone is a Volpone chuckling over his secret plans to disappoint a brood of ravenous relatives. The tragic dimension of this satiric episode has two aspects. One is the emptiness and futility of Featherstone's life, which has been devoted solely to acquisition and domination. The other is the hollowness of the life of Fred Vincy, whose will-o'-the-wisps include not only Featherstone's promised legacy but hopes for a "lucky break" in gambling, borrowing, and horse trading. Featherstone's machinations and Fred's great expectations are not only narrative ploys but are psychologically revealing as well.

Casaubon's will, like Featherstone's, represents an attempt to control the living from the grave. Again, the crucial element is not the narrative complication (that is, the question of what Dorothea will ultimately do) but the underlying motivation. The correct, unimpassioned scholar reveals himself to be an egocentric, jealous husband and at the same time more discerning of Dorothea's hidden emotional life than she is herself. If there is something of the soap opera in this gesture, there is also a strong element of pathos and cross-purposes as Casaubon's human weaknesses are displayed to the reader.

In some ways, the episode of Raffles and Bulstrode is the most melodramatic in the book. The sordid past of a self-righteous hypocrite coming home to roost through the drunken maunderings of an unsavory blackmailer is the very stuff of pulp fiction. However, Eliot's handling of the situation, especially her complex portrait of Bulstrode, turns the episode into a tragic study of psychology. Bulstrode's exacting conscience and penchant for self-examination, part of his dissenting creed, had preceded the fatal misstep which led him to "omit" the discovery of the missing heiress. Years later, the conscientious, self-abnegating streak has come to dominate the man in his daily attempts to reconcile self-interest with his religious aspirations. In allowing Raffles to die in a last desperate effort to retain his self-image, he founders on his own internal contradictions. Again the ostensible melodrama of murder and deceit masks an essentially moral fable whose point is that character is destiny.

The same enactment of a necessary fate characterizes Lydgate's involvement in Bulstrode's scheme to eliminate Raffles. Although the young doctor is, in fact, innocent of malpractice and conspiracy, he is guilty of allowing himself to become, to all intents and purposes, Bulstrode's tool. His desperate need for money, the outcome of his misguided marriage to an extravagant, willful girl, leads him to betray all the standards of independence and integrity he has set for himself. Lydgate's part in the Bulstrode scandal is the final way station on his road to a hollow, meaningless life as a doctor for the rich, a servant to men like Bulstrode.

Thus, in every instance of melodrama in Middlemarch, George Eliot's aim lies deeper than the obvious. The wellsprings of character are her true concern.

20.5 On its surface, Middlemarch is populated with a host of heroes and villains. For example, Dorothea Brooke has almost the aspect of a modern-day saint, while Bulstrode is a blackguard who has sold his soul to the devil in exchange for wealth and prestige. However, the drama of good and evil is enacted not only between characters but within characters. Discuss the characterization of Dorothea, Lydgate, Rosamond, Ladislaw, and Casaubon in terms of their inner conflicts.

Answer Dorothea Brooke is, at first glance, a creature of unblemished goodness, spontaneous, truthful, affectionate, and beautiful. At the end of the novel, Dorothea descends like an angel of mercy, attempting to save Lydgate from public censure, to arouse Rosamond's better instincts toward her husband, and to encourage her uncle in schemes for the improvement of the cottagers' lives. Her angelic nature is also apparent earlier in her aspiration to be a loving and devoted spiritual helpmate to Casaubon.

But Dorothea's goodness, although genuine, is founded throughout on romantic illusion and innocence, which ill equip her to deal with the real life of marriage and passionate attachment. In her attraction to Casaubon, she idealizes him as teacher and father and imagines herself as a spiritual acolyte, worshiping him and participating in his noble labors. She fails to see Casaubon's constricted egocentricity, the pedantic and limited nature of his *Key to All Mythologies*, and her own need for passionate fulfillment as well as cerebral enlightenment. Thus, her marriage is doomed to failure from the outset, a fact which the more practical-minded Celia immediately grasps.

It would be easy to view this failed relationship as a stereotypical case of innocence sacrificed on the altar of decrepit narcissism. In fact, this is precisely the view that Sir James Chettam, Mrs. Cadwallader, and Will Ladislaw take of the matter. However, as we have seen, Dorothea's character contributes to the tragic mismatch. As Dorothea is no mere victim, Casaubon is no mere villain. Eliot shows the pathetic side of this posturing academic, who is embarked on a lifelong search for self-justification and applause to soothe the tormented self-doubt at the heart of his existence. His wife, who he thought would flatter and comfort him through her adoration, instead stings him by her naive but pointed wit. At the same time, she fails to stimulate the current of tender feeling which he hoped to discover within himself late in life. He is trapped in the prison of his own preoccupations and rigidities, and the fear and disappointment which lie beneath his mask of self-importance make him a pitiable object.

Ladislaw is perhaps the simplest character in this love triangle. He, too, suffers from romantic self-deception, fancying himself a Byronic genius, but his "reform" is easy and instantaneous. Contact with Dorothea is sufficient to help him shed his grandiose self-image, and he settles down first to newspaper work and later to a career in politics. The keynote of his personality is a warm responsiveness which is the antithesis of Casaubon's rigidity and a parallel to Dorothea's openness.

Eliot's portrait of Lydgate represents another instance of complex layering. On the surface, he looks like a perfect hero: handsome, intelligent, of good birth, dedicated to his vocation, idealistic, and honest. But planted in the early descriptions of Lydgate's character are clues to his ultimate fate. His good breed-ing has accustomed him to the very best in material possessions, and his intel-lectual superiority has made him tactless and indiscreet with his fellow practitioners. His grandiose schemes for improving Middlemarch make him an easy prey for Bulstrode's manipulations, as in the matter of Tyke versus Farebrother. Fur-thermore, his inflated self-image as a dashing protector of helpless womanhood makes him equally the prey of Rosamond Vincy. Eliot constantly shows the close links between strength and weakness in Lydgate's character, stressing the inevitability of his destiny as he acts out his inner tendencies in his career and his marriage.

Rosamond Vincy is the least sympathetic character in the novel, precisely because she is all self-delusion, all "surface." Originally the imitator of genteel life at Miss Lemon's, she has become pure actress, intent on acquiring the props necessary to an elevated social position, from lace-edged handkerchiefs to a place at Sir Godwin Lydgate's table. Incapable of any genuine attachment to another, she is constantly absorbed with fantasies of self-aggrandizement. For example, Will Ladislaw becomes merely a character in her own domestic drama, providing her with the paramour "necessary" to a married woman. It is only when Will brutally shatters her fantasies that she must confront the real world, a world not designed for her convenience. Although she never truly changes, she does perform one generous act by telling Dorothea of Will's devotion to her.

Thus, for George Eliot, character provides a clue to destiny. In the universe of *Middlemarch*, the drama is acted out according to each character's inner directives. However, complications necessarily arise because there are no clear instances of black or white. Rather, the novel is fueled by the interplay of opposing impulses.

20.6 *Middlemarch* is a sprawling novel which interweaves the destinies of the Vincys, Lydgates, Garths, Brookes, Casaubons, and Bulstrodes as well as countless minor characters. However, despite the breadth of its canvas, the novel is coherently structured. Discuss the means by which Eliot imposes formal unity on her disparate materials.

Answer   Eliot unifies *Middlemarch* in two ways. First, she ties the complicated plot together by means of coincidence and family relationships; second, she creates thematic contrasts and parallels which link the lives of her characters in coherent patterns.

On the most superficial level, certain of the families of Middlemarch are loosely associated by intermarriage. Mrs. Bulstrode is Mr. Vincy's sister, Peter Featherstone's first wife was a Garth and his second a Vincy, and the Chettams and Casaubons are linked by marriage to the Brookes.

More crucial to the interweaving of the various plot strands are two figures, Lydgate and Ladislaw, who impinge on almost every other character's life. As a doctor, Lydgate is invited into every major household in the town. He treats Fred Vincy's typhoid, Casaubon's heart disease, Lady Chettam's complaints, Peter Featherstone's final ailment, and, at Bulstrode's request, Raffles's delirium tremens. Furthermore, the circumstances of his birth associate him with the landed gentry, while his profession places him within the middle class. He can thus talk on terms of equality with Dorothea Brooke and still play whist with the Vincys.

Ladislaw is perhaps the most important unifying agent in the plot. He is Casaubon's cousin and the son of the woman Bulstrode cheated of her inheritance. At the same time, he is Dorothea's ardent admirer and Rosamund's fantasy lover. The connection between the various stories is not merely arbitrary; rather, the coincidences suggest the mysterious operation of destiny, as Bulstrode's past returns to haunt him and as Ladislaw comes to Dorothea as her fated partner.

The thematic connections stress the operation of fate and pattern in human life. Apart from Book I, which is devoted almost entirely to Dorothea, the novel is organized according to thematic headings. "Old and Young" introduces major plot developments as a series of tableaux between youth and age. Thus, Mary and Fred are seen juxtaposed with the aged Peter Featherstone, Lydgate is presented as youthful idealism succumbing to the middle-aged Bulstrode, and the beautiful young Dorothea is poised between the aging Casaubon and his young cousin, Will Ladislaw. Book III, "Waiting for Death," and Book IV, "The Dead Hand," focus on the drama of mortality in the two different cases of Peter Featherstone and Edward Casaubon. Featherstone is a stereotyped miser who creates unbearable suspense among his greedy relatives but then is unable to control destiny as he had anticipated. Casaubon's illness and death are treated more in terms of pathos than satire. "Waiting for death" brings home to him the futility of both his life's work and his marriage, while the "dead hand" represents his vain attempt to clutch at his wife's loyalty and affection. The satire on greed and the fable of mortality illuminate a central dilemma of human existence in different but related ways.

In "Three Love Problems" (Book IV), another central human dilemma, the nature of love and marriage, is analyzed through three contrasting dramas. Fred Vincy's youthful irresponsibility and Mary Garth's clear-eyed realism constitute a clash of temperaments out of which will emerge a positive reconciliation. In contrast, Rosamond Vincy, with her egocentric willfulness, and Lydgate, with his romantic idealism, are a mismatched pair fated to an unhappy union. Dorothea and Casaubon, too, are mismatched, and Will's presence underlines the essential incompatibility of the couple. Further contrasts are developed in "The Widow and the Wife" (Book VI), with Dorothea's dawning self-awareness posed against Rosamond's stubborn self-righteousness. "Two Temptations" (Book VII) portrays the trial of conscience of two very different men: Lydgate, whose idealism is foundering on the rock of financial necessity and domestic misery, and Bulstrode, whose religious dogmatism cannot save him from his past. The final book, "Sunset and Sunrise," shows the characters living out the patterns of their lives, with marriages, births, and deaths suggesting the universal cycles of existence.

By organizing the Middlemarch stories in thematic patterns, Eliot emphasizes the philosophic and universal dimension of particular lives. She focuses on the problems of death, love, and belief common to all people, showing the various possibilities chosen by, or forced upon, any given individual.

20.7 In the midst of an analysis of the strains affecting Dorothea after her marriage to Casaubon, the narrator pauses to comment:

One morning, some weeks after her arrival at Lowick, Dorothea—but why always Dorothea? Was her point of view the only possible one with regard to this marriage? I protest against all our interest, all our effort at understanding being given to the young skins that look blooming in spite of trouble; for these too will get faded and will know the older and more eating griefs which we are helping to neglect.   (Chap. 29)

This aside, with its intrusion of the first person voice and its philosophical reflections, is typical of the narrative style of the novel. Analyze the effect of the manner of telling on the tale in *Middlemarch*.

Answer   The narrator of *Middlemarch* is an omniscient observer of her characters' inmost thoughts as well as their overt actions, of the vast spectacle of human life as well as the individuals of Middlemarch. In drawing conclusions and making generalizations about "human nature," she implicates the reader in the drama of the novel, forging an identification between readers and characters by stressing the common lot of humankind. None of us, she intimates, is immune from the illusions and errors which she so carefully documents in the lives of Dorothea, Lydgate, Casaubon, and others.

The narrator's sympathetic attitude toward her characters is perhaps most evident in her treatment of Casaubon. All the characters except Dorothea view him as an elderly, unattractive, dried-up pedant with no redeeming warmth or humor to mitigate his stiff-necked vanity. But the narrator tells us bluntly, "For my part I am very sorry for him" (Chap. 29). She helps us see his interior life, the "small hungry shivering self" which hides behind the stuffy rhetoric and stately pose. Bulstrode, too, though a criminal and a hypocrite, becomes sympathetic as Eliot portrays the tormented conscience and obsessive needs underlying his machinations.

The narrative voice provides not only a sympathetic medium but an ironic overview which stresses the blindness and ignorance of each individual caught in patterns he or she does not perceive. The two key instances of ironic foreshadowing occur in early descriptions of Dorothea and Lydgate. Without ever explicitly announcing that Dorothea is blindly romantic, the narrator describes her excessively sentimental responses to Casaubon's frigid gestures, contrasts her dreamy ideas of self-sacrifice with Celia's hardheaded common sense, and uses her nearsightedness metaphorically to suggest that she cannot see what is right in front of her. In characterizing Lydgate, the narrator contrasts his scientific idealism with his "spots of commonness": "That distinction of mind which belonged to his intellectual ardour, did not penetrate his feeling and judgment about furniture, or women, or the desirability of its being known (without his telling) that he was better born than other country surgeons" (Chap. 15).

By puncturing, from the outset, Lydgate's idealized self-image as a heroic savior and scientific prophet, the narrator foreshadows his ironic fate. The man of noble intellect becomes a slave to the petty whims of a beautiful woman and to the necessity of paying for his furniture.

Any omniscient narrator has the power to diminish the characters by irony or to bathe them in sympathetic understanding. Eliot's mark of distinction is her fusion of these two perspectives, eliciting both judgment and fellow feeling so that the reader sees both the limitations and the value of the characters.

L.R.

SUGGESTED READINGS

Haight, Gordon (ed.), *A Century of George Eliot Criticism* (1965).

Harvey, W. J., *The Art of George Eliot* (1962).

Levine, George, "Determinism and Responsibility in the Work of George Eliot," *PMLA* (1962).

SAMUEL BUTLER

C H R O N O L O G Y

1835   Born at Langar Rectory, Nottinghamshire, son of the Reverend Thomas Butler and grandson of Dr. Samuel Butler, headmaster of Shrewsbury School and then bishop of Lichfield.

1848   Enters Shrewsbury School.

1854   Enters St. John's College, Cambridge, where his father wishes him to take holy orders. Writes for *The Eagle*, his college magazine, and visits Italy on vacations. Learns Italian. Closely studies the New Testament in Greek. Begins to question the underpinnings of Christianity.

1859   Works as a lay assistant among the poor in a London parish. Loses his faith in dogma, refuses ordination, quarrels violently with his father, and leaves the church. Emigrates to New Zealand with £4200 from his father.

1860–   Buys a sheep run in the Canterbury Settlement and doubles his original
1864   investment. Discovers Darwin's *Origin of the Species* and is completely taken with it. Writes several articles for *The Press* in Christchurch, New Zealand, two of which will later be incorporated in *Erewhon*.

1863   Butler's father puts together some of his letters home and pieces of his published articles and publishes them under the title *A First Year in Canterbury Settlement*, a book Butler did not like.

1864   Returns to London with Charles Paine Pauli, an editor friend. Settles at 15 Clifford's Inn, London, his permanent residence for the rest of his life.

268

Studies art and paints his most famous picture, *Family Prayers*, showing eight adults in varying positions of boredom as they listen to a clergyman's prayers.

1865   Publishes pamphlet *The Evidence for the Resurrection of Jesus Christ as Given by the Four Evangelists*, which states his reasons for not becoming a clergyman.

1867–1869   Studies art at Heatherley's Art School; exhibits paintings occasionally; works on various writings. Meets Eliza Mary Ann Savage, a fellow student at the art school, beginning a friendship that will have a profound effect on his writings. She reads and comments on every one of his manuscripts and encourages his wit and satire. The model for the charming and witty Alethea in *The Way of All Flesh*, she inspires many of his writings.

1872   Publishes *Erewhon* anonymously, his only financially successful book. It establishes his reputation as a writer, going through nine editions in his lifetime. Meets Charles Darwin.

1873   Publishes *The Fair Haven*, an ironic defense of Christianity that satirizes its belief in miracles and many of its "superstitions."

1873–1875   Financial difficulties impede his writing.

1877–1887   Writes a series of books on evolution that reflect his doubts and skepticism.

1877   Publishes *Life and Habit*, speculations on Darwinism.

1879   Publishes *Evolution Old and New*, in which he attributes teleology to Darwin's theories by placing purpose in the organisms themselves rather than in an external God.

1880   Publishes *Unconscious Memory*, a further refinement of Darwinian thought.

1885   Eliza Savage's death is a great loss to him; he feels guilt for his egotistical behavior toward her.

1886   Publishes *Luck or Cunning*, reemphasizing the link between heredity and memory and urging a greater openness of mind toward scientific and religious thinking. His father dies; he inherits his grandfather's properties; his financial worries end.

1887–1901   Works on various projects: musical compositions, translations, lectures, paintings, notes and letters, literary criticism.

1901   Completes *Erewhon Revisited*, in which the hero, Higgs, returns thirty years later and is appalled by the religion that has been created in his name.

When Longmans refuses to publish it, George Bernard Shaw recommends it to Grant Richards, who becomes the first publisher to assume the financial burden for a Butler book.

1902   After falling ill in Italy, Butler returns home and dies suddenly in London, where he is buried.

1903   Butler's masterpiece, *The Way of All Flesh*, is published posthumously. An autobiographical novel, it traces the story of the George Pontifex family through five generations, ultimately undermining the very notions of inheritance and patriarchal tradition.

ESSAY QUESTIONS WITH ANSWERS

The Way of All Flesh

21.1 Ernest Pontifex, the central character of *The Way of All Flesh*, is not introduced until eighty pages into the book. Butler first spends considerable time chronicling the activities and personalities of the preceding three generations of Pontifexes. Why does he begin his story so early in the history of the family?

Answer The significant, mostly negative effect one generation has on the next is one of the main themes of the novel. Butler believed that one's life is influenced not only by one's parents but by all the generations that precede them. Consequently, the chronicle of John, George, and Theobald Pontifex functions as more than mere expository introduction; it describes Ernest's prenatal history in order to show the inheritance he receives at birth.

The chronicle begins with old Mr. Pontifex, who dies at the beginning of the nineteenth century. A brief biographical sketch establishes him as a benevolent patriarch. He is almost a prelapsarian figure, the kind of person we might imagine an unfallen Adam to be: "natural," alienated from neither his land, his work, nor his family. Although Mr. Pontifex works with his hands as a carpenter, his aesthetic side is also well developed, for he is an artist and musician as well. Our brief glimpse of this well-integrated and fulfilled figure, whose last act is to look at the sunset and then peacefully die, reveals an admirably uncomplicated patriarchal figure with whom future generations will be nostalgically compared.

George Pontifex, old Mr. Pontifex's son, is more successful than his father in worldly terms, but as Overton, the narrator, makes clear, he is more rigid, more conventional, and more unhappy. Lacking his father's creativity, George thinks in terms of convention and cliché, as Overton emphasizes in his description of George's stereotypically romantic response to the mountains of Switzerland. Although the portrait of George Pontifex is longer than that of his father, it is still brief, its purpose introductory; Butler's main interest lies in his

271

treatment of George's son, Theobald, the representative of the third generation. Terribly strict and controlling, George passes on to Theobald his rigidity and conventionality. After rebelling feebly against his father's wish to see him ordained, Theobald becomes merely a weaker version of his tyrannical father. He teaches his son, Ernest, the protagonist of the novel and the representative of the fourth generation of Pontifexes, to "kneel before he could crawl" (Chap. 20), and the cycle of tyranny and repression is renewed. The sins of the fathers are visited on their children.

But Ernest struggles against the direct legacy of his father and grandfather, trying to become more like his great-grandfather. He, too, enjoys music and art; he, too, wants to be part of the land around him. In the end, Ernest repudiates the whole patriarchal process of family and inheritance; he severs his bonds to his wife (since she is a bigamist) and gives his children away to a healthy peasant couple. At the end of the book, he has chosen the solitary life of a writer, content to analyze the institutions of marriage and the church from outside their confining nets. Thus the chronicle of the generations ends with Ernest repudiating the very notion of inheritance.

21.2 Although *The Way of All Flesh* is a realistic novel, many of the characters' names are symbolic. Discuss the significance of names in the book.

Answer The names of the main characters—Alethea, Christina, Theobald, Overton and Ernest—and even that of Towneley, a minor character, symbolically reveal something about the values and literary functions of the people they designate.

In Greek, Alethea means "truth," and indeed Ernest's spinster aunt represents a kind of wisdom that functions as an alternative to the inherited beliefs and conventions passed down from father to son in the Pontifex family. Her monetary legacy to Ernest frees him from the tyranny of patriarchal inheritance, and her encouragement of the artistic and instinctual sides of his nature counteracts the repressive influences of his parents. The Hellenic origin of Alethea's name is also important; her pagan name signifies her existence outside the rigid Christian institutions to which her brother, Theobald, and his wife, Christina, submit.

Unlike Alethea, Christina, the "little Christian," is the good Christian wife as conceived in the repressive world of the Pontifexes: submissive, dutiful, and totally devoted to her husband and to the church he represents. Theobald, her husband, is theological man in the worst sense: stark, severe, and lacking in any softening features ("bald").

Towneley and Overton also bear names appropriate to their roles in the novel. Towneley, whose parents died when he was young, leaving him a considerable inheritance, is a true child of the town, a sophisticated, bourgeois young man who has been freed from the kind of parental burden under which Ernest labors. Overton oversees the actions of the characters and, as narrator, provides a kind of overview for the reader. As an outsider to the Pontifex family, he remains above or aloof from the web of familial relations. His stance "above" the other characters is implied in the first part of his name.

Ernest's Christian name, too, is symbolic, but it is prescriptive rather than descriptive. "Ernest," a particularly popular name for young men in the nineteenth century (Oscar Wilde's play *The Importance of Being Earnest* puns on the meanings of the name), represented the moral seriousness and hard work generally valued during most of the century. Ernest's grandfather, George, suggests the name to Theobald in hopes that it will "have a permanent effect upon the boy's character, and influence him for good during the more critical periods of his life" (Chap. 18). The symbolism of the Christian name, combined with the patriarchal legacy conveyed by the surname Pontifex (Latin for "priest"), is almost more than Ernest can tolerate. He renounces his father's church, lands in prison, and marries a servant girl, actions embodying his rebellion against the middle-class Victorian values of his father and the Victorian ethic of duty and work. Thus, by his rebellious actions, Ernest tries to free himself from the yoke represented by the two halves of his name.

21.3 While Ernest attends Dr. Skinner's school for boys, he develops what Butler calls an "inner self" that opposes his "outer self." In Chapter 31, Butler even represents an unspoken and unconscious dialogue between the two Ernests. What exactly do these two selves represent?

Answer The dialogue between Ernest's inner and outer selves represents the struggle between his conscious, "reasoning" self, which has been molded by his parents, and his unconscious and inarticulate self, which is based on instinct rather than education, on desire rather than duty. Butler calls this latter self the "dumb" Ernest for two reasons. First, at this stage in his life, Ernest is unaware of its presence. Second, language for Ernest (including his own name) is in the service of powerful institutional forces. Names, sermons, interdictions—

all issue from the patriarchy, whether from Ernest's father, Theobald, his school-master, or the church.

The "dumb voice" warns Ernest to question the preachings of the institu-tional voices. In an ironic paraphrase of biblical language, the "true voice" calls for Ernest's obedience, for that voice is the "God" who made him. It admonishes Ernest that if he listens to the outer voice, he will be rent "in pieces even unto the third and fourth generation as one who has hated God" (Chap. 31). Calling Theobald's influence heretical, the "true voice" places Theobald's kind of Chris-tianity on the side of the devil, and instinct, joy, and desire on the side of God. Butler uses religious language here not merely to satirize the church but to suggest seriously that instinct is sacred and God-given. Although much of *The Way of All Flesh* is devoted to deflating certain institutions and values, it also presents an alternative: obedience to instinct, nature, and the other unconscious forces within the individual.

K.L.

SUGGESTED READINGS

Furbank, Philip Nicholas, *Samuel Butler, 1835–1902* (1971).
Jeffers, Thomas L., *Samuel Butler Revalued* (1981).

Part Four

MODERN POETRY

T I M E L I N E

The Age

1845:   Great Famine in Ireland

1848:   Revolutions in France, Italy, Austria; publication of *Communist Manifesto*

1854:   Outbreak of Crimean War

1859:   Publication of Darwin's *Origin of Species*

1860:   Outbreak of American Civil War

1865:   Assassination of Lincoln

1876:   Invention of the telephone

1886:   Publication in English of Marx's *Capital*

1887:   Golden Jubilee of Queen Victoria

1895:   Invention of motion picture camera

1900:   Publication of Freud's *Interpretation of Dreams*

1901:   Death of Victoria; accession of Edward VII

1903:   Wright brothers' flight at Kitty Hawk

1905:   Einstein's theory of relativity

1910:   Death of Edward VII; accession of George V

1914:   Outbreak of World War I

1917:   Russian Revolution

1919:   Treaty of Versailles

The Authors

1840

Gerard Manley Hopkins (1844–1889)

1850

1860

Rudyard Kipling (1865–1936)
W. B. Yeats (1865–1939)

1870

1880

T. S. Eliot (1888–1965)

1890

1900

W. H. Auden (1907–1973)

1910

Dylan Thomas (1914–1953)

1920

The Age

1921:   Irish independence

1922:   Publication of *The Waste Land*

1929:   U.S. stock market crash precipitates Great Depression

1933:   Hitler takes power in Germany

1936:   Death of George V; accession of Edward VIII, who abdicates in favor of George VI

1939:   Outbreak of World War II

1945:   End of World War II; invention of atomic bomb

1947:   Independence for India and Pakistan

1952:   Death of George VI; accession of Elizabeth II

1956:   Britain and France invade Egypt to seize the Suez Canal

1963:   Assassination of John F. Kennedy

1969:   Men land on moon

The Authors

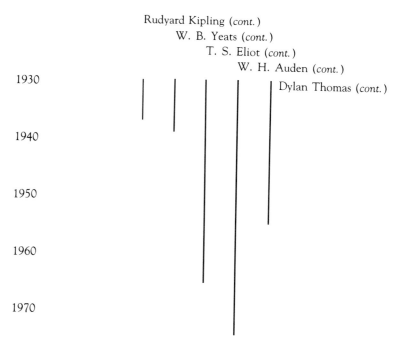

Rudyard Kipling (*cont.*)
W. B. Yeats (*cont.*)
T. S. Eliot (*cont.*)
W. H. Auden (*cont.*)
Dylan Thomas (*cont.*)

1930

1940

1950

1960

1970

1980

GERARD MANLEY HOPKINS

C H R O N O L O G Y

1844	Born at Stratford, Essex (now part of London), the oldest child of Manley Hopkins, consul general of Hawaii in Great Britain and himself a published poet.
1852–1853	Family moves to Oak Hill, Hampstead (northwest of London), where Gerard attends preparatory school. Shows unusual talent in music and painting.
1854–1862	Attends Sir Robert Cholmondeley's Grammar School in Highgate, where the poet R. W. Dixon is on the staff. Takes two trips to Germany with his father, in 1857 and 1860. Wins school prize for poetry in 1859 for "Escorial." Wins a second prize in 1862 for "A Vision of Mermaids."
1863	Matriculates at Balliol College, Oxford, with an exhibition. Walter Pater tutors him; Robert Bridges, future poet laureate, befriends him. Becomes involved in the Oxford Movement, a religious movement originally intended to return the established (Anglican) church to the beliefs and customs of the first Christians. One result was the conversion of many High Church Anglicans, such as John Henry Newman, to Roman Catholicism or "Anglo-Catholicism."
1865	With friend W. E. Addis visits Canon Raymond at Belmont Monastery in Hersford and becomes convinced of his calling to Roman Catholicism.

1866	Receives baptism in the Roman Catholic Church from John Henry Newman, later Cardinal Newman.
1867	Leaves Oxford with a double first in Honour Moderations and Greats. Benjamin Jowett, eminent Greek scholar, calls him the "star of Balliol." Works as an assistant to Newman at the Oratory School in Birmingham.
1868–1877	Enters Jesuit novitiate at Roehampton, London, and begins rigorous training for the priesthood. Studies philosophy at Stonyhurst, Lancashire, and theology at St. Bueno's College, North Wales. On becoming a Jesuit, he burns all his early poems. However, he begins writing poetry again as a novice, and in 1875 he produces the extraordinary long poem "The Wreck of the Deutschland." However, it is refused publication in the Jesuit magazine *The Month*.
1879	Is ordained a priest and preaches at several churches.
1881	Returns to Roehampton for tertianship, a third-year novitiate. As a Jesuit and a priest, he experiences terrible spiritual conflicts, not through doubts of faith or desire for worldly pleasures but through repression of his creative instincts, a discipline he feels is necessary to fulfill his vocation as a priest. Nevertheless, this conflict becomes the subject of some of his best poetry.
1884–1889	Accepts the chair of Greek at the Royal University of Ireland in Dublin. Is deeply moved by the terrible living conditions in the Dublin slums. Publishes no poems in his lifetime but sends them to friends R. W. Dixon, Robert Bridges, and Coventry Patmore. Also carries on lengthy correspondence with them explaining his poetry, which they only imperfectly appreciated. Develops his theories of poetry using the philosophy of Duns Scotus and his knowledge of Old English metrical patterns to explain his concepts of inscape, instress, and sprung rhythm.
1889	On June 8, dies of typhoid fever and is buried in the Jesuit cemetery at Glasnevin.
1918	Robert Bridges publishes a collection of Hopkins's poems. The technical and metrical innovations are better suited to the postwar sensibility than they had been to the time of their composition, but the poems still are hardly noticed.
1930	A second edition of Hopkins's poems with a critical introduction by Charles Williams creates more interest in Hopkins and widens his impact on a new generation of poets.

ESSAY QUESTIONS WITH ANSWERS

"The Windhover"

22.1 Discuss the symbolism of the falcon in the poem.

Answer Hopkins devotes the opening eight lines (octave) of the sonnet to a description of the falcon or kestrel, called windhover because of its ability to hover on the wind. He captures through vivid imagery, strings of adjectives, and aurally suggestive phrases the precise movements of the bird wheeling in midair, "his riding/Of the rolling level underneath him steady air" (lines 2–3). The poet further locates the event in reality by emphasizing his own relationship to the spectacle: "My heart in hiding/Stirred for a bird" (lines 7–8).

However, Hopkins prepares for the later symbolic transformation of the bird by means of images which hint at the falcon's identification with a prince or noble horseman. The references to "minion" and "dauphin" suggest an aristocratic knight riding out into battle. The phrase "how he rung upon the rein of a wimpling wing/In his ecstasy" (lines 4–5) condenses several complex ideas into an image of spiraling flight. In "ringing upon the rein" of his wing, the bird is both horse and rider, the perfect master of himself ("the achieve of, the mastery of the thing!" [line 8]). At the same time, the word "ecstasy" implies a kind of religious or spiritual transport, as though his flight were not merely physical but a rapturous ascension.

The first half of the sestet is the crucial turning point of the poem for the bird is transfigured in the poet's eyes as the literal and symbolic levels fuse. The lines "Brute beauty and valour and act, oh, air, pride, plume, here/Buckle!" (lines 8–9) bring together the abstract qualities of the bird's flight (beauty, valor, act, pride) and the concrete features of the bird as a physical being in a physical environment (air, plume). The word "buckle" suggests a sudden collapse, a condensation of all these qualities into the transcendent symbol of Christianity,

Jesus Christ, fringed with holy fire:

> . . . AND the fire that breaks from thee then, a billion
> Times told lovelier, more dangerous, O my chevalier!
>
> (lines 10–11)

"O my chevalier," an extension of the chivalric images earlier in the poem, thus becomes a direct apostrophe of Christ militant, the spiritual knight of the church descending to do battle on earth. The swooping falcon, seen as the savior of people's souls, is more beautiful and "dangerous," that is, powerful and overmastering, than he is when seen as a merely natural creature.

The second half of the sestet brings in two further images of shining or fire—the glinting of earth after the plow cuts through it and the breaking into flame of dying ash—which elaborate on "the fire that breaks" from the transfigured bird. These homely images suggest the possibility of transfiguration everywhere in the material world, while simultaneously recalling Christ's humble life of labor and poverty on earth and his miraculous transfiguration through death on the cross into "gold-vermilion."

"As kingfishers catch fire, dragonflies draw flame"

22.2   Paraphrase the poem.

Answer   As all the things of the world—kingfishers, dragonflies, stones, bells—assert their individual inner nature through a characteristic action (giving off sparks or flames, ringing or telling), so every living creature ("each mortal thing") announces its essential self through idiosyncratic activity (speech, behavior, bearing). Identity is thus manifested through action, which is also the proper end of human existence.

Furthermore, the upright person who is in a state of grace enacts his or her righteousness continually, confirming the individual's God-given identity as a reflection of Christ, for Christ is everywhere, inhabiting the bodies of people who are thus made beautiful in the eyes of God the Father.

22.3   Relate the content of the poem to Hopkins's aesthetic theory.

Answer   Hopkins begins the poem with the naming of concrete objects: kingfishers, dragonflies, stones, bells. The focus on particular sensory perceptions accords with his theory of inscape, which Hopkins identified as the distinctive, integrated form manifested by each object in nature. By describing these objects in metaphorical terms (kingfishers "burst into flame," dragonflies "attract fire," stones "echo," and bells "speak out their names"), Hopkins is alluding to their instress, that energy of being which defines them and which produces an answering instress, as a sense of mystical illumination, in the perceiver.

The intense focus on natural phenomena accords with the philosophy of the fourteenth-century Oxford theologian Duns Scotus, whom Hopkins deeply admired. Scotus's theory of *haecceitas* ("this-ness") proposed that human knowledge of the world rests in particular objects and that only by inductive reasoning can a person arrive at a notion of the abstract and universal. Instead of beginning, in deductive fashion, with general principles or universal ideas, the individual comprehends the world by means of discrete sensory impressions; by abstracting and comparing these impressions, one gradually achieves knowledge of a general category or principle. The logic of Hopkins's poem imitates Scotus's inductive process, moving from individual essences ("this" and "this" and "this") to a notion of integration and universality in Christ's omnipresence.

Finally, the poem suggests certain religious beliefs which are analogous to the aesthetic theory of instress. The perceiver's sudden awareness of pattern and significance in any being's inscape is like an epiphany. The "selving" of all living things is a transfiguration of matter into essence and is thus an analogue to the mystery of transubstantiation by which the wafer and wine become the body and blood of Christ. Hopkins emphasizes the infusion of spiritual significance into the mortal world by his closing reference to "Christ-in-men"; he expands the concept of communion beyond the ritual itself to the realm of purposeful activity. This activity takes the form of *imitatio*, the Roman Catholic doctrine of conscious imitation of the life of Christ.

All of these concepts indicate Hopkins's religious apprehension of the world around him; they are the philosophical framework underlying his poetic images of metamorphosis and epiphany.

"Carrion Comfort"

22.4   Discuss the technical devices Hopkins employs in the poem, including sprung rhythm, alliteration, the use of Anglo-Saxon words and compounds, wrenched syntax, and repetition.

Answer   Hopkins's use of these techniques contributes to the poem's vivid evocation of a tormented person locked in dramatic conflict with God. Hopkins creates an impression of intense, concentrated struggle by employing verbal "strangeness"; the poem's rhythms, diction, and grammar are all distorted and dislocated.

Although the poem is a sonnet, it lacks the iambic regularity which is conventional to the form. Hopkins uses instead a kind of rhythm he called sprung rhythm. Sprung rhythm, as described in the author's preface to *Poems 1876–1889*, allows up to four syllables in a foot, with the stress always on the first. In essence, this rhythm permits the greatest possible freedom in the distribution of accents. Any pattern of stresses and slacks can be created by mixing monosyllabic (´), trochaic (~), dactylic (~~), and paeonic (~~~) feet. The tendency of lines to run together with no break in their scansion and of certain words to hang outside the line (outride) with no place in the metrical pattern makes Hopkins's rhythmic units almost infinitely flexible. Although Hopkins emphasizes the "natural" quality of sprung rhythm, which he says is characteristic of common speech, prose, music, and nursery rhymes, his own use of it is idiosyncratic, creating a unique and distinctive effect of rhythmical surge and ebb. The sudden shifts in meter, together with the strained, gnarled, deliberately tangled syntax, project a distinctive poetic voice and convey the workings of a particular mind.

Despite the variability of each line's rhythm, Hopkins creates a recognizable music in his verse, reinforcing metrical pattern with alliteration, onomatopoeia, assonance, internal rhyme, and repetition. The following lines exhibit the acoustic patterns created by alliteration and internal rhyme:

> But ah, but O thou terrible, why wouldst thou rude on me
> Thy wring-world right foot rock? lay a lionlimb against me? scan
> With darksome devouring eyes my bruised bones? and fan,
> O in turns of tempest, me heaped there; me frantic to avoid thee and
>   flee?
>
>   (lines 5–8)

In addition to the somewhat submerged rhyme scheme (*abba*), the verse advances by means of clusters of like sounds ("wring-world right foot rock," "lay a lionlimb," "darksome devouring eyes," "bruised bones," "turns of tempest"). The acoustic patterns of these lines recall medieval alliterative verse and, more especially, the musical phrasings and alliterative interlockings of Welsh poetry (which Hopkins studied while reading theology in North Wales during 1874 and 1875). The diction also reflects an older native tradition of verse. "Lionlimb" and "darksome" as well as, later, "heaven-handling" are compounds which suggest the word-forming patterns of Old English, in which concrete nouns and active verbs were combined to produce sensuous word blends. The effect is of urgent utterance, with words wrenched out in short bursts.

Hopkins's sacrifice of normal word order and conventional syntax seems partly connected with his concern for sensuous music and rhythmic thrust. By dropping connectives and transposing phrases, he preserves a stress on internal rhymes and alliterations. But his elliptical and condensed style also constitutes an attempt to convey essences, or inscapes, and to project the simultaneous rush of many different ideas and impressions. The lines "Nay in all that toil, that coil, since (seems) I kissed the rod,/Hand rather, my heart lo! lapped strength, stole joy, would laugh, cheer" (lines 10–11) illustrate certain characteristic syntactic manipulations. The parenthetical "seems" condenses the complicated idea of an apparent devotion or pretended commitment. (The literal significance of "it seems" or "meseems"—that is, "In all that toil and coil which, it seems, have taken place"—is also present.) "Hand rather" is a shorthand correction for "rod" or cross ("rood"), indicating ritual submission to Christ in a kiss of the hand. (Again, there is also the more literal meaning of a child kissing the rod of chastisement wielded by a parent.) The syntax seems partly dictated by sound pattern: "seems" is juxtaposed with "since," "hand" with "heart." But the parenthesis and correction have the more important function of pointing up the ambiguities of the poet's commitment to a life of religious devotion. The aside has the effect of an admission of hypocrisy, while the correction ("Hand rather") hints at a conflict between rod, the symbol of Christ as a disciplining master, and hand, the symbol of his human, nurturing presence.

Further oppositions are latent in the repetition of "cheer" ("would laugh, cheer./Cheer whom though?" [lines 11–12]) and "me" ("the hero whose heaven-handling flung me, foot trod/Me? or me that fought him?" [lines 12–13]). The repetitions, with their quality of stammering, stumbling speech, seem to represent the poet's questioning of his own motives. Was his joy ("cheer") real or only seeming? Was his pleasure in himself rather than in his God ("Cheer whom though")? Was his God, the "hero" whose "foot trod/Me," one and the same with "Despair" [line 1], who "wouldst rude on me/Thy wring-world right foot rock"?

While the many repeated words in the sonnet create another kind of acoustical pattern, they chiefly serve a thematic function. The obsessive reiteration of the word "not" indicates the poet's profound struggle with his own negative emotions; he even phrases the rejection of suicide as a strained double negative ("not choose not to be"). "Me" and "my" become a steady refrain of self-reference, suggesting the depth of the introspective struggle. In the last line, the closing repetition "(my God!) my God" is simultaneously the naming of an opponent and the horrified recognition of who that opponent is.

Hopkins's technique is not only original but also, in certain ways, revolutionary. He "springs" rhythm free from tight metrical regularity, overrides the normal discreteness of words and ideas by his sweeping alliterative phrases, and dismantles the organized sentence with wrenched grammar and emphatic repetitions. His treatment of meter, acoustic pattern, and syntax manifests a struggle to give expression to complicated intuitions and recognitions. In attempting to render his experience faithfully, Hopkins overthrows the canons of lucidity and logical coherence in favor of a poetics of ambiguity, complexity, and tension.

B.S.

SUGGESTED READINGS

Gardner, W. H. (ed.), *Poems and Prose of Gerard Manley Hopkins* (1971).
Gardner, W. H., G. M. *Hopkins: A Study of Poetic Idiosyncrasy in Relation to Poetic Tradition* (1944, 1947).
Hartman, Geoffrey H. (ed.), *Hopkins: A Collection of Critical Essays* (1966).

RUDYARD KIPLING

C H R O N O L O G Y

1865	Born in Bombay, India, the only son of John Lockwood Kipling, a museum curator and illustrator, and Alice Macdonald Kipling, sister-in-law of painters Edward Poynter and Edward Burne-Jones and industrialist Alfred Baldwin.
1871	The Kiplings take their two small children, Rudyard (age 6) and Trix (age 3), to England and board them with strangers, Captain and Mrs. Holloway, in Southsea. It is a very unhappy household for the headstrong, precocious, ill-mannered Rudyard, to whom Mrs. Holloway takes a deep dislike.
1878–1882	Attends boarding school, the United Services College, in Westward Ho, Devon. After a horrible first year of severe bullying, he finds tolerance and acceptance there.
1882	Returns to India as a reporter. Easily regains command of the language, prowls the streets and bazaars at night, opens himself to "charge" of actually enjoying the company of Indians. His articles attract the attention of the viceroy.
1884	His mother and Trix rejoin him; the social status of the family improves.
1886	Publishes his first volume of verse, *Departmental Ditties*, clever, gossipy verse with no pretensions to poetry.
1887	Transfers to larger parent newspaper, the *Pioneer*, in Allahabad and edits its magazine supplement, *Week's News*.

1888   Publishes *Plain Tales from the Hills*, revised Lahore stories in book form, and several volumes of his Railway Series, popular light reading for train travelers.

1889   The *Pioneer* commissions him to write a series of travel articles while visiting friends in America.

1890   Arranges to have the Railway Series published in London; a great popular success; Kipling is hailed as a second Dickens. Publishes in America first version of *The Light That Failed*; it is unsuccessful. Collaborates on a romance set in India, *The Naulahka*, with American friend Wolcott Balestier. Meets his future wife, Wolcott's sister, Caroline Balestier.

1891   Publishes definitive London edition of *The Light That Failed* and a book of adult Indian stories, *Life's Handicap*. On doctor's orders, leaves on a trip around the world. Voyages to South Africa, Australia, and India. Hears of Wolcott's death in London and returns immediately.

1892   Marries Caroline Balestier on January 18; they honeymoon in Japan. Settles on his wife's property in Brattleboro, Vermont. Publishes *The Naulahka* and *Barrack-Room Ballads*.

1892–   Kipling's first daughter, Josephine, is born. Writes his famous children's
1896   books, *The Jungle Book* (1894) and *The Second Jungle Book* (1895), and other Indian stories, *Many Inventions* (1893). They move back to London.

1896–   A son is born, but Kipling's best-loved, oldest daughter dies. Publishes
1899   *Captains Courageous* (1897), a boy's romance of the sea. Publishes one of his best-known poems, "Recessional," in *The New York Times*. Widely regarded as an unofficial poet laureate, he is said to have intimated in 1895 that he would turn down the laureateship if offered. Publishes a collection of his early travel sketches of America, *From Sea to Shining Sea* (1899). Publishes *The Day's Work* (1898) and *Stalky & Co.* (1899), celebrating his years at the United Services College.

1900–   Settles for life in Bateman's, a house in Sussex, the scene of much of his
1910   later writing. Writes very successfully for children, especially *Kim* (1901), *Just So Stories* (1902), *Puck of Pook's Hill* (1906), and *Rewards and Fairies* (1910). Publishes other adult novels: *Traffics and Discoveries* (1904) and *Actions and Reactions* (1909). Turns down two offers of knighthood. Spends a few months every year in South Africa, where magnate Cecil Rhodes builds him a home on his estate. Receives the Nobel Prize for literature in 1907.

1915   His son, John, is killed in World War I barely six weeks after landing in

France. Kipling suffers for the rest of his life from gastritis caused by a stomach ulcer.

1921   Refuses the Order of Merit.

1923   Publishes *The Irish Guards in the Great War*, an official history in loving memory of his dead son who had served with the guards. Again refuses the Order of Merit.

1926–   Takes voyages to Brazil and the West Indies. Publishes *Debits and Credits*
1935   (1926), *Brazilian Sketches* (1927), *Thy Servant a Dog* (1930), and *Limits and Renewals* (1932).

1936   Dies in London almost unnoticed, while the world awaits the death of King George V. Buried in Poets' Corner in Westminster Abbey with a prime minister, an admiral, a general, and a Cambridge college master as his pallbearers.

ESSAY QUESTIONS WITH ANSWERS

"Danny Deever"

23.1 Discuss the use of dialect in the poem.

Answer In "Danny Deever," as in many of the poems in *Barrack-Room Ballads*, Kipling uses Cockney dialect to characterize the ordinary "tommies" who made up the rank and file of the nineteenth-century British army. Part of the effect of this special language is to stereotype the soldier as honest and well meaning; the Cockney speech, the symbolic opposite of the polished rhetoric of the upper classes, suggests the soldier's unsophisticated bluntness and candor. Significantly, the two characters whose conversation is reported in "Danny Deever" have no names but rather titles (Files-on-Parade and Color-Sergeant) which type them according to their army rank. These two representative observers offer a colloquial, intimate account of an army hanging; they are eyewitnesses whose reactions imply the general character of their social class.

The diction of the poem conveys the distinctive qualities of the lower classes as Kipling somewhat romantically perceives them. These soldiers describe the hanging in practical, concrete terms, referring to the bugle blast which calls them to the hanging ("To turn you out, to turn you out" [line 2]), the formation of the regiment ("in 'ollow square" [line 6]), and the stripping of Danny Deever's uniform ("They've taken of his buttons off an' cut his stripes away" [line 7]). They are professional men who know the special lingo and ritual of the army. They are also men who stand to their duty, whatever their personal feelings. The Color-Sergeant's pretense that "what makes the rear rank breathe so 'ard" (line 9) is the cold and that "what makes that front-rank man fall down" is the sun reflects the creed of manliness and courage which Kipling ascribes to ordinary soldiers. The repeated allusions to beer drinking (including "'E's drinkin' bitter beer alone," with its pun on "bitter," a variety of beer drunk in English pubs) suggest another virtue of the lower classes: their masculine camaraderie and good fellowship. The poem dramatizes Danny Deever's exclusion from this company of good fellows by an act of betrayal; he is "a sneakin' shootin' hound" (line 15) who "shot a comrade sleepin' " (line 22). These ordinary soldiers are thus men who know their job and do it and who prize courage, loyalty, and friendship; they speak a language that is concrete, homely, and practical.

In his essay on Kipling, George Orwell asserts that Kipling's use of Cockney speech has a humorous effect so that "the private soldier, though lovable and romantic, has to be a comic."[1] It is true that the back-and-forth exchanges between Files-on-Parade and the Color-Sergeant partially suggest a vaudeville turn, with Files playing straight man to the sergeant's ironic one-liners:

> " 'Is cot was right-'and cot to mine," said Files-on-Parade.
> " 'E's sleepin' out an' far tonight," the Color-Sergeant said.
> "I've drunk 'is beer a score o' times," said Files-on-Parade.
> " 'E's drinkin' bitter beer alone," the Color-Sergeant said.
>
> (lines 17–20)

Orwell points to the "underlying air of patronage" and "the facetiousness of [Kipling's] stage Cockney dialect," but it is possible to read Kipling's dialect poetry, as T. S. Eliot has done, as an inventive reworking of the music hall tradition of caricature, melodrama, and broad humor. The dialect may be exaggerated, even stagy, but it is at the same time a legitimate stylization, a poetic rendering of a special kind of speech which contributes to the mixed tone of pathos and humor which informs "Danny Deever."

23.2   Discuss ballad elements in "Danny Deever."

Answer   The poem has a typical ballad subject, the tragic end of a young man who is being punished for an awful crime. Its simple rhyme scheme (*ababcccd*), swinging iambic rhythm, and refrain ("For they're hangin' Danny Deever") are also elements associated with the ballad form. The concrete presentation of a single dramatic episode and the mixed tone of irony and humor indicate a connection with folklore and legend. Danny Deever is "one of us," a common man and a good fellow, who has made a fatal error; his death is reported with a combination of pity, fear, and gallows humor. All these elements recall the traditional ballad.

Kipling uses the ballad form to develop a distinctive theme: initiation. Characteristically, ballads present a dramatic incident simply and abruptly, without preamble or embellishment, leaving the background and details to the audience's imagination. Kipling reinforces the sense of being suddenly thrust

[1]George Orwell, A *Collection of Essays*, Harcourt Brace Jovanovich, New York, 1953, p. 122.

into an unfamiliar situation by recording the questions of Files-on-Parade. This ordinary tommy is the reader's surrogate in the poem as he wonders aloud about the bugles, the sergeant's pallor, and the stirrings in the ranks. Although we find out early in the poem that "they're hangin' Danny Deever," it is not until the second stanza that we discover that he has murdered someone, and not until the third are we given the precise circumstances: "'e shot a comrade sleepin'." The effect is of a puzzle which gradually becomes more clear. Like one of the rank and file, the reader is witnessing a particular army ritual which can be fully comprehended only in the course of confronting it:

> They are hangin' Danny Deever, you must mark 'im to his place,
> For 'e shot a comrade sleepin'—you must look 'im in the face;
> Nine 'undred of 'is country an' the Regiment's disgrace,
> While they're hangin' Danny Deever in the mornin'.
>
> (lines 21–24)

One of Kipling's major themes, not only in his army ballads but in such poems as "M'Andrew's Hymn," about a dour Scots engineer aboard a steamship, and "The Ballad of East and West," about a confrontation between a British colonel's son and an eastern bandit, is the theme of initiation into a mystery. All these poems document a rite of passage and the discovery of something secret and exotic, whether a craft like M'Andrew's, a way of life like that of the soldiers in "Danny Deever," or a general state of manhood, as in "The Ballad of East and West." The use of dialect in "Danny Deever," like the technical slang of M'Andrew and the oriental allusions of "The Ballad of East and West," is a sign of the special status of the characters and the special knowledge to which they lay claim.

In "Danny Deever," the ballad form, with its dramatic, abrupt mode of presentation, helps illustrate the process by which raw recruits become men and soldiers. In the last stanza, the sudden blackening of the sun and the pathetic whimpering of Danny's soul "that's passin' now" suggest the horror and shock associated with the spectacle of the hanging. Although "the young recruits are shakin', an' they'll want their beer today,/After hangin' Danny Deever in the mornin'," they have nonetheless marked him to his place and looked him in the face. They have done their duty, and in doing so they have become initiates.

"Recessional"

23.3 The form of "Recessional" is conventional, modeled on church hymn and patriotic anthem. Equally conventional are Kipling's themes: mutability in the political realm (*Sic transit gloria mundi*, "Thus passes the glory of the earth") and the transience of all human endeavors ("Ashes to ashes and dust to dust"). Given the formal and thematic orthodoxy of the lyric, how does Kipling rescue the poem from platitude?

Answer   Although many of the ideas in the poem are traditional and commonplace, Kipling's allusive, aphoristic style gives these ideas a striking effectiveness. His exploitation of the strong rhythms of church music and his use of the vocabulary of public oratory capitalize on the meanings associated with the genres of hymn and anthem to create an enduring statement of a powerful theme. But in a sense the theme works against the conventional form, for instead of military optimism or patriotic complacency the poem urges a rededication to spiritual values. "Recessional," then, is a truly religious hymn, not a battle hymn.

Thus the familiar forms of address to the deity—"God of our fathers," "Lord God of Hosts," "Judge of the Nations"—coupled with the urgent refrain "Lest we forget—lest we forget!" create a setting both recognizable and moving. Within this framework, Kipling introduces a series of brief images of the empire building which characterized the Britain of his day. The simple phrase "palm and pine" encapsulates the global spread of the British empire by allusion to the trees of south and north. "Captains and kings" is another alliterative unit which refers to empire builders, both the soldiers who go forth to do battle and the rulers who assert dominion.

However, only the first stanza of the poem implies imperial success and achievement. As the title suggests, the theme is the "receding" of the imperial tide. In stanza 2, the "captains and the kings" are already departing, as "the tumult and the shouting dies" (lines 7–8). What remains is "thine ancient sacrifice,/An humble and a contrite heart" (lines 9–10). In stanza 3, Kipling reinforces the idea that the empire is near dissolution:

> Far-called, our navies melt away—
>   On dune and headland sinks the fire—
> Lo, all our pomp of yesterday
>   Is one with Nineveh and Tyre!
>   (lines 13–16)

The condensed, gnomic diction has a riddling quality, as though the speaker were a prophet announcing doom and exhorting humility. Kipling's frequent use of paired nouns evokes not only the physical reaches of empire ("pine and

palm," "dune and headland," "Nineveh and Tyre") but the metaphoric significance of empire building. The tumult and shouting and the captains and kings
stand for the brief moment of imperial success, while the "reeking tube and iron
shard" are what is left behind as the empire builders depart and the "far-flung
battle-line" and "far-called navies" recede. Although at times the language of
the poem is relatively abstract, many of these doublets are concrete and evocative. The general and the particular are held in balance, producing a tone that
is at once familiar and arresting.

The prophetic, sermonizing tone continues in the last two stanzas, which
amplify the theme of "frantic boast and foolish word." This seems in part a
response to the shrinking of power alluded to in the earlier part of the poem
and in part an attack on temporal power itself as fragile and illusory in comparison
with the eternal realm of God. Although the imperial endeavor is both "valiant"
and compassionate ("guarding," not conquering), it is nonetheless "dust." The
aphoristic style condenses complex ideas into memorable phrases suggestive of
homiletic wisdom or biblical proverb:

> All valiant dust that builds on dust,
>   And guarding calls not Thee to guard—
> For frantic boast and foolish word,
> Thy mercy on Thy People, Lord!
>
>   (lines 27–30)

The originality of the poem lies in its reversal of the expected boasting and
propaganda of an anthem or national hymn. The references to "Gentiles," "lesser
breeds without the Law," and "heathen heart" delineate the danger of hubris
and godlessness even for a Christian nation. Although these are stock epithets,
they are unconventional when applied to the civilized British, who, "drunk
with sight of power," might yet "loose/Wild tongues that have not Thee in
awe" (lines 19–20). Kipling reserves the rhetoric of name-calling and insult for
the purpose of self-discipline, turning it on the empire builders themselves. His
prayer for the nation to turn away from "power" to "Thee" employs a controlled,
conscious diction which is the opposite of "frantic boast and foolish word."

23.4 Compare "Recessional" with "The White Man's Burden."

Answer Both "Recessional" and "The White Man's Burden" focus on the
responsibilities of imperial power. But while the focus of "Recessional" is upward,
to God, the focus of "The White Man's Burden" is downward, to the heathen
populations whom the empire has subdued. In "Recessional" Kipling

places the imperial endeavor in the perspective of eternity. Although the empire is "valiant" and God-ordained ("Lord of our far-flung battle-line—/Beneath whose awful Hand we hold/Dominion over palm and pine"), Kipling acknowledges that it is nonetheless "dust." It is this knowledge of transience and mutability, announced clearly in the poem itself, that makes the repeated invocation of humility seem genuine. There is, after all, much cause for humility.

In contrast, "The White Man's Burden" has a quality of complacency and self-congratulation as Kipling describes the responsibility of the conqueror to care for the conquered. The growth of empire is glorified as a religious and moral campaign "to seek another's profit/And work another's gain" (lines 15–16). Paradoxically, the white man must conduct "savage wars of peace" in order to "fill full the mouth of Famine/And bid the sickness cease" (lines 18–20). The paradox sounds strained, like a rhetorical evasion of a genuine, though unexamined, contradiction. In this poem, Kipling's rhetoric generally seems overextended, creating a suspiciously simplified polarity between the noble "White Man" who stoops, martyrlike, to pick up his heavy "burden" and the "new-caught, sullen peoples/Half-devil and half-child" (lines 7–8). The phrase "White Man's burden," with its obtrusive capitalization, has the effect of a slogan. Implied is the superiority and martyrlike authority of the white race. The characterization of the conquered peoples is equally stereotyped; they are like birds ("fluttered folk" [line 6]), animals ("new-caught"), demons, and children. The imagery is imprecise, implying only a generalized inferiority. This use of language to state a case rather than describe or dramatize gives the poem an air of propaganda.

It is interesting to see why for most readers "Recessional" succeeds as poetry where "The White Man's Burden" fails. It is not just that the sentiments of "Recessional" are more palatable to a liberal-minded reader (though they may be) but that its rhetoric is more effective than that of "The White Man's Burden." In "Recessional," the relatively abstract language of hymn and anthem alternates with telling, precise phrases which evoke the nature of the imperial enterprise. But the abstractions of "The White Man's Burden," dealing with the moral courage required of conquerors, have the opacity of clichés. The exhortation to

> Take up the White Man's burden—
> In patience to abide,
> To veil the threat of terror
> And check the show of pride.
> (lines 9–12)

consists of automatic phrases, and the capitalizations of Sloth, Folly, Famine, Freedom, and White Man suggest a kind of flaccid allegory, not fully realized. Part of the vividness of "Recessional" derives from its urgent attack on complacency, on drunken power and "foolish word," while the flatness of "The White Man's Burden" seems to stem from its self-satisfied point of view, leading to a use of language which is itself complacent.

B.S.

SUGGESTED READINGS

Dobree, Bonamy, *Rudyard Kipling: Realist and Fabulist* (1967).
Rutherford, A. (ed.), *Kipling's Mind and Art* (1964).
Sandison, Alan, *The Wheel of Empire* (1967).

W. B. YEATS

C H R O N O L O G Y

1865   Born in Dublin, Ireland. Son of J. B. Yeats, noted painter, and Susan Pollexfen Yeats, native of Sligo, a town steeped in Irish history and lore. Both are of Protestant background, though J. B. Yeats is a skeptic in religion. Until 1880, family will divide its time mainly between Sligo and London.

1880   Family settles in Howth, near Dublin.

1884   Encouraged by father, Yeats enters art school in Dublin. Lacking real talent, he abandons art studies after two years. Yeats never attends university.

1885   First published poems. Helps found Dublin Hermetic Society, early indication of lifelong mystical preoccupations.

1886   Begins narrative poem *The Wanderings of Oisin*, his first work based on Irish mythology.

1887   Moves to London with family. Joins London Lodge of Theosophists, mystical group headed by spiritualist Madame Blavatsky; remains a member until 1890.

1889   Meets and falls in love with Maud Gonne, Irish nationalist leader renowned for her beauty; subject of many of Yeats's greatest poems. Yeats remains captivated by her for years; he proposes marriage several times between 1891 and 1916, always to be refused. *The Wanderings of Oisin and Other Poems* published.

1890   Joins the Hermetic Order of the Golden Dawn, a secret society devoted to spiritualism and magic. He will remain an active member the rest of his life, drawing from his mystical studies symbols and themes used in his later poetry.

1891   Increasing interest in Irish politics and literary life. Joins Young Ireland League, nationalist group; helps form Irish Literary Society of London, the Rhymers Club, and National Literary Society in Dublin.

1892   *The Countess Cathleen* written.

1895   Publishes *Poems*, first collected edition of his writings.

1896   Meets Lady Augusta Gregory, Irish aristocrat, writer, and folklorist. She will be a collaborator and patron, especially in his work for an Irish national theater.

1897   Publishes *The Secret Rose*, a collection of "Pre-Raphaelite" poems.

1898   Beginning of gradual disengagement from political activism. Early planning for Irish theater with Lady Gregory.

1899   Publishes *The Wind Among the Reeds*. Founding of the Irish National Theatre.

1902   Begins work on series of plays on Irish themes and legends with Lady Gregory. President of Irish National Dramatic Society.

1904   Maud Gonne marries Roger MacBride, nationalist leader. Yeats publishes *In the Seven Woods*, in which his more mature, natural, colloquial style begins to appear.

1906–   Publishes *Stories of Red Hanrahan* (based on Irish legendry), *Poems 1895–*
1910   *1905*, *Collected Works* (eight volumes), and *The Green Helmet and Other Poems*.

1912   Meets American poet and critic Ezra Pound, who is to influence Yeats's increasingly modern style. Pound introduces Yeats to the spare, symbolic style of classic Japanese Noh drama.

1914   Publishes *Responsibilities*, first collection of poems to reflect Yeats's gradually developing system of personal mystic symbolism.

1915   Yeats refuses knighthood.

1916   Easter Rebellion. Roger MacBride is executed; Yeats gives him his grudging admiration ("Easter 1916"). Performance of *At the Hawk's Well*, first of several Noh-influenced dramas by Yeats.

1917   Yeats buys castle at Ballylee; he will renovate it and live most of his remaining life there. Proposes to Iseult Gonne, Maud's daughter, and is refused. Marries Georgie Hyde-Lees, who will share Yeats's spiritualist interests, engaging in "automatic writing" during trances from which Yeats will derive images and symbols for poetry. *The Wild Swans at Coole* published (Coole Park was Lady Gregory's home).

1921   Yeats publishes *Michael Robartes and the Dancer*.

1922   Appointed senator of the Irish Free State; plays only a minor political role. Outbreak of Irish Civil War, deeply troubling to Yeats. *Later Poems* published.

1923   Receives Nobel Prize for literature.

1925   Publishes *A Vision*, the result of seven years of work. It sets forth Yeats's mystical beliefs, including his theory of twenty-eight "phases" which help determine human history, personalities, culture.

1928–   Late outburst of creativity. Publishes *The Tower* (1928), *The Winding Stair*
1934   *and Other Poems*(1933), *Words for Music Perhaps* (1933), *Collected Poems* (1933), and *Collected Plays* (1934).

1935   Collaborates with Indian holy man Shri Purohit Swami on English translation of Hindu scriptures, the Upanishads. Publishes *A Full Moon in March*.

1939   Yeats dies in southern France; is buried at Roquebrune. *Last Poems and Two Plays* published posthumously.

1948   Yeats's remains are reinterred at Sligo in accordance with his wishes.

ESSAY QUESTIONS WITH ANSWERS

"To the Rose upon the Rood of Time"

24.1 What is the speaker's main dilemma in this poem?

Answer The speaker is an Irish poet who wishes to transcend the mundane world of modern Ireland by writing of ancient Irish myths. However, he fears that by doing so he will lose touch with both the common, natural world and his Irish audience. In addition, he wishes to reinfuse ordinary life with some of the grace and dignity of the ancient ways.

The red Rose, the symbol of eternal beauty, is invoked by the poet as his muse. Like other muses, she is implored by the poet to inspire him and help him elevate his poem. He longs to discover the eternal behind the transitory creatures of everyday life, just as he longs to sing of the mythic past instead of the lowly present. But in the second stanza, the dash in line 13 signals a reversal in the poet's attitude. After invoking the Rose once more, he suddenly begins to fear that he will become intoxicated with the Rose and overpowered by her inspiration: "Ah, leave me still/A little space for the rose-breath to fill!" he implores her. He fears that the beauty of myth and eternity will blot out the themes and sounds of human toil and mortality. The image evoked by the poem's title—the Rose of eternal beauty crucified on the Rood (cross) of Time—presents the paradoxical intersection of time and eternity.

The dilemma expressed in "The Rose upon the Rood of Time" reenacts, in a different form, the central problem of an earlier poem of Yeats's, "The Stolen Child," in which the faeries kidnap a young child away from the lowing calves, kettle on the hob, and brown mice of the Irish countryside. Again, the issue of the escape from mortal fears into an unchanging eternal realm is crucial. In the earlier poem, the speaker is a faery wooing the child to the other side; in the later poem, the speaker is the poet caught in a dilemma posed by the attractions of eternity and myth. Thus, "To the Rose upon the Rood of Time" is a poem specifically about poetry making; indeed, it is the inaugural poem for Yeats's 1893 collection of poems entitled *The Rose*. Rather than expressing the debate between the ideal and the actual in terms of a journey from one world to another, Yeats now expresses the conflict as a poetic dilemma: What is the Irish poet's proper subject, theme, language?

"Leda and the Swan"

24.2 Discuss the significance of the imagery in the following lines of the poem:

> A shudder in the loins engenders there
> The broken wall, the burning roof and tower
> And Agamemnon dead.
>
> (lines 9–11)

Answer   The images are striking in their radical compression: "The broken wall" and "burning roof" are both literal and symbolically sexual, suggesting the destruction of Leda's hymen as well as the destruction of the city of Troy. The rape paradoxically "engenders" destruction, for it results in the birth of the fatal female pair: Helen, whose capture by Paris led to the Trojan War, and Clytemnestra, whose murder of her husband, Agamemnon, led to the fall of the House of Atreus. Birth is eclipsed by death and destruction; the fires of Zeus's lust become the apocalyptic fires of Troy.

The compression in the lines also emphasizes the physical union of Zeus and Leda, violator and victim. The phrase "shudder in the loins" refers first to Zeus's orgasm, since this physical act is necessary to "engender" Helen and Clytemnestra. But the "shudder" also refers to Leda's emotional reaction of fear and dread. Although Zeus's physical force produces the central event, it is Leda's emotional reaction in which the poet seems most interested. In fact, the focus seems to shift here from a vivid description of the physical act to a consideration of its effect on Leda, not only in herself but as a representative of bewildered and violated humanity. The double reference of the phrase "a shudder in the loins" verbally unites the two very different central figures of the poem.

24.3   How does Yeats make use of the formal pattern of the sonnet in "Leda and the Swan"?

Answer   "Leda and the Swan" is a sonnet roughly in the Italian (or Pe-
trarchan) form: an octave (eight lines or two quatrains) and a sestet (six lines
or two triplets). The central division of a sonnet of this type—the break between
the octave and the sestet—usually signals some kind of logical reversal or at
least a change in the poet's course. For example, line 9, the first line of the
sestet, often begins with a transitional word, such as a conjunction like "but."
In "Leda and the Swan," although there is no abrupt logical turn, a shift of
emphasis does occur as the sestet begins. In the two quatrains of the octave,
Yeats describes the rape (quatrain 1) and asks two questions about Leda's terrified
reaction (quatrain 2); he then shifts in the sestet to the larger historical and
philosophical ramifications of the brutal act.

The question raised in the sestet is puzzling, but it seems to be a question
about the entrance of the divine (the god, Zeus) into human history as represented by Leda. Does humanity acquire knowledge or vision from the apocalyptic
intervention of a god in history? The question itself seems to assume that the
ultimate knowledge possessed by divinity may be transferable, at least in part,
to humanity. But rhetorically the problem is unresolved; the hope of vision or
understanding remains only a possibility the speaker posits, since the poem ends
with a question rather than a statement. Yeats uses the formal divisions of the
sonnet to shift from the more concrete and vivid imagery of the rape to more
abstract and philosophical considerations.

24.4   How does "Leda and the Swan" allude to other myths about the
intersection of the divine and human, and what does it say about the nature of
such events?

Answer   Yeats believed that history was composed of 2000-year cycles, each
initiated by a decisive intervention of the divine in human history. He also
believed that events in one cycle correspond to events in another, that history
repeats itself, with a difference. The brutal rape of Leda, which initiates one
2000-year cycle beginning with the downfall of Troy, is implicitly compared
and contrasted with the impregnation that initiates another 2000-year cycle:
the impregnation of Mary by the Holy Ghost. The myth of Leda's rape is a
myth of annunciation.

Unlike most other poetic treatments of divine intervention in history (for
example, T. S. Eliot's images of the Annunciation and Incarnation in "The
Dry Salvages"), Yeats's poem emphasizes the brutality and horror as well as the

significance of the event. The image of the girl's rape by the animal provides a metaphor for Yeats's sense of the violence and apocalyptic disruption which characterize the end of one cycle and the beginning of another. The combination of dread of and fascination with the impending change found in "Leda and the Swan" also appears in "The Second Coming." There, the speaker seems to welcome a change, a new birth; however, his excitement mingles with fear as he realizes that the "Second Coming" may bring a "rough," slouching, terrible beast rather than Christ, to whose return the title of the poem ironically alludes.

"Sailing to Byzantium"

24.5 Many of Yeats's poems are structured around a set of oppositions or antinomies. How does this structure appear in "Sailing to Byzantium"?

Answer The first opposition in the poem is given in a geographic metaphor: "that country," presumably Ireland, with its salmon falls, and this country, the early medieval imperial city of Byzantium. The two locations and the related motif of the journey between them, however, symbolize the fundamental thematic opposition in the poem: that between the natural, mortal world of process and aging and the unchanging, eternal realm of art. Yeats once wrote that Byzantium under the rule of Justinian (around A.D. 550) symbolized for him a unity of being, a state in which "religious, aesthetic and practical life were one." As opposed to the real world of natural processes, in which the aging poet feels himself to be in a hopeless decline, the aesthetic realm of Byzantium presents an image of stasis and harmony.

At the start of the poem, the speaker has already sailed to Byzantium, although he has still not been integrated into the mode of life he finds there. The world he has left is teeming with natural, sensuous life; in fact, every living thing sings praises to sensuality and mutability. On the other hand, the "artifice of eternity" (line 24) in Byzantium is spiritual and artificial; the songs in Byzantium, as opposed to the "sensual music" of "that country," are spiritual ones, products of art. Byzantium promises to be a place where the aging poet can concentrate on the exaltation of his spirit rather than his decaying body and on art rather than the processes of human sensuality.

However, one feels that the speaker, although in Byzantium, cannot yet relinquish his thoughts of the sensual music. He wishes to be "out of nature," imagining himself as an artificial bird, yet paradoxically the subject of the golden bird's song is time and the natural process. He chooses to sing "to lords and ladies of Byzantium/Of what is past, or passing, or to come" (lines 31–32). The poet's reluctance to abandon the realm of sensuality and time distinguishes this poem from its successor, "Byzantium," in which the speaker is in fact "out of nature," a mummy whose detached, visionary, posthumous voice differs greatly from the troubled, human voice of the speaker of this poem.

24.6   Yeats was in his sixties when he published "Sailing to Byzantium." To what extent can it be said that the poem's subject is aging and the suffering it brings?

Answer   It is basically true that the poem's subject is the aging process, although the statement should probably be amended slightly. The situation of the poem, or, to paraphrase Wordsworth, the occasion of its cry, is the speaker's awareness of growing older. The situation of aging serves both as a premise for the poem and as a metaphor for the dilemma of an individual divided against himself; for, as he ages, the once vital poet feels a split within himself between his desires and abilities. His heart is "sick with desire/And fastened to a dying animal" (lines 21–22); he is caught in the prison of his own decrepitude and must find some means of escape.

Describing an aged man as "but a paltry thing," the speaker seems to have reached a point where he can neither satisfy nor sublimate his desires. The poet's admission that his heart is still "sick with desire" suggests that the journey to Byzantium, and the search for transcendence through art, constitutes an attempt to sublimate his sensual desires. He begs the Byzantine sages to gather him "into the artifice of eternity," a request that may be interpreted as a plea for help to be a poet. He feels he can be freed of his agonizing state only if, as a poet, he can sing of time without being tyrannized by it.

24.7   How does the image of the bird unify the different parts of the poem?

Answer   The image of the bird occurs, in various forms, in stanzas I, II, and IV. As is true of many of the details and symbols here, the recurrent bird image emphasizes the contrasts between the various "worlds" presented in the poem: the world of the young, full of "sensual music," the plight of the old man, and the eternal realm of Byzantium.

In line 2, the phrase "birds in the trees" is only one of a triplet of phrases used to epitomize the sensuality and mutability of the natural world. Just as the description of "the young in one another's arms" serves as an emblem of the hot, crowded, intense world of sensuality and sexuality, the phrase "birds in the trees" symbolizes a kind of mindless celebration of natural process. The image of the birds, however, moves the poet closer to another important image in the poem—that of music making. As line 7 makes explicit, the birds' song celebrates the very sensuality in which they participate, or to put it more strongly, in which they are "caught."

This introduction of the motif of song through the image of the birds sets the stage for the new and contrasting image of the poet as scarecrow in stanza II. The poet now sees himself as "a tattered coat upon a stick" (line 10), a straw man to scare away the birds. He sees himself this way, that is, unless his soul can rejoice ("clap its hands and sing") despite the decrepitude of the body.

The final image of the bird appears in stanza IV. The transcendent form the poet desires to take is that of a golden bird, sitting on "a golden bough," singing his song. We have come far from the image of the natural birds of stanza I, yet both the image of the bird and its song of time unite the beginning and the end of the poem. The final line, giving the subject of the bird's song ("Of what is past, or passing, or to come"), echoes the triad of line 6 ("Whatever is begotten, born, and dies"). The image of the golden bird is meant to contrast with the natural birds of the first stanza; unlike the natural birds, it is an aesthetic object separate from the process of which it sings. It serves as an image of the speaker transformed from an old man into an artist.

"Among School Children"

24.8 In the first stanza of this poem, the poet situates himself in time and space. He is 60 years old and is walking through a classroom full of children. By the last stanza, the dramatic setting seems to have vanished. Why does Yeats abandon the scene by the end of the poem?

Answer Like Wordsworth's "Tintern Abbey," "Among School Children" begins in a specific location which reminds the poet of scenes and images from his past. The specific setting in both poems functions as a stimulus to memory and imagination. In "Among School Children," the contrast between the aging poet and the young children propels the poet on his journey back into his past.

The "sixty-year-old smiling public man" (line 8) is reminded of himself as a child and of the Ledaean (that is, sensually opulent) image of Maud Gonne, Yeats's ever-admired ideal woman, in her childhood and youth. The gap between the promise, freshness, and beauty of these childhood images and the decrepit reality of the aged man and hollowcheeked woman leads the poet to a consideration of the perplexities of the imagination. How, he seems to ask, can one reconcile the image with the reality? Are the knowledge and experience gained in life worth the price one has to pay to acquire them? These questions and this theme provide the center of the poem. The physical setting becomes unimportant as memories give way to a meditation on the imagination itself.

In stanzas V, VI, and VII, the poet considers various examples of the gap between promise and fulfillment and the role of the image of the ideal in a world of time and change. Philosophers—represented in stanza VI by Plato, Aristotle, and Pythagoras—have vainly contemplated the elusive relationship between essence and existence or between paradigm and circumstance. Nuns and mothers, in different ways, have been betrayed by the imagination, which has produced images for worship that "break hearts" because they promise too much. The icons worshiped by nuns and the fond images of the child that mothers adore "mock" humanity because the image cannot be reconciled with the reality which unfolds in time.

The second major question Yeats seems to be asking throughout the poem is, Is it all worth it? At the end of the poem, he seeks an image of a realm where the vision of ideal beauty is not purchased at such great cost.

24.9   In his search for an image of human possibilities that unifies the ideal with the real, why does the poet offer two different images in stanza VIII: the tree and the dancer?

Answer   The final stanza of the poem is a very difficult one. It offers two ecstatic images of unity, but they are cast in the form of questions rather than statements. What do the images at the end of the poem mean, and what is the significance of the fact that the poem concludes with two questions?

Throughout the poem, the poet has seemed to disparage the images that "mock" the human enterprise, images that philosophy, religion, or parenthood provide for worship. In the last stanza, he asserts, perhaps desperately, that there must be a place where Adam's curse (the pain of labor) can be avoided, where "the body is not bruised to pleasure soul" (reading "pleasure" as a verb).

He offers two images of unity which do not present a tragic split between promise and fulfillment: the chestnut tree and the dancer.

In the world of nature, he finds an image, the chestnut tree, which expresses a perfect congruence between origin and end, intention and reality. The tree is the leaf, the blossom, and the bole; it is all of its stages of creation. There is no ironic discrepancy between bole and blossom as there is between the childhood image and the smiling 60-year-old "scarecrow." But the image of the tree is inanimate and inhuman, and the poet looks to a second image, a human one, to perhaps better express a unity for humanity itself. The dancer is both a living body and a work of art, an aesthetic image; as Eliot says in "The Dry Salvages" in *Four Quartets* (perhaps with Yeats's dancer in mind), "You are the music/While the music lasts." The dancer is an image of labor and pleasure, of body and spirit, reconciled and unified.

Yet the ecstatic images which sweep us to the poem's conclusion are contained in two questions; the images themselves are addressed directly, asked whether in fact they do represent this unity. The conflict between these beautiful images of harmony and the rhetorical form in which they are presented leaves us with uncertainty. The poem ends ecstatically, but we wonder if there is not a certain evasion or irresolution in the leap of imagination that concludes the poem.

"The Circus Animals' Desertion"

24.10 What is the central opposition that gives this poem its structure?

Answer The central opposition, developed in section II and resolved in section III, is that between the heart and the dream. In enumerating the "old themes" of his earlier poetry, the poet "measures the lot" (as he says in "A Dialogue of Self and Soul") of his life and art. Although the source of his poetry was his own emotions and desires, and its themes were those of the "embittered heart," he realizes that he had sublimated his life too fully in his art; the "heart-mysteries" became less important than the art itself. The "dream" or poetic realization of the experience substituted for the experience. The dreams themselves enchanted him, he says; his love was taken by the dreams, "and not these things that they were emblems of" (line 32).

In enumerating the "old themes," the speaker cites three phases of his art, three examples of the split between heart and dream, in the three stanzas of section II. "Starved for the bosom of his faery bride," that is, possessed by desire and sensual longing, the young Yeats had written in 1889 *The Wanderings of Oisin*, a long poem about a mythological Irish poet and warrior. Apprehensive over the political activities of Maud Gonne (the woman he loved and to whom he unsuccessfully proposed marriage), in 1892 he had written his play *The Countess Cathleen* about a woman who sells her soul to the devil in exchange for food for the poor. In a later play, *On Baile's Strand* (1904), Yeats had written of Cuchulain, another Irish mythological hero. The people and events of the poet's life became the sources of his art but in the process were lost to him as real objects of love and affection. Throughout sections I and II, he reproaches himself with the division he sees between his life and his art.

24.11   At what conclusion does the poet arrive in section III? Is the central opposition of the poem resolved?

Answer   The final section of the poem at first seems to signal merely a swing from one pole to the other of the central opposition, from the "dream" to the "foul rag-and-bone shop of the heart." (line 40). One of the central metaphors in this section is the ladder, which represents talent and inspiration. Now, the poet says, the "ladder's gone"; the talent and inspiration seem to have vanished. The circus animals—the images and inspirations of Yeats's earlier poetic career—have abandoned him. Although referring to them as "circus animals" and "stilted boys" can be seen as disparaging, the tone of the poem conveys the sense that the poet is deeply grieved and frustrated over their loss: "Being but a broken man," he says, "I must be satisfied with my heart."

Yet somehow, out of the despair and bitterness, the poetic inspiration emerges and enables the aging poet to create once again, as he is able to write this poem about the loss of inspiration. Upon further study of the final section, it becomes clear that the poet offers an image of the connection between life and art, or the heart and the dream. For in the final stanza, the poet suggests that the mind connects the heart and the dream; they are not a pair of opposites that can be finally separated. Although the final word of the poem is "heart," and the heart is given its due, it is no longer sentimentalized as the exclusive province of truth. The images of art come out of experience and are nurtured in the mind; they are not mere chimeras but visions which bring together emotion and symbol, life and art. The dream comes from that "foul rag-and-bone shop of the heart." The image of the reconciliation of opposites in "The Circus Animals' Desertion" is a far cry from the lyrical images of tree and dancer in "Among School Children," written twelve years earlier. Instead, it is closer to the sardonic, tough, even bitter images expressed in the poems spoken by one of Yeats's other personas, Crazy Jane, who insists that "fair needs foul" (see "Crazy Jane Talks with the Bishop").

K.L.

SUGGESTED READINGS

Donoghue, Denis, and J. R. Mulryne (eds.), *An Honoured Guest: New Essays on W. B. Yeats* (1965).

Ellmann, Richard, *Yeats, the Man and the Masks* (1948).

Ellmann, Richard, *The Identity of Yeats* (1954).

Jeffares, Alexander Norman, *A Commentary on the Collected Poems of W. B. Yeats* (1968).

Kermode, Frank, *Romantic Image* (1957).

Rosenthal, Macha Louis, *Sailing into the Unknown: Yeats, Pound, and Eliot* (1978).

T. S. ELIOT

C H R O N O L O G Y

1888   Born Thomas Stearns Eliot in St. Louis, Missouri, seventh and youngest child of Henry Ware Eliot and Charlotte Chauncey Stearns. His father is president of the Hydraulic-Press Brick Company, and his mother is an intellectual and writer. His earlier ancestors had come to Massachusetts from England about 1670.

1906–   Studies at Harvard with scholars Irving Babbitt and George Santayana.
1909   Develops enthusiasm for Elizabethan and Jacobean literature, the Italian Renaissance, and Indian philosophy. Early poems include "Portrait of a Lady" and the beginning of "Prufrock."

1910–   Completes M.A. and goes to Paris, where, under tutoring of Alain-Fournier,
1911   attends philosopher Henri Bergson's lectures at the Sorbonne. Completes first great poem, "The Love Song of J. Alfred Prufrock."

1911   Resumes graduate work at Harvard in philosophy with Josiah Royce, studying metaphysics, logic and psychology. Studies Sanskrit.

1914   Traveling summer fellowship in Germany, then finishes his formal studies at Merton College, Oxford.

1915   Marries Vivienne Haigh-Wood, daughter of painter Charles Haigh-Wood. Teaches at High Wycombe Grammar School. Ezra Pound arranges to have Harriet Monroe publish "The Love Song of J. Alfred Prufrock" in *Poetry* magazine.

1916   Completes doctoral dissertation, "Experience and the Objects of Knowledge in the Philosophy of F. H. Bradley." Harvard accepts the dissertation immediately because, Eliot later said, it was "unreadable." Bradley's emphasis on the private nature of individual experience greatly influences Eliot's literary theory. Teaches at Highgate School near London. Obtains a position with Lloyd's Bank, which he holds for nine years.

1917   Becomes assistant editor for the *Egoist*. Harriet Weaver's Egoist Press publishes his first volume of poems, *Prufrock and Other Observations*.

1920   Publishes *The Sacred Wood*, his first collection of critical essays. The main issue of the essays is the integrity of poetry.

1922   Becomes founding editor of *The Criterion*, the leading English literary review until 1939. Becomes London correspondent for *The Dial* and for *La Revue Française*. Publishes *The Waste Land* in *The Criterion* and *The Dial*; it wins $2000 Dial Award. The impact of this poem on the literary establishment is sudden and far-reaching.

1925   Publishes *Poems, 1909–1925*. Joins publishing firm of Faber and Gwyer (later Faber and Faber).

1926   Gives the Clark Lectures at Trinity College, Cambridge.

1927   Becomes a British citizen and joins the Church of England.

1930   Publishes the whole of *Ash-Wednesday*, which had been previously published in parts.

1932   Publishes *Selected Essays*, which includes essays from several volumes since *The Sacred Wood*, addressing a new problem, "that of the relation of poetry to the spiritual and social life of its time and of other times." Returns to Harvard as the Charles Eliot Norton Professor of Poetry.

1933   Separates from his wife, who suffers from a nervous disorder. Lectures at the University of Virginia.

1934   Writes *The Rock*, a religious pageant play about the building of a church.

1935   Writes his first major play, *Murder in the Cathedral*, for the Canterbury Cathedral Festival. Play celebrates the martyrdom of Thomas à Becket in 1170 and explores the personal, social, and political meaning of martyrdom.

1939   Writes *The Family Reunion*, a tragicomic verse drama, which opens at the Westminster Theatre in London. His first venture into commercial theater, it is not a success. Gives up editorship of *The Criterion*, which discontinues publication.

1943   Publishes his most ambitious poem, *Four Quartets*. The first "quartet," "Burnt Norton," appeared in 1934; the second, "East Coker," in 1940; the third, "Dry Salvages," in 1941; the fourth, "Little Gidding," in 1942. These long meditations in quasi-musical form contain Eliot's most profound insights into time, history, and the moment of illumination that transcends time and history with intimations of an eternal, immutable reality. The poem represents the completion of a spiritual journey begun in *The Waste Land* and developed in *Ash Wednesday*.

1947   His wife, Vivienne, dies after a long illness.

1948   Receives the Nobel Prize for literature and the Order of Merit. Reportedly declines knighthood.

1949   Writes *The Cocktail Party*, a very successful verse drawing-room comedy for the Edinburgh Festival. Under the burlesque of trivial, upper middle-class small talk, the play dramatizes serious modern spiritual quests.

1950   *The Cocktail Party* is produced commercially in New York and London with even greater success. Lectures at the University of Chicago.

1953   Writes play *The Confidential Clerk* for the Edinburgh Festival.

1957   Marries his secretary, Valerie Fletcher.

1959   Publishes *The Elder Statesman*, a play that explores the meaning of tradition; it is a popular success.

1965   Dies in London. His ashes are buried in St. Michael's Church in East Coker, thus fulfilling one refrain of the "East Coker" quartet, "in my beginning is my end," since his ancestors had emigrated from East Coker to the Massachusetts Bay Colony. A memorial service is conducted in Westminster Abbey, where a memorial stone is placed.

ESSAY QUESTIONS WITH ANSWERS

"The Love Song of J. Alfred Prufrock"

25.1   How does the imagery of the first fourteen lines of the poem create its psychological and emotional atmosphere?

Answer   The imagery of the first fourteen lines establishes the atmosphere of disillusionment and passivity that suffuses the poem. The conceit in which the speaker compares the evening to an etherized patient violates the reader's expectations concerning the lyrical landscape and offers instead an image of sterility in an urban landscape which seems inimical to human life. The modifiers in the next few lines, too, heighten the sense of isolation and frustration: the "half-deserted streets" express the speaker's isolation, and although he tries to find a refuge or retreat in these lonely avenues, they seem to be "muttering" to him, as if reminding him of his predicament.

   The physical journey suggested by the speaker to his audience (possibly a woman, the reader, or an alter ego) is also a mental journey. The dirty, urban streets are not only the ugly spaces of the city but also the spaces of the speaker's mind, the wandering paths of his undirected thought. Thus, the streets which are "like a tedious argument" are also the twists and turns of an inner argument that Prufrock conducts with himself. Prufrock is afraid of the destination of his mental journey, that overwhelming question which will force him to confront the meaninglessness of his life. Throughout the poem, he is torn between a desire to change his life and a fear of change, between allowing himself to recognize how unhappy he is and burying himself in the triviality of polite society and the anonymity of the desolate urban landscape.

   The couplet at the end of the first fourteen-line passage reinforces the sense of meaninglessness and trivialization. Several times during the poem, Eliot uses rhyme to juxtapose the grand and mundane ironically, and here the rhyming of "Michelangelo" and the singsong phrase "come and go" suggests a general trivialization of culture. In the image of the women speaking of Michelangelo as they would of any item of gossip, Eliot satirizes the trivial, social interest in the aesthetic. Real beauty has become only a subject for society's chitchat.

25.2   One of the major difficulties that "Prufrock" presents to the reader is its disjointed and fragmented form. Although it is presented as a dramatic monologue, its form is radically different from the more coherent and continuous dramatic monologues of the Victorians, for example, Browning's "My Last Duchess" or "Fra Lippo Lippi" and Tennyson's "Ulysses" or "Tithonus." What is the purpose of the poem's fragmentation?

Answer   "Prufrock" is not a soliloquy spoken on a particular occasion to a particular audience like Browning's revealing psychological portrait of the duke of Ferrara in "My Last Duchess." It is meant to present a series of metaphors for a state of mind. The consciousness presented in the poem is an intensely anxious and impotent one in that the speaker is unable to draw conclusions about anything. The division of the poem into short and disjointed sections, the succession of short, anxious questions, and the ellipses are formal elements that contribute to the general atmosphere of mental confusion, anxiety, and frustration.

For example, the first verse paragraph, in which the speaker proposes a visit to his audience, is followed by a pair of short, rhyming lines that fail to locate us in relation to the preceding lines: "In the room the women come and go/ Talking of Michelangelo" (lines 13–14). What room? What women? The sing-song lines surface eerily, only to give way to eight lines of a description of the autumnal fog that shrouds some urban street. The effect of the crosscutting of scene and the formal disjointedness is to wrench us from any specific locale and place us somewhere in the mind of a person who experiences life in this disconnected, unintegrated way. The barrage of short questions—"Do I dare?" "Do I dare?" "So how should I presume?" "And how should I begin?"—is another important formal feature that conveys the neurotic indecision and anxiety in Prufrock's mind. No direct answers are given to these questions—a sift of attention invariably occurs.

The ellipses which follow the image of the ragged claws in the middle of the poem also function to represent Prufrock's suppression of painful thoughts. The self-loathing and wish for oblivion implicit in his self-image as a "pair of ragged claws/Scuttling across the floor of silent seas" are too terrible for the speaker to face; he switches abruptly to the more soothing image of the sleeping evening. Thus, Prufrock's fear of self-revelation and general anxiety about life are conveyed as much by the fragmentation of form as by the imagery and diction. Although the poem contains echoes of traditional verse forms, the destruction of narrative continuity gives it a decidedly modern flavor.

25.3 Is there any language in the poem that seems lyrical or romantic or that would justify Eliot's naming the poem a love song?

Answer Juxtaposed to the deliberately antipoetic and antiromantic images—evening as an etherized patient, and life measured out "with coffee spoons"—the reader finds the erotic, lovely image of the mermaids at the end of the poem. The diction here becomes more lyrical; the alliteration in the words "waves," "white," "wind," and "water" is soothing. The mermaids seem to evoke a more primitive and mysterious life. But although Prufrock can imagine them singing their alluring song, he dismisses the idea that they could actually be singing to him. The image conveys Prufrock's longing for beauty or, perhaps, love, but the poem returns us to the trivial chitchat, the "human voices" which wake us from the lovely, mysterious fantasy.

The title, then, is ironic. Prufrock is never able to sustain a relationship with another human being, or even his desire for beauty or love. The women in the poem appear as fragmented bodies and disconnected gestures, "braceleted arms" that "lie along a table" or faceless people who settle a pillow or throw off a shawl.

The Waste Land

25.4 In a 1923 essay entitled *"Ulysses, Order, and Myth,"* T. S. Eliot defended James Joyce's *Ulysses* against the charge of meaninglessness and lack of unity by pointing out that Joyce's "mythical method" unifies the work. To what extent can Eliot's defense of the unity in *Ulysses* be used to defend *The Waste Land* against a similar charge of formlessness?

Answer The fragmentary form of the poem is itself one projection of a modern myth that the world is moving toward crisis and chaos. In fact, encouraged by his fellow poet, friend, and editor Ezra Pound, Eliot courted formal discontinuity in this poem to convey his sense of the fragmentation of modern life. The division of the poem into five separate parts with different titles, the truncated lines, and the collage of voices all function to portray the lack of integration in the modern experience and the individual's abortive and frustrated attempts to find meaning.

But interestingly, this abortive quest for value in life becomes a theme which is itself unified by myth. At the heart of the poem is the theme of the spiritual impotence of society, a theme shared by numerous myths alluded to in the poem. The medieval grail legends catalogued in Jessie Weston's *From Ritual to Romance* and mentioned prominently in Eliot's footnotes merge in the poem with the older pagan vegetation myths discussed in Frazer's *The Golden Bough*. Building on pagan vegetation myths which attribute the seasonal cycle of vegetation to the death and rebirth of a god, the medieval myths tell of a society whose land is infertile and dry because its king has received a wound, often of a sexual nature. In the myth of the Fisher King, for example, the king is impotent and the land barren; society waits for salvation in the person of a knight (looking for the Holy Grail) who will come and ask the right question and so bring the much-needed rain.

The community's impotence and degradation, sexual and spiritual, is conveyed in almost every section of the poem: in one speaker's inarticulate encounter with the Hyacinth girl, in Lil's abortion to save her degrading marriage, in the young man's indifferent sexual conquest of the typist, and in the once-handsome Phlebas's drowned corpse. The failed sexual encounters, like the physical barrenness of the landscape, function as symptoms of the spiritual impotence of the community, a relationship represented by the multiple myths alluded to in the poem. The central condition of drought, the situation of waiting for rain which attends the various myths, becomes the dominant condition in the poem, in which "rain" is that nourishment which will revive a dying culture in body and spirit.

All the times and places alluded to (modern and medieval England, India, classical Greece) merge in one myth: the quest for salvation.

25.5   What is the meaning of the following lines from *The Waste Land?*

> What are the roots that clutch, what branches grow
> Out of this stony rubbish? Son of man,
> You cannot say, or guess, for you know only
> A heap of broken images, where the sun beats,
> And the dead tree gives no shelter, the cricket no relief,
> And the dry stone no sound of water. Only

There is shadow under this red rock,
(Come in under the shadow of this red rock),
And I will show you something different from either
Your shadow at morning striding behind you
Or your shadow at evening rising to meet you;
I will show you fear in a handful of dust.

(lines 19–30)

Answer This passage from Part I, "The Burial of the Dead," is probably the most explicit portrayal of the physical landscape of the wasteland: a hot, dry, stony place in which one can find no relief. The sun, instead of offering a source of energy, merely parches the landscape further; the trees, which might once have offered shelter from the intensity of the sun, are now dead branches which can provide no relief. The decay and destruction of human values in the world is evoked in this passage. Images which once gave meaning to our experience have now become meaningless bits and pieces, piled in a refuse heap, a jumble which we call culture.

The images, however, are poetic as well as cultural. The passage refers to the tattered and worn poetic images which are the resources of poetry and of this poem in particular. The speaker's question, "What are the roots that clutch, what branches grow/Out of this stony rubbish?" asks both what sort of meaningful spiritual life can grow in this wasteland experience, and what sort of modern poem can be created out of the fragments of the past at the poet's disposal. For example, the passage contains a number of biblical references: "Son of man" refers to God's address to Ezekiel in Ezekiel 2; the "shadow under this red rock" probably alludes to Isaiah, which depicts the righteous king "as rivers of water in a dry place, as the shadow of a great rock in a weary land." But the biblical references are severed from the system of belief that gave them coherence and meaning. The world depicted in these lines of the poem is godless and barren.

The only promise of relief in the passage is the speaker's offer of shelter under the red rock, a promise of some kind of revelation ("And I will show you something different"). But the hope of revelation or relief is dashed in the last line of the passage, in which our own mortality is frighteningly revealed: "fear in a handful of dust." As in Yeats's "The Second Coming," in which the speaker who longs for revelation sees instead, in horror and awe, the beast of the Apocalypse "slouching toward Bethlehem," in *The Waste Land* the search for salvation can bring only the painful knowledge of our vulnerability and impotence.

25.6 Does the image of the speaker, near the end of *The Waste Land*, "fishing, with the arid plain behind" him provide a hopeful resolution to the poem?

Answer Two sharply contrasting views of this conclusion can be taken. According to the first view, the final image of the speaker, fishing, with his back to the wasteland, does provide a hopeful resolution to the poem. The crucial words here are "the arid plain behind me," because this phrase suggests that the searcher has completed his journey through the wasteland. He is now on the threshold of a new experience, the "shore" being an image for this borderline condition; he is approaching a new vision of harmony and meaning. The fish for which he angles are a traditional symbol of life, the renewed vitality of the natural world; in primitive Christianity, the fish was also a symbol of Christ.

The final two lines complete this sense of resolution; the poem ends with the three words from the Hindu Scriptures, the Upanishads, "Datta, Dayadhvam, Damyatta" (Give, Sympathize, Control), and then the Hindu word for peace, "shantih," repeated three times. The Hindu words promise, in Eliot's paraphrase, a "peace which passeth understanding." The poem, having found the words to express value and meaning, must end, and "shantih" represents both the limit of thought and the limit of language. All the "fragments" of culture, the quotations and allusions used in the poem, have somehow come together to create a glimpse of significance; they provide protection from the sight of the ruins of contemporary culture. The Fisher King and the poet merge; both figures have passed from desolation to new inspiration.

According to the second view, the final image of the speaker fishing with his back to the "arid plain" does not provide any resolution to the poem, let alone a hopeful one. The speaker, who merges at this point with the Fisher King, asks whether he should set his lands in order; in other words, the land is still arid, the community's condition still one of despair and fragmentation. Just as the "gaiety" of the heart is in the conditional tense only ("Your heart would have responded/Gaily"), the restoration of order to the wasteland is at best in the future, at worst merely hypothetical.

In this view, the language of the poem, far from "resolving" the problems introduced previously, instead disintegrates into fragments of quotations, a babel of voices. In this context, even the final words quoted from the Upanishads are only additional fragments in the "heap of broken images." The language at the end of the poem is itself an example of fragments, and although we are told that these fragments are shored "against my ruins," we are not convinced.

The fact that such opposing views can be supported by the text illustrates a feature of much twentieth-century literature, both poetry and prose: an ambiguity which eschews conventional closure.

Four Quartets

25.7 What does the rose garden represent in the first of the *Four Quartets*, "Burnt Norton"?

Answer Before he describes the vision of the rose garden, the poet states: "What might have been is an abstraction/Remaining a perpetual possibility/Only in a world of speculation." The vision of the rose garden, when it occurs in the poem, represents this kind of "perpetual possibility"; it is a beautiful vision at the "heart of light," a paradise of joy and meaning. But whereas the somber poet at first claims that this possibility exists only as "speculation," the sudden and vivid presentation of the rose garden in the subsequent lines contradicts his original assertion. This kind of vision is possible, if only for one fleeting moment.

In fact, by describing the "location" of the rose garden as "Through the first gate,/Into our first world," the poet suggests that this garden paradise is Eden; "what might have been" is actually "paradise lost." The importance of this garden to the human imagination, however, transcends myth or history. It is a paradise which exists as a vision of possibility in the imaginations of all people. At the end of the poem, the fleeting vision is again evoked: "Sudden in a shaft of sunlight/Even while the dust moves/There rises the hidden laughter/Of children in the foliage/Quick now, here, now, always——." The "here and now" exist in the timeless realm of the imagination rather than in any specific time or place.

25.8 The first line of "East Coker" is "In my beginning is my end," and the last line is "In my end is my beginning." What does this reversal mean? What has occurred during the course of the poem?

Answer The first line of "East Coker" takes up the "waste sad time" with which "Burnt Norton" ends; darkly, it reminds us that we begin to die as soon as we are born. Echoing Ecclesiastes ("There is a time for building") in the first paragraph of the poem, the poet shows us that all of humanity's creations are "vanity," impotent before the destructive force of time.

In the course of the poem, the poet presents further images of our dying civilization. The pastoral vision of rustic life, fertility, and concord ends in "dung and death"; the possible healers of our illness are themselves "wounded" and "dying"; the wisdom of age turns out to be an illusion created by old men.

Yet "in my beginning is my end" can also refer to Eliot's return to his origins in "East Coker," which was the Eliot family's ancestral home. "Home is where one starts from," the poet says in section V, and home is where one returns— the origins are the "end" in the sense of goal. Section V is more personal than the others, as the poet, echoing the opening line of Dante's *Inferno*, locates himself in time ("So here I am in the middle way") and speaks explicitly of the difficulties of his poetic vocation ("trying to learn to use words"). He acknowledges that getting older means recognizing the confusing complexities of life rather than finding a clarifying, simplifying truth. Yet there is hope for "old men" and for the modern poet, who feels that everything has already been said and said better. "In my end is my beginning" looks forward to the new life which, for a Christian, begins with death: the "further union, a deeper communion" that the poet mentions. The paradox of life in death refers most significantly to the death and resurrection of Christ. The unhappy travelers in this life are now active "explorers," seeking in Christianity the kind of purpose, end, union that life has not provided previously. The allusion to Dante's confused predicament at the beginning of the *Inferno* may implicitly, by the end of the poem, suggest *La Vita Nuova*, the new life which both Christian poets eventually found.

25.9 Of all the Christian symbols used in *Four Quartets*, perhaps the most central is that of the Incarnation of Christ. How does Eliot use this event symbolically, specifically in "The Dry Salvages" and in the poem as a whole?

Answer Throughout *Four Quartets*, Eliot struggles to find a symbol for the point of intersection of the timeless with time. In "Burnt Norton," the only quartet without a central religious symbol, he describes this point as "the still point of the turning world" (sections II and IV). Seeking a more concrete symbol for this reconciliation of opposites, he suggests that of a Chinese jar in section V of "Burnt Norton," which "still/Moves perpetually in its stillness." In section

V of "The Dry Salvages," the poet finds the perfect Christian symbol for his central paradox: the Incarnation (Christ's birth), the event in which the divine and human, the word and the flesh, the timeless and time are reconciled.

Many of the images and scenes in Eliot's long poem depict time as a sad waste, essentially unredeemable. For most people, the cycle of life is an endless repetition of meaningless rituals, "Feet rising and falling./Eating and drinking. Dung and death" ("East Coker" [section I]). For Eliot, the Incarnation, or the coming of Christ, was a historical moment that transformed all of history, giving it meaning. This moment represents the "impossible union" of the timeless with time. In the final section of "The Dry Salvages," the poet makes a distinction between the saint and everyone else. The saint is he who actually apprehends the intersection of the timeless with time; he lives this revelation of divinity through his lifetime occupation of self-surrender to God. Most people, however, and this includes both the poet and his audience, are not saints. They must content themselves with something less than a lifetime of vision. They must settle for random moments of vision, "hints and guesses" as the poet calls them, and "the rest/Is prayer, observance, discipline, thought and action." For most people, the Christian life involves hard work and much discipline. It is graced only by moments when its meaning is dimly apprehended: "The hint half guessed, the gift half understood, is Incarnation," the poet tells us. This momentous event in the Christian calendar, then, functions as Eliot's central symbol for vision, for meaning, and for the paradoxical intersection of earth and heaven, the timeless with time.

K.L.

SUGGESTED READINGS

Drew, Elizabeth, *T.S. Eliot: The Design of His Poetry* (1961).

Gardner, Helen, *The Art of T.S. Eliot* (1959).

Kenner, Hugh, *The Invisible Poet: T.S. Eliot* (1969).

Matthiessen, F. O., *The Achievement of T.S. Eliot: An Essay on the Nature of Poetry* (1958).

Rosenthal, Macha Louis, *Sailing into the Unknown: Yeats, Pound, and Eliot* (1978).

Spender, Stephen, *T.S. Eliot* (1975).

Unger, Leonard, *T.S. Eliot: Moments and Patterns* (1967).

W. H. AUDEN

C H R O N O L O G Y

1907	Wystan Hugh Auden born at York, the third and youngest son of George Augustus Auden, a distinguished and scholarly physician of Icelandic descent, and Constance Rosalie Bicknell Auden, a trained nurse.
1908	Family moves to Birmingham, where his father becomes medical officer and professor of public health at Birmingham University. His father reads him Icelandic folktales and sagas, and so he learns more northern mythology than Roman or Greek.
1914– 1918	His father goes away to war. Auden develops a passion for science and longs to be a mining engineer. Acquires a strong sense of musical form and becomes an accomplished pianist. In 1915, enters St. Edmund's, a boarding school, where he first meets Christopher Isherwood.
1920– 1925	Attends Gresham's School in Norfolk, where he specializes in biology. In 1922, when he is 15, a friend suggests that he write poetry. Never having considered it before, Auden tries his hand at it.
1925– 1928	Enters Christ Church College, Oxford, where he discovers Anglo-Saxon, Middle English, Thomas Hardy, and modern literature. Wants to spend all his time reading. Helps edit two volumes of *Oxford Poetry* (1926 and 1927). Writes poetry; his friend Stephen Spender prints copies of twenty-six of his poems on a hand press. Early poems deal mainly with personal relationships: love, hatred, family conflicts, alienation.

1928–
1929

Lives in Berlin; writes a verse play, *Paid on Both Sides*, and sends it to T. S. Eliot at *The Criterion*.

1930

The Criterion publishes *Paid on Both Sides*, and Faber and Faber publishes *Poems*, his first important book.

1930–
1935

Teaches first at Larchfield Academy in Helensburg, Scotland, then at Downs School in Colwall, near Malvern. Publishes *The Orators: An English Study* (1922), a difficult, partly satirical analysis of a sick culture. His social consciousness and technological imagery link him with Stephen Spender, Cecil Day Lewis, and Louis MacNeice. Founds the Group Theatre (1932) with Rupert Doone and Robert Medley. Writes his first play for production, *The Dance of Death* (1933), but does not produce it until 1935. Publishes *Poems*, second edition (1933), with seven new poems. Marries Erica Mann, daughter of Thomas Mann, to secure her British passport so that she can flee Nazi Germany (1936). The couple never live together but remain legally married and friendly until Erica's death in 1971.

1935–
1938

Collaborates with Christopher Isherwood on three plays: *The Dog beneath the Skin* (1935), *The Ascent of F6* (1936), and *On the Frontier* (1938). Visits Iceland with Louis MacNeice in 1936 and publishes *Letters from Iceland* (1937), a travel book of prose and poetry. Travels in Spain (1937) during the civil war and espouses the Republican cause. Visits China (1938) with Isherwood during the Sino-Japanese War and publishes *Journey to a War* (1938). Returns by way of Japan and America.

1939

Moves permanently to the United States and becomes convinced of the lack of effect of poetry on politics. Turns attention to spiritual problems. Teaches at St. Mark's School in Massachusetts. Meets Chester Kallman, an 18-year-old New York poet, who becomes his lover for some years and his friend for life.

1940–
1956

Teaches at several American colleges: New School for Social Research (1940–1941), University of Michigan (1941–1942), Swarthmore College (1942–1943), Bryn Mawr College (1943–1945), Bennington College (1946), New School for Social Research (1946–1947), Barnard College (1947), University of Virginia (1949), Smith College (1953).

1940

Publishes *Another Time*; begins a new phase of poems showing the progress of his thinking from social and political problems to religious concerns. In the autumn, after reading Charles Williams and Kierkegaard and Niebuhr, he takes the "leap of faith" and becomes a Christian. Turns away from Freud and Marx.

1941–
1947

Publishes four long poems that continue his progression from detached abstraction to involved engagement in everyday life: *New Year Letter* (American title *The Double Man*) (1941), an analysis of the metaphysical limitations of art and reason; *For the Time Being*, including "The Sea and the Mirror," a "Christmas Oratorio," and a "Commentary on Shakespeare's *The Tempest*"; and *The Age of Anxiety* (1947), a "Baroque Eclogue."

1945   Publishes *Collected Poetry* in the United States. Investigates for the U.S. Air Force the effects of allied bombings on German morale.

1946   Becomes a United States citizen.

1950–
1955   Publishes several volumes of poetry: *Collected Shorter Poems* (1950), *Nones* (1951), and *The Shield of Achilles* (1955). A book of critical essays, *The Enchafèd Flood*, appears in 1950. Collaborates with Chester Kallman on opera librettos: *The Rake's Progress* (1951) and "Delia, or a Masque of Night" (1953).

1956–
1961   Professor of poetry at Oxford, where he becomes an extremely popular lecturer and something of an institution. Publishes *In Homage to Clio* (1960) and libretto *Elegy for Young Lovers* (with Chester Kallman [1961]). Buys a house in Kirchstetten, Austria, where he spends springs and summers with Chester Kallman.

1962–
1969   Publishes *About the House* (1965) and *City Without Walls* (1969). Also opera libretto *The Bassanids* (with Chester Kallman [1966]).

1972   Leaves New York to move to Oxford as a fellow of Christ Church College, where he plans to spend fall and winter every year. Publishes *Epistle to a Godson.*

1973   Dies in Vienna, during his sleep, of heart failure. Buried in Kirchstetten's village churchyard, about thirty miles from Vienna.

1974   *Thank You, Fog: Last Poems* published posthumously.

1976   *Collected Poems* published.

ESSAY QUESTIONS WITH ANSWERS

"In Memory of W. B. Yeats"

26.1 Discuss the function of landscape in the poem.

Answer   In the first line, Auden prosaically identifies the season of Yeats's death: "He disappeared in the dead of winter." The whole first stanza is devoted to a description of a winter landscape, and the references to frozen brooks, snow-covered statues, the sinking mercury, darkness, and cold become metaphors for the death of Yeats. By transferring the attributes of death to nature, Auden creates a sympathetic relationship between the dead poet and the living world, which has put on winter mourning in commemoration of the loss. In this instance, landscape has the traditional elegiac function of symbolizing mortality, with winter as a symbol for extinction, and of emphasizing the extent of the loss through a use of the classical theme "all nature mourns."

In the second stanza, Auden sketches a different landscape, a distant rural scene where nature continues in its usual round, unchanged by Yeats's death. Landscape here offers the consolation that the world goes on; this idea of continuity leads to the further point that the poet, in particular, survives death in the poems he has created: "By mourning tongues/The death of the poet was kept from his poems" (lines 10–11). This punning line latently suggests the idea of sympathetic mourners hiding the loss—keeping it—from the "bereaved," that is, the poems; but it also implies that the utterance of the poems by living tongues keeps mortality at bay, allowing the poems to go on as though they too were a part of nature, a permanent feature of the landscape.

In stanza 3, Auden returns to the man Yeats himself and to the physical fact of death. He creates a personified cityscape to represent Yeats's last moments on earth. The provinces, squares, and suburbs of his body are scenes of insurrection and desertion, a kind of war which ends not in death but in metamorphosis: "He became his admirers." The admirers are those "mourning tongues" who keep death from the poems and thus from the poet. At the moment of his physical death, Yeats "became" his admirers, surviving in each person who reads

his words. Stanza 4 further develops this sense of physical continuation, describing the poet as a pervasive presence in a landscape of cities and woods,
undergoing experiences which extend beyond his literal death:

> Now he is scattered among a hundred cities
> And wholly given over to unfamiliar affections;
> To find his happiness in another kind of wood
> And to be punished under a foreign code of conscience.
>
> (lines 18–21)

Yeats is at once himself and all those others who alter his "happiness" and
"punish" him by their "unfamiliar" readings of him. The return in the fifth
stanza to the "dark cold day" of Yeats's death rounds out the first section of the
elegy, reintroducing the restrained, poignant, allusive style of the opening and
posing the "slightly unusual" winter's day against the diurnal round of mundane
life.

The second section elaborates on the idea of landscape as a metaphor for
poetry. The words of the poet become a river, flowing south from its origins in
a secluded valley through outposts of civilization ("ranches of isolation," "raw
towns"). Poetry is thus treated as a natural phenomenon which, though it has
no power to alter the world, is part of it, surviving as "a way of happening, a
mouth" (line 41).

In section 3, the allusions to seas, vineyard, and deserts once again analyze
the effects of poetry in terms of landscape. (It should be noted that an earlier
version of the poem includes three verses on the theme of the power of language
to transcend and even justify inhumane views on the part of the writer. The
specific references to Kipling, whom Auden regarded as an imperialist, and Paul
Claudel, whom he considered a fascist, seem to represent an attempt to excuse
Yeats for his antidemocratic sentiments on the basis of the beauty of his writing.
The omission of these verses, which have the effect of a somewhat strained
apology, makes the elegy more consistent in tone. In the final version, the
theme of the relationship between art and humanity is treated in universal
terms, under the controlling metaphor of landscape.)

Thus, in the closing section, the central contrast between imprisonment,
hatred, and suspicion on the one hand and freedom, self-expression, and joy
on the other is represented in natural images: a sterile curse becomes a vineyard
through "the farming of a verse," and the desiccated "deserts of the heart" are
watered by "the healing fountain" of the poet's words. Writing on the eve of
World War II, Auden makes the point that although poetry "makes nothing

happen" on the level of world history, it humanizes people and stimulates them to oppose "the nightmare of the dark" where "all the dogs of Europe bark."

In general, Auden draws on the data of the physical world to perform the elegaic functions of commemoration and consolation. He uses landscape to convey an intense experience of loss and at the same time suggest the power of poetry to renew and revitalize the world. The political and historical perspective of the final section is particularly appropriate in a poem commemorating Yeats, who was in many respects a public poet, writing lyrics which addressed issues not only of Irish politics but of world history.

26.2   The poem has three distinct sections, each markedly different in meter and style. Analyze the tonal shifts in the poem produced by this tripartite structure.

Answer   The three sections of the poem imply different speakers or styles of speaking. The first section suggests the voice of the modern poet, musing, objective, somewhat scientific and detached; the second section is more personal, passionate, and engaged as Auden addresses Yeats as his colleague in the art of poetry; the third is a formal public utterance, like an epitaph or elegaic song delivered at a funeral rite. (It is relevant that Auden ultimately omitted from this section the verses which betrayed his personal ambivalence about Yeats's politics in favor of a general celebration of the power of poetry to move, instruct, and delight humanity.)

Auden produces these different tonal effects through rhythm, diction, and imagery. The first two sections have a colloquial quality deriving from a loose syllabic pattern. Irregular unrhymed lines of four, five, and six stresses emphasize syntactic structure over meter so that the net effect is one of pausing speech. However, the two sections differ in style. The use of scientific-sounding description, condensed metaphor, and prosaic statement makes the opening section a restrained and partly ironic obituary. In contrast, the direct address, epigrammatic phrases ("mad Ireland hurt you into poetry," "Poetry makes nothing happen"), and fully developed metaphor of the second section produce the more lyrical, intense tone of personal commemoration.

In section 3, the tone shifts radically. Auden's use of a four-beat line and a regular *aabb* rhyme recalls the classical conventions of epitaph and elegy. "Earth, receive an honoured guest;/William Yeats is laid to rest" (lines 42–43) has the chiseled simplicity of words on a gravestone, while the descriptions of "Europe," "the living nations," and "every human face" link this single death to the role of poetry in the fate of the entire world. The prosody and diction also echo, as in homage, Yeats's own poetic epitaph, "Under Ben Bulben," with its hortatory tone and its celebration of the artist's humanizing mission:

> Poet and sculptor, do the work,
> Nor let the modish painter shirk
> What his great forefathers did,
> Bring the soul of man to God.
> Make him fill the cradles right.
> ("Under Ben Bulben," [lines 37–41])

Auden again stresses the public dimension of his elegy in the closing address to the "poet" whose function it is to "persuade us to rejoice" even in the midst of "night." The final apostrophe, which seems directed both to Yeats as he survives in his poetry and to all living poets as well, has the aspect of a prayer for future joy, fruitfulness, and freedom.

By juxtaposing these three sections, Auden produces a series of perspectives on Yeats's death. The modernistic attempt to quantify, measure, and analyze death, the lyrical address to the honored dead, and the public epitaph are all included here. Thus, Auden offers different kinds of significance and different modes of consolation, creating a composite portrait of the dead poet as a man among men, subject to mortality; a poetic colleague who practiced a craft; and a public figure who, through the power of his words, was an oracle for all humankind.

"Musée des Beaux Arts"

26.3 Analyze the relationship between the two parts of the poem.

Answer The two parts have a relationship somewhat like that between the octave and sestet of a sonnet. Like a conventional sonnet, Auden's lyric produces a sense of contained logic with a definite break or turn in thought. Here the first stanza performs the function of generalization, while the second offers a specific example of the general idea.

The generalizing quality of the opening section is evident from the first line, "About suffering they were never wrong." Auden deals with the "Old Masters" as a group, describing their pictorial art in generic terms. By insisting on a broad historical perspective, he establishes the universality of Renaissance art and the truth of its message. The idea that human suffering is a solitary burden to which the world is largely indifferent is implied in each of the descriptions of paintings that Auden offers in the first stanza. The effect of the multiple allusions is to suggest that the theme has been depicted countless times by countless artists. The desultory tone of the poem, with its loose syntax and colloquial diction, reinforces the impression that the speaker is discussing a familiar idea.

In describing one convention of Renaissance art, the poet is in a sense ignoring another, that of the religious altarpiece which depicts sacred subjects in heroic tableaux. The "Old Masters" he seems to have in mind are northern painters rather than Italian, for the latter placed human suffering—that of Christ—squarely in the center of their compositions. (The title of the poem refers to the Museum of Fine Arts in Brussels, which contains Brueghel's *Icarus*, the picture described in the second stanza.) However, the implication is that the Old Masters as described represent all artists, who agree on the theme of suffering. The ironic counterpoint between individual disaster and ordinary experience is stated as a commonplace, universally known and accepted.

The anonymous illustrations in Part 1 are linked to the particular example in Part 2 by the common theme of the contrast between the miraculous and the everyday. In Part 1, the "miraculous birth" is visually displaced by the image of children skating on a pond and the "dreadful martyrdom" by the spectacle of dogs going on with "their doggy life" and the torturer's horse scratching "its innocent behind on a tree." In the second section, Auden dwells at greater length on one canvas, Brueghel's *Icarus*. The images of plowman, sun, and ship occupy the foreground of both the picture and the poet's description of it, while the boy Icarus himself is referred to only as a splash, a cry, "white legs disappearing into the green/Water" (lines 17–18). The sense of indifference implied by the images of turning away in the first half of the poem (the children at the edge of the wood, the horse's "behind") is here made explicit: "How everything turns away/Quite leisurely from the disaster" (lines 14–15). The fullness and precision of the description of Brueghel's picture reinforce the poignant insignificance of individual tragedy in the scheme of nature. The fall of Icarus is counterposed against the busy plowman, the necessary shining of the sun, and the preordained route of the ship. Although the allusions in the first section are to religious events—the Nativity and the Crucifixion—while the picture described in the second section depicts a Greek myth of human aspiration, in both cases the world ignores the fateful implications.

The visual displacements described in the poem suggest an ironic perspective. Auden and the Old Masters of the northern Renaissance as well seem to be implying that the historical and "fateful" events on which we usually focus are less significant than the enduring rhythms of human existence. High drama and portentous tableaux properly belong in the background, where the Old Masters have placed them. While the poem seems to be purely descriptive, illustrating the artistic rendering of a familiar theme, it subtly argues for a particular attitude. The poem, and the pictures in it, celebrate not the extraordinary and the miraculous but the ordinary. The truly "sacred" subjects are the skating children, the restless animals, and the sailing ship, not Christ or Icarus.

"In Praise of Limestone"

26.4   Describing the limestone landscape, Auden asks, "What could be more like Mother. . . ?" Does this humorous analogy have a serious dimension in Auden's scheme of "psychological geography"?

Answer   The comparison of limestone to a mother is used to suggest what Auden saw as the nurturing properties of limestone and its malleable and responsive nature, which encourages the child reared in such a landscape to take the "ingenious but short steps" of development and achievement. Not only does the landscape have a "psychology" of its own as a kind of doting mother, it produces a psychology in its offspring. Those who live amid limestone are, in Auden's scheme, forever children, playing games against a shifting backdrop of "secret" caves, "private pools," and "little ravines." The image of a child's playground of "short distances and definite places" merges with the suggestion of a pastoral golden world or Eden where temples, fountains, and vineyards magically appear. Auden thus speaks to the "homesickness" of "we, the inconstant ones": the longing for childhood innocence and ease that affects the uprooted modern person. The deities of this earthly paradise are like pagan gods, indulgent and human, easily pacified "by a clever line/Or a good lay," while the inhabitants are ordinary sinful mortals, neither the best nor the worst but always "comprehensible."

In part, these children of paradise fit into a Freudian scheme, with the Oedipal son ("the nude young male" showing off his "dildo") and the competitive siblings ("the band of rivals") all seeking to achieve their wishes through their "power to charm."

At the close of the poem, it is the unselfconscious, "blessed" ease of those living in a limestone landscape that "calls into question" the absolutist ideologies and psychological anxieties of modern culture. In contrast to the solipsistic poet or the obsessional neurotic, "the blessed will not care what angle they are regarded from,/Having nothing to hide. . . ." Limestone is thus the terrain of pleasure, gratification, and wish fulfillment associated with our dreams of perfect love and heavenly bliss.

26.5 Auden defines the meaning of limestone by comparison with other, very different landscapes. What is the significance of the other vistas introduced in the poem?

Answer The other landscapes in the poem are the "immoderate soils" sought by the "best and worst," those beings dissatisfied with the easy pastoral life associated with limestone. The "granite wastes" symbolize the spiritual yearning of "saints-to-be," "clays and gravels" appeal to "intendant Caesars" who plan to alter the face of the globe, and the "oceanic whisper" speaks to the nihilist, or self-absorbed loner, promising freedom from the "illusion" of love yet offering nothing. All these hostile landscapes are metaphors for extreme psychological tendencies toward self-abnegation, power lust, disillusioned emptiness. There is the additional suggestion that they are causal, that the "nomad's comb" and the "monstrous forms" of the jungle help shape human character, influencing people to seek out what is fixed, absolute, or unyielding. In contrast to these terrains, limestone embodies a golden mean, where human life is flexible, harmonious, balanced. At the same time, because granite, clay, and ocean are more awesome and magnificent than the rounded slopes of limestone, they seem to "show up" limestone as a "backward/And dilapidated province," unconnected to the modern world.

The interplay between the two kinds of landscape thus becomes significant. Desert and clay lead people to conceive of visions and empires and so contribute a kind of grandeur to human life. But limestone performs an important function, reminding people of life's contingency and frailty and of its abundant blessings. The fragility of limestone, easily weathered and eroded, suggests an affinity with human experience, which is in a sense a continual process of weathering and change. However, that people can easily modify this transient, changing landscape into pleasing artifacts ("From weathered outcrop/To hill-top temple") implies that even ordinary human beings—who are not "saints-to-be," "intendant Caesars," or "the really reckless"—have, as a birthright, a certain power and nobility. The child of a limestone landscape is comfortable with both nature and himself because of the ease with which he can impress himself on his surroundings. Society depends not solely on saints and sinners but on the child in us, who is most at home in a limestone landscape.

26.6 What do the following phrases contribute to the tone of the poem?

"displaying his dildo" (line 13)
"thank God" (line 23)

"a good lay" (line 29)
"born lucky" (line 35)
"I suppose" (line 43)
"a mad camp" (line 47)
"habit of calling/The sun the sun, his mind Puzzle" (lines 70–71)
"His antimythological myth" (line 73)

Answer   These phrases suggest the range of diction in the poem, from colloquial and even slang expressions to complicated rhetorical constructions. At neither end of the spectrum is the language particularly lyrical or decorative. Instead, the poet uses conversational tags ("thank God," "I suppose"), clichés ("born lucky," "nothing in common"), and slang ("dildo," "a good lay"—which is also a pun, referring to a narrative poem as well as to sexual intercourse—and "a mad camp") to establish a sense of the intimacy, directness, and ordinariness of conversation. Thus, the basic language of the poem is "native" to a limestone landscape, the easygoing, unselfconscious, oral style suggesting human, even all-too-human, speech. The sexual references in particular contribute to the poem's relaxed, permissive environment, where a flippant and off-color allusion is a pleasant indulgence rather than an impropriety.

The more obscure passages also suggest spoken language in that they are condensed and elliptical, but instead of drawing on the familiar phrases of slang or cliché, as speech might, they offer oddly arresting paradoxes. "The sun the sun, his mind Puzzle" is in itself a puzzle which must be unraveled, just as the obvious contradiction of "antimythological myth" must somehow be interpreted. These phrases are connected with the portrait of the poet, who insists on the concrete reality of the external world (calling "the sun the sun") and mythologizes his own imagination, insisting that his mind is godlike and oracular (a "Puzzle"). The stumbling of the language seems to imply that the poet is creating subjective muddles and complexities while denying the mythic power inherent in the objective world. After all, limestone has its own gods, its "solid statues," "innocent athletes," and "gesticulating fountains," and it promises the blessedness of "the life to come" without the meddling metamorphoses of poets. In contrast to the self-conscious obscurity of "poetic" language, the basic diction of the poem is straightforward, easy, and humorous, helping to create an image of limestone as a place of pleasurable moderation and natural grace.

B.S.

SUGGESTED READINGS

Beach, J. Warren, *The Making of the Auden Canon* (1957).
Fuller, John, *A Reader's Guide to W.H. Auden* (1970).
Hoggart, Richard A., *An Introductory Essay* (1951).
Spears, Monroe K., *The Poetry of W.H. Auden: The Disenchanted Island* (1963).

DYLAN THOMAS

C H R O N O L O G Y

1914	Born Dylan Marlais Thomas at Swansea, South Wales, the only son and younger child of David John Thomas, an English master at Swansea Grammar School, and Florence Hannah Williams Thomas, daughter of a local railway inspector. Marlais is the name of a stream in his parents' native county.
1925— 1931	Attends Swansea Grammar School, where he edits the school magazine. Leaves school at 16 with an undistinguished academic record but an impressive amount of creative writing.
1931– 1932	Works as a proofreader, then reporter for the South Wales *Evening Post*. Leaves the newspaper toward the end of 1932 to begin career as a professional poet.
1932– 1934	Does amateur acting with Swansea Little Theatre. The *New England Weekly* publishes his first adult poem in May 1933; in 1934, the *Sunday Referee* awards him its major prize for poetry, which leads to the publication of his first book, *18 Poems*. All the major themes of his later poetry are found here, especially the Genesis myth, the Adam theme, and the creative word. Meets Pamela Hansford Johnson, an aspiring poet with whom he corresponded, and a romance develops. Moves to London to work as a free-lance writer. Lives the legend of poet as hard-drinking bohemian. Ends his romance with Pamela, but not their friendship.
1935– 1936	Wins a second publication prize from the *Sunday Referee*. Takes a summer trip to the west coast of Ireland with friend Geoffrey Grigson. In March

342

1936, accepts Mrs. Wyn Henderson's invitation to be "mascot and very welcome guest" at her home in Cornwall. Meets in a London pub his future wife, Caitlin Macnamara, the fourth child of Francis and Yvonne Macnamara, brilliant middle-class Londoners with literary aspirations. Caitlin at 18 had run away from home to go on stage and joined the chorus line at the Palladium. Attends the International Surrealist Exhibition in London in July; thereafter his stories show varying degree of surrealist influence. Publishes *Twenty-five Poems* (1936), continuing his probe into the nature of humanity and into the sacramental nature of the universe.

1937–
1940

Marries Caitlin Macnamara at Penzance, Cornwall. They settle first at Ringwood, Hampshire, with Caitlin's mother, then in Swansea with his parents, and finally at Laugharne. A period of little money but great happiness. Renews his friendship with Vernon Watkins, his constant poetic mentor for the next ten years. Signs contract with Europa Press to publish sixteen short stories under the title *The Burning Baby*. However, the London printers balk at printing a story about a preacher who seduces his daughter, attends the birth of their child, and then burns the baby. When a second set of printers refuses it, Dylan turns the book over to agent David Higham, who remains his agent for life. Higham agrees to eliminate the "Baby" story, and J.M. Dent agrees to publish sixteen other stories and sixteen poems as *The Map of Love* (1939). New Directions in America publishes *The World I Breathe* (1939), poetry selections from previous books and some additional new stories. This book introduces him to American readers. Opposed on principle to the war, he nevertheless reports when called up and receives a medical exemption as an acute asthmatic. Publishes *Portrait of the Artist as a Young Dog* (1940), a collection of autobiographical short stories.

1941–
1945

Moves to London and writes scenarios for documentary films for Donald Taylor. Also works as a scriptwriter on feature films such as *The Doctor and the Devils*, *Life of Robert Burns*, and *Twenty Years A-Growing*. Uses his considerable talents for acting and reading to read poetry for the BBC with a "sensitivity which enabled him to ally himself, as it were, with the poet, in the very act of creating." Two of his three children are born.

1946–
1950

Moves to Oxford. Continues his broadcasts with the BBC. Publishes *Deaths and Entrances* (1946), the volume that assures him a place in the tradition of English poetry. Contracts with Sydney Box, executive producer for J. Arthur Rank, to produce three feature film scripts: *Rebecca's Daughters*, *The Beach of Falesa*, and *Me and My Bike*. None of the films are produced.

1950

Tours America at the invitation of John Malcolm Brinnin, giving readings at the Poetry Center of the 92nd St. Y in New York City and at many universities. The tour is a great success. Publishes *Twenty-six Poems*.

1951   The Anglo-Iranian Oil Company, now known as the British Petroleum Company, flies him to Iran to write a propaganda script, but he does not follow the company line. The film is not made.

1952   Visits America for the second time, this time with Caitlin. The trip is a public relations success but a financial failure, because of the spendthrift ways of both Thomases. Makes extensive commercial recordings of his poems, including the first record for Caedmon Records. New Directions publishes six new poems in *Country Sleep*. J.M. Dent publishes in London his *Collected Poems*, containing all the poems he wishes to preserve.

1953   In May, visits America for the third time. The tour is a creative success, but the drinking, partying, and sexual escapades undermine his already fragile health. Gives the world premiere of his play *Under Milk Wood* at the Fogg Museum under the sponsorship of The Poet's Theatre of Cambridge. He has been working on this play since 1933 and keeps revising it until his death. In the fall, returns to America for a fourth visit, against Caitlin's wishes; he is seriously ill. Reads *Under Milk Wood* again at the 92nd St. Y in New York City, in what has been called the finest performance the play ever had. Days later, he dies of alcohol poisoning in New York City. After a memorial service in Trinity Church attended by hundreds, his body is brought back to Wales and buried in the cemetery of St. Martin's Church, Laugharne. He had just turned thirty-nine years old.

1955   *Adventures in the Skin Trade*, his unfinished novel describing a young poet's arrival in London, is published posthumously.

ESSAY QUESTIONS WITH ANSWERS

"The Force That Through the Green Fuse Drives the Flower"

27.1 Thomas defines "the force" by means of a series of conceits or metaphors. Analyze these metaphors and their interrelationships.

Answer   The metaphors Thomas uses to describe "the force" have in common an underlying violence. Part of their violence comes from the merging of opposites: on the one hand, life, growth, activity, and sexuality; on the other, death, desiccation, paralysis, and decay. The imagery is thus like that of the seventeenth-century metaphysical poets, insisting in forceful and sometimes shocking language on similarities between widely disparate things, for example, water and blood or flesh and birdlime. The vivid fusion of literal and figurative terms creates a surrealistic effect, with grotesque or disturbing conjunctions given tangible form by the sensuous diction.

In the opening image, the latent reference is to an explosive, an ignited spark driving its way through a "fuse," blasting and destroying. Paradoxically, this force explodes into life ("drives the flower," "drives my green age") on its way to destruction ("blasts the roots of trees"). The paradoxical nature of the life principle, inextricably linked with death, is also implied in the phrase "wintry fever" (line 5): the force is both cold and hot, a crippling, deathlike chill and a pulsing fever, as well as a driving energy which burgeons and flowers.

Throughout the poem, Thomas uses images with multiple connotations; instead of tightly controlling the logic of his comparisons, he piles up metaphors and allows meanings to proliferate, often in opposing directions. The sense of tension in the speaker, whose mind spills over with so many ideas at once, is made explicit in the repeated refrain "And I am dumb to tell." He is, of course, telling of the connections he sees between himself and flower, water, wind, hanging man, lover's tomb, between humanity and nature, living organism and dead thing. But a quality of paradox and strain imbues the conceits, as though he is struggling to communicate a mystery. There is a hint of romantic despair in the poet's feeling of being unable to commune with nature; although he can tell us of the patterns he sees, he is "dumb to tell" the rose, or even his own "veins," of his sense of organic oneness. He is somehow isolated from the living world and from his own body even as he declares his connection to them.

The images also convey a tone of wonder mixed with dread or horror. For example, in the second stanza, the image relating the rushing of mountain streams to the coursing of "my red blood" and the drying up of the "mountain spring" to the hardening of "my veins" to "wax" suggests biological process, the intricacies of circulation and the natural effects of aging. At the same time, the diction hints at vampirism. The force is here a mouth that "sucks"; it "dries the mouthing streams" and makes the poet "dumb to mouth unto my veins." The imagery implies the insidiousness of "the force." Its "mouth," in draining the mountain streams and the veins of the poet, silences them, too.

The opening lines of the third stanza also contain a latent image of sucking or suction: the hand idly whirling the pool of water is, in fact, stirring quicksand. The idea is of a violent force, a "whirlpool" of quicksand, drawing the speaker into its vortex. The roping of the wind, implying a gesture of control—the hauling to of a sail against the breeze—becomes another image of victimization as the speaker becomes entangled in his own "shroud sail." The pun on "hanging man" reinforces the confusion between actor and victim in that the phrase suggests both the hangman and the hanged man. The man who does and acts is also the man who dies, violently, and the body's "clay" or flesh is also "lime," the sticky resin of a trap.

In stanza 4, there is an echo of the earlier vampire conceit: "The lips of time leech to the fountain head;/Love drips and gathers" (lines 16–17). The conclusion of this passage, "but the fallen blood/Shall calm her sores" (lines 17–18) marks a shift in the diction from the violent imagery of driving, sucking, whirling, and hauling to more subdued language. Although the "leech" sucks and drains, it also, according to medical lore, heals; and the reference to "fallen blood" which calms love's "sores" evokes, delicately and elliptically, the image of Christ, whose blood is a sacrifice and whose wounds heal humanity's moral wounds. At the same time, the language suggests the sexual act (the "lips" of the female genitals and the "fountain head" of the male), which is somehow healing. The conjunction of Christian and sexual imagery is one instance of the bold synthesis and collision of ideas which characterizes the poem as a whole. Although there may be no stopping "the force," no end to the paradoxical cycle of growth and decay, either in a resurrection of the flesh or a sexual consummation, Thomas here conveys a sense of continuity and unity that is somehow religious. A similar mood of quiet acceptance pervades the closing of stanza 4, which suggests a locus of meaning in the midst of headlong violence: "And I am dumb to tell a weather's wind/How time has ticked a heaven round the stars" (lines 19–20). Time is not only a leech, a kind of horrifying suction or vortex, but a peacefully ticking clock which marks out and orders the cosmos. Any given moment ("a weather's wind") implies the eternal, circular movement of the spheres ("a heaven round the stars").

The closing couplet is reminiscent of seventeenth-century metaphysical poetry in its punning allusions to sex and death. The "lover's tomb" is an allusion to the vagina, the "crooked worm" suggests the penis, and the "sheet" is a bed sheet as well as a winding sheet. The act of intercourse, although it may be transiently healing, as suggested in stanza 4, is nonetheless part of the progress toward death.

The final merging of images of sex and death illustrates the basic trope of the whole lyric, that is, paradox, the assertion of seeming contradictions. "The Force" is about the irony of process, how the life force is also a destroyer, a mouth that both issues forth like a fountainhead and sucks dry like a vampire or leech. The lyric offers a profusion of images and conceits, conveying both the diversity and the unity of organic life. Flower, mountain stream, whirlpool, sail, hanging man, and lips all illustrate the same process by which growth becomes decay and the ostensibly active agent becomes a passive victim. Stanza 4 constitutes the exception, for it suggests a temporary halting of the rush toward destruction. Time the destroyer is seen, for a moment, as a healer, and the driving force of life and death is stilled as "love drips and gathers." The concluding couplet returns to the major theme, but it has an almost nonchalant tone. It is a sardonic admission that even the most life-enhancing act cannot keep death at bay. This final image, in which the "crooked worm" is both phallus and maggot, reinforces the idea of the individual as the victim rather than the master of his or her life. But the truncated concluding stanza has the effect of a jaunty coda, giving the speaker, as it were, the last laugh. The poet, though isolated in his knowledge and "dumb to tell" the living universe what he has comprehended, is nonetheless master insofar as he is able to preserve a grim humor as he considers "the same crooked worm."

27.2 Discuss aural effects in the poem, including meter, alliteration, syntactical repetition, and slant rhyme.

Answer Rhythmic patterns are crucial to the meaning of the lyric; in a fundamental way, they contribute to the definition of "the force that through the green fuse drives the flower" by giving us its beat or pulse. The rhythmic structure of the stanzas (two iambic pentameter lines, a two-beat line, and two more iambic pentameter lines) enacts a process of expansion, contraction, and expansion. The central short line completes the turn in the thought, begun after the semicolon in the second line, from the ideas of growth and life to those of decay and death. The contracted line of each stanza provides a halt in the rhythm which imitates the thematic content; it brings the reader up short, just as the force does. In stanza 3, the phrase "hauls my shroud sail," with its two spondees (a foot with two accented syllables), is only the most pronounced instance of the metrical slowing the short line produces.

The syntactic repetitions have somewhat the same function as the repeated metrical pattern in that they too define the nature of the force. The reiterated grammatical structures underscore the sameness of the life principle in all its manifestations and indicate how its opposing actions (for example, driving and blasting or driving and drying) are actually one action. The last two lines of each stanza function as a refrain ("And I am dumb to tell") which, while repeating the major theme of the irony of the natural process, stresses the poet's isolation from nature. Ironically, he is separated from the life of other organisms because of his inability to communicate with these fellow victims of the "force." The repetitions underscore his singular, isolated consciousness as he witnesses the teeming processes which surround him.

The controlled structures of the rhythm and grammar are overlaid by the less predictable patterns of alliteration and slant rhyme. To the beat of the iambic line Thomas sometimes adds the musical emphasis of alliterated units: "force"/"fuse"/"flower" (line 1), "mountain spring"/"mouth sucks" (line 10), "whirls the water" (line 11), "lips . . . leech" (line 16), "weather's wind" (line 19), and "time has ticked" (line 20). A kind of lilt is introduced at these points, suggesting an incantation or song.

Though the poem lacks conventional rhyme, chiming effects result from assonance and consonance. The conjunctions of "flower"/"destroyer"/"fever" (stanza 1), "rocks"/"wax"/"sucks" (stanza 2), "pool"/"sail" (stanza 3), "dead"/"blood" and "sores"/"stars" (stanza 4), and "tomb"/"worm" (stanza 5) convey a sense of delicate, shifting interrelationship among all the disparate things and actions in the poem. Within lines, such repetitions as "mouthing"/"to mouth"/"same mouth" (stanza 2) and "hanging man"/"hangman's" (stanza 3) imply the identification between actor and victim, the force and what it acts on.

The aural effects of the poem contribute to its music; it is like a chant, with a prophetic air. The sound patterns of the lyric also reinforce the theme of fusion and organic unity. The deliberate patterns of the rhythm and sentence structure as well as the more local effects of slant rhyme, alliteration, and verbal repetition create the effect of complication integrated and diversity contained. The fragments of "the force," exploding into its various manifestations, are synthesized by the formal discipline of the lyric.

"A Refusal to Mourn the Death, by Fire, of a Child in London"

27.3 Discuss the religious imagery of the lyric.

Answer In reworking the conventions of the elegy, Thomas avoids traditional Christian consolations, but his more pagan or naturalistic approach to the death of the child nonetheless employs religious imagery. Thus, the first two stanzas invoke the whole cycle of Christian history from Genesis, when humanity was created, to the Day of Judgment, when it shall be resurrected. However, the poet's scriptural allusions merge with a secular vision of biological process and activity. The first stanza alludes not to God the Creator but to a fertile, generative chaos in which living things are tumbled together in rich profusion:

> . . . the mankind making
> Bird beast and flower
> Fathering and all humbling darkness
> (lines 1–3)

Despite the lack of hyphens, the sense is of a single rushing phrase, characterizing "darkness" as the originator, the one.

In a scriptural context, the "mankind" made in the darkness was Adam and Eve. In a related poem about a burned child, "Ceremony after a Fire Raid," Thomas says:

> I know the legend
> Of Adam and Eve is never for a second
> Silent in my service
> Over the dead infants
>
> . . . .
> Man and woman undone,
> Beginning crumbled back to darkness
> Bare as the nurseries
> Of the garden of wilderness.
> (stanza II, lines 48–51; 58–61)

In "A Refusal," the "mankind making . . . darkness" implies both Eden and
the Fall. The last line of the poem, "After the first death there is no other,"
refers, at least in part, to Adam's fall, which introduced death into paradise.
This "first death" is the only one in the sense that it is sufficient to destroy all
mortals; it is our mortality. The line is also a questioning of eschatology. Thomas
suggests that the belief in a Judgment Day in the orthodox sense is an illusion;
just as there is no second life to be achieved in the final "still hour," there is
at least no second death in the form of damnation either.

Thomas's description of the Day of Judgment, "the last light breaking" and
"the still hour/. . . of the sea tumbling in harness" (lines 4–6) includes an image
of second life, but it is life in a naturalistic and biological sense rather than an
orthodox resurrection. In stanza 2, the poet alludes to the decay of the body
into organic matter:

> And I must enter again the round
> Zion of the water bead
> And the synagogue of the ear of corn
>   (lines 7–9)

The concept is, in part, one of ashes to ashes and dust to dust. At the same
time, the lines convey a sacramental quality, as though the poet's death were
an act of worship or a consummation; the water is a promised land and the
grain a temple. There is even a hint of the sacrament of communion, in which
wine and wafer are the blood and body of Christ. The naturalistic treatment of
death is thus colored with religious feeling. This purely organic resurrection
somehow partakes of the divine, partially fulfilling the Christian promise of
eternal life.

The refusal of conventional rites of mourning is connected with this vision
of the resurrected being in "water bead" and "ear of corn." The idea of a continual
cycle of growth and fructification prohibits tears, that is, the sowing of "salt
seed," which is barren and infertile. Also forbidden is "a grave truth"—the pun
suggests both a somber epitaph and a specious truth which would consign the
dead child to the grave—for an emphasis on the grave would "murder/The
mankind of her going" (lines 14–15). The child was conceived in the "mankind
making . . . darkness" of genesis, and as the last stanza implies, in death she
grows again in the dark earth. Similarly, to elegize would be to "blaspheme
down the stations of the breath" (line 16). The phrase suggests several things,
among them the holy, truth-telling power of words and speech conceived as
vital "inspiration" (from the Latin inspirare, "to breathe in"). The rhetoric of

formal mourning is a violation of the prophet's holy function. But the phrase also echoes the "stations of the cross," the symbolic moments of anguish or relief which Christ experienced as he bore the cross toward Calvary. It is blasphemy to grieve, even for "innocence and youth," when what lies at the end of suffering is not only crucifixion and death but future life in a resurrected being. Although Thomas subtly refers to the passion of Christ, he is not suggesting the usual consolations: "Christ died for our sins," "we die to live." But he draws on Christian symbolism to contribute to his image of a natural resurrection and the vital continuity which persists even in death.

The last stanza describes the nature of the resurrected being which the dead child has achieved. "London's daughter" is ceremonially clothed in "the long friends," which are

> The grains beyond age, the dark veins of her mother,
> Secret by the unmourning water
> Of the riding Thames.
>
> (lines 21–23)

These "long friends," the "grains beyond age" and "dark veins," are eternal, springing from the same original darkness of chaotic life that engendered mankind, beast, bird, and flower. This is the consolation that Thomas offers, an image of being gathered into the earth and of becoming a body of earth, with flesh of grain and veins of water. The death is described as a return to friends and an embrace by a mother who is at once the city of London, Mother Earth, and also Eve, the "first dead" (line 19). The child is "secret" in the earth because she is secreted in earth, hidden there in a new form, and also because she bears the secret of eternal life. The Thames is "unmourning" because this consumption of the self to matter is a consummation, wholly natural. Like the death Thomas imagines for himself in the second stanza ("And I must enter again"), there is a sense of an entrance rather than an exit. There is also a sense of completion, as this "daughter" lies with her parents, the "first dead," Adam and Eve.

27.4 Discuss the significance of the title.

Answer The title is paradoxical, with the first part of the phrase—"A Refusal to Mourn"—contradicted by the closing words—"The Death, by Fire, of a Child in London." The end of the title suggests how great a cause there is for mourning this violent, premature, unnatural death. By refusing to express grief, Thomas powerfully suggests that he has a consolation which is equal to the tragedy. At the same time, the word "refusal" implies the effort required to stand up against such a loss.

Although all elegies in some sense ultimately "refuse to mourn," most reserve the consolation for a definite "turn" in the poetic structure. For example, Milton does not make a shift from grief to joy until three-quarters of the way through "Lycidas": "Weep no more, woeful shepherds, weep no more,/For Lycidas your sorrow is not dead" (lines 165–166). In contrast, Thomas begins with the word "Never"; his denial of grief is immediate and emphatic. The structure of his opening statement implies that his "Never" extends until the end of time, "the still hour" which is both the apocalypse and the moment of his personal dis- solution. The assertion is a vow to remain true to the splendor of this loss, "the majesty and burning of the child's death." There is no need to suggest, as classical elegy does, a resurrection of the dead person in a structural progression from ceremonial grief to the celebration of eternal life. As the first stanza implies and the final stanza confirms, the dead child is never truly dead but is part of the generative darkness of fecund nature.

The rejection of mourning includes the renunciation of funeral rites: prayer, tears, sackcloth, epitaph ("a grave truth"), and formal elegy. Throughout the poem, the rhetoric of lamentation is attacked as spurious and slanderous; the usual talk of death is both a lie and a libel. For example, in declaring that he will not "let pray the shadow of a sound/Or sow my salt seed/In the least valley of sackcloth," the poet echoes, and rejects, the language of the Twenty-third Psalm ("Yea, though I walk through the valley of the shadow of death"). The allusion has the effect of denying the consolation to be found in trusting the Lord as a shepherd. The implication is that there are other, greater consolations for this loss than the conventional religious ones. Similarly, the poet asserts that epitaphs "murder" and elegies "blaspheme"; the traditional language of commemoration paradoxically does violence to the slain child by means of its very emphasis on death and its offer of false symbols of eternal life.

The rejection of the rhetoric of mourning is accompanied by a subversion or transformation of certain conventions of formal elegy. The usual elegaic theme of "all nature mourns," with the landscape depicted as grieving sympathetically for human mortality, is replaced in "A Refusal" by an image of a fertile chaos: "the mankind making/Bird beast and flower/Fathering and all humbling dark- ness" (lines 1–3). The rush and tumble of the language suggests that this darkness will go on about its makings and unmakings until the end of time. The Thames is thus "unmourning" (line 22) in a double sense. Nature is unconscious, a rich generative force rather than an extension or reflection of human values; it also has no cause to mourn.

Another *topos*, or theme, of classical elegy is the merging of the dead person with the forms of nature. Thus Milton's Lycidas becomes a "genius of the shore" (line 183) and Shelley's Adonais "is made one with Nature" (line 370). This diffusion of the spirit in the living world is for Milton the sign of the soul's immortality and for Shelley the symbol of a kind of pantheistic animism. Thomas's dead child, too, is made one with nature, but not in any metaphoric sense. She is literally "grains" and "veins," earth and water, just as the poet describes his own decomposition in terms of "water bead" and "ear of corn." Thomas thus celebrates continuing life in terms of elemental matter and organic process, transforming metaphor into literal statement.

It is clear that "A Refusal to Mourn" in many respects conforms to classical elegy. The poem celebrates the eternal life of the dead child in the forms of nature, performing the traditional functions of consolation and commemoration. But in the poem's preemption of grief, its attack on conventional elegiac gestures and symbols, and its emphasis on matter and flesh, Thomas makes a claim for the uniqueness of this child and this death. His powerful rhetoric of refusal and attack creates a tone of defiance which sharply contrasts with the pathos of the death. The lyric's special poignance derives from this tension of opposites, the poet's emphatic assertions and denials weighed against the tragic circumstances which have occasioned his defiant joy.

B.S.

SUGGESTED READINGS

Cox, Charles B., *Dylan Thomas: A Collection of Critical Essays* (1966).
Daiches, David, "The Poetry of Dylan Thomas," in *Literary Essays* (1956).
Moynihan, William T., *The Craft and Art of Dylan Thomas* (1966).
Stearns, Marshall W., "Unsex the Skeleton," *Sewanee Review* (July 1944).

Part Five

THE MODERN
NOVEL AND
DRAMA

T I M E L I N E

The Age

1845:	Great Famine in Ireland
1848:	Revolutions in France, Italy, Austria; publication of *Communist Manifesto*
1854:	Outbreak of Crimean War
1859:	Publication of Darwin's *Origin of Species*
1860:	Outbreak of American Civil War
1865:	Assassination of Lincoln
1876:	Invention of the telephone
1886:	Publication in English of Marx's *Capital*
1887:	Golden Jubilee of Queen Victoria
1895:	Invention of motion picture camera
1900:	Publication of Freud's *Interpretation of Dreams*
1901:	Death of Victoria; accession of Edward VII
1903:	Wright brothers' flight at Kitty Hawk
1905:	Einstein's theory of relativity
1910:	Death of Edward VII; accession of George V
1914:	Outbreak of World War I
1917:	Russian Revolution
1919:	Treaty of Versailles

The Authors

1840	Thomas Hardy (1840–1928)
	Henry James (1843–1916)
1850	
	George Bernard Shaw (1856–1950)
	Joseph Conrad (1857–1924)
1860	
1870	
	E. M. Forster (1879–1969)
	Virginia Woolf (1882–1941)
1880	James Joyce (1882–1941)
	D. H. Lawrence (1885–1930)
1890	
1900	
1910	
1920	

The Age

1921: Irish independence

1922: Publication of *The Waste Land*

1929: U.S. stock market crash precipitates Great Depression

1933: Hitler takes power in Germany

1936: Death of George V; accession of Edward VIII, who abdicates in favor of George VI

1939: Outbreak of World War II

1945: End of World War II; invention of atomic bomb

1947: Independence for India and Pakistan

1952: Death of George VI; accession of Elizabeth II

1956: Britain and France invade Egypt to seize the Suez Canal

1963: Assassination of John F. Kennedy

1969: Men land on moon

The Authors

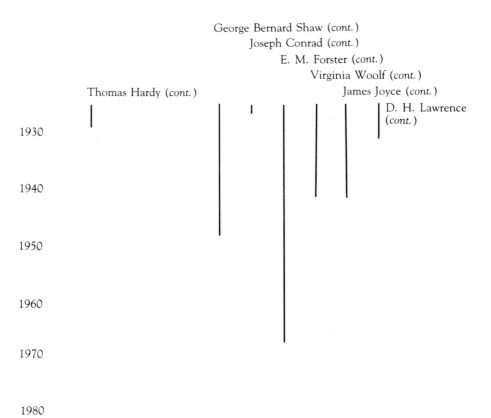

George Bernard Shaw (*cont.*)
Joseph Conrad (*cont.*)
E. M. Forster (*cont.*)
Virginia Woolf (*cont.*)
Thomas Hardy (*cont.*)
James Joyce (*cont.*)
D. H. Lawrence (*cont.*)

1930

1940

1950

1960

1970

1980

THOMAS HARDY

C H R O N O L O G Y

1840   Born at Upper Brockhampton, Dorset, near Egdon Heath, which he immortalizes in his novels; the oldest child of a prosperous stonemason and a bookish mother descended from a long line of Dorset farmers. Because of his delicate health, his mother tutors Hardy at home, where he learns to read before he can speak.

1848–
1856   Attends four schools in all, learning the fundamental subjects and Greek. Develops a love for poetry and classical learning.

1856–
1862   Works as apprentice to John Hicks, an ecclesiastical architect in Dorchester, who allows him to study more Greek than architecture. Also receives encouragement from William Barnes, a Dorset poet, and intellectual stimulus from Horace Moule, the brilliant son of a vicar. Writes some verse and essays but decides to pursue architecture.

1862–
1867   Works in London as assistant to the eminent architect Arthur (later Sir Arthur) Bloomfield.

1863   Wins the gold medal of the Royal Institute of British Architects in a national competition for his essay "The Application of Coloured Bricks and Terra Cotta in Modern Architecture." (Wins the medal but not the £10 offered, because his essay, though splendidly written, does not delve deeply into the subject.) Also wins the Architectural Association's prize for design.

1864   Publishes anonymously his first work, a humorous sketch, in *Chamber's Journal*.

1867–1874	Returns to work for John Hicks in Dorset and, after Hicks's death, for the architect who takes over the business. In 1870, he goes to Cornwall to restore a church and meets his future wife, the vicar's sister-in-law.
1868	Writes a novel, *The Poor Man and the Lady*, accepted by Chapman and Hall, but George Meredith, a Chapman reader, persuades him to withdraw it for lack of plot. Uses some parts later, and eventually destroys the original manuscript.
1871	Publishes anonymously the novel *Desperate Remedies*. Attracts little attention except for a few scathing reviews.
1872	Publishes anonymously *Under the Greenwood Tree*, subtitled "A Rural Painting of the Dutch School"; it is a modest financial success.
1873	Publishes *A Pair of Blue Eyes*, based on his own courtship in Cornwall; another financial success.
1874	Convinced he can now support a wife through his writings, he marries Emma Lavinia Gifford from Cornwall. Publishes *Far from the Madding Crowd*, his first popular success. When it is serialized anonymously in the *Cornhill Magazine*, some critics annoy Hardy by attributing it to George Eliot.
1874–1896	The first stage of Hardy's writing career, in which he writes the novels for which he is best remembered. Notable novels include *The Hand of Ethelberta* (1876); *The Return of the Native* (1878); *A Laodicean* (1881); *Two on a Tower* (1882); *The Mayor of Casterbridge* (1886); *The Woodlanders* (1887); *Tess of the d'Urbervilles* (1891), his best-known novel but one which brought down a storm of abuse for its "obscenity" and had to be bowdlerized for magazine publication; and *Jude the Obscure* (1896), his most controversial novel, roundly denounced as pornography. Disgusted with this reception, Hardy announces he will never write fiction again.
1897–1908	The second stage of Hardy's writing career, characterized by his poetic drama masterpiece *The Dynasts* (1904–1908). It begins as a celebration of England's part in the Napoleonic wars but deepens into a summation of Hardy's mature vision of life. He also publishes lyric poems in *Wessex Poems* (1898) and *Poems of the Past and Present* (1901).
1909–1928	In the third stage of his writing career, Hardy devotes himself exclusively to lyric poetry. His most important contributions are *Time's Laughing Stocks* (1909), *Satires of Circumstance* (1914), *Moments of Vision* (1917), *Late Lyrics and Earlier* (1922), *Human Shows, Far Phantasies* (1925), and *Winter Words* (1928), published posthumously.
1910–1920	Receives the Order of Merit and honors from Oxford, Cambridge, Bristol, Aberdeen, the Royal Society of Literature, and many others.

1912   His wife, Emma, dies, leaving him bereft.

1914   Marries his secretary, Florence, a successful journalist and writer of children's
            books, and his chief biographer.

1928   Dies of a cold at age 87. His heart is buried in his first wife's grave near
            Dorchester; the rest of his body is cremated and buried in Poets' Corner in
            Westminster Abbey at an impressive funeral service attended by thousands,
            including the most eminent people in England.

ESSAY QUESTIONS WITH ANSWERS

Tess of the d'Urbervilles

28. 1   In literature, descriptions of places often take on thematic or narrative significance, as well as providing a setting for the action of the plot. In *Tess of the d'Urbervilles*, important events occur in Tess's life at both Talbothays Dairy and Flintcomb-Ash. How do these settings add to the meaning of the novel?

Answer   The two landscapes pose a series of contrasts: summer versus winter, a fertile paradise versus a barren wasteland, Angel Clare versus Alec d'Urberville. At Talbothays Dairy, Tess is a milkmaid whose daily ritual of work occurs in an environment of rich natural abundance and warmth. At Flintcomb-Ash, she is a field hand, digging turnips from the frozen, unyielding earth in a setting dominated by the red threshing machine and the bleakness of the sky. In the earlier scene, Tess experiences the awakening of love for Angel Clare; in the later one, she undergoes a renewed threat from her seducer, Alec d'Urberville.

In both cases, the landscape serves as a projection of Tess's psychological state. The first reflects her feeling of hope and limitless possibility, the second her feeling of despair and deprivation. The contrast between the places suggests the movement from a paradise, much like the Garden of Eden, to a hell. The images used to depict Flintcomb-Ash are hellish; the red threshing machine is described as "the red tyrant that the women had come to serve," which keeps up "a despotic demand upon the endurance of their muscles and nerves" (Chap. XLVII). The engineman seems like "a creature from Tophet" who "serves fire and smoke." At Flintcomb-Ash, both the earth and the machines people have created to turn nature to their use seem inimical to the human laborers. Here Tess reaches the nadir in her loss of optimism and power; she seems to be just one of the sufferers trying to endure this infernolike atmosphere.

This neat dichotomy between the two landscapes, however, may obscure the fact that all through the novel, the earth acts as both a friend and a foe to humankind. The vistas that confront Hardy's characters as they stand poised upon a hill surveying the scene below sometimes represent what seems like limitless possibility, sometimes a vastness in nature that dwarfs humanity and reduces its significance. As Tess descends the Egdon slopes to reach the dairy, she is described in the following manner: "Not quite sure of her direction Tess stood still upon the hemmed expanse of verdant flatness like a fly on a billiard-table of indefinite length, and of no more consequence to the surroundings than that fly" (Chap. XVI). Although Talbothays is subsequently described as an abundant garden and the scene of Tess's renewed hope, the landscape in this passage reveals Tess as an insignificant creature operating in an arena where the gods play indifferently or even malevolently with human fate.

28.2 Certain scenes and episodes in *Tess of the d'Urbervilles* seem to violate the expectation of sober realism many readers bring to the novels of Hardy. How can these episodes be accounted for in terms of the themes of the novel?

Answer A number of incidents in *Tess of the d'Urbervilles* are melodramatic and improbable. The d'Urbervilles' horse, Prince, is stabbed through the heart by the pointed shaft of an oncoming mailcart in the dead of night; the cock crows three times the afternoon of Tess's and Angel's departure from Talbothays; a sleepwalking Angel carries his young wife Tess to the ruined abbey, laying her in an empty stone coffin; a story is told about the d'Urberville coach which makes the sound of the coach an ill omen connected with a long-ago murder; and Tess murders Alec, her seducer, as he sleeps by stabbing him through the heart with a dagger.

Collectively, these scenes suggest a strong streak of fatalism in the world of the novel. Certain episodes have a sensational quality: the sleepwalking scene and the seduction and murder. Others act as omens: the death of Prince, the cock's crowing, the telling of the d'Urberville legend. Both kinds of incidents derive from the earlier narrative tradition of the ballad. Although the use of the balladic elements in a modern novel may seem strange, the traditional flavor, the simplicity and melodrama of the basic plot, and the often pessimistic cast to the ballad all harmonize with Hardy's interest in tradition and ritual and in the mixture of human passion and cruel fate that operates in the universe. The ballad elements become symbols in the modern novel, thematic repetitions that convey the sense that mistakes are doomed to be repeated and that the best intentions often lead to disastrous results.

Thus the gruesome death of Prince at the beginning of the novel, for which

Tess feels responsible, regarding herself "in the light of a murderess" (Chap. IV), foreshadows her murder of Alec at the end of the novel. The ill omens of the crowing cock and the sound of the d'Urberville coach are fulfilled in that act of violence. Some of the melodramatic incidents cited reveal important psychological mechanisms; Angel's sleepwalking is highly revealing of his anger toward Tess after she tells him her story as well as his desire to bury that past.

28.3 Is Tess a victim?

Answer Hardy's narrator constantly offers comments which suggest that Tess is a pure, innocent girl undone by circumstances. The subtitle, "A Pure Woman Faithfully Presented," reinforces his thesis that Tess is basically good and that, consequently, her unhappy fate is not her fault. By comparing her to "a fly on a billiard table" (Chap. XVI), the narrator suggests her helplessness and insignificance. The omens, too, from the disastrous death of Prince to the eerie tale of the d'Urberville coach, symbolize the inevitability of Tess's tragic destiny.

However, other evidence in the text suggests that Tess is too prone to yield to circumstances. The fact that she drifts into sleep in the dark woods while alone with Alec implies a lack of caution and wisdom. When she goes to live with Alec after Angel has deserted her, she relinquishes her fidelity to her moral code out of hurt and despair. It is even possible to interpret her eleventh-hour confession to Angel, slipped under his door just before the wedding, as a sign of her unwillingness to accept the consequences of her actions.

Perhaps the most explicit reference to Tess's passive complicity in what occurs is found in Chapter XXXVII, when Tess submits to all Angel's conditions for their relationship: "But her mood of long-suffering made his way easy for him, and she herself was his best advocate. Pride, too, entered into her sub-mission—which perhaps was a symptom of that reckless acquiescence in chance too apparent in the whole d'Urberville family" (Chap. XXXVIII). Interestingly, there is something "reckless" in this kind of submission to circumstance that suggests almost a stubborn kind of gambling with one's own life.

28.4 A crucial episode in the novel is the seduction of Tess by Alec d'Urberville. From the following list of interpretations of the episode, select those which are plausible.

1. Tess, a member of the laboring classes, is defiled by the "aristocrat" Alec d'Urberville, symbolizing the exploitation of the poor by the capitalistic rich.

2. Tess is a victim of male egotism; she represents the oppression of women in the nineteenth century by a rigidly patriarchal society.

3. Tess's rape is a hallucination, occurring only in her own mind.

4. Tess's loss of virginity is a puberty rite signifying a stage in her development as a mature adult.

5. Tess's seduction represents the action of a hostile fate operating in the universe.

Answer Interpretations 1, 2, and 5 are the most logical interpretations of the incident, while interpretations 3 and 4 fail for various reasons.

Interpretation 3 is easily refuted by the birth of Tess's baby, Sorrow, nine months after the incident. Although the description of the seduction is deliberately hazy and left largely to the reader's imagination, the very real consequences of the incident prove that Tess's dreamy passivity is not the same as hallucination. Interpretation 4 is unsupported in the novel; narrative comments and the events of the story make it plain that a serious violation of morality has occurred. Tess is cruelly punished for her transgression; no one sees it as a mere rite of passage. Yet a puzzling narrative comment appears at the end of Chapter XV that seems, at least, to suggest the possibility of interpretation 4: "But for the world's opinion those experiences would have been simply a liberal education." The sentence seems callous in ignoring the violation of Tess's soul and body that occurs. It is hard to reconcile the statement with the real seriousness with which the event is treated. Perhaps the tone conveys bitterness, even sarcasm, that is meant to expose the difference, in society's view, between the "liberal education" of a woman and that of a man. In any case, interpretation 4 distorts the tragic tone of the novel as a whole.

The first interpretation, which implies a Marxist reading of the novel, is useful in stressing the book's economic and social aspects, particularly the theme of the powerlessness of the laboring class. There is much in the novel to support the idea that the Durbeyfield family, especially Tess, are victims of their economic and social condition. For example, the chain of events leading to Tess's employment by Alec d'Urberville and, ultimately, her seduction by her employer begins with the killing of the family horse, a resource crucial to their livelihood. Although Tess feels responsible for the death of the horse, her family's dire economic straits trap her into seeking a job and keeping it even after Alec's behavior has warned her to be on her guard. Throughout the novel, as in the case of Tess's return to Alec, economic conditions are influential in shaping Tess's decisions.

Yet this view of the class system does not quite do justice to the fact that Alec is a pseudo-aristocrat and that the Durbeyfield family (exclusive of Tess) are would-be social climbers. One must qualify the idealized portrait of the downtrodden poor somewhat when Mrs. Durbeyfield is willing virtually to sell her daughter in exchange for entrance into the ranks of the middle class.

Interpretation 2 also emphasizes the role of social and political power in the novel but puts less emphasis on purely economic factors. Instead, it sees Tess mainly as a victim of sexual oppression. There is much in the novel to support this view. Alec's role as sexual aggressor, for example, is made quite vivid in the following analysis of Tess's seduction:

> Why was it that upon this beautiful feminine tissue, sensitive as gossamer, and practically blank as snow as yet, there should have been traced such a coarse pattern as it was doomed to receive? (Chap. XI)

The description of the mostly female workers at Flintcomb-Ash as subordinated to the machine and the men who serve it also suggests the sexual politics in the world of Tess. Even the forbidding, cruel landscape is rendered at one point in sexual terms. The women are set hacking in one area described as "the outcrop of siliceous veins in the chalk formation, composed of myriads of loose white flints in bulbous, cusped, and phallic shapes" (Chap. XLII). In general, women in the novel are presented as victimized and powerless because of their sex.

Interpretation 5 represents Hardy's pessimistic view of the world, as expressed throughout the novel in both the cruel accidents that befall the characters (e.g., Angel's overlooking the envelope which contains Tess's confession) and the explicit narrative comment. Perhaps the most striking narrative summary of this attitude appears in the final paragraph: " 'Justice' was done, and the President of the Immortals, in Aeschylean phrase, had ended his sport with Tess." Ironically, the final chapter is called "The Fulfillment," emphasizing the fatalism in the book as a whole. Although Alec's cunning and duplicity are responsible for creating Tess's helpless situation in "The Chase" (the "wood of error" where she finds herself alone with Alec late at night), the strong sense of ironic fate in the world of the novel prepares us to see Tess as an inevitable victim. The name of the wood is prophetic of Tess's plight as the prey not only of Alec but of life itself.

Jude the Obscure

28.5   The theme of marriage dominates *Jude the Obscure*. Between them, Jude and Sue are married four times, and numerous other marriages are mentioned: Arabella's to Cartlett, the innkeeper; Jude's parents' unhappy union; and the wedding couples observed at the marriage registry and the parish church. How does the novel convey Hardy's attitude toward the institution of marriage?

Answer   Scattered throughout the novel are ominous references to past marriages in the Fawley family: Aunt Drusilla's vague allusions to Jude's parents, Sue and Jude's troubled exchanges about the familial curse, and Widow Edlin's gruesome ancestral tale of murder and madness. This thread of allusion, together with the many epigraphs on the relationship between the sexes, constitutes a dark background for the immediate relationships which Hardy portrays in the novel.

The marriage between Jude and Arabella, founded on sexual attraction, is doomed by the vast differences in their characters and intellect. The marriage between Sue and Phillotson, founded on intellectual sympathy, is doomed by their sexual incompatibility. All marriages in *Jude the Obscure* turn into bad marriages.

The relationship between Sue and Jude is more complicated. Sue, conscious of the destructive nature of marriage, avoids the legal bond; Jude, feeling the pressure of the ancestral curse, agrees to live with Sue outside the bounds of the conventional marriage sacrament. As a consequence of their decision, society hounds them, depriving the pair of work, lodgings, and general acceptance. Furthermore, their "marriage," like all the others in the novel, is disastrous: Sue is frightened of sex; Jude is frustrated by her coldness and excessive spirituality; their offspring commit suicide, and the last child is born dead. In a drunken stupor, Jude remarries Arabella, living out the short remainder of his life wracked by illness, misery, and despair. Sue remarries Phillotson, prostituting herself out of misguided religious belief and condemning herself to a life of unhappy submission.

The unhappy and often fatal consequences of these marriages point to some evil beyond the errors involved in these particular relationships. Unlike some of Hardy's earlier novels (*Far from the Madding Crowd*, for example), *Jude the Obscure* expresses a fatalistic view of marriage as an institution. It seems that in the world of the novel, love and sex hardly ever go together, and marriage seems merely to exacerbate the imbalance between the two. Unlike many nineteenth-century novels, which picture marriage as the final fulfillment of the preceding events and the final untangling of the novel's complications, Hardy's turn-of-the-century novel expresses deep pessimism about the institution of marriage.

28.6   The figure of Father Time, Jude and Sue's eldest child, has been attacked for its grotesque and melodramatic aspects. Instead of developing him as a real character, Hardy gives him an allegorical name and what seems to be a purely symbolic function. Discuss the character of Father Time and its contribution to the novel.

Answer   It is true that there is something slightly comic in the figure of the little old man, Father Time, as, perhaps, there must be in a child who seems prematurely aged and carries the troubles of the world on his shoulders. As a character, Father Time is not one of Hardy's more interesting creations. Yet the improbabilities of the aged child's character are themselves revealing of what appears to be a lack of faith in the basic conventions of the traditional novel. The ideas of family, inheritance, and the movement of life from generation to generation, so important to the nineteenth-century novel, to a large extent depend on the viability and energy of the children. The image of an aged child contradicts all that childhood conventionally means: hope, promise, continuity.

Furthermore, Father Time reinforces a theme established early in the novel in the character of Jude. Of Jude, Hardy writes: "If only he could prevent himself growing up! He did not want to be a man" (Part I). Whatever natural instincts Jude has for survival appear to have atrophied in Father Time. His suicide note, "Done because we are too menny," puns on the word "men," thus echoing his father's wish not to grow to adulthood. The horrific image of the four children hanged in the tenement flat emphasizes, in a particularly graphic way, the theme of hopelessness in the novel.

28.7   The title of each part of *Jude the Obscure* contains the name of a town or city: "At Marygreen," "At Christminster," "At Melchester," "At Shaston," "At Aldbrickham and Elsewhere," "At Christminster Again." Comment on the significance of these urban settings.

Answer   The series of chapter headings suggests the aimless wanderings of the chief characters. Apart from Marygreen, a point of departure, and Christminster, which for Jude is a goal or destination, the rest of the towns are arbitrary stopping places. In contrast to the rural, rooted folk cultures of Hardy's earlier Wessex novels, *Jude the Obscure* portrays a modern world where uprooted individuals take temporary lodgings in one town or another.

Christminster has a special meaning in the novel as a medieval center of learning, religion, and culture to which both Phillotson and Jude travel in order to fulfill their ambitions. As a child, Jude sees the town as a "mirage," a "new Jerusalem" hovering on the horizon, a Mecca which means escape from the stagnation of rural Marygreen. When he arrives in Christminster, he mentally converses with the spirits of the famous dead, thrilled by the weight of traditional culture which the very stones convey. Even when his attempts to pursue his theological vocation are thwarted and his infatuation with Sue draws him away to Melchester, the academic town (Hardy's version of Oxford) remains fixed in Jude's mind as a symbol of beauty and truth.

At the end of the novel, we see that Christminster, like all the other towns in the novel, is hostile to human aspirations and desires. Jude's illusions continue to the very end; his decorated Christminster cakes commemorate the gothic beauties of the town, and his bringing his family there on Remembrance Day constitutes a symbolic pilgrimage. But it is in Christminster that Sue is forced out of her lodgings and Father Time engineers the suicide of the children, and it is on another Remembrance Day in Christminster, with the graduates cheering in the streets, that Jude whispers his bitter dying words: "Let the day perish wherein I was born. . . ." The illusory city of beauty and truth has become the graveyard of hope.

28.8 Consider the following sequences of events in the novel.

1. At the beginning of the novel, Phillotson leaves his post as schoolmaster at Marygreen to pursue his intellectual ambitions; at the end of the novel, he is once again schoolmaster at Marygreen.

2. Jude marries Arabella Donn and divorces her. At the end of the book, he is once again married to her.

3. Sue marries Phillotson and divorces him. At the end of the book, she is once again married to him.

4. Early in the novel, Jude arrives in Christminster to seek his fortune there; at the end of the novel, he returns to Christminster, there to meet his tragic end.

Analyze the structural and thematic significance of these narrative strands.

Answer   All the sequences mentioned are circular; they lend a static quality to the plot of the novel. Although the characters appear to act and struggle, they are trapped in a pattern of fruitless repetition. Like people on a treadmill, Sue and Jude are forever running to stay in the same place. Their spatial movement from town to town forms an ironic contrast to the internal deadlock of their relationship.

Even minor events in the novel reflect Hardy's vision of cyclical repetition. For example, at the beginning of the novel, Jude assists his great-aunt Drusilla in her bakery at Marygreen; toward the end of the novel, Sue and Jude are selling their home-baked Christminster cakes at the Mennetbridge fair.

Furthermore, apparent changes turn out to be mere reversals with no net gain. When Sue and Jude meet, Sue is a skeptic and Jude a religious believer; when they part, Jude is a skeptic and Sue a religious believer. What remains constant beneath the alterations of conviction is the fundamental conflict between the two characters, who are mismatched at both beginning and end.

Hardy's earlier Wessex novels, such as *Far from the Madding Crowd* and *The Return of the Native*, also employ repetition as a structural device. However, they differ from the heavily ironic scheme of *Jude the Obscure* by implying the possibility of fruitful repetition: both Bathsheba and Thomasin move from unhappy marriages to happy ones. *Jude the Obscure* stands alone in its unrelieved pessimism, of which the purposeless repetitions are an emblem.

28.9   Discuss the relationships among Sue Bridehead, Jude Fawley, and Arabella Donn. How can this triangle be interpreted symbolically?

Answer   One way of interpreting these relationships is to see Arabella as pure flesh, Sue as pure mind, and Jude as the divided person torn between two poles. Arabella is introduced in the rural atmosphere of Marygreen, where her association with animal life—pigs, slop, butchery—and her seductive tactics identify her as a sensual woman motivated entirely by instinct. Sue, on the other hand, is associated with the scholarly environment of Christminster, the training school of Melchester, and intellectual men—the Christminster undergraduate and, later, Phillotson. Furthermore, the name Bridehead emphasizes both Sue's physical purity ("bridehead" or "maidenhead") and her cerebral nature ("head"). It is precisely this quality of disembodied intellect which attracts Jude, who is in revolt against the carnal desire which drove him to Arabella.

Throughout the novel, Jude struggles with his conflicting wishes, aspiring to an ideal spirituality like Sue's but ultimately returning to Arabella's bed in despair.

But this view of the two women characters is perhaps too schematic. Arabella is more than a negative emblem of carnal lust, for her sexuality has a positive significance as well. She has a kind of shrewd native common sense and a healthy acceptance of natural impulse which allow her to survive in Hardy's bleak universe. Sue is not merely the admirable embodiment of ideal purity, for she suffers from a repression of sexuality which appears in her rivalry with Arabella and in her manipulations of men. Because of their psychological complexity, these characters—especially Jude and Sue—cannot be seen merely as the playthings of fate or the scapegoats of society. They are also victims of their own internal conflicts and divided natures.

K.L.

"Hap"

28.10 What is the tone of the poem, and how is it conveyed?

Answer The dominant mood of "Hap" is ironic. The title suggests the central irony: "Hap" (chance or happenstance), which has dealt out sorrow to the speaker of the poem, could as readily have bestowed "Happiness." The painful truth is that neither ill fortune nor good luck has any inherent meaning. It is the impersonality, neutrality, and randomness of fate against which the speaker rails, in a voice both grim and sardonic.

In the octave of the sonnet, the poet posits the idea of a hostile god wreaking vengeance on him. This hypothetical deity speaks in a highly dramatic language:

> ". . . Thou suffering thing,
> Know that thy sorrow is my ecstasy
> And thy love's loss is my hate's profiting!"
> (lines 2–4)

This declaration, with its exulting epithet and stark, gloating antitheses, makes the god a concrete presence and the worthy antagonist for which the poet longs. The poet's response to the god is described in similarly dramatic rhetoric:

> Then would I bear it, clench myself and die,
> Steeled by the sense of ire unmerited;
> (lines 5–6)

Thus the poet personalizes fate as a tragic contest between clashing opponents, between an evil Nemesis and a suffering individual.

In the sestet, the speaker begins by undercutting his own illusion: "But not so" (line 9). These monosyllables stand in contrast to the luxuriant rhetoric of the octave, and the following question, which also contains many monosyllables, has a subdued tone: "How arrives it joy lies slain,/And why unblooms the best hope ever sown?" (lines 9–10). The coinage "unblooms" emphasizes, by the negative particle un, the obstructive and destructive quality of "hap," while at the same time suggesting that the workings of fate are as wholly natural as "blooming," an organic process rather than an expression of conscious will. The mindless neutrality of destiny is conveyed by the phrases "Crass Casualty," "dicing Time," and "purblind Doomsters"; the forces opposing humanity's joy and hope are undiscerning, frivolous, and half-blind. "They" are playing a game of chance rather than dealing a malignant blow, and to them "blisses" and "pain" are merely equivalent throws of the dice. There is no deity in the heavens, evil or otherwise, to announce that "thy love's loss is my hate's profiting!" The poem's irony derives from the substitution of an absurdity for a tragedy. Where there is motive, there is meaning; but instead of a "Powerfuller than I," who at least acknowledges the opposing "I," there is only "hap," gambling with human lives.

The tone of the poem, then, shifts from the dramatic defiance of the octave to the more resigned, sardonic tone of the close. Throughout the sonnet, the irony has a strangely double effect, wavering between bitterness and a kind of grim satisfaction. The general logic of the sonnet, with the hypothesis of the octave undercut by the reality of the sestet, has the quality of a bitter indictment. A sense of angry disillusionment colors the substitution of "Crass Casualty" and "dicing Time" for an exulting, powerful god, and the pun on "hap," with its echo of "happy," is a grim joke.

At the same time, the sonnet is tinged with something like complacency. In the octave, the image of a mighty contest between heroes has an air of pleasurable excitement, with the dramatic language suggesting a flight of fancy. There is also a sense of pleasure or satisfaction in the closing movement, where the poet answers his own question with a resounding affirmation of meaning-lessness. Underlying the irony of the absurd, to which the poet consciously points, is the subtler irony of pessimism, which has its own peculiar "happiness." The whole of the poem documents the contest which the speaker imagines in the octave, for the poet is the expressive "I" who bears it, clenches himself, and is steeled "by the sense of ire unmerited"; he is "half-eased" even by the "purblind Doomsters," who are as satisfyingly unfair as the "vengeful god." The sense of knowing martyrdom lightens the irony, giving it a sardonic edge.

28.11 Several impersonal "forces" are personified in the poem. Explain the function of these personifications.

Answer Throughout the poem, the poet personifies the forces of fate. The most fully developed of these personifications is that of the vengeful god who speaks in the octave, taunting the poet as his personal adversary. The poet calls him a being "Powerfuller than I," implying that he is an omnipotent god who determines fate. Furthermore, the poet suggests that the existence of this hypothetical power, however malevolent, would somehow make sense of his misery. The implication is that being bereaved of a sense of divine purpose in existence—even if that purpose is evil—is more painful than our earthly sufferings. There is also a sense that the stature of humanity, and its dignity, are diminished by the absence of God. Even a defiant and defeated person is a greater thing, for Hardy, than a person subject to the mere whims of a mechanistic, random universe.

In the sestet, "Crass Casualty" (accident or chance, as opposed to purposefulness) and "dicing Time" (time as a gambler) are depicted as "purblind Doomsters" (half-blind judges), impersonal forces acting randomly in a mechanistic universe. According to the logic of the poem, these forces contrast with the all-powerful god in the octave. However, because the poet personifies these forces as well, the effect is to transform them into personal antagonists much like the "vengeful god." Therefore, the contrast between a willfully malevolent god and the impersonal forces of chance tends to dissolve, because these latter forces acquire an aspect of personal animosity. What comes through in the poem, despite the poet's assertions, is his feeling that he is surrounded by hostile powers.

The line "How arrives it joy lies slain" (line 9) contributes to the paradoxical notion of the malevolence of chance. Though the sowing and "unblooming" of hope may be a purely natural process ("And why unblooms the best hope ever sown?"[line 10]), the "slaying" of joy implies some kind of battle or confrontation similar to that described in the octave. If joy is slain, there must be a slayer, an active agent who has "willed and meted" (line 8) this lot. In the concluding line, the reference to "my pilgrimage," like the personifications and the slaying of joy, runs counter to the theory of a mechanistic, absurdist universe. The word "pilgrimage," with its religious connotations, implies a journey with a goal, a progress toward some kind of enlightenment or significance. It would be paradoxical to attempt a pilgrimage in a world governed by chance, for the pilgrim in such a world is helpless to achieve any personal intention.

The tensions in the language of the poem suggest Hardy's solution to a characteristically modern dilemma. In the twentieth century, the poets of disillusionment have sometimes attempted to express their sense of absurdity and chaos by a deliberately fragmented technique (as, for example, in T. S. Eliot's *The Waste Land*). Some have sought solace in the order and beauty of nature (for example, Dylan Thomas), in the hints of God in nature (Eliot in *Four Quartets* and Gerard Manley Hopkins), in the construction of a personal mythology to replace traditional theology (W. B. Yeats), or in the celebration of the secular and everyday (W. H. Auden). Hardy's consolation is stated in the same terms as his disillusionment; he redeems absurdity by treating it, at least covertly, as significant. Despite its overt avowal of meaninglessness, the poem embodies the struggle for meaning. The poet makes this struggle personal, dramatic, and even noble by characterizing the universe not as a machine but as an active antagonist. Purblind or no, the "Doomsters" are foes to "my pilgrimage," against whom the poet clenches himself. His poem about the inevitable disappointments dealt out by happenstance "half-eases" him.

"A Darkling Thrush"

28.12   Explain how the visual descriptions in the first two stanzas of the poem convey the poet's feelings.

Answer   The most prominent images used in describing the landscape are metaphors for death or dying. In the first stanza, the language implies a state of enervation, impotence, and exhaustion. The frost is a ghostly presence, "specter-gray" (line 2); the year has been consumed, leaving only "Winter's dregs" (line 3); and the "eye" of day is "weakening" (line 4). The image of "bine-stems" (the twining stems of shrubs) as "strings of broken lyres" (line 6) suggests an instrument damaged, useless, and voiceless. These lyres, in contrast to the "darkling thrush," make no music. The final lines of the stanza offer an opposing image: the "household fires" at which "mankind" seeks refuge connote warmth, society, and animation—all that the bleak landscape fails to provide. The phrase "household fires" is reminiscent of "household gods"; there is the subtle implication that the huddling indoors is deluded, a hopeless attempt to turn away from the grim reality outside to false gods who offer an illusion of safety and order.

In the second stanza, the poet presents a developed metaphor linking the landscape with death. The terrain is depicted as a corpse, the sky as a crypt, and the wind as a dirge. In the phrase "the ancient pulse of germ and birth" (line 13), the poet evokes the life force of nature, the throbbing rhythm of conception and growth; this pulse is now "shrunken hard and dry" like the arteries of a dead organism. Part of the effect of this imagery of death is to suggest that the seasonal cycle of growth and decay has ended forever; not only the year but all life seems to have reached its final terminus. In this context, rebirth appears impossible.

These first two stanzas constitute the poet's projection of his emotional state onto the landscape. The diction is not neutral or objective but emotive, conveying the speaker's depression and despair. The poet explicitly states his mood in the lines "And every spirit upon earth/Seemed fervorless as I" (lines 15–16). The somewhat unusual word "fervorless" emphasizes, by means of the suffix *less*, the ideas of loss, negation, lack; the extension of the poet's condition to "every spirit upon earth" suggests the blanketing, pervasive quality of his depression. He projects this feeling onto the earth itself, which he perceives as a dead thing, and onto time, which he implies has reached an endpoint. It is significant that the poem was composed on December 31, 1900, for the poet sees the condition of nature ("the Century's corpse") as an emblem of the death of the nineteenth century.

The poet suggests in the last stanza that he has been reading the landscape, that is, describing what "was written on terrestrial things" (line 27). But the language of the opening stanzas produces the different impression that the poet has been writing a mood into the landscape rather than reading a meaning from it. In the tradition of the romantic poets, Hardy's concern is with the relationship between perceiver and perceived, subject and object. He touches on the question of where the origins of joy and significance lie without offering an explicit answer. Thus the poet initially presents himself as the victim, as it were, of a dying world which offers "little cause for carolings" (line 25). But the emotional diction of the poem's opening casts suspicion on the idea of a purely objective reality which can overpower the subject who views it. The perceiver is inevitably implicated in what he or she perceives.

28.13   The "darkling thrush" appears in the third and fourth stanzas, signaling a shift in the poet's mood. What does the bird symbolize?

Answer   The thrush is both part of the desolate landscape and separate from it. The title of the poem suggests his connection with the bleak winter dusk and the "weakening eye of day" (line 4). The thrush is "darkling" because he appears in the dark, at a moment of "growing gloom" (line 24). The poet describes him as an almost spectral presence who properly belongs in the dead world of the first two stanzas:

> An aged thrush, frail, gaunt, and small,
>   In blast-beruffled plume,
> Had chosen thus to fling his soul
>   Upon the growing gloom.
>
>   (lines 21–24)

But in several important respects the bird is opposed to the natural world, that "corpse" (line 10) whose "ancient pulse . . ./Was shrunken hard and dry" (lines 13–14). Instead of constriction and death, the thrush conveys a sense of the infinite and the immortal. His voice arises "in a fullhearted evensong/Of joy illimited" (lines 19–20). The connotations are of abundance and extravagance, of generosity without limit. The fact that he has "chosen to fling his soul" in this way implies a conscious act of bravery and bravado; it constitutes a choice, not an instinct. His song is "ecstatic" (line 26) because it stands outside of "terrestrial things," springing from somewhere other than the physical world with its silent "broken lyres." The "cause" of the song appears to be within the thrush, "some blessed Hope, whereof he knew/And I was unaware" (lines 30–31). Hardy ends on this note of mystery, affirming only the "trembling" of some unspecified possibility which the poet, in his limited consciousness, cannot fully comprehend. The capitalization of "Hope" suggests its symbolic significance, but it is a relatively abstract, open symbol. Like the thrush's "joy illimited," his "blessed Hope" is obscurely motivated.

The poem partially suggests the characteristic movement of the romantic lyric from description of the physical world to some intimation of immortality, some stirring of joy or momentary illumination. But the thrush does not suddenly animate the universe, and Hardy does not elaborate on the joy or hope which the bird conveys. He halts at the threshold of the transcendent significance that Wordsworth finds in nature ("a sense sublime/Of something far more deeply interfused" ["Tintern Abbey," lines 95–96]) and that Coleridge locates within the perceiver ("Joy is the sweet voice, Joy the luminous cloud—/We in ourselves rejoice!" ["Dejection: An Ode," lines 71–72]). Hardy's thrush, unlike Shelley's skylark ("Bird thou never wert" [line 2]) or Keats's nightingale ("Thou wast not born for death, immortal Bird!" [line 61]), remains primarily a bird, "frail, gaunt, and small" (line 21). There is little in the language to suggest that he

symbolizes a spiritual presence made flesh or the creative imagination as expressed in poetry. It is because the thrush is of the natural world and, at the
same time, beyond it, "ecstatic," that he has meaning. His joy and hope are a
"flinging" of the soul; he chooses to sing, despite the "growing gloom." He thus
represents the existential bravery required of people in the twentieth century,
who must live without the consolations of myth and religion, even the natural
religion of the romantics. Hardy's treatment of the thrush is modern in the sense
that he refuses any leap to affirmation, confining himself instead to what the
bird, as bird, can suggest to the despairing mind of the perceiver.

B.S.

SUGGESTED READINGS

Gregor, Ian, *The Great Web: The Form of Hardy's Major Fiction* (1974).
Guerard, Albert, *Hardy: A Collection of Critical Essays* (1963).
Hardy, Barbara, *The Appropriate Form* (1964).
Hardy, Florence Emily, *The Life of Thomas Hardy* (1962).
Miller, J. Hillis, *Thomas Hardy: Distance and Desire* (1970).

HENRY JAMES

1843   Born at 2 Washington Place, New York City, the second son of Henry James, Sr., inheritor of one of the three largest fortunes in New York State, who gave up the family business to study moral philosophy, and Mary Robertson Walsh James. Brother William, later an eminent philosopher, had been born a year earlier.

1843–   Family travels extensively in Europe. Henry is educated at home by gov-
1860   ernesses, at day schools in Albany and New York City, and then in Geneva, Paris, and Boulogne. Henry becomes a voracious reader and begins his youthful writing. Becomes friends with the artists John La Farge and Thomas Sergeant Perry.

1860   Family takes up residence in Newport, Rhode Island, where Henry studies art with William Morris Hunt. Translates Alfred de Musset's *Lorenzaccio* and Mérimée's *La Venus d'Ille*.

1861   Suffers a mysterious back injury while fighting a fire with the Newport Fire Department. May have incapacitated him sexually. Brothers Garth and Robertson join the Union Army.

1862–   Studies law at Harvard but gives it up. Family moves to Boston, where
1864   Henry becomes friends with Charles Eliot Norton, James Russell Lowell, and William Dean Howells.

1865–   Publishes his first tale, "The Story of a Year," in *The Atlantic Monthly*.
1870   Begins reviewing for *The Nation*. Travels to Europe for his first adult encounter with European culture. Hears of the death of his beloved cousin,

Minny Temple; she will be the inspiration for several of his heroines, notably Isabel Archer in *The Portrait of a Lady* and Milly Theale in *The Wings of the Dove*. Refuses editorship of the *North American Review*. Writes a group of "wonder tales" and a group of realistic tales.

1871–1884 Travels in Europe and continues writing for several magazines. Spends 1875 in Paris "listening brilliantly" to the writers Flaubert, Maupassant, Zola, the Goncourt brothers, Daudet, Turgenev, and others in Flaubert's circle. In 1876, settles more or less permanently in England, where he writes the major fiction of his middle years: *Watch and Ward* (1871), his first novel; *Roderick Hudson* (1876), the story of a young sculptor's struggle with his art and passions; *The American* (1877), his first really successful novel, about an American businessman in conflict with European culture; *Daisy Miller* (1878), the story of an ingenuous unconventional American girl in Rome, which makes him an international literary celebrity; *The Europeans* (1878), about European aristocrats come to America, a reversal in the international theme; *Washington Square* (1880), a brilliant psychological study of inverted family relationships; and *The Portrait of a Lady* (1881), an early masterpiece. Lionized in London society, he hobnobs with eminent Victorians such as Tennyson, Browning, Gladstone, Stevenson, Meredith, and Gosse. He returns briefly to America when his mother and father die in 1882.

1884–1890 Feeling he has exhausted the international theme, James turns to novels of social reform and politics: *The Bostonians* (1886), concerning women's suffrage; *The Princess Casamassima* (1886), dealing with the anarchist movements of the 1880s; *The Aspern Papers* (1888); and *The Tragic Muse* (1890). Also writes many tales and critical essays.

1890–1895 Devotes himself to writing plays until opening night of *Guy Domville* on January 5, 1895. On that disastrous first night, not realizing the hostility of the audience calling for the author, he takes a curtain call and is jeered off the stage. Deeply humiliated, he leaves the theater, vowing never to return.

1895–1901 The experience of writing for the theater leaves an indelible mark on his novelistic technique. He experiments with narrower angles, more dialogue, withholding of information from the reader until the appropriate dramatic moment, and alternation of dramatic scenes with pictorial scenes in *The Spoils of Poynton* (1897), *What Maisie Knew* (1897), *The Turn of the Screw* (1898), and *The Sacred Fount* (1901).

1902–1904 Writes three novels that represent the new psychological and moral direction of the novel in the twentieth century. He uses an increasingly allusive style suffused with symbolic imagery in *The Wings of the Dove* (1902). *The Ambassadors* (1903), the story of a middle-aged American who discovers in the richly civilized Parisian life a previously unknown dimension of life; and *The Golden Bowl* (1904), a highly symbolic novel in which James played a "small handful of values for all they were worth" ("Preface"). All three novels transcend their plots and characters in their insight into a social ethic that must preserve its forms while at the same time recognizing the absolute need for privacy and freedom.

1904–1905	Visits the United States for the first time in twenty years and travels extensively around the country.
1907–1910	Publishes *The American Scene* (1907), essays about his American travels. Writes eighteen important critical prefaces for twelve of his twenty novels and his principal tales. Publishes his revised novels and tales in twenty-four volumes as the New York Edition. Although ill, he goes with his brother William, also ill, on a trip to Germany in 1910. Accompanies William home to New Hampshire, where William dies.
1911–1914	Publishes several minor novels and some tales. Also publishes his autobiographical memoirs: *A Small Boy and Others* (1913), *Notes of a Son and Brother* (1914), and *The Middle Years* (1917), unfinished and published posthumously. Receives honorary degrees from Harvard (1911) and Oxford (1912).
1915	Becomes a naturalized British citizen in protest over America's delay in entering the Great War as England's ally. Suffers a stroke and catches pneumonia.
1916	Receives the Order of Merit from King George V. Dies in Chelsea. His funeral is held in Chelsea Old Church, London, and his ashes are interred in the family cemetery plot in Cambridge, Massachusetts.
1917	*The Ivory Tower* and *The Sense of the Past*, two unfinished novels, are published posthumously.

ESSAY QUESTIONS WITH ANSWERS

The Portrait of a Lady

29.1 Henry James's realism consists not only of his accurate and detailed presentation of human experience but also of his treatment of the conflict between the romantic imagination and reality. Discuss the treatment of this conflict in *The Portrait of a Lady*.

Answer Henrietta Stackpole, Isabel Archer's American friend, accuses her of living too much in the world of her dreams. The narrator, too, describes Isabel as possessing a "ridiculously active" imagination; "when the door was not open it [her imagination] jumped out of the window" (Chap. 4). *The Portrait of a Lady*, then, chronicles the education of a young, idealistic, rather egotistical American girl who learns about the ways of the world and comes to recognize her own idealism and egotism.

Isabel views the world in terms of the novels she has read. For example, Warburton, the wealthy Englishman who becomes her first suitor, appears to her as an appropriate hero for a novel, and Gardencourt, the symbolically named estate of the Touchetts, represents the kind of paradise of possibilities, dreams, and romantic excitement which she has experienced only vicariously in books. However, Isabel finds that life can be very different from romantic novels and comes to recognize the miscalculations and errors of judgment involved in some of the passionate choices she makes.

This movement of Isabel from romantic expectations to confrontation of the reality of her situation is mirrored in the structure of the novel, which can be divided in half at Chapter 36. In the first half, *The Portrait of a Lady* contains a basic romantic situation: a marriageable young girl surrounded by multiple suitors. A rich and manly English lord, a strapping American capitalist, a sensitive but sickly English cousin, and finally, an intriguing American expatriate and aesthete are the characters who want to marry Isabel. Of course, throughout the book, James rings changes on romantic conventions. Instead of being swept off her feet, as other girls might be, by the wealth and power of the English blue blood, Isabel rejects his money and title as potential limitations on her freedom. Clearly, although orphaned and needy, Isabel is no ordinary damsel in distress.

If the first part of the book treats Isabel's choices, the second part deals with the consequences of those choices. The first half ends with Isabel's choice of Gilbert Osmond and the various opinions of her friends on her selection. When Chapter 36 begins, a number of years have elapsed, and something has perceptibly altered in Isabel's situation. She is more subdued, disillusioned, and patient than the eager young girl of the first half, and we gradually learn that a chasm separates husband and wife, who now see each other without illusions. Ultimately, Isabel comes to two important realizations. First, her decision to marry Osmond, which had seemed to have been made in utter freedom, had been plotted by Madame Merle and Osmond. Second, the seemingly original and unusual Osmond is, in reality, the height of conventionality. At the end of the novel, Isabel decides to return to Rome to face the consequences of her mistaken perceptions.

29.2 In Chap. 1, Ralph Touchett repeats to Lord Warburton Mrs. Touchett's two "inscrutable" telegrams concerning Isabel Archer: "Tired America, hot weather awful, return England with niece, first steamer decent cabin" and "Changed hotel, very bad, impudent clerk, address here. Taken sister's girl, died last year, go to Europe, two sisters, quite independent." How do both the form and the content of these messages introduce important themes or questions in the novel?

Answer The cryptic form and ambiguous content of Mrs. Touchett's messages present in miniature some of the major themes and problems dramatized in the novel as a whole. Even the telegrams' obscurity typifies the general way language works in many of James's novels. James's narrative style is anything but condensed and cryptic like Mrs. Touchett's, but his elliptical periodic style nevertheless employs ambiguity, obscurity, and hidden meanings.

The telegram, as well as the narrative style of the book, suggests an important Jamesian theme: the difficulties of interpretation, particularly in the area of human relationships. These difficulties of style point to a difficulty in human relationships: their nature is to be ambiguous, expressed by implication, deceptive, and often intended to deceive. Ralph's comment on the telegram, "It seems to admit of so many interpretations," could describe the novel as a whole.

After quoting the telegrams to Warburton, Ralph lists their possible inter-pretations, and this scene is emblematic of a classic Jamesian process: a character pondering another character's speech or actions and trying to rescue meaning from obscurity. Such scenes occur throughout the novel. In a sense, Isabel's major problem is her naiveté in "reading" both Osmond and Madame Merle. She fails to do justice to the complexity of the "texts" before her and ignores the possibility of multiple interpretations.

The ambiguities of the second telegram in particular introduce important questions about the female protagonist. The choppy, ambiguous syntax with its misplaced modifiers (the verb "died," for example, is meant to refer to "sister" rather than "girl") creates several problems of interpretation in regard to Isabel. As Ralph points out, it is unclear who died, whose sister is mentioned, who is independent, and in what sense—both sisters or just one? independent finan-cially or morally? The question of Isabel's relationship to the Touchetts, raised by the ambiguous reference of "sister," and the question of her financial status gain in importance as the novel proceeds. For it is precisely because of Mr. Touchett's legacy to Isabel that she finds herself in the especially marriageable situation that makes her a prey to Gilbert Osmond. By the end of the novel, the initial question of independence raised in the telegram has received an ironic twist: The more financially independent Isabel has become, the less independent are her actions. Ironically, the Touchetts' kindly assistance to their niece makes her more vulnerable and, in a sense, less free. Her quest for knowledge and experience is initially aided by her inheritance, but ultimately, she discovers, it has placed her unwittingly at the mercy of the unscrupulous Osmond.

29.3   Money plays an important part in the plot of *The Portrait of a Lady*. Isabel's entire future is affected by her large inheritance and by Madame Merle's and Osmond's pecuniary desires. In addition, an implicit and more subtle sug-gestion of the importance of money is woven into the fabric of narrative and dialogue by means of metaphor. Discuss the use of this economic metaphor.

Answer   When Madame Merle encourages Osmond to make a new ac-quaintance (Isabel), he promptly and "crudely" asks what "good" it will do him, and she answers, subsequently, that he will indeed "profit" by his acquaintance with the young girl (Chap. 22). The word "good," which most often has a moral connotation, includes here more prominently an economic connotation (as in the word "goods"). Both Osmond and Madame Merle view people in terms of their usefulness, their value, their potential for bringing "profit." The whole question of value, then, is given a decidedly pecuniary twist by Madame Merle and Osmond, and this is evident in the metaphors they use.

Isabel attributes greatness to Madame Merle because she is able to affix a "value" to other people (Chap. 19); ironically, Madame Merle's ability to gauge someone's usefulness and profitability leads to Isabel's undoing. Isabel's only reservation about Madame Merle early in the novel is that she is too thoroughly the "social animal," so that Isabel wonders "what commerce she could possibly hold with her own spirit" (Chap. 22). Again, metaphor serves an ironic purpose, for the word "commerce," used innocently by Isabel to signify communication or connection, carries with it a second, more sinister meaning, that of economic trade. Madame Merle has indeed sacrificed one kind of commerce for another; one could say that her talent for using others has been received in exchange for her feelings of self-worth and self-approval.

But it is Gilbert Osmond who is the greatest materialist in the novel, the collector and appreciator of valuable objects, including his wife. James comments that Gilbert wants Isabel to be "as smooth to his general need of her as handled ivory to the palm" (Chap. 29). In this metaphor, the implicitly financial and material connotations of the word "need" are emphasized by the simile of the ivory. Isabel becomes a valuable object to be "handled," or managed.

Although, in a general sense, economic metaphors form part of the matrix of metaphorical analogy in many of James's novels, the calculating, utilitarian characters such as Madame Merle and Osmond tend to be the ones who see relationships as mediums of exchange and other characters as commodities.

29.4   Like other novels by James, *The Portrait of a Lady* contains numerous minor characters who function thematically in important ways. One such character is Pansy, the delicate young daughter of Gilbert Osmond. Discuss Pansy's function in the novel.

Answer   Gilbert Osmond's delicate flower, Pansy, contributes importantly to the intrigue of the plot, for her origin and her future are held in doubt until the conclusion of the story. She also represents an interesting contrast to Isabel, for unlike her more recalcitrant stepmother, she is the perfect product of Osmond's taste and artistry.

Pansy is the living link between Serena Merle and Gilbert Osmond and the hidden reason for Madame Merle's matchmaking. She is a pawn in a game played by powerful strategists. The star-crossed relationship of Pansy and Edward Rosier provides not only an interesting subplot but also an explicit form of that which is covert in the other male-female relationships in the novel—match-making, plotting, and calculation.

Pansy's greatest thematic or symbolic function, however, is to provide a contrast to Isabel in her relationship with Osmond: Osmond tries to make works of art of both his wife and his daughter but succeeds in molding only his daughter. If he sees Isabel as ivory to be handled, Pansy throughout remains the most malleable of clays. If in Isabel James paints the portrait of a lady, in Pansy he paints the portrait of, as Edward Rosier calls her, the model "jeune fille." Ultimately, Isabel finds that everything she says irritates her husband; Pansy, on the other hand, lives to please the father she adores. She is a "household angel" (Chap. 36), that peculiar product of a certain kind of male imagination. Isabel feels so much sympathy for Pansy partly because she recognizes the extent to which Osmond is trying to mold *her* as well.

How successfully Gilbert Osmond has molded his young daughter is proved by the attention she receives from Edward Rosier, another American expatriate pursuing the life of the aesthete. Rosier, like Osmond, is a collector of beautiful things; in one way, at least, he is the perfect young man to appreciate Pansy's style. But Rosier differs from Osmond in two major ways. He is ineffectual and foolish, whereas Osmond is powerful and calculating; and he genuinely loves the woman he intends to marry, whereas Osmond is incapable of love. When the two dilettantes conflict, Rosier, who, like Pansy, is a rather delicate flower, is no match for Osmond. Osmond's thwarting of this relationship between the two young people leads ultimately to Pansy's retreat to a convent. Her isolation and virtual imprisonment serve as images of the still more insidious, though less literal, forms of alienation and entrapment that Isabel experiences.

The Golden Bowl

29.5 Unlike most eighteenth- and nineteenth-century novels, twentieth-century novels tend to have symbolic titles, such as *A Passage to India, Ulysses,* and *To the Lighthouse.* Discuss the significance of the title of *The Golden Bowl.*

Answer The title refers to the cracked golden cup that Charlotte contemplates buying as a wedding present for Maggie and that Maggie buys innocently and Fanny smashes violently later in the novel. The golden bowl is, first, a kind of linchpin in the plot, as it is the "evidence" which finally brings about Maggie's awareness of the adulterous relationship of Charlotte and the Prince. It is also an important symbol.

In Book I, the first dialogue about the golden bowl occurs in the antique shop where the bowl is for sale. Charlotte's desire to spend some time with the Prince after his engagement and before his marriage leads to their trip together to the shop, where she hunts for an appropriate present for Maggie. The different perceptions of the bowl by Charlotte and the Prince symbolize differences in their characters and outlooks. Most important, Charlotte first mistakes the crystal bowl for solid gold and then fails to see its fatal flaw. The Prince, on the other hand, recognizes at a glance that the cup seems beautiful and tasteful but contains a crack that ruins its value. The golden bowl here represents both the beauty and the danger of Charlotte herself, a magnificent woman who nonetheless possesses a character flaw. Paradoxically, the Prince recognizes both the beauty and the danger of the *objet d'art* but only the exquisite beauty of Charlotte; he fails to see the real danger.

Once they leave the shop, the Prince confesses that he sees the cracked golden bowl as an omen; he shuns it partly because he sees it as a symbol of weakness in the structure of relationships he has created in his life. Charlotte asks him if he is afraid for his happiness and his marriage, and he acknowledges that he is. The Prince says that he protects himself from catastrophe by recognizing the weaknesses in people and in relationships. Ironically, he does not "protect" himself from his own impulses and Charlotte's later in the book.

In Book II, the full meaning of the symbol is exploited. After Maggie innocently comes across the cup in the shop, she learns from the shopkeeper of the secret relationship between her husband and her best friend. Maggie buys the cup, places it on the mantle, and determines to confront the Prince with it; she thus consciously desires the cup to reveal to him the terrible knowledge that she has recently acquired.

Fanny Assingham, however, cannot bear to have the truth exposed, for then the conventions that keep their intimate society together will come apart. She attempts to obliterate the truth by dashing the cup against the floor, where it smashes into three pieces. But the Prince walks in, and Maggie and he confront each other over the golden bowl; they confront, that is, the truth of their previous lives: that the exquisite surfaces of the lives of the Prince and Princess and their spouses have disguised a basic division between them. The bowl's three shattered pieces lie on the floor as a symbol of the love triangle that has existed all along.

In the first scene in the shop, Charlotte and the shopkeeper discuss the price of the cup in relation to its worth; in Book II, Maggie tells the Prince that although the artistic value of the bowl has been ruined by Fanny's violent act of smashing it to bits, its symbolic value as an agent of truth has remained intact. Whereas Charlotte worries about the monetary cost of the bowl, Maggie focuses on the terrible human price she has paid for the tragic knowledge of her husband's duplicity.

29.6   The essential structure of *The Golden Bowl* consists of a series of love triangles. The four main characters—the Prince, Maggie Verver, her father Adam Verver, and Charlotte Stant—arrange and rearrange themselves into four different triangles, each consisting of two men and a woman or two women and a man. Why does James, with almost mathematical precision, establish such a structure in the novel?

Answer   In his "Preface," James acknowledges how few are the players involved in the drama of *The Golden Bowl*, but he suggests that the limits of the group allowed him "to play the small handful of values really for all they were worth." The limited context of the respective marriages of a widowed father and his daughter makes the predicament of the characters both intense and inescapable. Unlike the large canvas used by Tolstoy in *War and Peace* or by George Eliot in *Middlemarch*, James's canvas is small enough to permit author and reader to concentrate on exquisitely subtle shadings and groupings.

The first circumstance of the plot which establishes the triangular groupings is the marriage of the Prince and Maggie, with which the book begins. What is unusual about the marriage is that Maggie marries the Prince without leaving her father; thus the first triangle—father, daughter, husband—is established. This opens the way for the formation of the second triangular relationship, that of the Prince, Maggie, and Charlotte, for if Maggie's marriage allows her to keep her father, it also ultimately allows the Prince to keep his former lover. The relationships among Charlotte, her husband, and her lover and among Charlotte, her husband, and his daughter are the two remaining triangles of interest. The main arenas for the playing out of these relationships are Portland Place (the home of Maggie and the Prince) and Eaton Square (the home of Adam Verver and Charlotte).

As in a game of chess, the characters maneuver back and forth, toward and away from each other. We see each character calculating his or her position in the battle of wits. It is primarily Maggie, however, who masterminds the interpersonal alliances in Book II; it is she who ultimately dissolves the triangular relationships by cutting off the ties between her father and herself. At the end of the novel, in place of the various threesomes, we find the two couples separated from each other literally by an ocean and metaphorically by the depth of the pain they have inflicted on each other. James shows us the price they have had to pay for the fullness of their former relationships. We see, as we do in many of James's novels, the price that must be paid by those who plot to have everything as well as those who are the unsuspecting victims of these plots.

29.7 Although the Prince, Maggie, her father, and Charlotte are the main characters of interest in *The Golden Bowl*, Fanny and Assingham are introduced early in the novel and play important roles throughout. What is their function in the novel?

Answer The Assinghams advance the plot in certain instances and inter-pret it in others. As actors in the drama, they facilitate meetings, relationships, and events in the story. As commentators, they conduct a series of dialogues about the other characters which provide both new information (e.g., it is Fanny who tells the reader of the Prince and Charlotte's former affair) and analysis.

In her role as a participant in the drama, Fanny figures more prominently than her husband, for she is a facilitator, a connector, even a manipulator of people, whereas he is more circumspect and aloof. Her chosen milieu is the drawing room, her own and her friends'; his is the club, which provides a male retreat from the embroilments of heterosexual relationships. Fanny, we discover, originally introduced Maggie and the Prince, and she unintentionally precipi-tates the confrontation between them over the pieces of the golden bowl. It is she who presides over much of the action like a mother hen.

But the differences between Fanny and Bob emerge most clearly in their dialogues with each other about the various love triangles of their friends. With great emotional involvement, Fanny tells her husband of past and present events, providing analysis and sometimes even prophecy. Her husband, on the other hand, although amused and curious, is emotionally detached. Although he is curious enough to question his wife on the details of the "situations" in which she is involved, he watches her as if she were a performer, like the "celebrated lady" in the tight bathing suit at the aquarium (Chap. 4). She, in turn, accuses him of being indifferent and immoral; she says he has witnessed the sacking of cities yet has never become agitated or involved in the events he has observed. In his disinterested curiosity and casual approach to personalities, however, Bob Assingham sometimes penetrates to the relevant aspects of the "situation"; he seems, for example, instinctively to understand Charlotte Verver.

The narrative situation established in the scenes between this husband and wife team is almost a surrogate for the relationship between narrator and reader. Fanny tells the story, adding little bits of commentary along the way; Bob is like a close reader who pays attention to the details related to him. Their reciprocal relationship of teller and listener provides a fictional representation within the book of the activity of interpretation so important in any reading but particularly crucial to the reading of James's novels.

29.8 James divides his spacious novel into two parts, entitling the first "The Prince" and the second "The Princess." How accurately do these titles reflect the content of the parts of the book, and why does James employ such a division?

Answer Commenting on the narrative mode of The Golden Bowl in his "Preface," James says that "the whole thing remains subject to the register, even so closely kept, of the consciousness of but two of the characters": the Prince and the Princess. Acknowledging certain inconsistencies in the execution of this plan—Fanny Assingham sometimes "supersedes" the Prince's knowledge in Part I, for example—James maintains that even where the Prince is not the actual perceiver, events are presented in terms of their impact on him. Similarly, the narration in Part II centers on Maggie's perceptions of the situation and its effect on her.

One feature of this use of "centered consciousness" is that instead of an omniscient presentation of the story we are given subjective impressions and thoughts. It is not plot that is most important in a Jamesian novel but the impact of the plot on the characters. Interpretation supersedes facts in importance; we are made to see different sides of the "truth."

The order of the narrative divisions in The Golden Bowl is also important, for if the Prince and Charlotte's affair, so to speak, creates the problem predicament, it is Maggie who must combat the deception with a plot of her own making. In Part II, Maggie appears to take over the author's function; she plots out the story carefully, with calculation, simultaneously playing her role in the drama she is writing. Although the Prince displays a fine aesthetic consciousness,

Maggie's is a more sensitive psychological and moral "register" and the reader shares this point of view until the end.

Near the end of the novel, Maggie glances through the smoking room window and fixes in her mind the little social group sitting inside. She realizes, in fact, that this view of things is only one interpretation, which might differ for another interpreter. It is this ability to analyze and interpret as well as participate that characterizes the most interesting of James's characters, who function almost as narrators of their own stories.

K.L.

SUGGESTED READINGS

Dupee, F. W., *Henry James* (1956).

Edel, Leon, *The Prefaces of Henry James* (1970).

————, *The Life of Henry James* (1977).

Holland, Laurence Bedwell, *The Expense of Vision: Essays on the Craft of Henry James* (1964).

Lebowitz, Naomi, *The Imagination of Loving: Henry James's Legacy to the Novel* (1965).

Matthiessen, F. O., *Henry James: The Major Phase* (1944).

Rimmon, Shlomith, *The Concept of Ambiguity—The Example of James* (1977).

GEORGE BERNARD SHAW

C H R O N O L O G Y

1856	Born in Dublin, Ireland, of English parents, the third child of George and Lucinda Shaw. His father is a failure in business and a drunkard with an outrageous sense of humor; his mother, an opera singer and music teacher.
1871	Leaves school to work as a clerk in a Dublin land agent's office.
1876	Moves to London, where his mother is supporting herself as a music teacher.
1878–1883	Writes five unsuccessful novels: *Immaturity, The Irrational Knot, Love among the Artists, Cashel Byron's Profession,* and *An Unsocial Socialist.*
1882	The importance of the economic basis of society dawns on him one night at a lecture on the single-tax theory by an American, Henry George. Reads Karl Marx's *Das Kapital* at the British Museum.
1884	Joins the new Fabian Society, an intellectual group of socialists working to bring about the socialist state gradually through education.
1886–1887	Writes art criticism for the London *Star* and then for the *World.*
1888–1894	Delights and shocks London readers with his ruthlessly honest music criticism for the *Star* and the *World.*
1891	Publishes the *Quintessence of Ibsenism,* which praises Norwegian playwright Henrik Ibsen as a reformer of the theater and of society. Sums up the stand against conventional morality which will inform Shaw's own plays.

1892   Produces his first play, *Widowers' Houses*.

1893   Writes *Mrs Warren's Profession*, a play that was banned from public theater because of its subject of prostitution.

1894   Writes plays *Arms and the Man* and *Candida*, which mock conventional romantic ideas about love, marriage, and war.

1895   Becomes London's foremost drama critic for the *Saturday Review*, edited by Frank Harris.

1898   Publishes collection of *Plays Pleasant and Unpleasant*. The long, provocative prefaces to each play further elaborate his attacks on conventional ideas. Marries Charlotte Payne-Townsend, a wealthy heiress and a fellow Fabian. Publishes *The Perfect Wagnerite* in an attempt to arouse interest in Wagner's music. Deals only with *The Ring*, one of Wagner's opera cycles, and attempts to prove that Wagner is the perfect revolutionist. Writes *Caesar and Cleopatra*.

1899   Writes *Captain Brassbound's Conversion*, a romantic comedy designed for Ellen Terry, the renowned actress.

1900   Writes *Fabianism and the Empire*, the first of his Fabian tracts to be published in book form.

1901–
1903   Writes *Man and Superman* (not produced until 1905) and begins his most brilliant dramatic phase. Dramatizes his ideas about the "Life Force" and its workings in the personal, social, and political life of ordinary people.

1904   Publishes play *John Bull's Other Island*, a treatment of Ireland's grievances against England.

1905   Writes *Major Barbara*.

1906–
1913   Writes and produces several plays, including *The Doctor's Dilemma* (1906), *Getting Married* (1908), *Androcles and the Lion* (1911), and *Pygmalion* (1912).

1913–
1916   Writes *Heartbreak House* (not produced until 1920), which suggests Chekhov in its dramatization of the imminent collapse of the social order. Shaw's old, optimistic faith in the Life Force has been shaken.

1921   Publishes *Back to Methuselah*, his own favorite and most ambitious play.

1923   Publishes *Saint Joan*, his only tragedy, considered by some his best drama.

1925   Receives the Nobel Prize for literature.

1928   Publishes *The Intelligent Woman's Guide to Socialism and Capitalism*, his most thorough treatment of socialist doctrine.

1929	Produces *The Apple Cart*, his last major play, a paradoxical satire on both democracy and monarchy.
1931–1942	Tours Russia, New Zealand, America, and other parts of the world. Writes several more works.
1943	His wife, Charlotte Payne-Townsend Shaw, dies.
1950	He dies at age 94 at his home, Shaw's Corner, in a blaze of publicity and admired by the world. His will asks that his body be cremated and that "its ashes (be) inseparably mixed with those of my late wife now in the custody of the Golders Green Crematorium," and then inurned or scattered "in the garden of the house in Ayot St. Lawrence where we lived together for some thirty-five years."

ESSAY QUESTIONS WITH ANSWERS

Major Barbara

30.1 Discuss the relationship between the "Preface" and the play.

Answer At one point in *Major Barbara*, Lady Britomart says to her husband, "Stop making speeches, Andrew. This is not the place for them" (Act III). Although *Major Barbara* has a remarkable number of set speeches expounding philosophical views and intellectual arguments, the constraints of the drama preclude Shaw's explaining his own views directly. The "Preface" not only provides a forum for the playwright but firmly grounds the dramatic argument in the world outside the theater.

The central paradox of the play is an inversion of good and evil through an attack on conventional ideas of piety, virtue, love, and charity. Undershaft, the munitions manufacturer, emerges as a more morally respectable man than his priggish son, Stephen, who is so supremely confident of what is morally right and wrong. Shaw uses the "Preface" in part to elaborate on his paradoxical views and thus further jolt readers out of their safe, comfortable opinions. He analyzes the significance of Undershaft, who is a typical Shavian hero in his intellectual vigor and unheroic posture. If Undershaft has "made good" in life, it is because he has discarded the traditional idea of merit and concentrated instead on more revolutionary ideas of enterprise. As he says to "poor but honest" Peter Shirley, "I wouldn't have your income, not for all your conscience, Mr. Shirley" (Act II). But Undershaft is not merely a rich villain. One of the consequences of his self-interest and energy, Shaw tries to show, is the improvement of other men's lives. This is the point Shaw emphasizes in the "Preface" when he attacks the traditional Christian view of poverty as a blessing and undercuts the unrealistic belief that charity can be insulated from the sources of worldly wealth.

Shaw also devotes space to the Bill Walker episode in his "Preface." Although Major Barbara almost succeeds in reforming and "saving" Bill, using the "spiritual" means of persuasion and prodding, Shaw brings his hardheaded materialism to bear on the case. Bill's conscience money is unacceptable because it is a pittance, while Bodger's bequest is sufficiently large to save his soul. The irony here reinforces Shaw's thesis that poverty is a crime because it robs people of self-respect and self-belief.

In the conclusion to the "Preface," Shaw attacks capitalism and the present system of law as well as the churches for supporting these institutions. He proposes within the play a "hygienic" rather than religious solution to people's ills: Let a person be well fed and well clothed, and that person will be a moral and upstanding citizen.

The "Preface," then, spells out in expository style what the play dramatizes. Furthermore, through the "Preface," Shaw is able to use the theater (traditionally a bourgeois and conservative medium) as a forum for his revolutionary ideas, thus preventing audiences and critics from wriggling off the hook of his satire.

30.2 Although *Major Barbara* deals with serious social problems, the play is a comedy. How do the plot and language of the play contribute to its humor?

Answer The plot of *Major Barbara* has many of the conventional features of a romantic comedy, with an inheritance plot as a means of reconciling the generations and pointing toward future happiness for the main characters. There are several sets of lovers, a legacy puzzle, and various stereotyped characters, including a bemused butler, a domineering wife, a lame-brained young aristocrat, and a priggish son. The conclusion of the play, with Adolphus Cusins coming into his proper fortune by means of a legal technicality, has the zany inconsequence of light comedy.

The play also has some of the specific features of a drawing room comedy. Apart from the literal drawing room setting of the first act, the play includes an examination of manners and mannerisms, style and speech. Paradox, a species of wit characteristic of drawing room comedy, is a feature not only of the intellectual positions of the play but of its language as well. The characters speak in witty epigrams and antitheses, scoring points against one another as though conversation were debate. A typical exchange demonstrating Shaw's paradoxical style occurs between Lady Britomart and Dolly Cusins regarding Undershaft's anonymous gift to the Salvation Army:

Lady Britomart.   That's Andrew all over. He never does a proper thing without giving an improper reason for it.

Cusins.   He convinced me that I have all my life been doing improper things for proper reasons.

(Act III)

Witty definitions which puncture conventional notions about politics, religion, and mores are scattered throughout the dialogue. For example, Undershaft comments on Stephen's inflated idealism: "He knows nothing and thinks he knows everything. That points clearly to a political career" (Act III). A similar instance of ironic deflation is seen in Cusins's definition of his academic profession: "Greek scholars are privileged men. Few of them know Greek; and none of them know anything else; but their position is unchallengeable" (Act I).

For the most part, the language of the play lacks the effervescent wit of, for example, a Wilde comedy, and the comedy of manners is at times submerged in the social drama. Shaw's characters are given to harangues, which may start out as frivolous, shocking mock rhetoric but end as earnest argument. This interplay of serious comment and drawing room patter is most characteristic of the Shavian style, but the comedy is a crucial ingredient in the recipe, for it makes the message palatable and entertaining. Comedy helps shape Shaw's message by emphasizing its tolerant humaneness and its emphasis on the puncturing of snobbery and hypocrisy. Furthermore, the humor suggests that Shaw is not so much a serious reformer (although he is that) as one concerned mainly with the demolition of outmoded ideas.

30.3   *Major Barbara* is a didactic play which attempts to reform the audience's attitude toward a variety of social institutions and customs. Is its argument convincing?

Answer   Shaw has designed the play carefully to lend dramatic support to the ideas he wishes to present. One way Shaw supports his thesis is by dramatizing Barbara's conversion to her father's point of view. The central action of the play is the bargain struck between father and daughter; Barbara agrees to visit the "death and destruction factory" after the munitions maker has visited her "salvation factory." Because Barbara is the play's most sympathetic character, combining fervent idealism with buoyant wit, the audience is able to identify first with her distrust of her father's philosophy and later with her enthusiasm for his projects.

The structure of the play also contributes to the persuasive message. Act II exposes the hypocrisy which conventional charity both demands and enacts. Rummy and Snobby only pretend to a moral reformation in exchange for food and shelter, while Mrs. Baines is happy to accept the "tainted" money of Bodger and Undershaft to keep the shelter open. Hard facts—the physical necessities of life and the financial needs of an institution—defeat "spiritual" considerations. Act III is thus a dramatic answer to the previous scene, offering a vision of the good life where facts are accommodated and people are thus free to pursue the salvation of their souls. The model village seems to vindicate the munitions industry which supports it.

The narrowness of the minor characters throws into high relief the breadth of vision of the "mad" trio of Undershaft, Barbara, and Dolly. The opinionated narcissism of Lady Britomart and the dim-witted clichés of Lomax and Stephen make a poor answer to the strong, realistic creed of Undershaft. Arguing against the false piety of the Salvation Army, he says that

> you have made for yourself something that you call a morality or a religion or what not. It doesn't fit the facts. Well, scrap it. Scrap it and get one that does fit. That is what is wrong with the world at present. (Act III)

L.R.

SUGGESTED READINGS

Bentley, Eric, *Bernard Shaw: A Reconsideration* (1947).
Kaufmann, R. J., (ed.), *G. B. Shaw: A Collection of Critical Essays* (1965).
Meisel, M., *Shaw and the 19th Century Theatre* (1963).

JOSEPH CONRAD

C H R O N O L O G Y

1857	Born Jozef Teodor Konrad Nalecz Korzeniowski near Kiev in Russian Poland, son of a Polish patriot.
1861	Father imprisoned by Russian authorities for Polish nationalist activities.
1862	Moves with his parents to Warsaw. His father is condemned to exile in Russia for activities in the secret Polish National Committee.
1865	Death of Conrad's mother. He goes to live with his uncle in the Polish Ukraine.
1869	His father dies in exile in Russia.
1874	Trip to Marseilles. Ships out on a French merchant ship to Martinique and the West Indies.
1878	Attempts suicide.
1878–1883	Without knowledge of English, he signs on an English ship and begins career in British merchant service. Learns English and works his way up through the ranks, taking third mate's papers in 1880 and first mate's papers in 1883.
1886	Takes master's certificate (captain's papers) and becomes a naturalized British subject.
1890	Takes a steamboat up the Congo River. Keeps a "Congo Diary" from which he will later derive *Heart of Darkness* and "An Outpost of Progress."

1895   Publishes his first novel, *Almayer's Folly*, with moderate success.

1896   On strength of first literary success, he marries an Englishwoman and retires from the sea. In London, takes up new career as a writer. Publishes *An Outcast of the Islands*, which is not well received.

1897   Publishes *The Nigger of the "Narcissus."* Conrad's famous "Preface" to the 1898 edition details his aims as an artist. Conrad called this "the story by which, as a creative artist, I stand or fall."

1898   Publishes *Tales of Unrest*, a collection of five short stories. Writes and publishes *Youth*, an autobiographical romance of the sea. This tale introduces Conrad's favorite narrator, Marlow.

1900   Publishes *Lord Jim*, the widely acclaimed novel that established Conrad as a literary craftsman.

1902   Publishes *The Heart of Darkness* and *Typhoon*, another romance of the sea.

1904   Publishes *Nostromo*, called by F. R. Leavis "one of the great novels of the language."

1907   Publishes *The Secret Agent*.

1910   Publishes *Under Western Eyes*.

1912   Publishes *The Secret Sharer*, a Dostoyevskian story of a young sea captain who gains control over his first command through a moral confrontation with his double.

1915   Publishes *Victory* and *The Shadow Line*.

1917–
1921   Publishes *The Arrow of Gold*, *The Rescue*, and *Notes on Life and Letters*.

1923   Works on *The Rover*, an unfinished romance about Napoleon on Elba. Published posthumously as *Suspense* (1925).

1924   Dies and is buried at Canterbury.

ESSAY QUESTIONS WITH ANSWERS

Lord Jim

31.1   In Marlow's letter to the "privileged listener," he speaks of the "terrifying logic" in the final events of Jim's life, "as if it were our imagination alone that could set loose upon us the might of an overwhelming destiny." How does imagination lead to destiny in *Lord Jim*?

Answer   Whereas the idea of external forces largely determining the fate of the character plays a major role in Thomas Hardy's novels, the idea of imagination as destiny dominates the world of *Lord Jim*. Jim's leap from the deck of the *Patna* in Part I and his violent death in Patusan in Part II are precipitated by his imaginative acts, not by powers outside him. The difference in the two episodes, however, is that in Part I, Jim's romantic self-conception leads to a destiny for which he is unprepared; in Part II, his romantic self-conception leads to the destiny he desires.

Before the hole is punctured in the *Patna*, Jim stands on deck immersed in dreams of heroism. As he did on the training ship two years earlier, he fantasizes about the valorous deeds he would perform on ship if trouble were to occur. His self-satisfied complacency, however, is precisely what leaves him unprepared to face sudden disaster; his heroic self-conception prevents him from anticipating his own cowardly impulses. When disaster strikes, his imagination works, in another way, to thwart his impulse toward decent behavior. He imagines the panic which will seize the pilgrims when they learn of the accident, and his vivid mental picture of the chaos on the ship finally impels him to jump to the lifeboat in order to escape the scene. Betrayed by his imagination, Jim leaps into the sea and into his destiny.

On Patusan, Jim's imagination again determines his destiny; as Marlow says, he forsakes a living woman for a "shadowy ideal of conduct." As a final gesture of bravery and duty, Jim faces unarmed the father of the friend whose death he has caused, in full knowledge that this action will lead to his death. The dream of honor becomes a reality for Jim, but at the expense of his life. In the end,

405

he holds to a code of ethics just as strongly as the French lieutenant, who cannot imagine a life without honor. Thus, although Jim's behavior is shaped by his imagination in both Part I and Part II, suggesting that people never radically or magically change, Jim's final gesture, unlike his leap from the *Patna*, reveals a conscious acceptance of the consequences of his actions.

31.2　In *Lord Jim*, Conrad employs multiple narrators. An omniscient narrator begins and ends the novel, Marlow narrates much of it directly, and the final episodes are recounted in a letter to the privileged listener. Marlow's knowledge of the story is itself pieced together from Jim's account, from Stein's, and from Brown's. Why doesn't Conrad either let Jim tell his own story or let Marlow tell Jim's story?

Answer　*Lord Jim* is the story of Jim's impact on Marlow as well as the story of Jim's struggle with his conscience. Marlow's attempt to piece together the facts of Jim's story and, more important, to understand these facts is a crucial element of the novel which would be lost in a first-person account of Jim's story. Through the decent, rational, and articulate Marlow, the reader learns that Jim is "one of us." The theme of the common guilt and the common illusions which unite Jim, Marlow, and the reader would be lost if the tale were told only by Jim.

　　In addition, Jim may not have either the understanding or rhetorical power to sustain his own narrative. His speeches to Marlow, as related by Marlow to the reader, are often halting and tentative; Jim tends to blurt out his feelings and then disavow the significance of his statements. Marlow is necessary as the storyteller for Jim, sometimes completing, sometimes commenting on, often interpreting Jim's story.

　　But Marlow is not alone as a narrator of Jim's story; even Marlow must piece together material from various sources in order to complete the tale. If *Lord Jim* is partly about Marlow as interpreter, it is also about the limitations of any individual's understanding and the impossibility of really knowing anyone else. As Marlow acknowledges, "It is when we try to grapple with another man's intimate need that we perceive how incomprehensible, wavering, and misty are the beings that share with us the sight of the stars and the warmth of the sun" (Chap. 16). The enigma of personality, an important theme in Conrad's work, is expressed formally in *Lord Jim* through the use of multiple narrators. The different stories told by Jim, Marlow, Brown, Stein, and the omniscient narrator all shed light on Jim's "case," but the figure of Jim never totally emerges from the obscurity, the shadow, that seems to shroud him in Marlow's eyes.

31.3 Discuss the moral relationship to Jim of the following characters: the French lieutenant, Captain Brierly, and Gentleman Brown.

Answer The three minor characters cast different lights on Jim's cowardice and guilt. Brierly and the French lieutenant are seamen who embody in various ways the honorable standard of conduct; Gentleman Brown embodies a criminality which ties him to Jim.

The elderly French lieutenant, one of the boarding officers on the *Patna* after it has been abandoned by its crew, is a man of correct behavior, one of the "steady, reliable men who are the raw material of great reputations" (Chap. 13). Although he perceptively recognizes that the fear in Jim is shared by all people, he cannot understand a life without honor. He acknowledges to Marlow that "Man is born a coward," and Marlow says that he is glad that the lieutenant takes "a lenient view" of Jim, but to Marlow's surprise, the lieutenant goes on to say that he could not live without honor. Marlow is deflated, for he thinks that an understanding of the pervasiveness of fear in all people should lead to some kind of exoneration of Jim. The Frenchman's Latin temperament is a sympathetic one, but since Jim has violated the code which the seaman views as the very basis of ethical behavior and manly pride, he cannot forgive Jim.

The Frenchman's imaginative identification with Jim's cowardice is not as strong as that of Captain Brierly, a man who has prided himself on never making a mistake. Brierly cannot face up to the possibility of weakness in himself, a possibility he recognizes as he sits in judgment of Jim. He suggests to Marlow that he help Jim run away before the end of the trial, an idea Marlow views as quite uncharacteristic of the brave and glorified captain. But for Brierly, the shame involved in Jim's affair is most significant; not the weakness itself but its exposure most agitates Brierly. "The only thing that holds us together is just the name for that kind of decency" (Chap. 6), Brierly says at one point. When the vulnerability and fallibility of public standards are exposed, as they are so resoundingly in Jim's case, Brierly feels there is nothing left. He commits suicide soon after Jim's hearing by leaping from his ship into the sea, a symbolic repetition of Jim's original leap from the *Patna*.

Just as Brierly identifies with Jim, Jim seems to identify with Gentleman Brown, a deserter and gun smuggler who comes to Patusan. Brown himself does everything to foster Jim's identification with him; as he speaks to Jim of his shady past and present troubles (the natives have tried to kill him from the moment he landed), there is in his talk "a vein of subtle reference to their common blood . . . a sickening suggestion of common guilt" (Chap. 42). When Brown asks Jim insinuatingly if there is not something in his past to make him understand Brown's mistakes, Jim is obviously much affected. Jim recognizes that his own guilt binds him to a criminal like Brown; he identifies with Brown's desire for another chance. He decides to let Brown go, to offer him safe conduct, and to assure the natives that Brown poses no threat. Jim's empathy for Brown is not the only reason for his behavior. He has no reason to mistrust Brown and has no idea that Brown is so evil that he would take his "revenge upon the world" (Chap. 43) by shooting Dain Waris. Jim cannot even imagine Brown's kind of treachery. Thus, although Brown is in some ways Jim's double, there are tremendous moral differences between them. Jim's leniency is a misjudgment, but it is not purely a result of some irrational identification in crime.

The Secret Agent

31.4   What is the thematic and symbolic significance of the explosion in which Stevie is killed?

Answer   The explosion is the violent conclusion both of Stevie's life and of the Professor's plan. As reconstructed by the chief inspector and his policemen, Stevie's demise occurs when he trips over a root of a tree. Instead of successfully completing his "mission" to blow up the Greenwich Observatory, the half-witted Stevie kills himself. His body is blown to bits; the label sewn inside his jacket, the one clue to his identity, becomes the piece of evidence which leads the inspector to Mr. Verloc.

As a symbol, however, the explosion carries a further significance. Stevie's death jolts Winnie Verloc out of her complacency. The death is both a tragic loss to Winnie and, in a sense, a symbol of her moral shock. Winnie believes that the facts of life "do not bear much looking into." It is desperate characters like Winnie who are afraid to see reality, as well as those, like Kurtz, who try to look too deeply into the dark face of reality, who are often ultimately destroyed in Conrad's novels. Finally, the violent explosion represents the violence at the heart of society and of individuals. It is an irrational act that cuts through all the laws and codes on which society is founded. In a way, the explosion of the network of consensus and rationality fundamental to society is central to Conrad's vision, whether it occurs in Kurtz's barbaric actions, too terrible to name, in *Heart of Darkness*; in Jim's cowardly leap from the *Patna* in *Lord Jim*; or in the grotesque, accidental death of the half-wit Stevie.

31.5 Discuss the significance of the following patterns of actions and consequences in *The Secret Agent*:

> Winnie's mother leaves the Verloc home so that Stevie will receive better treatment there; her action leads to Mr. Verloc's increased interest in the boy, which ultimately leads to his death.

> Mr. Verloc's ill-conceived efforts to assuage his wife's grief at Stevie's death lead to her sudden impulse to kill him.

> The revolutionaries' plan to bomb the Greenwich Observatory results instead in the death by explosion of a half-witted, pitiful, and harmless boy.

Answer   These three examples reflect the relentless dramatic irony in the novel: The actions of the characters bring about results precisely opposite to the intended ones. In the universe of the novel, no one gets what he or she expects; neither the altruism of Winnie's mother nor the treachery of the anarchists exempts the characters from suffering ironic reversals. At times in *Lord Jim* we are made to feel along with Jim that he is the object of cruel tricks of fate; similarly, in *The Secret Agent*, the sardonic narrator and the forces in the universe seem to conspire relentlessly against the characters, just as the characters conspire against one another.

Yet in *The Secret Agent* we often see that psychological factors as well as the forces of fate contribute to the pathetic ineffectiveness and tragic misconceptions of the characters. The characters constantly misinterpret each other, as illustrated most terribly and poignantly in the final scene between Mr. and Mrs. Verloc. Conrad develops a powerful tension between the surface actions and interior thoughts of the pair. For the first time in his life, Mr. Verloc confides in his wife and feels closer to her than ever, while she thinks only that her husband is the murderer of "the boy." When Mr. Verloc tells Winnie that he seeks revenge on the people in the embassy, he inadvertently puts the idea of revenge in her mind. The newly established intimacy that Mr. Verloc feels his confession has created leads him to call to her in a tone of "wooing." He says of Stevie's death, "Suppose it had been me." This insult is the last straw for

Mrs. Verloc. She stabs her husband, who recognizes, in the final second before his death, the extent of his misjudgments of his wife and of their relationship.

31.6 Mr. Verloc leads a double life as a middle-class shopkeeper and a secret agent. The novel represents both a domestic, bourgeois world and a world of intrigue and violence. How are these two worlds brought together in the metaphors and images in the novel?

Answer   The metaphors used in *The Secret Agent* integrate the realms of espionage and domesticity. In describing the benign activities occurring in the Verloc household, the narrator employs metaphors of violence which cast a sinister light on their domestic life. Revealing the violence just below the surface in the familial relationship of the Verlocs, the metaphors increase the suspense and foreshadow the transformation of domestic drama into murder mystery. For example, the narrator's description of Stevie, happily drawing circles on a piece of paper in the Verloc household, is ominous: "His thin neck, sunk into a deep hollow at the base of the skull, seemed ready to snap." In this metaphor, Conrad foreshadows both Stevie's death and Winnie's fear of the gallows which leads her to suicide. Similarly, when Mr. Verloc calls out his window to a policeman walking nearby, the policeman wheels around "as if prodded by a sharp instrument." The metaphor anticipates the stabbing of Mr. Verloc by his wife.

The central figure of Mr. Verloc, the secret agent who works for the anarchists, the Russian embassy, and the British police, is the main symbol of the duplicity, treachery, and danger at the heart of society. Through Conrad's middle-class, "respectably married" secret agent, we see the intrigue and secrecy that underlie personal as well as international relations. Every character in the book hides some of his or her deepest fears and desires and uses others as tools to achieve certain personal goals. Mr. Verloc simply carries this tendency to an extreme.

The city of London, like Mr. Verloc, has a veneer of civilization, but beneath this surface, too, lies treachery and duplicity. In his "Preface," Conrad describes the city as "a town of darkness, a cruel devourer of the world's light." Bound together by no social contract like that uniting the fraternity of sailors in *Lord Jim*, the dark city instead represents a web of conspiracies and plots, a dog-eat-dog society of nasty schemers. (Indeed, the image of cannibalism recurs throughout the novel.) Beneath its veneer of civility and law, London is revealed as a "heart of darkness."

K.L.

SUGGESTED READINGS

Graver, Lawrence, *Conrad's Short Fiction* (1969).

Guerard, Albert, *Conrad the Novelist* (1958).

Karl, Frederick R., *Joseph Conrad: The Three Lives* (1979).

Said, Edward, *Joseph Conrad and the Fiction of Autobiography* (1966).

Thorburn, David, *Conrad's Romanticism* (1974).

Watt, Ian, *Conrad in the Nineteenth Century* (1979).

E. M. FORSTER

C H R O N O L O G Y

1879   Born Edward Morgan Forster in Dorset Square, London, the only child of Edward Morgan Llewellyn Forster, descendant of the Thorntons, wealthy bankers and prominent members of the Clapham Sect, an evangelical group of social activists, and Alice Clara (Lily) Whichelo Forster.

1880   His father, a budding architect from Cambridge who studied with Thomas Hardy's mentor, Sir Arthur Blomfield, dies unexpectedly. The boy's early upbringing is dominated by three women: his overprotective mother, his adored maternal grandmother (Louisa Whichelo), and his influential great-aunt, Marianne Thornton.

1883–   Moves to Rooksnest, a house in Hertfordshire, the model for the house in
1893   *Howard's End.* This period represents to him an earthly paradise ruined only by an Irish tutor who tries to discipline the spoiled boy. At age 11, he is sent to a preparatory school, Kent House, where he is bullied and unhappy. One day, an unidentified man exposes himself to the impressionable boy, causing a sexual trauma that puzzles him even in his old age.

1893–   Attends Tonbridge School as a day boy, an even more unhappy period than
1897   the previous one. This experience confirms him in a lifelong loathing for the English public school system (privately owned schools for the privileged), representing what he hated in English life: philistinism, snobbery, bland assumption of racial and class superiority, and an "undeveloped heart." Marianne Thornton, his great-aunt, dies and leaves him a legacy of £8000,

making it possible for him to go to Cambridge and to travel in Europe and India later on.

1897–1901	Matriculates at King's College, Cambridge, where he finds liberation in the spiritual, intellectual, and cultural life of the university. Takes a second in classics, then switches to history and takes another second. Comes under the influence of Nathaniel Wedd, classics tutor, who introduces him to the moderns, encourages his antiauthoritarianism, and encourages him to write. Elected to the Society of Apostles, an intellectual discussion group that greatly influences his thinking.
1901–1904	Travels on the Continent with his mother. Settles with her in a London flat. Studies Latin at the Working Men's College in Bloomsbury in preparation for a teaching career. Writes reviews for the *Independent Review*.
1905–1910	Publishes his first four novels: *Where Angels Fear to Tread* (1905); *The Longest Journey* (1907); *A Room with a View* (1908); and *Howard's End* (1910). This highly successful novel brings him literary fame.
1912–1923	Visits India (1912–1913 and 1921). Works for the Red Cross during the war years (1915–1919) in Alexandria, Egypt. Falls in love and finds sexual fulfillment with an Egyptian tram conductor, Mohammed-el-Adl. Develops a second important friendship, though not an intimate one, with C. P. Cavafy, the Alexandrian poet. Publishes three minor works: *The Government of Egypt* (1920), *Alexandria: A History and a Guide* (1922), and *The Pharos and Pharillon* (1923).
1924	Publishes *A Passage to India*, his final novel, begun in 1913, put aside, and completed in England after his return from India in 1921. It is both a critical and a popular success.
1924–1946	Inherits lease from his aunt of house in West Hackhurst, Abinger Hammer, near Dorset, and lives there with his mother until she dies in 1945 and his lease is not renewed. Gives the Clark Lectures at Cambridge and publishes them as *Aspects of the Novel* (1927). Is elected supernumerary fellow to King's College, Cambridge (1927–1933). Meets in 1929 a young married policeman, Bob Buckingham, who becomes his closest friend for life. Publishes his first full-length biography, that of his friend, *Goldsworthy Lowes Dickinson* (1934), a Cambridge don whom he admired. Publishes his first collection of essays, *Abinger Harvest* (1936), which carries on his attack against English smugness and self-righteousness. Collaborates with the composer Vaughan Williams on two pageants: *The Abinger Pageant* and *England's Pleasant Land*. Serves as broadcaster for the BBC, president of the National Council for Civil Liberties, and president of PEN conference in London.

1947 Evicted from his West Hackhurst flat, he is elected an honorary fellow at King's College. Visits America and lectures at Harvard and Hamilton College.

1949 Returns to America and collaborates with Benjamin Britten on the libretto for the opera *Billy Budd.*

1951 Publishes his second collection of essays, *Two Cheers for Democracy,* divided into two sections, "The Second Darkness" and "What I Believe," and unified by his concern for the survival of western culture and freedom.

1953 Publishes *The Hill of Devi,* largely a collection of his letters from India detailing his experience there.

1956 Publishes his second biography, *Marianne Thornton,* his affectionate tribute to his great-aunt, to whom he attributes an extended life in her creative influence on him and others.

1970 Dies in Coventry at the home of his friends Bob and May Buckingham. His ashes are scattered over their rose garden.

1971 *Maurice* is published posthumously—Forster's homosexual novel, written in 1913–1914 but suppressed because he did not want his sexual preference known. The novel was inspired by his friend Edward Carpenter and Carpenter's working-class lover George Merrill.

1972 *The Life to Come and Other Stories* published posthumously, fourteen stories that span his writing career and reveal much about his hidden, private life.

ESSAY QUESTIONS WITH ANSWERS

A *Passage to India*

32.1 The title of Forster's novel alludes to the poem "Passage to India" by the nineteenth-century American poet Walt Whitman. Using the following excerpt from the poem as a springboard, discuss Forster's treatment of Whitman's theme.

> Passage O soul to India!
>
> . . . .
>
> Lo, soul, seest thou not God's purpose from the first?
> The earth to be spann'd, connected by network,
> The races, neighbors, to marry and be given in marriage,
> The oceans to be cross'd, the distant brought near,
> The lands to be welded together.
>
> . . . .
>
> Passage indeed O soul to primal thought,
> Not lands and seas alone, thy own clear freshness,
> The young maturity of brood and bloom,
> To realms of budding bibles.[1]

Answer Forster's allusion to Whitman's poem is basically ironic; in *A Passage to India*, Forster transforms Whitman's expression of profound faith in humanism and in the spiritual connections among people into a vision of their separateness and their spiritual frustration. For Whitman, the passage to India symbolizes the soul's journey to the understanding of its own past, since each soul embraces the collective memory of all humanity, past and present. In *A Passage to India*, on the other hand, there is a spiritual chasm between the two peoples, the English and the Indians. The image of Aziz and Fielding on horseback at the end of the novel suggests that the hostile Indian earth itself keeps

---

[1]*Complete Poetry and Selected Prose*, James E. Miller, Jr. (ed.), Houghton Mifflin, Boston, 1959, pp. 288–294.

them apart ("the earth didn't want it, sending up rocks"). Although India represents an appeal to spiritual fulfillment in the novel—"She is not a promise, only an appeal" (Chap. XIV)—the English ignore this appeal.

In fact, Mrs. Moore, who yearns for Whitman's sense of "oneness" in India, experiences psychic trauma in the caves of Marabar and ultimately dies. Although she does establish a sympathetic relationship with Aziz in the Mosque in Part I, her experience in the caves subverts her belief in Christianity and in humanism. She is overwhelmed by the nihilistic message of the echo in the caves: In its "boum" she hears the voice of India saying, "Everything exists, nothing has value." The effect of the echo is to "blur all distinctions," a grotesque parody of Whitman's image of personal, national, and racial interconnection. Immediately following her exit from the cave, Mrs. Moore thinks, "No one could romanticize the Marabar because it robbed infinity and eternity of their vastness, the only quality that accommodates them to mankind" (Chap. XIV). The Marabar caves provide a negative answer to Whitman's romantic dream.

32.2   The Marabar caves seem to murmur to Mrs. Moore, "Everything exists, nothing has value." Does *A Passage to India* present this as an adequate summary of the "message" of India?

Answer   "Everything exists, nothing has value" is Mrs. Moore's "translation" of the echo in the cave. That message negates for her all the values in which she has believed. "Pathos, piety, courage—they exist, but are identical, and so is filth." But it is Mrs. Moore herself who makes the equation between existence and meaninglessness; we hear the voice of the caves through her ears.

Mrs. Moore's approach to the world has been conditioned by the particular mentality and sensibility of western civilization; like other westerners, she structures her world by making discriminations and categorizing people and situations. However, whereas the other English people in the story who come to India manage to impose their British categories on that nation, Mrs. Moore is more open to the world of India. Thus, when she finally experiences the echo in the caves, she is lost. It confirms and strengthens the feelings she has had during her visit to India, that personal relations are less important than they once seemed and that Christianity and the Christian God no longer satisfy her search for meaning. The experience in the cave completely disorients Mrs. Moore, increasing the despair and lassitude she has begun to experience.

Yet it is important to stress that this nihilism is Mrs. Moore's reaction to her experience. Most of the colonial English people would not bother to enter the caves and, if they did, would probably find the experience stifling and annoying rather than shattering. Even Fielding, who seems to possess genuine goodwill and affection for India and the experiences it affords, still feels he can rely on the English values of courage, loyalty, and honesty to get him by. Although by the end of the book he seems to sense certain limits in this view, Fielding never really allows India to undermine his hold on English values. But for Mrs. Moore, the caves radically subvert her already vulnerable system of belief; when confronted with an utterly incomprehensible universe, she reacts with fear and dread.

The Indians confront the irrational and inexplicable with more equanimity. Godbole, for example, has the ability to live acceptingly with mystery, as revealed in his half-mysterious, half-comical attempts to describe the caves by describing what they are not but never saying what they are. For Godbole and many other Indians, mystery enriches the world. Thus Mrs. Moore's is not the only profound reaction to the caves; her pessimism is balanced, in a sense, by the Hindu attitude, as expressed by Godbole.

The Hindu ceremony in Part III conveys this Indian attitude toward confusion and irrationality; "[t]hey [the Hindus] did not one thing which the non-Hindu would feel dramatically correct," and yet to the Hindus participating in the festival, it fully achieves the desired sense of love and communion.

32.3 The novel is divided into three main parts: "Mosque," "Caves," and "Temple." What is the significance of this structure? How does the simplicity of the structure contrast with the "muddle and mystery" which is one of the book's main themes?

Answer Each part of the novel is associated with a specific dramatic episode: the meeting of Mrs. Moore and Aziz in the mosque, Mrs. Moore's and Adela Quested's experiences in the cave; and the ceremony of Krishna at which Godbole presides. The tripartite division of the novel also corresponds to three philosophies of life: Islam, nihilism, and Hinduism. In Part I, the Moslem and Christian faith in God as love is supported by the moment of communion between Aziz and Mrs. Moore; in Part II, the adequacy of these religions of "pathos" and love is undermined by the echo in the caves; and in Part III, Hinduism is presented as an alternative to the faith of Part I and the nihilism of Part II. For Forster, Hinduism represents "mystery" rather than "muddle," that is, a profound yet paradoxical religious insight rather than chaos. In Hinduism, good and evil are both accepted as aspects of each other.

But the suggestion of synthesis in Part III is not a final solution for the intellectual problems posed in the novel. The Hindu synthesis cannot provide a resolution for the English characters. Hinduism is an eastern answer which the westerners cannot really accept; for them the experience of nullity, so powerfully symbolized in the novel's longest section (Part II), seems to prevail. Behind the neatness of the book's formal divisions lies the "muddle" of India, of which the cave, which blurs all distinctions, is a symbol. It represents the impossibility of creating neat "fictions" that adequately contain the world, both for the characters in the novel and for the novelist.

Ultimately, the formal neatness of the novel's structure is at odds with the breakdown of rationality represented by the "boum" of the caves. To this extent, the tripartite structure plays a role similar to that of the narrative voice in the novel, which also seems to express a faith in distinctions and categories that events seem to render obsolete. Although much in the novel suggests a questioning of rationality, formalism, and humanism, the narrative voice and the structure mitigate the uneasy questions; they attach themselves, that is, to an older, more traditional vision.

32.4   What is the significance of the various allusions in the novel to the "wasp"? How do they acquire symbolic significance?

Answer   The wasp is first mentioned at the end of Part I, when Mrs. Moore, going to hang up her coat, finds a wasp on the coat rack. The incident takes on thematic importance through Mrs. Moore's reaction to it; instead of fear or repulsion, she feels sympathy for the creature, a sympathy like that which she has already manifested in her meeting with Aziz. In addition, the narrator's comment that in India insects have no sense of interior or exterior spaces has symbolic resonance. In India, according to the novel's vision, conventional boundaries between humanity and nature, private and public, are obscured.

But it is in the description of the wasp in Part III of the novel that the meaning of the earlier incident with Mrs. Moore is "fulfilled." In a moment of meditation, Godbole, the Hindu professor, links Mrs. Moore and the wasp in an expression of Krishna's love of all creatures: "One old Englishwoman and one little, little wasp" (Chap. XXXII). The spiritual affinity between Mrs. Moore and Godbole, two characters with a special ability for sympathetic identification with others and with nature, is thus suggested. Furthermore, an implicit contrast is established between these two characters and the English missionaries in Part I who feel the need to exclude others ("We must exclude something, or we will be left with nothing").

Ralph's bee stings in Part III are another variation on the thematic use of the wasp. In this case, Ralph's contact with the bee leads him to accept treatment from Dr. Aziz, thereby echoing a moment between his mother and Aziz. This formal repetition of detail contributes to the sense of a spiritual communion, even telepathy, between the characters in the novel.

32.5 In both Conrad's *Lord Jim* and Forster's *A Passage to India*, a seemingly inexplicable event lies at the heart of the novel. In *Lord Jim*, it is Jim's desertion of his ship; in *A Passage to India*, it is Adela Quested's "assault" in the Marabar Caves. In both novels, someone attempts to collect the facts of the case to determine what really happened. Compare and contrast Forster's and Conrad's treatments of this motif.

Answer The central enigmatic event in each novel represents the essential mystery at the heart of human behavior. Both Conrad and Forster employ a rational, honorable Englishman as the collector of the facts of the case. In *Lord Jim*, it is Marlow, the major narrator; in *A Passage to India*, it is the character of the collector, Mr. Turnball. Much of *Lord Jim* is devoted to Marlow's often tortured attempts to understand Jim's behavior. The collector in *A Passage to India*, on the other hand, is only a minor representative of the English wish to comprehend events rationally, specifically the event in the cave, itself a symbol of the irrationality of India. More priggish than Marlow, who recognizes his kinship with Jim's act of cowardice, the collector prides himself on being "unemotional" and objective: "He was still after facts, though the herd had decided on emotion" (Chap. XVII).

   In both novels, it becomes apparent that the objective record of the "facts" of the case omits almost everything important about the event. Although in Conrad's novel Jim at first believes that "only a meticulous precision of statement would bring out the true horror behind the appalling face of things" (Chap. IV), the idea of objective truth itself ultimately becomes suspect in both novels. Truth itself seems to become deeply relative for both writers; hence the old English standards for evaluating the truth are called into question. We may never glimpse what is in the hearts of others; even our loyalty and friendship cannot ensure that we shall understand the conduct of another human being. Despite the presence in *A Passage to India* of the ironic, sometimes comic narrative voice that we associate with Forster's earlier novels, the novel has a darkness to it, a basic questioning of values and truths that can be fruitfully likened to Conrad's. Despite the tremendous difference in the tone of these writers and Conrad's more intense focus on the interiors of his characters, both Forster and Conrad explore the darkness and mystery which underlie the surface of things.

                                                                              K.L

SUGGESTED READINGS

Bradbury, Malcolm (ed.), A *Passage to India: A Selection of Critical Essays* (1970).
Colmer, John, *E. M. Forster: The Personal Voice* (1975).
Crews, Frederick, *E. M. Forster: The Perils of Humanism* (1962).
Furbank, P. N., *E. M. Forster.* (1978).
Trilling, Lionel, *E. M. Forster* (1943).
Wilde, Alan, *Art and Order: A Study of E. M. Forster* (1964).

VIRGINIA WOOLF

C H R O N O L O G Y

1882   Born at 22 Hyde Park Gate, London, daughter of Sir Leslie Stephen, eminent scholar, philosopher, and editor, and Julia Duckworth Stephen, noted beauty and widow of Herbert Duckworth. Her background gives Virginia a sense of being born into an aristocracy of intellect. She is the third of the couple's four children; she also has several half brothers and sisters from both parents' previous marriages. Sir Leslie was married to Thackeray's daughter, who went insane and died. Their daughter, Laura, also insane, lives with the Stephen family and disturbs Virginia with her bizarre behavior. An older half brother on her mother's side sexually molests her, beginning when she is 6 years old.

1895   Her mother dies. Virginia suffers her first mental breakdown.

1897   Stella Duckworth, her older half sister, who had assumed her mother's responsibilities, dies. Virginia becomes ill again.

1899   Virginia studies Greek.

1904   Her father dies. Suffers another mental breakdown and attempts suicide. Moves to Bloomsbury. Publishes her first review in *The Guardian*. Her brother Thoby introduces her to his Cambridge friends, including Clive Bell, the art critic, who marries her sister (Vanessa), Lytton Strachey, the future biographer, and Leonard Woolf.

1906   Her brother Thoby dies of typhoid. She begins her first novel, *The Voyage Out*, which takes seven years to finish.

1909   Lytton Strachey, who is homosexual, becomes engaged to her, then breaks it off. She receives a legacy of £2500.

1912–
1915   Marries Leonard Woolf (1912) after his return from Ceylon, where he spent seven years as a government administrator. Various illnesses. Discovers she cannot have children. Attempts suicide with veronal.

1915–
1918   Resides with Leonard at Hogarth House, Richmond. Publishes *The Voyage Out* (1915). Begins keeping a diary which she will maintain, with some interruptions, until her death. She and Leonard found the Hogarth Press (1917). At first she reads manuscripts, sets type by hand, and binds books. Success of the press forces her to turn over manual labor to others, but she keeps reading manuscripts by such authors as Joyce, Auden, Freud, E. M. Forster, T. S. Eliot, and many others. Publishes her own and Leonard's books. Becomes very close to worldly, self-assured women of strong, in-dependent spirit, such as Katherine Mansfield.

1919–
1923   Publishes her second novel, *Night and Day* (1919). Publishes *Jacob's Room* (1922). Meets Vita Sackville-West (Mrs. Harold Nicolson). Moves to Monk's House.

1924–
1932   Woolf's most creative period. She and Leonard move their household and the press to Bloomsbury (52 Tavistock Square), where she flourishes in a large intellectual circle. The Bloomsbury group is a heterogeneous circle of artists and intellectuals who had been Thoby's and Leonard's friends at Cambridge. In addition to those already mentioned, John Maynard Keynes, the economist, and E. M. Forster, the novelist are prominent. Publishes several important critical works, such as "Mr. Bennett and Mrs. Brown" (1924), her famous dissent from the fictional view of reality presented by the established novelists of her day, Bennett, Wells, and Galsworthy, *The Common Reader* (1925), and *The Common Reader: Second Series* (1932). During this period, Woolf also publishes the bulk of those novels for which she is chiefly remembered today: *Mrs. Dalloway* (1925), *To the Lighthouse* (1927), her fictional depiction of her parents; *Orlando* (1928), a historical fantasy; and *The Waves* (1931), a lyrical novel comprising the soliloquies of six characters. Also publishes a distinguished work of feminism and social protest, *A Room of One's Own* (1929).

1937–
1938   Publishes *The Years* (1937). Also writes *Three Guineas* (1938). In 1938, she sells her half of the press to John Lehmann, her manager.

1940   Publishes biography *Roger Fry*, in which she shows convincingly that he altered the artistic tastes of his time for the better.

1941   Completes *Between the Acts*, her last novel. On March 28, after severe recurrence of mental illness, she walks to the river near her house in Sussex and drowns herself.

1953   Leonard publishes A *Writer's Diary*, excerpts from the journal she kept since 1917, revealing her art, her purposes, the intense psychic toll exacted by her creative activity, and the severe depression she suffered at the completion of each novel.

ESSAY QUESTIONS WITH ANSWERS

Mrs. Dalloway

33.1 Many critics have seen Clarissa Dalloway and Septimus Smith as "doubles" for each other, a view supported by Woolf's original plans for the novel. What evidence in the text would reinforce this reading?

Answer Clarissa and Septimus are partners in suffering who find the tasks of daily life burdensome and painful. These two characters share an apocalyptic view of existence: Clarissa waits suspiciously for Big Ben to strike, as if something terrible and important were about to happen; Septimus, whose apprehension of the future takes a more extreme form, thinks, "The world has raised its whip; where will it descend?" This sense of anticipation for both characters becomes so intense that it leads them at times to wish for death; both Septimus and Clarissa yearn to escape the struggles of life.

The doubling of the characters is made explicit when Clarissa learns of Septimus's death. She feels "somehow very like him—the young man who had killed himself." She sees his suicide as an act of defiance against those powers of society which "force the soul" (like Bradshaw, the psychiatrist). For as conventional as Clarissa seems to be in much of the novel, she feels herself to be different, on "the outside, looking on." Although she guards her difference more carefully and successfully than Septimus, both are vulnerable to the heartless authority of a Bradshaw or a Holmes.

When Clarissa learns of Septimus's suicide, she sees him as a kind of savior who has died for others, herself included. She feels that his death has given something to her. The thought of his suicide somehow spurs Clarissa into her own vision. As she ponders Septimus's leap from the railing, Clarissa opens her bedroom curtains and sees an old lady across the way preparing for bed. The sight of the old woman, combined with her spiritual bond with the dead young man, enables Clarissa to feel a connection with others, a sympathy of which she has seemed incapable. She realizes that she is related to others in life because she is related to them in death.

424

33.2 The plot of the modern novel develops in part by means of recurring images and motifs as well as through the dramatic action of the characters. One such recurring motif is a line from Shakespeare's *Cymbeline*, "Fear no more the heat of the sun," which Clarissa remembers at various points in her day. How is this motif used to record changes in Clarissa's consciousness?

Answer In *Cymbeline*, these words are spoken over the body of Imogen, whom the other characters believe to be dead. In this context the words are consolatory; life's pain is ended in the oblivion of death. Clarissa first recites the line from Shakespeare when she has just learned that her husband, Richard, is lunching without her at Lady Briton's. Her exclusion from the party disconcerts her greatly, and the line from Shakespeare reveals her wish to escape from the pain of her present circumstances.

Later, while window-shopping in town, Clarissa sees the text of the play in a window, opened to the page of the quotation. Although the sun is usually an image of warmth and light, in *Mrs. Dalloway* it also represents an intensity which is frightening (Septimus's apocalyptic vision is of the sun bursting into flames). When Clarissa reads the lines, their promise of an escape from pain comforts her.

Finally, at the end of the novel, the lines recur again as Clarissa watches the old lady across the way extinguish her light. Somehow, the vision of the old lady and the news of Septimus's death combine to give Clarissa, at least momentarily, a renewed sense of life as well as an acceptance of the knowledge of death. In this final appearance, the quotation symbolizes for Clarissa the momentary subsiding of her intense fears and anxieties about death. In her vision of the old lady, Clarissa comes to an understanding of death. Each time the words of the quotation are repeated, their meaning for Clarissa changes as a function of her immediate feelings about life and death.

33.3 A repeated symbol in *Mrs. Dalloway* is Big Ben, the London clock. What is the symbolic significance of Big Ben?

Answer Big Ben, the famous London landmark, symbolizes British authority, order, and proportion. Its more personal function for Clarissa is to remind her of her own mortality.

Throughout the book, the sound of the bell on the clock marks the passing of the hours. Clarissa, we are told, waits in dread for each stroke, as if it signaled her inevitable death. This oppressive reminder of her own death generalizes to an awareness of the common fate which unites all people, the finger of death which points at everyone.

But the inevitable ticking of the clock also represents humankind's conformity and submission to society's laws. The tick of the clock, "shredding and slicing, dividing and subdividing," promises the smooth functioning of society at the expense of individuals like Septimus and Clarissa. Like Dr. Bradshaw, who occupies a position of authority and who "forces the soul," Big Ben is a British institution which represents society's attempt to extirpate creativity and human differences in the service of proportion and order.

To the Lighthouse

33.4 In *To the Lighthouse*, Virginia Woolf dispenses almost entirely with the omniscient narration found in most nineteenth-century novels. As one consequence, Woolf often uses images to represent a character symbolically rather than employing more conventional description. Interpret the significance of the following passages in which one character views another:

> William Bankes thought of Ramsay . . . striding along a road by himself. . . . But this was suddenly interrupted, William Bankes remembered (and this must refer to some actual incident), by a hen, straddling her wings out in protection of a covey of little chicks, upon which Ramsay, stopping, pointed his stick and said "Pretty-pretty." . . . (Part I, Chap. IV)

> Whenever Lily "thought of his work" she always saw clearly before her a large kitchen table. It was Andrew's doing. She asked him what his father's books were about. "Subject and object and the nature of reality," Andrew had said. And when she said Heavens, she had no notion what that meant, "Think of a kitchen table then," he told her, "when you're not there." (Part I, Chap. IV)

> . . . as she [Mrs. Ramsay] sat in the wicker arm-chair in the drawing-room window she wore, to Lily's eyes, an august shape; the shape of a dome. (Part I, Chap. IX)

Answer In all three passages, the image both captures an important quality of the character and reveals something about the perceiver as well. To Mr. Bankes, Mr. Ramsay's solitary walk interrupted by the passage of a hen with her covey of chicks symbolizes Ramsay's loss of independence and his domestication. The kernel of Mr. Ramsay's relationship with his wife is symbolized in this image: his appreciation of his wife as beautiful woman, mother of his children, and protector of his ruffled ego. Mrs. Ramsay is like a mother hen to her husband as well as her children; in fact, his confident strides through the world seem to depend on her nurturing presence at home. For Bankes, a lonely bachelor, the episode represents the beginning of the end of his friendship with Ramsay.

The second paragraph employs a complex layering of perception. Lily remembers Andrew's illustration of his father's work. Andrew glibly reduces his father's epistemological inquiries to the problem of the kitchen table. The angular lines of the table symbolize the tough, no-nonsense, empirical approach Mr. Ramsay seems to take toward reality. The image, remembered by Lily, conveys the ambivalence she feels toward Mr. Ramsay; picturing the rather comic domestic image of a kitchen table when she thinks of Ramsay's work, Lily sees him as both an important male philosopher and a somewhat inept husband and father of eight children. Ramsay's intense absorption in the weighty problems of philosophy makes him seem a very distracted member of the domestic group which revolves, instead, around the strength of Mrs. Ramsay.

The sexual role playing in the world of the novel is also revealed in this image. The phrase "Heavens, she had no notion of what that meant" illustrates Lily's conformity to the role of the unintellectual female stymied by the male world of philosophy. In part, Andrew's choice of example displays the typical male condescension toward the intellect of women in the book. It aptly captures, therefore, something about "subject and object" and the nature of relationships between men and women.

The use of the image of the dome, one of protection and stability, to describe Mrs. Ramsay symbolizes to Lily her attractiveness and awesome power. Sitting in the window, knitting a brown stocking, Mrs. Ramsay is a picture of domesticity, but Lily perceptively sees beyond the mere trappings of the maternal role to the "august" power which a woman like Mrs. Ramsay has over the lives of her family and friends. The dome suggests an almost religious edifice whose beauty and majesty must be held in awe by the viewer, and all those who know Mrs. Ramsay are held in her spell in this way.

33.5 "Who knows what we are, what we feel? Who knows even at the moment of intimacy this knowledge?" (Part II). In this statement, Lily is concerned, as she is throughout the novel, with the essential enigma of personality. What view of personality is reflected in the narrative technique of *To the Lighthouse*?

Answer In Parts I and III of *To the Lighthouse*, the narrative moves grace-fully in and out of the minds of the various characters, from one to the other, from dialogue through description to inner thought. The stability of traditional omniscient narration, which carefully separates the inner from the outer and one character's thoughts from another's, is replaced by a kind of disembodied narrative voice which circles in and out of minds so unobtrusively that readers are startled to find themselves continually in different places. In the first section of the novel, the reader is given, in quick succession, Mr. Bankes's thoughts on Mr. Ramsay, Lily's thoughts on Mr. Ramsay, and Lily's thoughts on Mr. Bankes. Lacking the single controlling point of view of an omniscient narrator, the reader must weave together the various points of view.

At times, this mode of narration makes it obvious that one character misreads another. For instance, Mr. Bankes thinks that Mrs. Ramsay is totally uncon-scious of her beauty, but a few pages lager, Mrs. Ramsay thinks of the effect her beauty has on those who surround her. In general, however, the multiple views of a character are not directly contradictory; they are merely difficult to integrate into one coherent picture. In her abandonment of the explanatory narrative voice, a traditional component of the Victorian novel, Woolf displays artistically the twentieth century's skepticism about a person's ability to know the essence of someone else. Like Conrad's use of narrative frames in his novels, Woolf's use of a disembodied narrative voice is a technical device which reflects the assumption that no one point of view is definitive, that no one person can give us a complete picture of the truth.

33.6 In the course of the novel, certain moments of heightened meaning— "epiphanies"—occur, moments conceived of as transcending the daily passage of time. How do these moments confer meaning specifically on the life of Mrs. Ramsay?

Answer Two kinds of significant moments occur in *To the Lighthouse*, those which take place when the character is alone and those which occur in a social environment.

In the moments of solitary experience, the Woolfean character comes closest to achieving self-knowledge; in the social experience, he or she participates in a momentary act of communion with others. In the first kind of experience, the social self is shed; in the second, it merges with the social self of others. Mrs. Ramsay experiences two of these significant moments, one as she is alone by the window, "sitting and looking" at the beam of the lighthouse, and another as she is sitting at the dinner table with her family and guests.

Mrs. Ramsay becomes mesmerized as she gazes at the lighthouse beam. Suddenly, she feels an identification with the impersonality of the beam of light: "the pitiless, the remorseless [light] which was so much her, yet so little her." Part of the meaning of this enigmatic phrase is that the beam of light is so little like her personal, warm, "social," and maternal self but so much like her inner self in its impersonality. The beam of light penetrates the barrier she has created to the inviolate core of her selfhood, which no one sees, that "wedge-shaped core of darkness." The moment is at once exhilarating and terrifying for Mrs. Ramsay, for it reveals to her a side of her personality that she hides from herself as well as from others.

Opposed to this dark moment of self-knowledge is the moment of communion Mrs. Ramsay feels when the people around the dinner table finally come together in a social unit, no longer hostile to one another. Here, she suddenly experiences a sense of stability and coherence in the midst of time's passing. Suddenly, she feels the "still space that lies about the heart of things." As in her previous epiphanic experience, she welcomes this moment, in which time seems to stand still. Mrs. Ramsay is, at this moment, like an artist who has composed the scene, a social artist who has arranged the figures around the table. Years later, Lily thinks of Mrs. Ramsay's ability to make "of the moment something permanent" (Part II) and compares Mrs. Ramsay's talent for this to her own attempt to create permanence through her art.

33.7 How does the middle section, "Time Passes," invert the relationship between man and nature established in Part I, "The Window"?

Answer The complex relationships among the characters dominate the narrative in Part I; the passing of time, symbolized by the pounding of the waves on the shore outside the windows, only momentarily invades the consciousness of the characters and the reader. In Part II, this relationship between humanity and nature is reversed as the wind and darkness invade the house abandoned by the Ramsay family. The bulk of the narrative in Part II is a lyrical description of the effect of time and nature on the Ramsay house.

This reversal of the preeminence of humanity over nature is reflected technically in Woolf's use of parentheses. In Part II, the most important events of the human drama, such as the death of three members of the Ramsay family (including Mrs. Ramsay), are reported parenthetically. The characters are put into a new perspective; the reader sees the insignificance of human lives in the context of the larger world and becomes aware of humanity's pitiful powerlessness in face of time and nature. The loosening of the shawl which Mrs. Ramsay had so carefully and solicitously placed around the boar's head is a symbol of this powerlessness.

However, at the end of Chapter II, the characters again begin to assert their control over the destructive forces of nature, and the plot is again dominated by the human action. Mrs. McNab, who had abandoned the house to the forces of nature, now returns to prepare it for its other human inhabitants. The dangers represented by the "airs" which circulate through the house recede; the characters once more appear to control time and dominate the narrative. At the end of Part II, we are prepared for the resumption of the main events of the "plot" in the next chapter: the Ramsays' sailing to the lighthouse and Lily's painting of her picture.

K.L.

SUGGESTED READINGS

Bell, Quentin, *Virginia Woolf: A Biography* (1972).
DiBattista, Maria, *Virginia Woolf's Major Novels: The Fables of Anon* (1980).
Naremore, James, *The World without a Self: Virginia Woolf and the Novel* (1973).
Rose, Phyllis, *Woman of Letters: A Life of Virginia Woolf* (1978).

JAMES JOYCE

C H R O N O L O G Y

1882	Born in Dublin, the oldest of fourteen children of Mary Jane Murray Joyce and John Stanislaus Joyce, a tax collector.
1884	Birth of Stanislaus Joyce, closest to James of all his brothers and sisters in later life.
1888	Enters Clongowes Wood College, a Jesuit boarding school.
1891	Withdraws from Clongowes because of family financial difficulties. Deeply affected by the death of Charles Stewart Parnell, a popular politician who championed Irish home rule, he writes a poem denouncing Parnell's betrayer, Tim Healy, "Et Tu, Healy."
1893	Enters Belvedere College, another Jesuit school, where he compiles a brilliant academic record.
1898	Enters University College, Dublin, yet another Jesuit institution, where his difficult individuality begins to emerge. He revolts against Catholicism and Irish nationalism, refusing to learn Gaelic, to sign letter attacking "heresy" of Yeats, or to join the student nationalist groups. Writes essays praising Ibsen and criticizing the provincialism of the Irish theater.
1902	After graduation, leaves Dublin for Paris to study medicine.
1903	Recalled to Dublin by his mother's fatal illness.
1904	Writes a story-essay, "A Portrait of an Artist." It is rejected. Rewrites it as

an autobiographical novel, *Stephen Hero*. Meets and falls in love with Nora Barnacle, an uneducated country girl. Opposed to marriage, he travels through Europe with Nora to Pola, Yugoslavia. Publishes separately the first stories of *Dubliners*.

1905   Moves to Trieste, where his son, Giorgio, is born. Ekes out a living teaching English. Brother Stanislaus joins him and Nora.

1906   *Dubliners* is accepted for publication by Grant Richards but is rejected after a long controversy over certain words the publisher wishes to delete. Moves to Rome and works as a bank clerk.

1907   Moves back to Trieste. Publishes in London a slim volume of verse, *Chamber Music*. Daughter, Lucia Anna, is born.

1909   Returns to Dublin to open the Cinematograph Volta, a movie house. Maunsel and Company agrees to publish *Dubliners*.

1910   Controversy over certain passages delays publication of *Dubliners*. Returns to Trieste. Cinema venture collapses.

1911   Throws manuscript of *Stephen Hero* into fire. Nora Joyce retrieves it and puts it away.

1912   Last trip to Dublin. Unable to publish *Dubliners*, he returns to Trieste in bitterness. Writes a savage broadside, *Gas from a Burner*.

1914   Grant Richards finally publishes *Dubliners*. Ezra Pound publishes serial installments of *A Portrait of the Artist as a Young Man* in journal *The Egoist*. Begins drafting *Ulysses*.

1915   Completes play *Exiles*. Moves to Zurich, Switzerland.

1916   Publishes *A Portrait of the Artist as a Young Man* in book form.

1917   First operation for lifelong eye ailment. Drafts first three episodes of *Ulysses*.

1918   Publishes *Exiles*. Begins serialization of *Ulysses* in the *Little Review*.

1919   Returns to Trieste and works on *Ulysses*.

1920   Moves to Paris to join Pound. Society for Suppression of Vice stops publication of *Ulysses* in the *Little Review*.

1922   Sylvia Beach, Paris bookseller and publisher, publishes *Ulysses*, Joyce's modern epic based on Homer's *Odyssey*.

1923   Begins *Finnegans Wake* (known at the time as *Work in Progress*). Fragments are published at various times throughout the 1920s.

1931   Travels to London and marries Nora. His father dies.

1932   Joyce's grandson, Stephen Joyce, is born to Giorgio; Joyce writes poem to celebrate occasion, "Ecce Puer." Lucia suffers nervous breakdown, which saddens Joyce's last years.

1933   U.S. Court rules that *Ulysses* is not pornographic in a landmark decision that establishes legal limits of pornography in America.

1934   Spends time with Lucia in sanitorium near Zurich. Consults Zurich specialist for his failing eyesight.

1939   Publishes *Finnegans Wake,* after fourteen years of meticulous craftsmanship. Joyce considers this his masterpiece, though it is little read.

1940   Takes family to Zurich after the fall of France but is forced to leave Lucia in La Baule.

1941   Dies in Zurich after abdominal operation for perforated ulcer. Buried at Allmend Fluntern Cemetery near Zurich.

1944   Stanislaus Joyce publishes *Stephen Hero* posthumously.

ESSAY QUESTIONS WITH ANSWERS

"The Dead"

34.1 How is Gabriel's confrontation with his wife, Gretta, near the end of the story anticipated in other confrontations at the party?

Answer Gabriel's confrontation with Gretta is anticipated in his encounters with two different women at the Christmas party: Lily, the servant who takes his coat when he enters, and Molly Ivors, a former schoolmate, who chides him for publishing literary reviews in a pro-English newspaper. In both instances, Gabriel's carefully constructed self-image is punctured by the comments of the women, prefiguring the jolt he will receive from his wife at the end of the story.

Although the confrontation with Lily may appear trivial, it is out of just such seemingly insignificant occurrences that Joyce establishes our sense of Gabriel's character. Lily's bitter retort to Gabriel's banter about marriage catches him off guard, and he reacts in a manner that the reader will come to recognize as characteristic of him. Realizing that he has "made a mistake," he immediately busies himself with removing his galoshes and flicking the snow from his clothes. His attention to the details of his person is a psychologically revealing gesture of avoidance as well as a symbol of his preoccupation with the way he presents himself to the world.

Later on, when Molly Ivors criticizes him, Gabriel again becomes defensive and tries to "cover his agitation" by absorbing himself in the dancing. Again, Gabriel is deflated. Molly Ivors's criticism punctures his image of himself as a cosmopolitan literary critic and transforms it into the image of a disloyal son of Ireland.

These confrontations establish the pattern of Gabriel's responses and anticipate, thematically, his wife's startling revelation at the end of the story. Gabriel's limited understanding both of marriage and of Irish culture, which precipitates the earlier confrontations, also forms the basis for his personal upheaval when Gretta tells him of the death of Michael Furey. He realizes that he has failed to understand the extent of Gretta's romantic longings or the extent of her emotional connection to her rural Irish past.

34.2 What is the meaning of the clause at the end of the story "the time had come for him to set out on his journey westward"?

Answer The clause cited has several possible meanings, all relevant to the significance of the story as a whole.

First, it may mean that Gabriel has realized he cannot escape his Irish ancestry and decides to go "westward" to the Aran Islands to recover a sense of his cultural past. This interpretation draws on Miss Ivors's reference to the western islands; thus, its validity rests on a specific reference in the text. Miss Ivors challenges Gabriel's plans for a Continental summer vacation by demanding to know why he does not visit the Aran Islands in the west of Ireland instead. She argues that he should get in touch with his own land, people, and language rather than visit a foreign country.

Throughout the story, although Gabriel praises the unique qualities of Ireland (such as its hospitality), the English literature of Browning and Shakespeare along with Continental culture (such as Greek myths), saturates his thoughts. At the end of the story, his desire to journey westward represents his sincere interest in Irish rather than European culture.

In addition, this interpretation illustrates the stripping away of Gabriel's pretensions and brings out his new feelings of love for his wife, Gretta, who is a country girl from the west of Ireland. Since the culture indigenous to the west of Ireland is a peasant or folk culture, Gabriel's decision to journey westward reveals that he is no longer trying to impress himself and others with his erudition and exposure to European high culture. Gabriel's acceptance of his Irish roots symbolizes, then, a greater acceptance of his identity and an affirmation of a new bond with his wife.

By the end of the story, Gabriel realizes how profoundly he has misinterpreted his wife, seeing in her only a reflection of his own desire. For the first time, he sees his wife as a person with her own profound desires and regrets; his resolve to journey westward thus expresses his empathy with Gretta and at least the partial breakdown of the egotism we have seen throughout the story.

Second, the westward journey suggest death. From this standpoint, the clause suggests that Gabriel has begun to fall asleep and expresses to himself a death wish; journeying westward is traditionally associated with death, as symbolized by the setting sun. In the final moments of the story, Gabriel feels that his soul is approaching "that region where dwell the vast hosts of the dead." He imagines that he sees the figure of the dead Michael Furey. Gabriel sees the contrast between his own passionless life and the brief but passionate existence of Michael Furey, who "died" for Gretta, and he wishes to blend into sleep and the night, to exchange a death-in-life for a real death.

Third, the passage may represent Gabriel's symbolic death; his old identity is destroyed and a new one is born. The journey westward is a metaphor for the death of Gabriel's old identity, which he feels fading at the end of the story. "The Dead" has recorded a profound shock to a character's ego and his carefully constructed defenses. By the end of the story, the old pompous and conceited Gabriel is dead. Joyce leaves us at this point with a new identity for Gabriel about to emerge.

34.3 What is the narrative point of view of the story?

Answer The point of view of "The Dead" is one of "centered conscious-ness"; third-person narration is used, but Gabriel is the predominant center of interest. It is through his eyes that we see much of the story. However, the answer should be qualified to reflect the changing focus of narration in the story. The story begins in third-person narration not associated with Gabriel, focuses particularly on Gabriel once he enters the story, and intensifies this focus as the story progresses. The lyricism of the final paragraphs stylistically expresses the intensity of Gabriel's feelings.

The tone of the first paragraph of the story is casual and chatty; the breathless quality of the narration echoes the mind of Lily, the caretaker's daughter, as she scampers to and fro preparing for the guests. The stage is set for Gabriel's entrance, and when he appears, the narration is largely concerned with pre-senting his thoughts and actions. We move in and out of Gabriel's mind as he reacts to Lily and Miss Ivors, prepares his speech, and sees his wife on the stairs. Once we leave the social setting of the party in which many characters are presented dramatically, the narrative focus narrows even further.

The final section of the story concentrates on Gabriel's thoughts and feelings. Although the dialogue between husband and wife punctuates the narrative, Gabriel's perceptions dominate our attention. The style of narration shifts at this point to a heightened lyricism which reflects the intensity of Gabriel's emotions. To penetrate his psyche, a new kind of language—a more fluid and poetic medium—is introduced into the story. In this way, the narrator tries to give metaphoric expression to Gabriel's consciousness. Thus, although the focus of narration and style changes in "The Dead," the primary narrative point of view is Gabriel's.

A Portrait of the Artist as a Young Man

34.4   What is the significance of the title A Portrait of the Artist as a Young Man?

Answer   The use of the definite article "the" in the title illustrates Joyce's attempt to present Stephen as an exemplum of the developing artist, just as, for example, Wordsworth in The Prelude represents the growth of the poet's soul. The story of Stephen Dedalus depicts the growth of the artistic consciousness; the significance of his development transcends that of a single artist and represents a prototypical process. If Stephen were merely an artist, the factors which contribute to his choice of vocation could be regarded as idiosyncratic or novel. Instead, Joyce wants to show that his sensitivity to language, his status as an outsider, and his sacrifices for art are basic to the creation and development of the artist. Yet Joyce never lets us forget the specific Irishness of Stephen's struggle, the particular "nets" that Ireland casts over its young artists and intellectuals. England and Rome, the twin "masters" of the Irish to which Stephen Dedalus refers in Ulysses, pose tremendous obstacles to the development of the young Irish artist.

The last four words of the title, "as a Young Man," remind us that what we observe in the book is the developing artist, not the mature artist. In adding these words, Joyce reserved the right to present Stephen ironically at times, to show the adolescent posturing which is as much a part of Stephen's story as his courageous final decision to leave Ireland. By stressing the youth of the artist, Joyce could present Stephen's foibles without reducing his artist to fatuousness; he could present Stephen's pretensions without creating a portrait of the artist as Narcissus.

In A Portrait of the Artist as a Young Man, Joyce created a serious, often ironic portrait of the developing artist. But the irony never reduces the significance of Stephen's process of development. Particularly since the book is a fictional treatment of autobiographical materials, the mixture of sympathy and irony implied in the title is an appropriate, perhaps necessary ingredient.

34.5
Once Stephen has decided to become an artist, he resolves to become "a priest of the eternal imagination." What is the meaning of this phrase and why is it appropriate, given Stephen's background?

Answer The use of this religious metaphor to describe Stephen's view of the role of the artist aptly conveys Stephen's (and Joyce's) conception of the sacramental quality of art. Just as the priest presides over the sacrament of communion in which bread and wine become the body and blood of Christ, so the artist transforms the ordinary into the universal, the mundane into the eternal. Unlike the priest, however, whose symbols are established by scripture and tradition, the artist creates personal symbols out of imagination.

Applied to art, the religious metaphor links the artist's profession with the basically religious idea of a vocation or a calling; like the priest, the artist responds to a higher sense of purpose than does an ordinary person. Summoned by a divine voice within, the artist has no choice but to obey; the artist must accept the challenge of this vocation.

Stephen's calling to the priesthood of art, however, reflects ironically on his rejection of the Catholic priesthood in Chapter IV. Stephen decides finally that the life of the Catholic priest is dry and sterile; he chooses the aesthetic truth rather than the religious, the artist's life rather than the priest's. The religious metaphor, then, reflects the seriousness and awe with which Stephen regards the aesthetic; his religious allegiance is transferred from Catholicism to art.

34.6
Why does the style of narration change in the course of the novel?

Answer A *Portrait of the Artist as a Young Man* is a *Bildungsroman*, or "novel of education," a fictional form particularly favored in the nineteenth century. One of Joyce's contributions to this genre was to have his style develop along with his protagonist; the style imitates the general education of the artist, and matures to reflect the growth of the artist's mind.

The narration begins with the childlike rhythms and images of a fairy tale

("Once upon a time and a very good time it was . . ."). The style of the opening evokes Stephen's child's-eye view of the world; he is the "nicens little boy named baby tuckoo." A few pages later, the prose reflects the consciousness of Stephen as a small boy, sensitive and isolated, responding to his surroundings. The short, simple sentences express sensation after sensation with few logical transitions between them, a technique which reflects both Stephen's responsiveness and his immaturity ("That was not a nice expression. His mother had told him not to speak with the rough boys in the college. Nice mother!").

The more sophisticated prose of Chapters III, IV, and V reflects not only Stephen's chronological growth but also his increasing facility with language. The increasingly precise, educated diction of the third-person narration mirrors Stephen's sensibility and often presents the world as Stephen himself sees it ("He stood still in deference to their calls and parried their banter with easy words"). In the final pages, the style of narration and Stephen's consciousness converge in first-person diary entries. The book ends with Stephen's actual jottings to himself rather than a narration of his thoughts.

34.7   Why does Stephen respond with such intensity to the word "foetus" carved on a school desk which he sees on his visit to Cork with his father?

Answer   The carved word "foetus" represents to Stephen his own adolescent sexual curiosity. The word, carved by another schoolboy long ago, reminds Stephen of his own lurid imagination and precipitates his disturbing realization that the external world confirms the seamy images flashing through his mind. Earlier in the novel, Stephen longed to "meet in the real world the unsubstantial image which his soul so constantly beheld" (Chapter II). Ironically, what he meets in the real world is not the strange, wonderful woman he has fantasized about but the sordid trace of another adolescent imagination. The intensity of Stephen's response to the carving may seem disproportionate, but it comes at a time when he is engaged in a constant unsuccessful battle to repress his sexual longings. Soon after this episode, the chapter culminates in Stephen's first visit to a prostitute.

The circumstances of this episode are also relevant to its interpretation. Stephen's trip to Cork with his father represents a ritual of father and son returning to the father's roots, for Simon Dedalus had come from Cork as a boy. As Stephen accompanies his father to the bar he used to frequent and meets some of Simon's old friends, he is constantly compared with his father, who was reputed (at least by his cronies) to be a ladies' man, a sexual conqueror.

Thus, Stephen's resentment of his father as well as his sexual insecurity are tapped in this seemingly insignificant incident.

Ulysses

34.8 What important symbolic roles are conferred on Leopold Bloom by virtue of his being Jewish?

Answer In choosing to make his main character a Jew, Joyce placed Bloom in the symbolic roles of outsider, scapegoat, and wanderer. As a Jew in a predominantly Catholic and anti-Semitic culture, Bloom wanders through the streets of Dublin, an Odysseus ironically exiled and outcast in his own hometown.

The Wandering Jew, a popular and literary type that Joyce alludes to in his portrayal of Bloom, is based on the legend of a Jew who mocked Christ and was doomed to an eternity of wandering the earth. Bloom, whose factual statement that Christ was a Jew infuriates the patriotic Irish citizen with whom he debates in the "Cyclops" chapter, can be said to "wander" through Dublin in two senses. First, knowing that his wife, Molly, will be entertaining a lover at home at 4:00 P.M., Bloom tries to occupy himself with vacuous tasks throughout the day and evening. Bloom, like Stephen, has his reason for feeling that "Home I cannot go." Secondly, as an outsider, he wanders among his fellow Dubliners, like the Wandering Jew a solitary figure on the fringes of his society.

The ride to Dignam's funeral in the morning also shows Bloom in his role as outsider. Last to enter the carriage, frequently interrupted in conversation by the others, and isolated in his attitudes toward life and death, Bloom does not belong to the group. Bantam Lyons's suspicions that Bloom has won a bet on the Gold Cup race but is too cheap to stand a round of drinks reveals the anti-Semitic stereotyping to which Bloom is subject. Finally, the blatant anti-Semitism of the Citizen and the narrator in "Cyclops" illustrates how Bloom, as a Jew, is made a scapegoat by at least some of his peers.

Bloom's Jewishness also relates to the connection in Joyce's mind between Homer's Odysseus and Semitism. Joyce was intrigued by Victor Bérard's idea that Odysseus was a Phoenician or Semite rather than a Greek. The truth of this theory is less important than the use Joyce was able to make of it in his novel.

34.9   The leitmotif, or repeated phrase of thematic significance, is an element of much modern literature. *Ulysses* contains many such leitmotifs. Among them is the phrase "Plumtree's Potted Meat," which is mentioned at least five different times in the novel. What is the thematic importance of this leitmotif?

Answer   The phrase "Plumtree's Potted Meat" first appears in an advertisement Bloom reads in the morning newspaper: "What is home without/ Plumtree's Potted Meat?/Incomplete./With it an abode of bliss" ("Lotus Eaters"). The advertisement's promise of domestic bliss provides an ironic counterpoint to Bloom's actual, less than blissful situation at home. By the end of the novel, the phrase is associated with death, sex, and usurpation; it becomes one psychological index to the state of mind of Leopold Bloom.

The phrase becomes linked with the idea of death partly through its placement on the newspaper's obituary page (which Bloom peruses for the notice of his friend Paddy Dignam) and partly through the image of an interred corpse evoked in Bloom's fertile imagination by the phrase "potted meat." In the "Lestrygonians" chapter, under the influence of his hunger, Bloom associates the phrase with cannibalism: "Dignam's potted meat. Cannibals would with lemon and rice." The phrase echoes in Bloom's mind, but this time its associations reflect his melancholy mood and "eat or be eaten" view of the human race.

But most important for Bloom are the phrase's associations and its applicability to his own domestic situation. The meat in the pot becomes a metaphor for sexual intercourse, the most important occurrence of which involves Molly and Blazes Boylan in Bloom's own bed. Bloom's marriage has indeed been "incomplete" in this sense; Bloom has not had intercourse with Molly since their son, Rudy, died. When Bloom finally returns home in the early hours of the morning, he spies an empty pot of Plumtree's Potted Meat. In bed, he finds flakes of potted meat, and this suggests that Boylan and Molly have been feasting together. The presence of these crumbs in his bed triggers Bloom's thought that he is neither the first nor the last of Molly's suitors. Thus, in its final appearance in the novel, the phrase leads subtly and indirectly to the acknowledgment of Molly's infidelity, which Bloom has tried so hard to avoid.

34.10   Although Joyce at one time planned to assign titles to the chapters in *Ulysses*, he ultimately decided instead to leave them out. His title for the third chapter, and the one Joyce critics use in speaking of the chapter, is "Proteus." Why is this an appropriate name?

Answer   Proteus is the name of a Greek god of the sea, a relative of Neptune and a master of disguise who elusively changes shape in order to evade capture. The adjective "protean" is derived from that name. According to the myth, if Proteus is finally captured, he is forced to tell the truth. In *The Odyssey*, Homer's Odysseus captures Proteus and forces him to say what has happened in Ithaca while Odysseus has been away.

The title "Proteus" is appropriate to the setting, theme, and style of the third chapter of *Ulysses*. The setting of the chapter is Sandymount Strand, a beachfront along which Stephen Dedalus strolls alone. Gazing at the beach and sea, Stephen muses about his identity and relationship to his past life and to the world around him; he seems changed from the arrogant and sensitive boy he used to be, and he questions whether he can find a stable identity within the protean roles he has played in his life.

In his mind, Stephen searches for some kind of pattern within the flux: "I am I," he tells himself, acting, in a sense, like Odysseus, attempting to pin down some kind of truth. According to Joyce's symbolic schema for the chapter (published in Stuart Gilbert's *James Joyce's Ulysses*, [1952]), its "art" is "philology," which also relates to the namesake of the chapter, Proteus. Philology is the study of linguistic change, and the style of the chapter includes both foreign and archaic words, that is, words which have changed with changes in time and space. Thus the language of the chapter is also protean, displaying a flexibility that is appropriate to its artist-protagonist whose vocation depends on the malleability of language. Neither the setting of the chapter, then, nor its Homeric title is accidental; both express the theme and style of the chapter.

34.11   Most of the chapters of *Ulysses* appear to be written in styles and forms appropriate to their theme and content. Is there such a thematic or situational significance to the form of the "Ithaca" chapter?

Answer   The "Ithaca" chapter is cast in the form of a catechism, or series of questions and answers. Its style is pseudo-scientific (i.e., "What discrete succession of images did Stephen meanwhile perceive?" "Reclined against the area railings he perceived through the transparent kitchen panes . . .").

At the end of the chapter, the questions and answers of the "catechism" represent Molly's questions and Bloom's answers as they both lie in bed. The merging of the narrative questions and answers and the characters' dialogue is the only real link between the characters' situation and the form of the chapter. Of all the techniques or styles used in *Ulysses*, the catechism of "Ithaca" seems most deliberately arbitrary, designed purposely by Joyce to reveal the essential arbitrariness of stylistic choices.

The catechism is reminiscent of both the Catholic catechism, in which children answer questions about the relationship between God and his church, and the classroom texts used in many nineteenth-century schools. These two kinds of associations of the form of the chapter seem curiously inappropriate to the setting of the dramatic action, in contrast to, for example, the headlines and rhetorical tropes of the "Aeolus" chapter, whose setting is a newspaper office.

As *Ulysses* progresses, Joyce uses a different style for almost every chapter. By the penultimate chapter, the reader may begin to question the reliability of any one style or narrative mode. The arbitrariness of the catechetical form to the dramatic, even symbolic, situation of the chapter serves to reinforce the idea of the relativity of any style. The chapter also represents a kind of tour de force for Joyce. He seems to be saying that he is able to tell the story of his characters in any style, however unpoetic or mathematical it may be.

K.L.

SUGGESTED READINGS

Blamires, Harry, *The Bloomsday Book: A Guide through Joyce's Ulysses* (1966).
Budgen, Frank, *James Joyce and the Making of Ulysses* (1960).
Ellmann, Richard, *James Joyce* (1982).
Gilbert, Stuart, *James Joyce's Ulysses: A Study* (1952).
Kenner, Hugh, *Ulysses* (1980).
Lawrence, Karen, *The Odyssey of Style in Ulysses* (1981).
Peake, C. H., *James Joyce: The Citizen and the Artist* (1977).

D. H. LAWRENCE

C H R O N O L O G Y

1885	Born in Eastwood, Nottinghamshire, the younger son of Arthur John Lawrence, a coal miner, and Lydia Beardsall Lawrence, a former schoolteacher.
1898	Wins a scholarship to the Nottingham High School. Meets and becomes engaged to Jessie Chambers, the Miriam of *Sons and Lovers*.
1901–1906	Clerks in a surgical appliance factory, then becomes student-teacher at Ilkeston, Devonshire. Falls gravely ill of pneumonia. Takes job as an uncertified teacher at Eastwood.
1906	Enters University College, Nottingham. Publishes first poems in the *English Review*, edited by Ford Madox Hueffer (his first literary friend) and first stories in the *Nottinghamshire Guardian*. Awarded a teaching certificate at Nottingham, he goes to teach at the Davidson Road School in Eastwood.
1910	Breaks his engagement with Jessie Chambers and becomes engaged to Louie Burrows. His mother, an unusually strong influence in his education and his attitudes toward women, dies of cancer. He says that her death "wiped out everything else—books published, or stories in magazines. It was the great crash and the end of my youth." With the help of Ford Madox Hueffer, publishes his first novel, *The White Peacock*, setting forth his basic vision of humanity trapped between nature and culture.
1912	Publishes his second novel, *The Trespasser*. Elopes to Germany with Frieda von Richthofen Weekly, the aristocratic German wife of one of his former

professors at Nottingham. Begins the restless, nomadic life and intense marital relationship that form the basis of much of his later work.

1913   Returns to England and forms a lasting but difficult friendship with John Middleton Murry, and Murry's wife, the short story writer Katherine Mansfield. Publishes the masterpiece of his early work, the autobiographical novel *Sons and Lovers*. Also publishes his first volume of poems, *Love Poems and Others*.

1914   Goes to Italy, where he conceives and drafts *The Rainbow*. Returns to England to marry Frieda once her divorce becomes final. Publishes his first volume of short stories, *The Prussian Officer and Other Stories*.

1915   Publishes *The Rainbow*, perhaps his most important work, which charts a new direction for the novel. After five weeks, the magistrate's court suppresses it as obscene. Disillusioned by World War I and his book's reception, Lawrence dreams of founding a utopian community, Rananim, with a small band of creative people dissociating themselves from corrupt society. He interests in the project Ottoline Morrell, flamboyant wife of a member of Parliament and patron of the arts. Plans a series of lectures with Bertrand Russell, but they soon quarrel and part. *The Rainbow* alienates Lawrence's friends Murry, Mansfield, and Garnett.

1916   After unsuccessfully trying to emigrate to America, moves to Cornwall. The Murrys move nearby despite the friction between the couples. Katherine becomes the model for Gudrun in *Women in Love*, which Lawrence completes at this time.

1915–   Persecuted by neighbors, leaves Cornwall on order from police (cause of
1920   the trouble: his wife is German). Lives in Berkshire, Derbyshire, and London. Frieda goes to Germany alone for a while.

1920   They live in Florence, Capri, and Taormina. Publishes *Women in Love*, sequel to *The Rainbow*. Meets Norman Douglas in Florence. Publishes *The Lost Girl*. They stay with Frieda's mother in Germany, where he writes *Fantasia of the Unconscious*, explaining his complex psychological theories.

1921–   The Lawrences sail to Ceylon and Australia. Publishes *The Captain's Doll*
1922   and *The Ladybird*. Accepts invitation from Mabel Dodge, a rich American, to join her in Taos, New Mexico. Publishes *Aaron's Rod*.

1923   Leaves for Mexico to study Aztec civilization. Publishes *Kangaroo*, a "leadership" novel set in Australia, and *Studies in Classic American Literature*, a brilliant, erratic critical work written to finance his trip to America. Publishes a collection of poems, *Birds, Beasts and Flowers*. Frieda returns to

London alone, but Lawrence joins her there in December. Katherine Mansfield dies, and Lawrence and Murry are reconciled.

1924   With Frieda and Dorothy Brett, leaves London for Taos, New Mexico. Jealous complications between Frieda, Dorothy, and Mabel. Falls seriously ill.

1925   Returns to Europe and publishes the short novel *St. Mawr*.

1926   Moves to Florence and publishes *The Plumed Serpent*, a Mexican novel. Becomes friendly with novelist Aldous Huxley. Paints and works on *Lady Chatterley's Lover*. Visits England for the last time.

1928   Publishes *Lady Chatterley's Lover* privately in Florence, then in Paris (1929). An expurgated edition appears after his death in 1932; the full text is not published until 1959 in New York and 1960 in London. Publishes *The Woman Who Rode Away*, another collection of influential short stories.

1929   Travels to Majorca, Florence, Germany, and returns to France. Police seize two of his manuscripts in the mail and confiscate his paintings in the Warren Gallery. Publishes *Pornography and Obscenity*, essays explaining the creative literary use of sex and distinguishing it from sexual exploitation. Publishes a volume of light verse, *Pansies*.

1930   Moves to a sanatorium in Vence, France, near Antibes, and dies of tuberculosis. His remains are later exhumed from the French cemetery and moved to a Lawrence shrine in Taos, New Mexico, by Frieda and her third husband, Angelo Ravagli. Shortly after his death, his last novel, *The Virgin and the Gypsy*, appears.

1931   *The Man Who Died* is published posthumously, along with *Apocalypse*, his commentary on the Book of Revelation and his last attempt to explain his beliefs.

1932   *Last Poems* is published.

ESSAY QUESTIONS WITH ANSWERS

The Rainbow

35.1 *The Rainbow* begins with a description of the Marsh Farm and the generations of Brangwens who have inhabited it. Lawrence refers to this description as a "poem" ("The male part of the poem was filled in by such men as the vicar" [Chap. I]. How does this prose description resemble a poem? How does it introduce the novel?

Answer The description of the Marsh Farm is poetic in its rhythmic repetitions, its vivid imagery, and its symbolism. Evoking the fertility and the richness of life on the marsh, the description sets the stage for the story of the Brangwen men and women who are the main characters of the book.

The images of the passage are erotic. The "intercourse" between heaven and earth is described in sexual terms: "Sunshine drawn into the breast and bowels, the rain sucked up in the daytime. . . ." The relationship between the Brangwen men and the land is almost one of sexual possession: "Their life and interrelations were such; feeling the pulse and body of the soil, that opened to their furrow for the grain, and became smooth and supple after their ploughing, and clung to their feet with a weight that pulled like desire, lying hard and unresponsive." Transforming the landscape of the marsh into a kind of primeval garden of fecundity, the imagery anticipates the story of marriage, sexual struggle, and procreation which follows.

The sexual imagery is accompanied by the repetition of phrases, which echo biblical rhythms (in particular the Book of Psalms). Certain phrases operate like poetic refrains: "It was enough for the men, that the earth heaved and opened its furrows . . . it was enough that they helped the cow in labour, or ferreted the rats from under the barn. . . ." The cadence of the prose also imitates the rhythms of the activity described: The repetition of the phrases evokes the seasonal cycles of fertility on the farm. The "prose poem" provides a mythic introduction which places the relationships between men and women in the center of the larger, impersonal, yet erotic forces in nature. The ritual flavor of the writing suggests that we are reading a kind of history of humankind. The central opposition between men and women, introduced in the prose poem, is developed throughout the novel. The men represent the physical "knowledge" of the earth; the women strive for an intellectual "knowledge" which transcends their life on the farm. Thus, the opening pages of the novel are also poetic— or, perhaps, musical—in the way they introduce themes or motifs which the rest of the book will develop, underscore, and modify.

35.2   What is the significance of Lydia Brangwen's foreign ancestry?

Answer   The importance of Lydia Brangwen's Polish ancestry is emphasized in the title of Chapter I, "How Brangwen Married a Polish Lady." Lydia's foreignness is anticipated in the plot by the foreign gentleman who dines with a local girl Tom fancies. To Tom this meeting with a foreigner is more significant than his relationship with the girl. In this episode, the stage is set for Tom's encounter with new experiences which will expand his narrow, provincial life.

When Tom first sees Lydia on the road, he says to himself, "That's her." When he discovers that she is the widow of a Polish doctor, her foreignness is "a profound satisfaction" to him and enhances her mystery and wonder. Yet there is a curious mixture of kinship and strangeness in his relationship to her. "She was strange, from far off, yet so intimate." "She was from far away, a presence, so close to his soul." This kind of grammatically simple sentence, which connects almost antithetical ideas merely with commas, characterizes Lawrence's treatment of the tensions between men and women. The uneasy combination of a sense of "otherness" and a sense of intimacy in Tom and Lydia's relationship is found in the successive generations of Brangwen couples as well. Men and women are polar opposites even when they come from the same narrow culture, since, ultimately, Lawrence refers to something far beneath cultural differences or personal preferences. Yet the tension between the sexes is also magnetic, as it is in the relationship of Lydia and Tom.

35.3   *The Rainbow* paints a portrait of marriage in three successive generations. How does the depiction of marriage change in the course of the book?

Answer   The first two generations of Brangwens are depicted in the marriages between Tom and Lydia and between Anna and Will; the third generation is represented in the perverse marriage of Tom Brangwen and Winifred Inger and the bitter love affair between Ursula and Anton Skrebensky, which fails to issue in marriage. The progression from the first chapter entitled "How Brangwen Married a Polish Lady" to the penultimate chapter entitled "The Bitterness of Ecstasy" reveals the increasing difficulties and strains in these relationships between men and women. Yet Lawrence does not simply depict a declining happiness and sense of falling off from the pure values of the past. He also presents the increased expectations of his characters and an expansion in their consciousness that makes them unhappy with the same goals sought by their parents.

After uncertainty and struggle in its initial stages, the marriage of Tom and Lydia becomes a fruitful union allowing freedom within the ties of the marriage bonds. The marsh becomes a place of domestic fulfillment. Through his wife, Tom feels he submits to his "transformation." He feels their union is somehow sanctified, a feeling expressed at Anna's wedding, when he describes their relationship as "he and his wife, two little upright figures walking across this plain, whilst the heavens shimmered and roared about them" (Chap. V).

Although Will Brangwen and Anna will also participate in a creative union, by the second generation marriage involves a greater battle of the wills. Taunting and criticizing each other, Anna and Will struggle to achieve the kind of balance which defined Tom and Lydia's relationship. Will tries to assert his power over her; Will's interior struggles, unlike Tom Brangwen's, lead him to a certain brutality with Anna. She challenges his attempts to control her by dancing naked and pregnant in front of him and by belittling his miniature sculpture of Eve. She feels that he is like a weight upon her, so discontented is he in himself. Although this second generation does achieve moments of ecstasy and peace, the battle of wills seems more dangerous and brutal.

By the third generation, the representative marriage has become a destructive tie between two perverse individuals, Tom Brangwen and Winifred Inger. In stark contrast to the elder Brangwens' attitude toward marriage, the younger Tom Brangwen describes marriage as "a little side-show." Marriage has been displaced from the center of experience and has acquired an almost freakish aspect. No longer a lifelong, creative relationship, marriage is only the fitting conclusion to two unhappy and unfulfilled lives.

Finally, in the relationship between Ursula Brangwen and Anton Skrebensky we see a "modern" relationship which consists of each partner's attempt to "annihilate" the other. Both characters demand more from a relationship than their predecessors; both know more of the world outside rural English life. As a modern man, Skrebensky suffers from some of the perils that Lawrence finds in industrial society; enormously egotistical in some ways, he still sees himself as only a part in the war machine, a brick in the edifice of modern society. However, in ending her affair with Skrebensky, Ursula, in contrast to Tom Brangwen, escapes from the destructive relationship. In the final use of the image of the rainbow at the end of the novel, Lawrence suggests that there is hope for Ursula in her quest for the right partner in marriage. Although the prognosis for marital relations worsens with each successive generation, Lawrence still seems to retain his faith in the possibility of a fruitful union between the sexes.

35.4   Chapters X and XIV of *The Rainbow* bear the same title, "The Widening Circle." What is the significance of this image and of its repetition?

Answer   The image of a widening circle represents the expansion of Ursula Brangwen's sphere of experience and knowledge. In Chapter X, the phrase refers to Ursula's early adolescent experiences, which include her exposure to literature and mathematics at school during the week and to the Christian mysteries on Sundays. Chapter XIV records Ursula's infatuation with Anthony Schofield and her decision to reject him. She feels she must transcend his kind of existence, an existence rooted in the natural processes which dominated and fulfilled the first generation of Brangwens. At the end of the chapter, the Brangwen family moves to Beldover, a middle-class suburb of Nottingham, and the idea of the widening circle becomes slightly ironic. Instead of the cultured life to which Ursula aspires, she is forced into a sterile bourgeois existence; instead of achieving liberation, she is chained to the petty responsibilities of suburban family life.

The image of the widening circle captures the process of expansion so crucial in the lives of Lawrence's characters. In general terms, it conveys not only the passage to maturity of a character such as Ursula but also the breakthrough from adult provincialism achieved by Tom in his relationship with Lydia. The most important and "alive" characters in Lawrence's fiction engage in constant struggle to push themselves beyond the limits which circumscribe each stage of life, hence the repetition of the title. Yet although the circle expands, it still encloses an area within which the characters operate; the widening circle is an image of insecurity or boundary as well as expansion. Compared with the more modern, frantic world portrayed in *Women in Love*, the traditional, largely agricultural world of *The Rainbow* gives a sense of roots and boundaries as well as growth.

The image of the widening circle is also related to the image of the rainbow in the title. The arch of the rainbow is richer with traditional associations than the widening circle; its reference to the covenant between God and humankind after the flood in Genesis and its natural architecture that unites earth and sky convey the sense of promise, sacredness, and tradition that underlies the struggles in the novel. The image is given structural prominence at the end of Chapters III and VI, where it symbolizes the passage from one generation to another; the parents are seen as the pillars between which the children of the next generation pass on to the world beyond. At the end of the novel, the arch of the rainbow again represents a promise of a new order, or, as Ursula experiences it, "the earth's new architecture, the old, brittle corruption of houses and factories swept away, the world built up in a living fabric of Truth, fitting to the overarching heaven."

Women in Love

35.5 In 1914, D. H. Lawrence wrote to his friend Edward Garnett:

> You mustn't look in my novel for the old stable *ego*—of the character. There is another *ego*, according to whose action the individual is unrecognisable, and passes through, as it were, allotropic states which it needs a deeper sense than any we've been used to exercise, to discover are states of the same single radically unchanged element. (Like as diamond and coal are the same pure single element of carbon. The ordinary novel would trace the history of the diamond—but I say, "Diamond, what! This is carbon." And my diamond might be coal or soot, and my theme is carbon.)[1]

How does this quotation apply to character portrayal in *Women in Love*?

Answer The passage is extremely difficult. How, exactly, can the characters in the novel reveal something beneath the "old stable ego," and what is the essence or "radically unchanged element" Lawrence mentions? By "old stable ego," Lawrence seems to refer to character as presented in the nineteenth-century novel or in an early twentieth-century writer like Galsworthy: consistent, stable, and fairly predictable in its actions. Without denying these novels their complexity of characterization, Lawrence nevertheless suggests that they fail to represent the more fluid but essential core of the person beneath his or her thoughts and actions.

[1]*The Collected Letters of D. H. Lawrence*, Vol. 1, Harry T. Moore (ed.), Viking Press, New York, 1962, pp. 281–283.

The difficult concepts to reconcile are the idea of the instability of character and the sense of a core or unchanged element. The instability Lawrence posits as antithetical to the stability of the traditional novel perhaps refers to the general unrest, the struggles, the sometimes tortured questioning of a Rupert Birkin. In *Women in Love*, even more than in *The Rainbow*, Lawrence is interested in those moments of least stability, the moments of transformation, tension, excitement, sometimes annihilation. In order to portray these moments, Lawrence often uses metaphor to get at something beneath even the conscious thoughts of the characters, let alone their actions. For example, at one point he describes the hatred between Birkin and Ursula as "beyond words": "It was as if he were a beam of essential enmity, a beam of light . . . a strange gem-like being whose existence defined her own non-existence" (Chap. XV). Both characters here are stripped of their everyday, rational, recognizable identities to reveal something deeper and more terrifying. Here, Ursula worries that if the old stable ego is stripped away, nothing may take its place.

Although Birkin is often treated ironically by Lawrence, perhaps most frequently when he is preaching to the other characters, he is, nevertheless, the character in the novel who is most dedicated to stripping away social masks and exposing the essence of the characters. When he speaks to Ursula of "a final me which is stark and impersonal and beyond responsibility" (Chap. XIII), he refers to the "core," the essential unchanging element that Lawrence describes in his letter to Garnett.

35.6 How does the short chapter "Rabbit" establish a symbolic communication between Gudrun and Gerald?

Answer   In this chapter, Winifred's rabbit, freed from its cage, explodes into a frenzy of violent action, and the violence precipitates a recognition scene between Gudrun and Gerald. First Gudrun tries to subdue the frantic animal and is clawed in the process; then Gerald takes over and finally overpowers the animal. In witnessing Gerald's masterful treatment of the rabbit and, earlier, his treatment of his horse, Gudrun recognizes both his sexual force and his brutality. In turn, the convulsive struggling of the rabbit, soft yet surprisingly powerful, attracts Gerald to the same qualities in Gudrun. The red gash in her forearm becomes like a rent in his own consciousness: "The long, shallow red rip seemed torn across his own brain, tearing the surface of his ultimate consciousness, unthinkable red ether of the beyond, the obscene beyond" (Chap.

XVIII). In the secret smiles that the pair exchange, they communicate their awareness of the cruelty and sexual attraction that bind them together. They realize that in some mysterious way they are each other's violent "fate."

K.L.

35.7 In *The Rainbow*, the coal mines provide a backdrop for the novel and represent the encroachment of technology on the agricultural environment. In *Women in Love*, the presence of the mines is more pervasive; indeed, one of the major characters, Gerald Crich, is a mine owner described as "the Industrial Magnate." How does Gerald's administration of the Crich coal mine reveal his character?

Answer Throughout the novel, Gerald is described as a man with an iron will. The depiction of Gerald wielding power over his miners in "The Industrial Magnate" reveals this will in a larger social context. When Gerald takes charge of the mines, the more casual and personal regime of his father gives way to an autocratic domination: Gerald demands that the men operate as one perfect machine. Gerald deifies the concept of the machine; the individual wills of his men are broken as they submit to the god of production.

Thomas Crich's rule and his son's represent two stages in the development of industrial capitalism. The change from father to son represents a change from the benevolent, patriarchal figure who is personally concerned with the well-being of his employees to the "new" industrial magnate who seeks to dehumanize the workers into mere instruments. Gerald's tragic end illustrates what happens to a person who becomes pure will, dedicated to using people in every circumstance, from industrial confrontation to sexual encounter.

"The Blind Man"

35.8 Discuss the function of "place" in "The Blind Man." How does Lawrence make the house and the barn symbolic centers of the action?

Answer Isabel Pervin and Bertie Reid are comfortable in the well-lit, refined atmosphere of the Pervin house; Maurice feels at ease in the darkness of the stable. The characters change emotionally according to their movement between the two places: Isabel feels "desperate" in the barn when she goes to look for Maurice, and Bertie, too, feels "nervous" when he ventures first into the darkness of the night and then into the barn. Maurice, on the other hand, wavers when he enters the house, moving cautiously in the more constricting surroundings.

These reactions to the physical environment reveal the essences of these characters. Maurice, in his blindness, has developed a new consciousness, a tactile sense of the physical, animal world around him; Isabel and Bertie are afraid that this consciousness will destroy their intellectual control and balance. It is as if the blind man can see beneath their social pretenses and defenses. Lawrence often creates opposing groups of characters who represent different ways of knowing and experiencing life. In "The Blind Man," he creates an antithesis between the barn, Maurice, and physical consciousness, on the one hand, and the house, Isabel and Bertie, and intellect and culture, on the other.

35.9 In Lawrence's "The Blind Man," very little actually happens. Old friends, a man and woman, visit together after many years, in the presence of the woman's blind husband; later, the sighted man goes out in the barn to find the blind man and they touch each other's faces. Of course, this synopsis of plot tells almost nothing about what really happens in the story, which occurs on the level of reactions rather than actions and involves revelation and recognition rather than outcome. Discuss what "really" happens in the story.

Answer The real story told in "The Blind Man" exists in the altered consciousness of the characters rather than in any overt change in their lives. The climax of the story occurs when Maurice and Bertie touch each other's faces in the barn. The touch creates intimacy between the men, yet ironically, it produces totally different reactions in the two. Maurice is exhilarated by the contact; Bertie is devastated by it.

The climax at the end of the story is anticipated in the characters' earlier reactions to each other. Bertie's sense of horror in the final scene is in some way prepared for by his anxiety during dinner, where the silent presence of the blind man makes him nervous. Intellectual and insecure, Bertie feels at a loss when conversation ceases. The drama of the scene exists in the unspoken tension among the characters; even the smallest gesture of contact, Maurice's touching Bertie when receiving a bowl of flowers from him, causes a strong reaction in Bertie. There is a disproportion between the slightness of the gesture and the significance it assumes for the characters.

In the final scene, this emotional movement reaches a climax. Bertie feels annihilated by his physical contact with Maurice, "like a mollusc whose shell is broken." The metaphor suggests that Bertie's defenses have been destroyed; the witty mask he wears in his social encounters has been cracked. He feels violated in some way; perhaps even sexual violation is suggested, since Maurice is a man who luxuriates in his own physicality, and his touch of Bertie, earlier described as "neuter," threatens to penetrate Bertie's sexual as well as social defenses. By the end of the story, nothing and everything has happened. Two men have merely touched each other, but the psychological significance of that touch is enormous.

"Piano"

35.10 One reader had the following response to the poem:

> If this, on further inspection, should prove not to be *silly, maudlin, sentimental twaddle,* I have missed the point. Such it certainly seems to me, and I loathe it. *It is a revelling in emotion for its own sake, that is nothing short of nauseating.* Moreover, it's badly done.[1]

Discuss the issue of sentimentality in the poem. Has this reader, indeed, missed the point?

Answer The reader's response to "Piano" is not altogether surprising; the picture of a child seated at his mother's dainty feet, listening to her play the piano on a Sunday evening, may suggest as old-fashioned illustration of Home Sweet Home out of Currier and Ives. At times the diction seems to lapse into cliché; "vista of years," "cozy parlor," and "tinkling piano" are phrases which evoke stock responses.

Yet the romance and even cliché in such a picture of domestic bliss do not escape the poet himself. The clichéd nature of the family portrait is less of an artistic lapse on his part than a tacit acknowledgment of the romance inherent in our memories of childhood; no matter what happens to us later in life, we have a need to retain the myth of a secure and nurturing past.

The angry reader also ignores the poet's own ambivalence about his nostalgic response to the music. In stanza 2, the poet speaks of the "insidious mastery of song" that "betrays" him back to his childhood. Although he gives in to the

---

[1] Quoted in I. A. Richards, *Practical Criticism: A Study of Literary Judgment*, New York, Harcourt, Brace & World, 1929, p. 99.

spell of the past and weeps "like a child" again, he is embarrassed and surprised by the power of music to evoke such buried feelings. Thus, his is not an unchecked "revelling in emotion for its own sake," for his feelings are delicately balanced between tenderness for the past and awareness of his own nostalgia and romanticism.

Finally, not only the poet's note of ambivalence but the rhyming couplets and brevity of the poem as well check the flow of uncontrolled emotion. We are not asked to dwell on this moment of feelings, only to note it, perhaps to empathize, and then to pass on.

"Bavarian Gentians"

35.11 Discuss the use of the Persephone myth in the poem.

Answer The Greek myth, which recounts Persephone's descent every autumn into Hades and her return every spring to earth, is associated with ancient fertility rites and with Christian resurrection. However, Lawrence does not merely exploit the conventional meanings of the myth but personalizes it in order to convey the experience of death.

When the poet says, "Reach me a gentian, give me a torch," he becomes a companion of Persephone in her journey toward death. Death itself is described in the imagery of sexual consummation: Persephone is embraced by Pluto and is "pierced with the passion of dense gloom." Furthermore, death is envisioned as a kind of marriage between "the lost bride and her groom."

Although there is no overt allusion to any Christian concept of resurrection, the sexual suggestions of the language which ends the poem convey the notion of vitality, the paradox of life in death.

35.12 The word "dark" is repeated in varying forms eighteen times in the course of the poem. What does the darkness signify, and what is the effect of the repetition?

Answer On the most literal level, the darkness is associated with the deep blue of the gentians. But almost immediately in the poem, "dark" is also associated with death ("Pluto's gloom" [line 4]) and, paradoxically, with light ("torchlike" [line 4]). The image of the torch connotes the fire and heat of hell, thus uniting the motifs of darkness, light, and death.

The repeated use of "dark" and of various forms of the word gives the poem some of the quality of an incantation or chant, which increases in intensity as the poem continues. This deepening intensity evokes a sense of ritual progression, a mythic descent into hell. The journey climaxes in the strikingly paradoxical fusion of light with darkness: "the splendor of torches of darkness, shedding darkness on the lost bride and her groom" (line 19).

K.L.

SUGGESTED READINGS

Ford, George, *Double Measure: A Study of the Novels and Stories of D. H. Lawrence* (1965).

Kermode, Frank, *D. H. Lawrence* (1973).

Leavis, F. R., *D. H. Lawrence: Novelist* (1955).

Nehls, Edward, *D. H. Lawrence: A Composite Biography* (1957).

Spender, Stephen (ed.), *D. H. Lawrence: Novelist, Poet, Prophet* (1973).

INDEX

INDEX

ABOUT THE AUTHORS

Karen Lawrence is currently associate professor and chairperson of the English department at the University of Utah. She received a B.A. from Yale University (1971), and a Ph.D. from Columbia University (1978). Her areas of specialization include twentieth-century British literature and women's studies, and she has published articles on Virginia Woolf and James Joyce. In addition to the *McGraw-Hill Guide to English Literature,* Professor Lawrence is the author of *The Odyssey of Style in Ulysses* published by Princeton University Press. She is a member of the editorial board of *The James Joyce Quarterly.*

Betsy W. Seifter received a B.A. (1969) from Swarthmore College and a Ph.D. (1979) in English literature from Columbia University, where she was the Marjorie H. Nicolson Scholar for 1974–1975. Dr. Seifter's dissertation was "The Rhetoric of Thomas Nashe." She is currently at work on a study of tonal ambiguity in the plays of Shakespeare. Dr. Seifter is a member of the Renaissance Society of America and the Alliance of Independent Scholars. She lives and works in Wellesley, Massachusetts.

Lois Slatin Ratner received a B.A. from Goucher College (1972) and an M.A. (1973) and M. Phil. (1975) from Columbia University. She is at work on her doctoral dissertation, a study of the origins of the detective novel. Mrs. Ratner is also currently completing a novel of her own. She lives and works in New York City.

Catalog

If you are interested in a list of fine **Paperback**
books, covering a wide range of subjects
and interests, send your name and address,
requesting your free catalog, to:

McGraw-Hill Paperbacks
1221 Avenue of Americas
New York, N. Y. 10020